Ad Hoc
Networking

Ad Hoc
Networking

Charles E. Perkins

Editor

Addison–Wesley

Boston · San Francisco · New York · Toronto · Montreal
London · Munich · Paris · Madrid
Capetown · Sydney · Tokyo · Singapore · Mexico City

The publisher offers discounts on this book when ordered in quantity for special sales.
For more information, please contact:

    Pearson Education Corporate Sales Division
    One Lake Street
    Upper Saddle River, NJ 07458
    (800) 382-3419
    corpsales@pearsontechgroup.com

    Visit us on the Web at *www.awl.com/cseng/*

Library of Congress Cataloging-in-Publication Data

Ad hoc networking/Charles Perkins, editor.
    p. cm.
  Includes bibliographical references and index.
  ISBN 0-201-30976-9
    1. Computer networks.   I. Perkins, Charles.
  TK5105.5 .A28 2000
  004.6--dc21   00-048524

ISBN 0-201-30976-9

Text printed on recycled paper.
1 2 3 4 5 6 7 8 9 10 – CRW – 04 03 02 01 00
First printing, December 2000

Contents

Preface

The field of ad hoc networking is reemerging amid unprecedented growth in the scale and diversity of computer networking. New horizons for wireless connectivity have come into view along with a new sense of the inevitability of wireless data transmission over IP, the Internet Protocol that patches the Internet together. With new wireless products and research have come a more widespread familiarity between network protocol engineers and wireless media and some recognition that wireless media are *almost* as good as wired media for transmitting data—as long as one can overlook the differences in transmission speed. *Almost*—or perhaps *even better*—because of the dramatically greater convenience promised by mobile computing.

Unfortunately, there is another reason that mobile computing is often not *truly* as convenient as conventional computing. The Internet cannot yet handle mobile computers very well. Although this situation is changing quickly, almost no one would disagree that a fixed computer with wired media offers a better computing and communications environment than a mobile wireless computer—even more so for PDAs. The task set before today's network engineers is to eliminate the shortcomings of mobile computers and wireless media so that the inherent convenience of mobility will no longer suffer the burden of inadequate or inappropriate system design.

Part of the inadequacy of current system design starts with the outdated assumptions made in the network and routing protocols deployed in the Internet today. Many efforts to repair these outdated assumptions rely on additional infrastructure elements for managing data related to mobile computers—for example, Mobile IP—and various proxy architectures. These efforts and others offer new design perspectives that either preserve the time-honored end-to-end model of Internet communications or that offer new models aimed at improving user experience.

Perhaps naturally, the wide deployment of the Internet has provided additional impetus for exploring the benefits of computer internetworking even for situations in which neither the Internet per se nor any other internetwork is reachable. In such situations, one might still wish to use familiar network programs to carry on the same kinds of interactive computing with neighbors and associates in the area. Network programs can typically continue to work as long as they can identify the IP address of the desired destination and a path of one or more network links toward the destination.

Finding such paths is the job of ad hoc network algorithms and protocols. Exploring that design space has been an increasingly active area of research in the last few years. It is our hope that the diverse algorithms and protocols described in this book will give the reader a good idea of the current state of the art in ad hoc networking. The authors of each chapter are among the foremost practitioners in the field, and each one will no doubt try to convince the reader that his or her approach is best. The result may be as confusing or as delightful as trying to order the best meal in a fabulous restaurant with a menu created by a crew of creative and distinctively different chefs. *Bon Appetit!*

1

Ad Hoc Networking
An Introduction

Charles E. Perkins
Nokia Research Center

In recent years, mobile computing has enjoyed a tremendous rise in popularity. The continued miniaturization of mobile computing devices and the extraordinary rise of processing power available in mobile laptop computers combine to put more and better computer-based applications into the hands of a growing segment of the population. At the same time, the markets for wireless telephones and communication devices are experiencing rapid growth. Projections have been made that, by the year 2002, there will be more than a billion wireless communication devices in use, and more than 200 million wireless telephone handsets will be purchased annually. The rise of wireless telephony will change what it means to be "in touch"; already many people use their office telephone for taking messages while they are away and rely on their mobile telephone for more important or timely messages. Indeed, mobile phones are used for tasks as simple and as convenient as finding one's associates in a crowded shopping mall or at a conference. A similar transformation awaits mobile computer users, and we can expect new applications to be built for equally mundane but immediately convenient uses.

Much of the context for the transformation has to do with keeping in touch with the Internet. We expect to have "the network" at our disposal for the innumerable little conveniences that we have begun to integrate into our professional lives. We might wish to download a roadmap on the spur of the moment so that we can see what is available in the local area. We might wish to have driving suggestions sent to us, based on information from the global positioning system (GPS) in our car, using the services offered by various web sites. The combination of sufficiently fast and inexpensive wireless communication links and cheap mobile computing devices makes this a reality for many people today. In the future, the average traveler is likely to take such services for granted.

Today we see a great expansion in the production of technology to support mobile computing. Not only are the computers themselves getting more and more capable, but many new applications are being developed and wireless data communications products are becoming available that are much improved over those available in the past. The bandwidth now available to laptop computers over radio and infrared links is easily 10 to 100 times more than that available just ten years ago.

Such rapid technological advance has spurred equally impressive growth in mobile connectivity to the Internet. In the wired Ethernet domain, we have plug-and-play hardware and software so that laptop computers can be reconnected with ease according to the form factors of the local network outlets. The Internet is available around the world to those willing to make a dial-up connection to a local phone number. People are getting used to the advantages of having frequent and convenient Internet access. As a result, more and more network functionality will be taken for granted by typical laptop users.

As wireless network nodes proliferate and as applications using the Internet become familiar to a wider class of customers, those customers will expect to use networking applications even in situations where the Internet itself is not available. For instance, people using laptop computers at a conference in a hotel might wish to communicate in a variety of ways, without the mediation of routing across the global Internet. Yet today such obvious communications requirements cannot be easily met using Internet protocols. Providing solutions to meet such requirements is the subject of this book. The proposals to be described allow mobile computer users with (compatible) wireless communication devices to set up a possibly short-lived network just for the communication needs of the moment—in other words, an *ad hoc* network.

At the same time, there is a huge potential market for embedded network devices in our vehicles, our mobile telephones, and perhaps even in our toys and personal appliances. Surely the day is not far off when a typical child's doll will have a microprocessor and a remote control device and will depend on network access to interact with the home's television and computer games. Embedded networking could represent the "killer app" for wireless networks.

Anyone reading this book will agree that the modern age of networking represents one of the great achievements of humanity. We already take many aspects of it for granted. In particular, we often take for granted the infrastructure currently needed to support our vast networking enterprise. The things we do with our networks do not inherently depend on the network infrastructure; rather, having the infrastructure extends the reach of network applications immeasurably.

Once we have grown accustomed to the power of network communications and to accomplishing our daily tasks with the aid of applications that rely on networking, we will want the applications to be available at all times. In fact, many network researchers predict that some day in the not too distant future we will put our applications to use "anytime, anywhere," perhaps by way of the rapidly expanding satellite communications systems now under construction. The communications satellites girding the earth will complement the cellular (wireless) telephone infrastructure, which is itself growing even more rapidly in most developed countries.

Indeed, the authors of this book suggest that mobile computers and applications will become indispensable even at times when and at places where the necessary infrastructure is not available. Wireless computing devices should physically be able to communicate with each other, even when no routers or base stations or Internet service providers (ISPs) can be found. In the absence of infrastructure, what is needed is that the wireless devices themselves take on the missing functions.

In this introductory chapter, we consider some general topics that provide context for the rest of the chapters in this book. In the next section, we describe a general model of operation for ad hoc networks and some of the factors affecting the design decisions that various approaches have taken. In Section 1.2, we list a few of the commercial opportunities that may await vendors of wireless products when the necessary protocols are available. This will naturally include a look at some of the applications enabled by ad hoc networking. Following that, Section 1.3 will discuss some of the technical drivers for the resurgence of interest in ad hoc networking. The needs of military communications have been very influential in creating this renewed interest. Discussion of military ad hoc networking, however, is not included in that section because it is covered much more completely in Chapter 2. Because many of the approaches to ad hoc networks use variations on existing routing protocols, some very general comments about routing protocols are presented in Section 1.4. Finally, a capsule summary of each chapter in the book is presented in Section 1.5.

1.1 MODEL OF OPERATION

This book is concerned with ways (past and present) that wireless mobile computing devices can perform critical network topology functions that are normally the job of routers within the Internet infrastructure. Keeping track of the connections between computers is something so basic that a computer network, almost by definition, cannot exist without it.

There are many kinds of protocols available today that are supported by network infrastructure, either in a particular enterprise or in the Internet at large. These other protocols deserve consideration, but need adaptation before they can be useful within a network no longer connected to the Internet infrastructure. Some of them may not be appropriate for use when the infrastructure is unavailable; credit card validation and network management protocols come to mind.

As a matter of definition, an ad hoc network is one that comes together as needed, not necessarily with any assistance from the existing Internet infrastructure. For instance, one could turn on 15 laptop computers, each with the same kind of infrared data communications adapter, and hope that they could form a network among themselves. In fact, such a feature would be useful even if the laptops were stationary.

There are a bewildering variety of dimensions to the design space of ad hoc networks. We take a particular slice of that design space that should serve a large number of user requirements and yet allow discussion of a number of interesting and illuminating techniques. Besides *ad hoc networking,* similar techniques have been proposed under the names *instant infrastructure* [Bagrodia+ 1996] and *mobile-mesh networking* [SDT 1995].

Consider, for example, whether the range of wireless transmission should be large or small compared to the geographic distribution of the mobile wireless nodes. If all of the wireless nodes are within range of each other, no routing is needed, and the ad hoc network is, by definition, fully connected. While this might be a fortunate situation in practice, it is not a very interesting routing problem to solve. Plus, the power needed to obtain complete connectivity may be impractical, wasteful of battery power, too vulnerable to detection, or even illegal.

Thus, we discuss only proposals that offer solutions to the case in which some of the wireless nodes are not within range of each other. Combined with the lack of infrastructure routers, the restricted range of wireless transmission indicates the need for *multihop* routing.

As another example, we might suppose that wireless computer users could measure their relative positions and subsequently configure their laptop computers using the measured distances, so that the appropriate link information could be available at each mobile node. This would work, but it would not be very convenient. Worse yet, the link information would be likely to change whenever the users moved relative to each other. We are not interested in simplifying the problem space at the expense of user convenience, however, so we restrict our attention only to those proposals that provide automatic topology establishment (eschewing user configuration steps) and dynamic topology maintenance (enabling user mobility). In fact, we make the slight additional restriction of considering only proposals that are self-starting, except possibly for an enabling or mode setting step performed by the user, who should be able to exert necessary controls over the performance of the ad hoc networking operation.

In this book, most of the discussion focuses on the interesting cases that have the following characteristics:

- The nodes are using IP, the Internet Protocol [Postel 1981a], and they have IP addresses that are assigned by some usually unspecified means.
- The nodes are far enough apart so that not all of them are within range of each other.
- The nodes may be mobile so that two nodes within range at one point in time may be out of range moments later.
- The nodes are able to assist each other in the process of delivering packets of data.

The discussion in this book focuses on the protocol engineering that underlies the establishment of the paths by which the ad hoc network nodes can communicate with each other. Thus, address autoconfiguration in particular, a very interesting subject, is largely absent from this book, but is ripe for exploration very soon.

As an example of a small ad hoc network, consider Figure 1.1 (taken from Chapter 3), illustrating a collection of eight nodes along with the links between them. The nodes are able to move relative to each other; as that happens, the links between them are broken and other links may be established. In the picture, MH_1 moves away from MH_2 and establishes new links with MH_7 and MH_8. Most algorithms also allow for the appearance of new mobile nodes and the disappearance of previously available nodes.

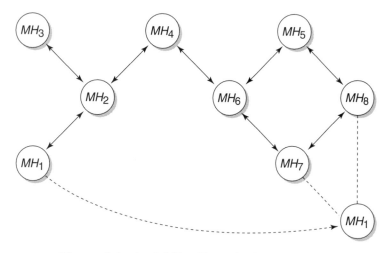

Figure 1.1. An Ad Hoc Network of Mobile Nodes

1.1.1 Symmetric Links

Some of the models considered in this book depend on the existence of symmetric communication links between the nodes in the ad hoc work. Unfortunately, wireless links in the real world do not necessarily conform to this assumption. This assumption of symmetry is made because routing in networks with unidirectional links is known to be quite difficult. Recent analysis has yielded a mathematical result of interest that characterizes this difficulty [Prakash 1999]. As it turns out, there are such networks in which two system-wide (i.e., all-node) broadcasts are needed for a source to find a route to a particular destination. On the other hand, not all networks with unidirectional links exhibit this characteristic. If the network has a sufficiently high degree of connectivity and relatively few unidirectional links, alternative routes comprising only symmetric links can usually be found.

There is another factor that mitigates the decision to ignore possible asymmetric routes. A unidirectional link is sometimes on the verge of failure anyway. In such cases, extending the basic ad hoc network protocol to deal with unidirectional links may cause less robust routes to be discovered, leading to early failure and the subsequent need for a new (and more complicated) route discovery cycle.

1.1.2 Layer-2 Ad Hoc Solutions

The ad hoc networking protocols in this book are mainly targeted at layer-3 operation. It is possible, in practically every case, to retool the protocol for use at layer 2. Doing so requires first that IP address fields be enlarged to contain 48 (or more) bits instead of 32, as needed for IP, because the IEEE MAC address is typically 48 or 64 bits long. This is not a problem, especially in view of the fact that such retooling will be needed anyway to enable the protocols to handle ad hoc networks of IPv6 addressable computers.

However, given the universal deployment of IP applications for networking today, every application eventually causes the communication subsystem to resolve an IP address into a neighboring layer-2 address, or else into the layer-2 address of a node in the neighborhood that can forward the application protocol data units (packets) toward the IP address of the desired application endpoint. When the route table at the application's source node has IP addresses of desired endpoints, IP forwarding naturally takes care of framing the data with a layer-2 header containing the layer-2 destination address of the next hop along a path toward the destination.

This happy circumstance evaporates, however, when the routing is based on layer-2 addresses. In that case, as a matter of consistent terminology, the route table is presumably indexed by layer-2 destination addresses.

That implies that the IP address of the destination has to be resolved to the layer-2 address of the destination, even for destinations that are multiple hops away. Then, unless the layer-2 route discovery is equipped with suitable layer-3 address information in appropriate extensions, additional broadcast discovery operations will be needed. If the layer-3 information is included for better performance, the entire operation can be viewed as a layer-3 route discovery anyway, albeit with an odd data structure for the route storage.

1.1.3 Proactive versus Reactive Protocols

One of the most interesting aspects of recent investigations concerns whether or not nodes in an ad hoc network should keep track of routes to all possible destinations, or instead keep track of only those destinations of immediate interest. A node in an ad hoc network does not need a route to a destination until that destination is to be the recipient of packets sent by the node, either as the actual source of the packet or as an intermediate node along a path from the source to the destination.

Protocols that keep track of routes for all destinations in the ad hoc network have the advantage that communications with arbitrary destinations experience minimal initial delay from the point of view of the application. When the application starts, a route can be immediately selected from the route table. Such protocols are called *proactive* because they store route information even before it is needed. They are also called *table driven* [Royer+ 1999] because we can imagine that routes are available as part of a well-maintained table.

However, proactive protocols suffer the disadvantage of additional control traffic that is needed to continually update stale route entries. The ad hoc network we are trying to support is presumed to contain numerous mobile nodes. Therefore, routes are likely to be broken frequently, as two mobile nodes that had established a link between them will no longer be able to support that link and thus no longer be able to support any routes that had depended on that link. If the broken route has to be repaired, even though no applications are using it, the repair effort can be considered wasted. This wasted effort can cause scarce bandwidth resources to be wasted and can cause further congestion at intermediate network points as the control packets occupy valuable queue space. Since control packets are often put at the head of the queue, the likely result will be data loss at congested network points. Data loss often translates to retransmission, delays, and further congestion.

As a result, *on-demand,* or *reactive,* protocols have been designed so that routing information is acquired only when it is actually needed. Reactive routing protocols may often use far less bandwidth for maintaining the route tables at each node, but the latency for many applications will drastically increase. Most applications are likely to suffer a long delay when they start because a route to the destination will have to be acquired before the communications can begin.

One reasonable middle point between proactive and reactive protocols might be to keep track of multiple routes between a source and a destination node. This "multipath routing" might involve some way to purge stale routes even if they are not in active use. Otherwise, when a known broken route is discarded, one of the other members of the set of routes may be attempted. If the other routes are likely to be stale, the application may experience a long delay as each stale route is tried and discarded.

1.1.4 Multicast

Ad hoc networks are interesting to a large extent because of the challenge of maintaining a communication path between a source and a destination, even when some of the intermediate forwarding nodes are unable to continue participating in packet forwarding and must be replaced by nodes along another path. It turns out that maintaining paths between a single source and multiple destinations is somewhat more difficult, but not excessively so. Given the growing importance of multicast as a means to reduce the bandwidth utilization for mass distribution of data, and the pressing need to conserve scarce bandwidth over wireless media, it is natural that multicast routing should receive some attention for ad hoc networks.

It is an open question whether or not the multicast routing algorithm should be integrated with the routing algorithm used to establish communication paths between single endpoints. On the one hand, the problems may be sufficiently different so that trying to make a single routing algorithm serve for both may be unnaturally difficult. On the other hand, the problem of reestablishing paths caused by movement of intermediate points in a routing path or tree may dominate both situations. In this latter case, careful attention to path reestablishment for both contexts at once may be much easier than re-examining solutions in multiple disparate contexts, as would be necessary if multicast routing were unrelated to unicast routing.

1.2 COMMERCIAL APPLICATIONS OF AD HOC NETWORKING

In this section, we look at some of the potential applications for ad hoc networks that might provide the basis for commercially successful products. In fact, any commercially successful network application can be considered a candidate for useful deployment with nodes that can form ad hoc networks.

For example, users of nodes in an ad hoc network are likely to wish to transfer electronic mail. If some nodes in an ad hoc network offer web service, the other nodes that wish to make use of the service will still need to connect to the web server and support the usual HTTP traffic.

1.2.1 Conferencing

Perhaps the prototypical application requiring the establishment of an ad hoc network is mobile conferencing. When mobile computer users gather outside their normal office environment, the business network infrastructure is often missing. But the need for collaborative computing might be even more important here than in the everyday office environment. Indeed, the whole point of the meeting might be to make some further progress on a particular collaborative project. Given that today's project environments are heavily computerized, for projects in a very broad range of industries the need for being able to create an ad hoc network seems clear.

As it turns out, the establishment of an ad hoc network for collaborative mobile computer users is needed even when there may be Internet infrastructure support available. This results from the likely overhead required when utilizing infrastructure links, which might entail drastically suboptimal routing back and forth between widely separated office environments. Current solutions for mobile networking (e.g., Mobile IP [Perkins 1996]) are not well suited for efficiently supporting ad hoc networks, although the techniques are not wholly incompatible.

This interplay between the immediacy of ad hoc networks and the possible performance loss inherent in relying on Internet infrastructure routing is a recurring theme that should be considered in connection with each approach described in the chapters of this book.

1.2.2 Home Networking

As another example, consider the scenario that will likely result if wireless computers become popular at home. These computers will probably be taken to and from the office work environment and on business trips. It is quite possible that such computers will not have topologically related IP addresses, especially if they are connected at the offices of each parent or at the children's school. Keeping in mind the convenience that an unchanging IP address affords to the user, it would be nice to allow the various mobile computers to operate an ad hoc network in the home, even if the home maintains its own subnet with more or less permanently situated network nodes.

Add to this the fact that assigning multiple IP addresses to each wireless node for identification purposes would add an administrative burden (a job that most people do not want), and the alternative of deploying an ad hoc network (automatically created as needed) seems more attractive. Ad hoc networking offers the prospect of reachability to all the nodes at home regardless of their "normal" point of attachment, which would otherwise be indicated by the network prefix that is part of every IP address. Furthermore, by using protocols such as Mobile IP, the nodes in the home ad hoc network can operate as if they were still connected to their standard computing environment *in addition* to participating (with higher performance) in the residential ad hoc network.

1.2.3 Emergency Services

When created at home or away from home at a meeting, an ad hoc network makes up for the lack of an existing Internet infrastructure. But, what about cases in which the existing infrastructure is damaged or out of service for other reasons? We are all familiar with situations in which loss of local power causes loss of electricity, and each year natural disasters wreak havoc with people's lives around the world. As the Internet grows in importance, the loss of network connectivity during such natural disasters will become an ever more noticeable consequence of the calamity. Furthermore, network applications will become increasingly important for emergency services, and thus it will be important to find ways to enable the operations of networks even when infrastructure elements have been disabled as part of the effects of a disaster.

Ad hoc networks can help to overcome network impairment during disaster emergencies. Mobile units will probably carry networking equipment in support of routine operations for the times when the Internet is available and the infrastructure has not been impaired. With the techniques and protocols in this book, emergency mobile units can greatly extend the usefulness of their networking equipment during times of lost infrastructure support. For instance, police squad cars and firefighting equipment can remain in touch longer and provide information more quickly if they can cooperate to form an ad hoc network in places not otherwise offering connectivity to the global Internet.

1.2.4 Personal Area Networks and Bluetooth

The idea of a personal area network (PAN) is to create a very localized network populated by some network nodes that are closely associated with a single person. These nodes may be attached to the person's belt or carried in a purse. More exotic visions of the future include virtual reality devices attached around the head and other devices more oriented toward the sense of touch. These devices may or may not need to have an attachment to the wide area Internet, but they will almost certainly need to communicate with each other while they are associated with their users' activities. In this scenario, mobility is not the overriding consideration.

However, mobility suddenly becomes much more important when interactions between several PANs are needed. In other words, when people meet in real life, their PANs are likely to become aware of each other also. Since people usually do not stay in a fixed location with respect to each other for very long, the dynamic nature of this inter-PAN communication should be obvious. Methods for establishing communications between nodes on separate PANs could benefit from the technologies of ad hoc networks.

No current discussion about PANs would be complete without at least some mention of Bluetooth [Haartsen 1998]. Bluetooth is an emerging short-range radio technology targeted at eliminating wires between personal digital assistants (PDAs). If each PDA is equipped with a Bluetooth radio, it is possible for up to eight devices to organize themselves into what is called a *piconet,* with slotted communications controlled by a master. Bluetooth protocols at the physical and MAC layers are focused on saving battery power, as PDAs are much more useful if people do not have to be continually changing dead batteries.

When there are more than eight devices, Bluetooth requires that multiple piconets be formed. These piconets can be connected together into a *scatternet* if one of the slaves agrees to relay data between two of the masters. This suggests that the slave should have separate time slots in each piconet to reduce latencies for data transfers. It may even be necessary to form scatternets for the PAN that is associated with a single person. It is almost guaranteed that scatternets will be required for the interaction of multiple PANs.

1.2.5 Embedded Computing Applications

The world is full of machines that move, and future intelligent mobile machines will be able to process a great deal more information about the environment in which they operate. The "environment" itself will increasingly be a virtual one created by fixed and mobile computers. Some researchers [Weiser 1993] predict a world of *ubiquitous computing,* in which computers will be all around us, constantly performing mundane tasks to make our lives a little easier. These ubiquitous computers will often react to the changing environment in which they are situated and will themselves cause changes to the environment in ways that are, we hope, predictable and planned.

Many of these intelligent machines will be both mobile and connected by wireless data communications devices. The Bluetooth short-range radio device is expected to cost less than $5 within four years and to be incorporated into millions of wireless communications devices. Already, many computers and PDAs are equipped with inexpensive wireless ports. These are being used for synchronizing data between machines owned by the same person, for exchanging virtual business cards, for printing out small files on local printers, and so on.

Ubiquitous intelligent internetworking devices that detect their environment, interact with each other, and respond to changing environmental conditions will create a future that is as challenging to imagine as a science fiction scenario. Our world will change so much that it is hard to predict the kinds of applications that might predominate. Security considerations must be taken into account, of course, to prevent unwarranted intrusions into our privacy and to protect against the possibility of impersonation by other people. However, these security matters are well known in other contexts, and they are not the particular subject of this book.

These capabilities can be provided with or without the use of ad hoc networks, but ad hoc networking is likely to be more flexible and convenient than, say, continual allocation and reallocation of endpoint IP addresses whenever a new wireless communication link is established. Furthermore, once we become used to having these simple and easily imagined features, it seems a sure bet that new applications will be invented. In fact, we may become so enamored of ad hoc computing that we will begin to presume the presence of appropriate support environments. These environments would be made available to ad hoc mobile nodes and could be considered a new form of micro-infrastructure. We might normally expect our ad hoc computers to have access to local information about temperature, light-switch controls, traffic information, or the way toward a water fountain [Hodes+ 1997]. Infrastructure elements that make their information available by way of standard TCP/IP client–server applications could operate in dual mode so that they participate in ad hoc networks as well, depending on the circumstances.

1.2.6 Sensor Dust

Recent attention has been focused on ideas involving the possibility of coordinating the activities and reports of a large collection of tiny sensor devices [Estrin+ 1999, Kahn+ 1999]. Such devices, cheap to manufacture and able to be strewn about in large numbers of identical units, could offer detailed information about terrain or environmental dangerous conditions. They might be equipped with positional indicators; alternatively, positional information could be inferred for network information such as the number of hops between various sensors and a well-known data collection node.

Such sensor network nodes have two characteristics that will strongly influence the design of networks to facilitate data acquisition:

- Once situated, the sensors remain stationary.
- Population may be largely homogeneous.
- Power is likely to be a scarce resource, so sophisticated communications scheduling will be important (see Section 1.3.2 and Chapter 10).
- In fact, the lifetime of the battery may define the node's lifetime.

As an example, suppose some hazardous chemicals were dispersed in an unknown manner because of an explosion or some other sort of accident. Instead of sending in emergency personnel who might be subjected to lethal gas and forced to work in unwieldy protective clothing, it would be better to distribute sensors containing wireless transceivers (perhaps by dropping them from a low-flying plane). The sensors could then form an ad hoc network and cooperate to gather the desired information about chemical concentrations and identification. Military applications are also of great interest.

1.2.7 Automotive/PC Interaction

In a somewhat different vein, consider the possible uses of ad hoc networks between automotive computers and laptops or PDAs that may accompany us as we travel in our cars. Suppose that when we start the car, we have an indication on our display that there may be a mechanical difficulty that needs attention. We may expect our mobile telephone to provide a link between our car and some local repair service advertised in a local service directory available by way of our PDA. Alternatively, once the service needs from the car's network have been loaded onto a laptop computer that we happen to be carrying, the laptop might take charge of finding directions to the repair shop. A laptop computer is likely to have a superior display monitor, and we might even want to take a little extra time to evaluate reports from various satisfied or dissatisfied customers before selecting one of several repair shops. The selection of display device and the urgency of making the decision are still matters for personal attention, but our computing devices can make matters much easier by cooperation and automatic discovery of relevant information for our consideration.

There are other interesting interactions that can be programmed between automobiles and their occupants. Positional information will likely be available to drivers and passengers, allowing those in the back seat to easily find answers to their typical questions. That might become a concern in communications between cars that are trying to arrange a meeting place. Wireless communication between cars could become the logical successor to citizen's band (CB) radio. Indeed, with both audio and video over wireless within reach of today's wireless technologies, countless possibilities for both useful and frivolous communications are easily imaginable. Browsing the web pages of nearby cars might become a new national pastime.

1.2.8 Other Envisioned Applications

Once they become conveniently available by way of widely deployed dynamic routing protocols as described in this book, ad hoc networks might be useful in many ways we cannot fully understand given our current experience. For instance, university campuses might well become large ad hoc networks as students and faculty learn to rely on their handheld and laptop computers for their communication and computing needs. Messaging and browsing could be managed either by available wireless infrastructure or by ad hoc connectivity, according to whatever is most convenient at the moment.

Similarly, at hospitals busy doctors and nurses will want to rely on the administrative infrastructure at times and to instantiate direct links outside the infrastructure at other times. Visiting staff and paramedics will need to confer with residents and transfer data to and from patient equipment. These operations will often be facilitated by infrastructure support, but the same communications needs can sometimes be met without interaction with the infrastructure.

Viewed from another perspective, however, searching for applications to justify the development of ad hoc networks may be putting the cart before the horse. What really matters is making communications technology useful for people everywhere regardless of the nature or availability of backbone infrastructure. We do not require a killer app for ad hoc networking any more than we needed a killer app for the success of the backbone Internet.

When people are within wireless range of each other, it becomes merely an unfortunate artifact of decades-old technology that their communication devices require remote infrastructures. With ad hoc networking, local communications can instead depend only on local communications channels and transmission technologies and protocols. As this localized technology gains significant mindshare, it is to be hoped that sufficient spectrum will be allocated for local use, given that the current ISM spectrum bands will not serve future needs. Furthermore, we can hope that such localized communications will rekindle the public's interest in reasserting its right to use the spectrum, which is supposed to be a resource managed for the public good. The rise of wireless cellular telephony, combined with ad hoc networks, could provide a new paradigm of public use of the public airwaves.

1.3 TECHNICAL AND MARKET FACTORS AFFECTING AD HOC NETWORKS

Nodes in an ad hoc network are often assumed to have IP addresses that are preassigned, or assigned in a way that is not directly related to their current position relative to the rest of the network topology. This differs substantially from the way that IP addresses are assigned to nodes in the global Internet. Routing within today's Internet depends on the ability to *aggregate* reachability information to IP nodes. This aggregation is based on the assignment of IP addresses to nodes so that all the nodes on the same network link share the same *routing prefix*. In practice, good network administration requires that networks that are nearby should have similar prefixes. Classless Inter-Domain Routing (CIDR) [Rekhter+ 1993] has been very effective in helping to reduce the number of routing prefixes that have to be advertised across the Internet, thus enabling today's router hardware to continue to maintain the Internet's global addressability. Using CIDR, when the prefixes themselves can be aggregated, reachability to all the networks within a site can be described by advertising a prefix that is itself the initial part of all the (longer) prefixes for the networks within the site. The process of aggregation can be iterated if network administrators for nearby sites cooperate to use networks with prefixes that share a common initial bit string (i.e., a common smaller prefix).

This creates a hierarchy of network prefixes—smaller prefixes that fit at higher levels of the hierarchy. Reachability to all nodes within the hierarchy can be described by advertising a single, smallest routing prefix. This drastically reduces the amount of routing information that has to be advertised and provides the necessary economy for the Internet to continue to grow. We can say that aggregating routing information is the key to Internet *scalability*.

With ad hoc networks, however, such aggregation is typically not available. Some proposed methods attempt to reintroduce aggregation by controlling the IP addresses of the mobile nodes, but this requires that the IP addresses (and, subsequently, routing information relevant to the mobile node) be changed depending on the relative movement of the node. It is not at all clear that the benefit of improved aggregation is worth the cost of complicated re-addressing and route table revisions. Thus, the scalability afforded by aggregation within the Internet is not likely to be available for ad hoc networks. This means that there may be major limitations on the viability of ad hoc network algorithms for extremely large populations of mobile nodes. The limits will also depend on the relative speed of movement between the mobile nodes. More movement means more maintenance so that the available routing information remains useful. In the face of uncontrolled increases in node mobility, any ad hoc routing algorithm will eventually require so much route maintenance that no bandwidth remains for the transmission of data packets [Corson+ 1996].

1.3.1 Scalability

Because ad hoc networks do not typically allow the same kinds of aggregation techniques that are available to standard Internet routing protocols, they are vulnerable to scalability problems. In particular, loss of aggregation leads to bigger route tables. There are ways to maintain aggregation for ad hoc networks, and some of them are discussed in Chapter 4. Aggregation can be very easily used for mobile networks, but the aggregation and addressing used for routing within the structure are not IP based. Consequently IP-based ad hoc protocols often must use additional memory for storing the route tables and processor cycles for searching them.

Node mobility introduces other kinds of scalability problems for ad hoc networking protocols. Since the routing changes as the nodes move, control messages have to be sent around the network to represent current connectivity information. These control messages are likely to be transmitted more often if the nodes move more quickly relative to each other, because then links will be lost or established more often between the nodes. This usually happens be true unless the movements of the mobile nodes are highly correlated.

The increased number of control messages places additional load on the available bandwidth, which is usually already a constraining factor for communication between wireless nodes. Thus, ad hoc protocols are typically designed to reduce the number of control messages, often by maintaining appropriate state information at designated mobile nodes. The downside of maintaining state information, however, is that it can become stale; the only cure for updating stale information is the introduction of more control messages.

Depending on the details of the algorithm, transmission of control messages may cause undesirable loads on the individual processing elements as well as on the available network bandwidth. For instance, protocols that cause a recomputation of the entire network topology whenever a new routing update is received may be subject to long convergence times whenever a node makes or breaks a link with one of its neighbors. The data in such a route update must be processed in far less time than the average time between network events caused by node mobility; otherwise, the ad hoc network may never stabilize. Route instability is a likely cause of routing loops, which can cause unnecessary bandwidth consumption. By Murphy's Law, such problems always arise at exactly the moment when they are least welcome or at exactly the time when communication is most critical.

Algorithms for ad hoc networking must be carefully evaluated and compared for their relative scalability in the face of node population growth and increased node mobility. If maximum values are known for those numbers, it is reasonable to calculate how many control messages may be required to manage the ad hoc network and to compare the total traffic due to control messages against the total bandwidth availability. As long as the control traffic takes up a manageable proportion of the overall bandwidth, a candidate protocol can be considered acceptable. Similarly, the time taken for convergence should be calculated for a given maximum value for node mobility if such a value is known.

1.3.2 Power Budget versus Latency

In many kinds of ad hoc networks, the mobile nodes operate on battery power. There are two ways that they do this. First, they might transmit data to a desired recipient. This use of battery power is not part of the overhead of ad hoc networking. Second, a mobile node might offer itself as an intermediate forwarding node for data going between two other nodes in the network. Providing such a service is likely to be costly in terms of power consumption, but without the availability of such forwarding nodes there can be no ad hoc network.

There are interesting questions about when a node should or should not forward traffic. For instance, perhaps a node with full battery power should be more willing to forward data for its neighbors than a node whose battery power is almost depleted. Nodes with reduced power might limit their activities to transmitting and receiving only emergency or high-priority messages. Server nodes may attempt to reserve bandwidth for sourcing data and rely on their other neighbors for enabling route establishment between other endpoints. Other nodes may attempt to "freeload" from their neighbors, taking advantage of their forwarding services without offering anything in return. If this potential bad behavior is of concern, steps should be taken to isolate the offending nodes and to offer forwarding services only to cooperative nodes. Detecting the offense, however, can be problematic or impossible. For instance, the behavior of any leaf node might be indistinguishable from that of a selfish node.

The behavior of the nodes in the ad hoc network given their power budget is likely to affect the ease with which routes can be established between endpoints. If it takes more control messages to find or maintain a route, communication latency might be increased. If route information is periodically transmitted throughout the network, further demands will be placed on the power budget of each individual node. However, the more route information that is made available, the more likely it is that a good route between endpoints can be found as soon as it is needed without any additional control operations. This is especially true as the frequency of periodic transmissions increases, because then it is more likely that existing (cached) route information is still valid. The tradeoff between frequency of route update dissemination and battery power utilization is one of the major engineering design decisions for ad hoc network protocols.

1.3.3 Protocol Deployment and Incompatible Standards

Wireless ad hoc network protocols may be susceptible to forces working against standardization. If the experience of the IEEE 802.11 committee is any guide, we can expect to see a plethora of engineering solutions, all incompatible and all solving a slightly different part of the problem. In the

IEEE, this was in part due to the huge design space for physical wireless channel access and coding techniques. Unfortunately, the design space for wireless routing protocols is also impressively large, as will become evident from the discussion in Section 1.4 and in the rest of this book. Furthermore, the need for standardization in routing protocols at the network layer is almost as great as the need at the lower protocol layers.

At least when neighbors share the same physical medium and method of utilizing it (e.g., MAC layer), there is hope for communication within a local neighborhood. Communication between nodes not in the same neighborhood (e.g., not sharing the same physical medium) will not be possible unless the nodes also agree on some higher-level protocol by which they can interchange connectivity information about links outside their respective neighborhoods. Unless a miracle happens (e.g., the IETF `manet` working group is able to promulgate a widely deployed ad hoc networking protocol), ad hoc networks will gain momentum only gradually because users will have to load software or take additional steps to ensure interoperability. But sooner or later, just as with the IEEE 802.11 standardization process, some useful standards are bound to emerge.

1.3.4 Wireless Data Rates

One of the biggest obstacles to the adoption of ad hoc networks may be reduced data rates—the same problem that slowed the adoption of wireless computing during the last decade. We can typically observe an order of magnitude difference in the speed of wired and wireless networks. For instance, while many enterprise users are accustomed to 100 Mbit/sec from the local Ethernet, wireless users must struggle to get a reliable 10 Mbit/sec over the air: 1 to 2 Mbit/sec is much more common.

The overall effect tends to be that wireless computers are no longer *general purpose*. The wireless user has to be careful not to invoke applications that require a lot of bandwidth. As many of today's applications involve transactions over the Web, it may not be so easy for the user to avoid this problem. At any moment, the next hyperlink selection may attempt to load some beautiful dancing alphabetic letters on fire, at great cost in bandwidth or at great cost in frustration as the user tries to figure out what went wrong. It is often hard to tell whether the network itself has failed or whether the implicitly selected image is huge and is tying up the available communication paths.

A related problem has to do with the higher error rates experienced by wireless media in comparison with today's wired network media. Because TCP was mostly designed to classify a lost packet as a sign of network congestion, it tends to respond poorly when data errors cause a packet to be lost or dropped. Thus, the hapless wireless user is stuck with an even greater performance loss whenever transient noise or obstacles cause a temporary increase in errors. This problem, while receiving quite a bit of recent attention, is not close to any solution at all, much less a widely deployed one. Furthermore, there are indications that TCP itself performs even worse than expected across multiple wireless hops.

Several IETF efforts have been aimed at identifying a working group charter for reaching a solution, but as of this writing no working group has been formed. There is no agreement about where to start searching for a solution to consider for standardization. As existing Internet applications use TCP, and as the same applications are likely to find use in ad hoc networks, TCP will probably be the first transport protocol of interest for ad hoc networks. Thus, the problems with wireless error rates are of central importance for ad hoc network designers.

1.3.5 User Education and Acculturation

Many of the obstacles to widespread deployment of wireless data devices stem from user education and acculturation. Menu selection, avoidance of web pages with huge image files, and alphanumeric data entry on small user input devices are all problematic for the uninitiated. However, these obstacles are slowly disappearing as PDAs such as the wireless Palm Pilot, WAP terminals, and iMode devices continue to grow in popularity. User input restrictions are mitigated either by special input modalities or by simplified menu selection from specially engineered web pages. The storage of convenient user profiles on the Web also helps reduce the requirements for data entry on bandwidth- and space-constrained devices.

Sometimes the obstacles to user acceptance are the most prosaic and mundane features. Current wireless devices depend on an external or exposed antenna for reliable operation. The antenna turns out to be expected and yet a pet peeve and object of frequent irritation. It is so much expected that some wireless telephones have a false antenna that can be pulled out by the user in order to "improve" the perceived voice quality. However, any such exposed device is constantly in the way and vulnerable to breakage.

1.3.6 Additional Security Exposure

As with any wireless communications, traffic across an ad hoc network can be highly vulnerable to security threats. What distinguishes an ad hoc network is that the additional threats extend even to the basic structure of the network. Thus, existing techniques for securing network protocol transactions for wired networks (see Section 1.4) must also be applied to the techniques of ad hoc networking. Unfortunately, this is easier said than done.

In the first place, security for routing protocols almost always depends on proper distribution of some key that allows the creation of unforgeable credentials. Designing secure key distribution in an ad hoc network might be a frightening prospect. Any reliance on a certificate authority seems doomed from the outset, for the same reason that reliance on any centralized authority is problematic. Centralization is antithetical to ad hoc networking, if not outright contradictory.

Beyond that, however, there are additional problems with the increased packet sizes required by authentication extensions. It is likely that the more secure a protocol is made to be, the slower and more cumbersome it will become. This combination of poor performance and tedious, inconvenient key distribution and configuration probably means that ad hoc networks will remain characteristically insecure. Diffie-Hellman key exchange techniques will help establish some temporary security between particular endpoints, but they are vulnerable to *man-in-the-middle* attacks that are hard to defeat in an ad hoc environment.

1.3.7 Spotty Coverage

Gaps in wireless coverage are both a problem and an opportunity for peer-to-peer devices capable of forming ad hoc networks. On the one hand, the coverage gaps make it unlikely that people in the affected regions will invest in most existing wireless devices, because such devices depend on infrastructure support for their operation.

On the other hand, people who are used to wireless connectivity to the Internet will often have to travel through regions of poor connectivity. These are likely to be the people who are motivated to put ad hoc network products into place so that they can continue to use local intercommunications even when the wide area infrastructure is inoperative.

1.4 GENERAL COMMENTS ON ROUTING PROTOCOLS

Each node in an ad hoc network, if it volunteers to carry traffic, participates in the formation of the network topology. This is quite similar to the way that intermediate nodes within the Internet, or within a corporate intranet, cooperate to form a routing infrastructure. Routing protocols within the Internet provide the information necessary for each node to forward packets to the next hop along the way from the source to the destination.

This observation motivates attempts to adapt existing routing protocols for use in ad hoc networks. Routing protocols are self-starting, adapt to changing network conditions, and almost by definition offer multihop paths across a network from a source to the destination. From this description, it is easy to see why we might wish to manage topology changes in an ad hoc network by requiring all forwarding nodes to operate some kind of routing protocol.

The wired Internet uses routing protocols based on network broadcast, such as OSPF [Moy 1997]. OSPF is an example of a *link-state* protocol, so named because each node gathers information about the state of the links that have been established between the other nodes in the network. Dijkstra's shortest path first (SPF) algorithm [Dijkstra 1959] can be used to construct routes as needed between sources and destinations for which the link-state information is available. Traditional link-state protocols may not be suitable for highly dynamic networks because of the relatively large bandwidth required to maintain a current view of the network state. Experiments have shown that OSPF can consume a very substantial percentage of the available bandwidth while trying to maintain adequate link information for routing in a typical military ad hoc network (Chapter 2, [Strater+ 1996]).

However, there are alternatives to table-driven link-state routing approaches. Some current link-state algorithms do not require all nodes to have identical link-state information and route selection algorithms, and generate routes on demand. Examples of these appear in Chapters 4 and 10.

Instead, nodes distribute link-state information (usually in the form of a statistical, not an instantaneous, characterization) only when there has been a significant change. Furthermore, this link-state information is distributed only to nodes that might be affected by the change—for example, those in close proximity to the place where the change occurred or, in a clustered network, those within the same cluster. It is not necessary for all nodes to receive all link-state information intended for them in order to compute routes.

Routing in multihop packet radio networks was based in the past on shortest-path routing algorithms [Leiner+ 1987], such as the Distributed Bellman-Ford (DBF) algorithm [Ford+ 1962]. DBF algorithms typically store very little information about links that are not directly connected to the node running the algorithm. For each destination, the node typically stores just a single route table entry, containing among other things the next hop toward that destination. DBF algorithms are also known as *distance-vector* (DV) algorithms because the route table entry for a destination contains a *metric,* which is often just the *distance* from the node to the destination, as well as the next hop (or *vector*) toward the destination.

Distance-vector algorithms have many advantages. They are easy to program. UC Berkeley offered a free implementation of the Routing Information Protocol (RIP) [Malkin 1994], which is easy to understand and modify. However, these algorithms can suffer from very slow convergence (the "counting to infinity" problem). This is because neighboring nodes can confuse each other by passing stale information back and forth, increment-ing the distance to a destination each time, until the recorded distance exceeds the maximum allowable (i.e., infinity). Techniques such as *split-horizon* and *poisoned-reverse* are used to mitigate the danger of counting to infinity; unfortunately, they do not eliminate it. Early implementations tried to solve the problem by defining infinity to be 15, but that clearly was a very short-term solution.

Compared to link-state algorithms, distance-vector algorithms use less memory and, since state information is not stored at every node, more lo-calized updates. However, when the distance to a particular destination changes, the effect can still ripple through every routing node in the net-work.

DBF-like protocols incur large update message penalties, although not as large as those incurred by link-state protocols. Attempts to fix some of the shortcomings of DBF, such as Destination-Sequenced Distance-Vector routing (DSDV) (see Chapter 3) have been proposed. However, synchroniza-tion and extra processing overhead are common in these protocols. Other protocols that rely on the information from the predecessor of the short-est path solve the slow convergence problem of DBF (e.g., [Cheng+ 1989, Garcia-Luna-Aceves 1993]). The processing requirements of these protocols may be quite high because of the way they process the update messages.

Scaling by grouping nodes into clusters, abstracting state information for the clusters, and selecting routes according to this abstracted state form a very old concept in networking, starting in the early 1970s with MacQuil-lan, Kamoun, and Kleinrock. Moreover, this hierarchical structure of nested clusters yields a natural addressing structure, such that a node's address is based on the labels of its ancestral clusters (i.e., the clusters in which it is contained). Routing within such a hierarchical clustering structure is what is usually termed *hierarchical routing*. Hierarchical routing addresses the in-efficiency of globally propagating local topology information. Most schemes using hierarchical routing are designed to avoid routing only through the clusterhead, which otherwise would introduce overhead not found in flat routing schemes. One approach to hierarchical routing is the Landmark Hi-erarchy [Tsuchiya 1988], which is discussed in Chapter 4 along with many other useful variants.

Other routing protocols have been adapted for use with ad hoc net-works, notably source routing (see Chapter 5) and link-reversal algorithms (see Chapter 8). Ad hoc networks can be viewed as the "acid test" of net-work protocol design, and so they are likely to continue to be of major interest. It may turn out that routing protocols designed for ad hoc net-works can be adapted to greatly improve the scalability of routing protocols designed for use in the global Internet. That would be an enormous payoff for ad hoc network research.

1.5 DESCRIPTION OF THE MATERIAL PRESENTED

The actual technical material follows this introductory chapter. Most of the chapters focus on a particular ad hoc networking protocol. It is fortunate that we can include in this book the descriptions presented in detail by the person or persons responsible for the creation of the protocol. Frequently, simulation results accompany the description of the algorithms and protocols. Each chapter and protocol has been selected to offer the reader the most diversity of opinion. The reader must decide separately how to make the comparisons.

Chapter 2—A DoD Perspective on Mobile Ad Hoc Networks

Chapter 2 describes the background of ad hoc networking from the military point of view and gives some ideas about how ad hoc network protocols are important for the armed forces. During combat, every design parameter for the communications network is stressed to, and sometimes beyond, the breaking point. There are many reasons for failure of military networks beyond the workaday problems of traffic congestion and crashing network nodes.

The military needs for communication engendered some of the earliest and best research into ad hoc networks, so this chapter seems almost mandatory for the reader to gain the fullest understanding of the subject.

Chapter 3—DSDV: Routing over a Multihop Wireless Network of Mobile Computers

My own involvement with ad hoc networks began with the design of the Destination-Sequenced Distance-Vector (DSDV) protocol. This protocol was designed in an ad hoc fashion; with Pravin Bhagwat, I started with Berkeley's routed and fixed problems one by one as they cropped up. I was surprised when Pravin could not find any previous work that included the idea of a destination sequence number to eliminate the counting to infinity problem. Because we thought we had found a very easy solution to a well-known problem, and because the solution was also easy to program, we decided to push it as far as we could. This was quite a while before we thought about doing anything "on-demand," so DSDV looks primitive by comparison with modern protocols.

Chapter 3, on DSDV, is presented with very few updates from the original.[1] I decided to include it in this book mainly for historical purposes. It was very instructive to build the protocol, and the protocol has

---

[1]In *Mobile Computing* edited by Tomasz Imielinski and Henry F. Korth. Norwood, MA: Kluwer, 1996—Chapter 6, pp. 183–206, by Perkins and Bhagwat.

some features that may be considered innovative even today. There have been numerous comparisons with DSDV, and I often think that is so because DSDV is so easy to beat in performance in many applications. Even now, papers propose new slants on how to outperform DSDV. Nevertheless, DSDV is still possibly a good contender for scenarios in which almost all nodes are mutually involved in communications with almost all other nodes and in which the mobility factor is neither very low nor very high.

Chapter 4—Cluster-Based Networks

Chapter 4 emphasizes routing within networks that have been organized according to cluster-based control structures, where the purpose of a cluster-based control structure may be for transmission management, backbone formation, or routing efficiency. The algorithms for forming and using these clusters and the structure and interconnectivity of the resulting clusters depend strongly on the purpose for which they are intended. The chapter presents various approaches, grouped according to the three purposes here and to show similarities and differences in the approaches and the advantages and disadvantages of each. In addition, a fine list of references is provided.

Chapter 5—DSR: The Dynamic Source Routing Protocol for Multihop Wireless Ad Hoc Networks

The Dynamic Source Routing (DSR) algorithm is another innovative approach to ad hoc networking, whereby nodes communicate along paths stored in source routes carried along with the data packets. DSR explores the many advantages of source routing and enjoys the benefits of some of the most extensive testing and deployment of any of the protocols in this book. It is one of the purest examples of an *on-demand* protocol, in which all actions are taken only when a route is actually needed. While reading Chapter 5, the reader should think about the ways that the additional path information in source routes can be applied to get a fuller description of the network topology even as it is changing over time.

Chapter 6—AODV: The Ad Hoc On-Demand Distance-Vector Protocol

Having experience with distance-vector routing and sequence numbering from DSDV, several researchers and I took up the task of shaping an *on-demand* version of that distance-vector protocol, called Ad Hoc On-Demand Distance-Vector (AODV). We were confident that nobody else had used that particular acronym, so we were safe at least on that count.

AODV offers a pure distance-vector approach to the problems of ad hoc networking, which means reduced memory and processing requirements. Because it acquires and maintains routes only on demand, the control traffic is reduced compared to most table-driven protocols. AODV takes care to cache routes, as long as the routes are likely to remain valid, to reduce unnecessary route acquisition; on the other hand, routes are purged soon after they no longer appear to be useful so that no additional control traffic will be wasted to maintain unused route information. AODV also offers multicast that benefits from the same route caching algorithms, address aggregation, some quality of service, and address autoconfiguration.

Over the years, AODV has benefited (as have many of the other protocols in this book) from the storehouse of knowledge built up in the IETF `manet` Working Group. As each Internet draft is published, new discussion ensues, identifying problems and possible solutions. This new and cooperative way of defining network protocols has been a very satisfying experiment in collaborative design, with the principal protocol designers borrowing the expertise of some of the best talents available.

Chapter 7—ZRP: A Hybrid Framework for Rerouting in Ad Hoc Networks

The Zone Routing Protocol (ZRP) takes a fresh yet time-tested approach to protocol improvement by constructing a way to hybridize table-driven protocols (such as DSDV) with on-demand protocols. ZRP uses zones that are similar to clusters, but instead of hierarchical routing between clusters being used, special border nodes are dynamically selected that connect adjacent zones. A zone radius parameter dynamically adjusts the size of the zone, in terms of the number of hops, as the network topology changes. A different routing protocol can be used between zones as compared to the one used within a zone. A proactive scheme is used inside the zone, and outside the zone routes are discovered only reactively.

This approach is almost guaranteed to find a happy medium between the two extremes that exhibits improved properties. The chapter first describes how the hybrid protocol can be parameterized to yield the extreme design points and then defines metrics for taking measurements. It is instructive to think about other extremes and how they might be hybridized to produce still other variants.

Chapter 8—Link-Reversal Routing

The Temporally Ordered Routing Algorithm (TORA) is the newest descendent of several *link-reversal* protocols derived from the original Gafni-Bertsekas algorithm, which is also described in this chapter. Creating a route between nodes is accomplished by building a directed acyclic graph (DAG). A packet is routed on the basis of information at each node (router) in the network, and routes are selected through evaluation of a sophisticated *height* function.

This innovative design will surely convince the reader that there is no realistic limit to the creative protocol design that can be brought to bear on the problems of ad hoc networking. I have often wondered if there is a simple transformation that would reduce TORA to, for instance, AODV or DSDV. Alternatively, if the height function were augmented with a source route, then perhaps TORA could also be considered a generalization of DSR. It is a fascinating mental exercise to imagine such protocol transformations and the generalities that must be extracted to produce each such specialization. I also believe that TORA can be specialized to produce each preceding descendant from the original Gafni-Bertsekas algorithm.

Chapter 9—The Effects of Beaconing on the Battery Life of Ad Hoc Mobile Computers

Chapter 9, on Associative Bit Routing (ABR), focuses on battery life, but I think that ABR is an example of yet another diverse design point for ad hoc network protocols. Like each preceding approach, ABR is a natural development of a protocol based on a sensible and intuitive model for route selection. Because battery life is improving at a rate far slower than that of improvements in processor speed and memory density, we will eventually face the prospect that caring for battery life may become the prime justification for many protocol design features. This is especially true for applications with tiny and very inexpensive devices like sensor dust, as described in section 1.2.6.

Chapter 10—Bandwidth-Efficient Link-State Routing in Wireless Networks

The most well-known link-state algorithms, such as the original ARPANet and the later OSPF and IS-IS, are table driven and require complete link-state information. Derived from these algorithms is a new type of link-state algorithm—a partial link-state algorithm that is not table driven.

Chapter 10, the last technical chapter, presents STAR as an example of a partial link-state algorithm. It also explores several other design innovations that enable maintenance of multiple routes between source and destination. The protocol in this chapter also has been extended to manage additional link-state parameters such as bandwidth availability and queue length; the latter quantity is directly related to average delay. In keeping with our theme, STAR bears little resemblance to the other protocols in this book. Thus, this last protocol chapter offers further convincing proof that the design space for ad hoc network protocols is huge indeed.

Chapter 11—Summary and Future Work

Finally, I close the book with some modest observations about possible futures for the field of ad hoc networking. I hope that the reader will be gentle in his or her criticism, for my attempt at identifying an ad hoc future is only one possibility out of the huge space of design and contingency that awaits all designers of ad hoc network protocols.

I hope that this book will delight and invigorate those who read it with the many divergent intuitions and creative energies that emerge from each chapter. At the end of the last chapter, I have made a list of relevant mailing lists and some other resources for participation. This, combined with the references in each chapter, should provide a resource with something to offer everyone.

References

[Bagrodia+ 1996] R. Bagrodia, M. Gerla, L. Kleinrock, J. Short, and T.-C. Tsai. *A Hierarchical Simulation Environment for Mobile Wireless Networks.* Technical report, Computer Science Department, University of California at Los Angeles, 1996.

[Cheng+ 1989] C. Cheng, R. Riley, S.P.R. Kumar, and J.J. Garcia-Luna-Aceves. A Loop-Free Extended Bellman-Ford Routing Protocol without Bouncing Effect. *ACM Computer Communication Review* 19(4):224–236, May 1989.

[Corson+ 1996] M.S. Corson, J. Macker, and S. Batsell. Architectural Considerations for Mobile Mesh Networking. In *Proceedings of the IEEE Military Communications Conference (MILCOM '96)*, October 1996.

[Dijkstra 1959] E.W. Dijkstra. A Note on Two Problems in Connection with Graphs. *Numerische Math.* 1:269–271, 1959.

[Estrin+ 1999] D. Estrin, R. Govindan, J. Heidemann, and S. Kumar. Scalable Coordination in Sensor Networks. In *Proceedings of the Fifth Annual ACM/IEEE International Conference on Mobile Computing and Networking (MOBICOM)*, August 1999, 263–270.

[Ford+ 1962] L.R. Ford, Jr., and D. R. Fulkerson. *Flows in Networks.* Princeton University Press, Princeton, N.J., 1962.

[Garcia-Luna-Aceves 1993] J.J. Garcia-Luna-Aceves. Loop-Free Routing Using Diffusing Computations. *IEEE/ACM Transactions on Networking* 1(1):130–141, February 1993.

[Haartsen 1998] J. Haartsen. Bluetooth—The Universal Radio Interface for Ad Hoc Wireless Connectivity. *Ericsson Review* (3), 1998.

[Hodes+ 1997] T. Hodes, R. Katz, E. Servan-Schreiber, and L. Rowe. Composable Ad Hoc Mobile Services for Universal Interaction. In *Proceedings of the Third ACM/IEEE International Conference on Mobile Computing and Networking (MOBICOM),* September 1997, 1–12.

[Kahn+ 1999] J.M. Kahn, R.H. Katz, and K.S.J. Pister. Mobile Networking for "Smart Dust." In *Proceedings of the Fifth ACM/IEEE International Conference on Mobile Computing and Networking (MOBICOM),* August 1999, 271–278.

[Leiner+ 1987] B.M. Leiner, D.L. Nielson, and F.A. Tobagi. Issues in Packet Radio Network Design. *Proceedings of the IEEE (Special Issue, Packet Radio Networks)* 75(1):6–20, January 1987.

[Malkin 1994] G. Malkin. RIP Version 2—Carrying Additional Information. RFC 1723 (draft standard). Internet Engineering Task Force, November 1994.

[Moy 1997] J. Moy. OSPF Version 2. RFC 2178 (draft standard). Internet Engineering Task Force, July 1997.

[Perkins 1996] C. Perkins. IP Mobility Support. RFC 2002 (proposed standard). Internet Engineering Task Force, October 1996.

[Postel 1981] J. Postel. Internet Protocol. RFC 791 (standard). Internet Engineering Task Force, September 1981.

[Prakash 1999] R. Prakash. Unidirectional Links Prove Costly in Wireless Ad Hoc Networks. In *Proceedings of the Third International Workshop on Discrete Algorithms and Methods for Mobile Computing and Communications (DIAL M),* August 1999, 15–22.

[Rekhter+ 1993] Y. Rekhter and T. Li. An Architecture for IP Address Allocation with CIDR. RFC 1518 (proposed standard). Internet Engineering Task Force, September 1993.

[Royer+ 1999] E.M. Royer and C.-K. Toh. A Review of Current Routing Protocols for Ad-Hoc Mobile Networks. *IEEE Personal Communications* 6(2):46–55, April 1999.

[SDT 1995] A Survey of Defence Technology: The Software Revolution—"To Dissolve, to Disappear." *The Economist,* June 1995.

[Strater+ 1996] J. Strater and B. Wollman. *OSPF Modeling and Test Results and Recommendations.* Mitre technical report 96W0000017, Xerox Office Products Division, March 1996.

[Tsuchiya 1988] P.F. Tsuchiya. The Landmark Hierarchy: A New Hierarchy for Routing in Very Large Networks. In *Proceedings of ACM SIGCOMM '88,* August 1988, 35–42.

[Weiser 1993] M. Weiser. Some Computer Science Issues in Ubiquitous Computing. *Communications of the ACM* 36(7), July 1993.

A DoD Perspective on Mobile Ad Hoc Networks

James A. Freebersyser
Office of Naval Research

Barry Leiner
*Research Institute for Advanced
Computer Science*

Within the last few years there has been a surge of interest in mobile ad hoc networks (MANET).[1] A MANET is defined as a collection of mobile platforms or nodes where each node is free to move about arbitrarily [Macker+ 1998a]. Each node logically consists of a router that may have multiple hosts and that also may have multiple wireless communications devices (Figure 2.1). (Note that nodes may be connected to other networks, for example, an Ethernet in a mobile vehicle.)

The term *MANET* describes distributed, mobile, wireless, multihop networks that operate without the benefit of any existing infrastructure except for the nodes themselves. A MANET expands the present Internet vision in which wireless nodes on the edge of the network cloud are typically connected and supported by a single wireless hop to the fixed, wired infrastructure. A MANET network cloud is composed of autonomous, potentially mobile, wireless nodes that may be connected at the edges to the fixed, wired Internet (Figure 2.2).

The acronym *MANET* is relatively new, but the concept of mobile packet radio networks, where every node in the network is mobile and where

---

[1]Special panel sessions on MANET were held at the 1996 IEEE Workshop on Computer Communications, MOBICOM '96, MOBICOM '97, NOMADIC '97, and MILCOM '97. The ARO/DARPA Workshop on MANET was held at the University of Maryland, March 1996.

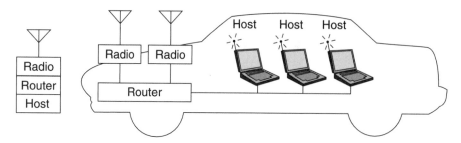

Figure 2.1. An Example of a **MANET**

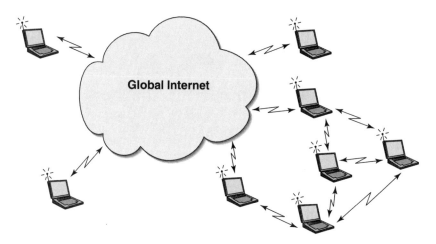

Figure 2.2. A **MANET** Connected to the Internet

wireless multihop (store-and-forward) routing is utilized, is not. Since the early 1970s, not long after the initial development of the packet switching technology that grew into what we now know as the Internet, the U.S. Department of Defense (DoD) sponsored research to enable packet switching technology to operate without the restrictions of fixed or wired infrastructure. In this chapter, we first examine the DoD motivation behind the development of MANET. Next we review some of the past foundational DoD-sponsored MANET work. Then we review current DoD-sponsored MANET work. Finally, we close the chapter with a few thoughts about MANET's future.

2.1 MOTIVATION

One of the original motivations for MANET is found in the military need for battlefield survivability. To survive under battlefield conditions, warfighters and their mobile platforms must be able to move about freely without any of the restrictions imposed by wired communications devices. Thus, the need for battlefield survivability translates into a mobile wireless communications system for coordinating group actions which operates in a distributed manner, avoiding single points of failure such as centralized control stations.

An additional motivation for MANET is that the military cannot rely on access to a fixed, preplaced communications infrastructure in battlefield environments. In some regions, such as the desert or the jungle, there is no terrestrial communications infrastructure. In other regions, access is unavailable because of destruction of or damage to the local communications infrastructure. A rapidly deployable, self-organizing mobile infrastructure is the primary factor that differentiates MANET design issues from those associated with commercial cellular systems.

A third motivating factor is derived from the physics of electromagnetic propagation, which results in the inability of frequencies much higher than 100 MHz to propagate beyond line of sight (LOS). Terrain, foliage, and man-made obstacles can also prevent LOS connectivity. Therefore, multihop (store-and-forward) packet routing must be used to exchange messages between users who are not within LOS of each other.

In summary, mobile wireless, distributed, multihop networking— MANET—developed out of the military need for survivability, operation without preplaced infrastructure, and connectivity beyond LOS.

A plethora of design parameters must be considered and a myriad of assumptions made about users and operational environments before undertaking the design of a MANET. We highlight the discussion of MANET design issues in Leiner et al. [Leiner+ 1987a] and Macker and Corson [Macker+ 1998a] to introduce a few of the salient issues that must be examined.

Network size   Network size usually refers to the number of network nodes, but it can also refer to the geographical area covered by the network; both are critical parameters for coordinating network actions with distributed control mechanisms. Taken together, the number of nodes over a given geographic area defines the network density. It is important to distinguish between the number of network nodes and the number of endpoints, since some platforms, such as a ship, may be a single node in the network, with a sub-network of many endpoints at that node.

Connectivity   Connectivity refers to a variety of issues. It may refer to the number of neighbors that each node can link to directly, which may or may not be bidirectional links because of, for example, local interference conditions. Connectivity may also refer to the link capacity between two nodes. Also related to connectivity are specialized military operating modes, such as emission-controlled (EMCON) operation. During EMCON operation, nodes do not transmit to prevent detection by the enemy, yet must still be able to receive critical messages.

Network topology   User mobility can directly affect how fast the node connectivity and hence the network topology changes; thus, it influences how and when the network protocol must adapt to changes. However, it is possible to have cases of very high user mobility that do not result in a change in link connectivity, such as when military units move in one direction in a set formation. Conversely, it is possible to have very rapid changes in link connectivity that result in changes in the network topology without user mobility, such as when nodes become inoperative because of dead batteries or destruction during combat.

User traffic   The characteristics and types of user-generated traffic heavily influence the design of a MANET. Does the user traffic consist of short, bursty packets that are without strict delay bounds but intolerant of loss? Or does it consist of longer packets that are generated periodically with strict delay bounds but tolerant of loss? Is it a combination of both? Does one type of traffic have priority over another type? Do all nodes generate traffic in the same manner? Whereas such knowledge is obviously important to the design of the network layer, it is also important to the design of the medium access control (MAC) layer because efficient access to the spectrum can be a performance bottleneck in a MANET.

Operational environment   Operational environment refers to the terrain (urban, rural, maritime, etc.) that may prevent LOS operation. It also refers to potential sources of interference in the radio channel, which is especially relevant in military environments where the potential for intentional enemy interference necessitates that design of the physical, data link, MAC, and network layers be resistant to such attacks.

Energy   Unlike a commercial cellular communications system, there are no fixed base stations in a MANET. All MANET nodes have roughly equal status, so, the energy burden cannot be transferred to energy-advantaged nodes such as fixed base stations, although nodes that are in platforms do have an energy advantage over those that are battery operated. Specifically, battery-operated store-and-forward nodes present a significant challenge in developing low-energy networking approaches. Often overlooked in the design of a MANET is the impact on energy consumption of the layers above the physical layer. An inefficient data link, MAC, or network layer design can result in additional packets being transmitted and hence in more energy being used. Shutting down a node in a MANET if it hasn't participated in the network for a given period of time is one energy-saving technique. Of course, the designer is then faced with the difficult task of determining how and when to wake up a sleeping node when it is needed by the network to forward other users' data packets.

Regulatory   A MANET must adhere to existing regulations for emitted power, for both legal and public health reasons. Because of the present state of the crowded spectrum below 100 MHz, it is unlikely that any future MANET will have the capability of connecting beyond LOS. If an unlicensed frequency band is selected, such as any of the Unlicensed National Information Infrastructure (UNII) and Industrial, Scientific, and Medical (ISM) bands, the existing power spectral density (PSD) requirements for noninterference must be met, although destructive interference can still result between users even if PSD regulations are followed.

Performance metrics   After determining the basic framework of a MANET, the designer must choose the important performance metrics to satisfy user needs. Typically, throughput and delay, along with their associated mean, variance, and distribution, are used as performance metrics for user data. Efficiency, in terms of the protocol overhead and data packets delivered correctly, is used to measure the goodness of the network protocol itself.

Cost   Ultimately, cost-versus-performance trades must be made if the MANET design is to be implemented. The designer must determine how cost affects the most critical aspects of the design, especially the performance as perceived by the user.

One observation about the design of a MANET is that the different layers of the system are highly interdependent. That is, the standard OSI layers cannot be decoupled with an optimal design made for each layer independent of the function of the other layers [Leiner+ 1987a]. Even in wired networks, there is coupling, particularly when working at the performance limits. Another observation is that a single protocol will likely not be able to operate efficiently across the entire spectrum of design parameters and operating conditions [Macker+ 1998a].

2.2 THE PAST

Packet switching technology, first demonstrated by the ARPANet in the 1960s, provided great promise for dynamically sharing bandwidth among multiple users, and it offered a means for adaptively routing traffic in response to changing network conditions and user demands. Recognizing the advantages of packet switching in a mobile wireless environment, in 1972 DARPA initiated a research effort to develop and demonstrate a packet radio network (PRNet). The PRNet was to provide an efficient means of sharing a broadcast radio channel as well as coping with changing and incomplete connectivity [Kahn+ 1978].

As interest in PRNets grew, the core ideas of the DARPA PRNet were applied in a number of environments: terrestrial and airborne; narrowband and wideband; amateur radio; and satellite. These networks shared a number of characteristics of a MANET. They were all based on the notion of packet switching applied to a broadcast radio usually sharing a common channel. Overall, they were aimed at the support of mobile users, although some of the amateur and commercial applications downplayed this capability. Most were based on store-and-forward operation, although the simpler satellite networks used a single satellite [Leiner+ 1987b].

In this section, we discuss the two phases of DARPA efforts in the 1970s and 1980s and related activities pursued by the Army, Navy, Air Force, and other communities.

2.2.1 DARPA Packet Radio Network

In 1972, when the DARPA PRNet program was initiated, packet switching had just recently been demonstrated as an efficient means for sharing bandwidth using store-and-forward routing to provide reliable computer communications. Although the initial PRNet protocols used a centralized control station, the core PRNet concept quickly evolved into a distributed architecture consisting of a network of broadcast radios with minimal central control, using multihop store-and-forward routing techniques to create complete end-user connectivity from incomplete radio connectivity. Broadcast radios were used for three reasons:

- Mobile users do not need pointing antennas.
- There is simpler channel management in that no coordinated frequency allocations are needed beyond the setting of the frequency for the network.
- Theoretical results indicated that for bursty traffic it is better to share a larger channel dynamically than to divide it into sub-channels [Tobagi 1987].

Dynamically sharing the channel required the development of sophisticated yet simple channel access protocols. The PRNet used a combination of the Aloha and Carrier Sense Multiple Access (CSMA) approaches. The use of CSMA, in particular, was made possible through development of advanced radio and controller hardware. Careful attention to issues such as receive/transmit switching time was necessary. To achieve these goals, special hardware combining spread-spectrum radios with computer controllers were built. A series of these units (experimental, improved, and value-engineered packet radios) were developed as part of the program. These units provided a number of relatively advanced features, including a variable data rate of 100 or 400 Kbps and direct-sequence (DS) spread spectrum at 12.8 Mcps. The spread-spectrum approach helped mitigate multipath fading and aided in discriminating between signals from different radios. In addition, advanced spread-spectrum radio technology was developed [Fischer+ 1987] to provide very wideband spread spectrum. These upgraded packet radios provided spreading at roughly 90 Mcps and also provided forward error correction, adaptive antenna nulling, and a variety of additional robustness features.

Given the basic connectivity provided by mobile, spread-spectrum, broadcast radios, the challenge was then to develop network management algorithms that would provide the needed connectivity assessment, route determination, and packet forwarding functions in a continually changing environment. The PRNet protocols were a sophisticated combination of algorithms that provided this function with no centralized control. A short description of these protocols along with pointers to more detailed descriptions of the individual algorithms is found in [Jubin+ 1987].

Development of the PRNet required sophisticated design and debugging tools. For example, a method was needed to update the software in the network nodes while the network was operating. Techniques ranging from dynamic loading and debugging to sophisticated test jigs that allowed laboratory testing of network dynamics were developed as part of the PRNet program [Jubin+ 1987].

The DARPA PRNet program demonstrated the technologies to create a MANET supporting mobile users from a collection of broadcast, spread-spectrum radios. It did so by exploiting the earlier lessons of packet switching combined with sophisticated radio hardware and software and network management algorithms. As the PRNet was being developed, in parallel with another DARPA effort involving packet switching over satellites (SatNet) [Jacobs+ 1978], it was recognized that there was a need to tie various networks together (ARPANet, PRNet, and SatNet). This was the origin of the Internet program, launched in 1974 [Leiner+ 1997], and the PRNet was the first network whose design was "Internet aware."

2.2.2 Survivable Radio Networks

The basic PRNet's feasibility was demonstrated by the early 1980s, but several major issues remained to be resolved before the DoD could fully exploit MANET technology. The initial versions of the radios and associated controllers were large, power hungry, and limited in their processing. They had sophisticated capabilities but needed considerable enhancement, for example, in the area of spread-spectrum management. In addition, the network management algorithms were demonstrated on relatively small networks but needed to support large networks. The robustness of the network against electronic attack also needed to be enhanced.

DARPA initiated the Survivable Radio Networks (SURAN) program in 1983 to address these issues. The SURAN program had three goals:

- To develop a small, low-cost, low-power radio that would support more sophisticated packet radio protocols
- To develop and demonstrate algorithms that could scale to tens of thousands of nodes
- To develop and demonstrate techniques for robust and survivable packet radio networking in the face of sophisticated electronic attacks

A linchpin of this effort was the low-cost packet radio (LPR) [Fifer+ 1987]—a digitally controlled DS spread-spectrum radio with an integrated microprocessor-based packet switch. LPR used the state-of-the-art micro-processor—an Intel 8086! Building on prior packet radio designs, it added a number of sophisticated features, such as the ability to change the spreading code on a bit-by-bit basis under program control, adaptive forward error correction, and coherent recursive integration of spread-spectrum signals.

On the foundation of the LPR, a family of advanced network management protocols was developed. To handle networks of large scale, a hierarchical approach to network topology, based on dynamic clustering, was proposed to support virtually unlimited network scaling. Techniques were developed for management of the spreading keys, both for security and for increasing capacity through generation of multiple channels, and for dynamically adapting radio parameters on the basis of measurements of both radio parameters and network traffic [Shacham+ 1987].

2.2.3 Other DoD Efforts in MANET

Once the basic ideas of packet radio networking were demonstrated in the DARPA programs, interest grew in directly applying these ideas to the needs of the U.S. military.

Army

Within the Army, the Army Research Office (ARO) provided sustained basic research funding to many of the university researchers associated with the larger DARPA programs. The Communications-Electronics Command (CECOM) Research, Development, and Engineering Center (RDEC) assisted in the management and direction of the DARPA programs and also advocated the transitioning of the technology to Army programs. Initially, as with any large and conservative organization, the operational branch of the Army did not embrace the new packet radio concepts. However, with the maturation of MANET technology and the demonstration of its utility in a series of user experiments in the mid-1980s, the benefits of MANET became increasingly apparent and the Army as a whole began to support it.

During the 1980s, the demonstration PRNet, based on ground-mobile spread-spectrum radios, had the most direct fit to the Army environment, and there were a number of Army efforts to exploit PRNet technology. DARPA and the Army partnered in a series of testbeds at Fort Bragg, North Carolina, to demonstrate how ground command and control could be improved through use of PRNet and Internet technologies [Leiner+ 1986, Frankel 1986]. One particularly interesting experiment was the use of PRNet technology to automate information flow in support of tactical fire control, demonstrated in the 1981 HELBAT exercise.

The approach initially taken by the Army was to add a packet over-lay capability to existing circuit- or broadcast-oriented radio systems. First came the overlay to the multichannel LOS radio system that eventually evolved into the Mobile Subscriber Equipment (MSE) overlay or Tactical Packet Network (TPN). Next was the overlay for the Single Channel Ground-Airborne Radio System (SINCGARS), which is currently the standard Army combat net radio. SINCGARS is a frequency-hopped spread-spectrum radio operating in the VHF band that is capable of sending and receiving data at a few kilobits per second. SINCGARS radios were used to provide the basic wireless connectivity, which was then managed by the SURAN algorithms to provide packet data communications to the users. Because of the limited data rate of SINCGARS, new algorithms were needed to reduce the overhead of individual packets as well as network management overhead. Finally, the Tactical Multinet Gateway (TMG), which used standard Internet protocols, was developed as part of the Army's 1993 Survivable Adaptive System (SAS) Advanced Technology Demonstration (ATD), which also used LPRs. The systems just mentioned demonstrated capabilities eventually deployed in the Army's recent Task Force XXI experiment, which will be discussed later in this chapter [Sass 1999].

Navy

While the Army developed packet radio networks primarily for land-based application, the U.S. Naval Research Laboratory (NRL), with funding provided by the Office of Naval Research (ONR), developed a different type of packet radio network for use by ships at sea [Ephremides+ 1987]. The challenge in such a ship-based network was to provide an adaptive network management structure and end-to-end user data communications using a low data rate (< 10 Kbps) channel for connectivity. Since individual Navy ships within a task force are often beyond LOS communications range, the resulting intra-taskforce (ITF) network does not have the denser connectivity of ground-based packet radio networks, which resulted in a design optimized to operate in the limited spectrum of the HF band. Distributed network control is used to increase survivability, whereas frequency hopping (FH) is used for resistance against jamming. A link-clustered architecture (LCA) was developed in which ordinary nodes cluster around dynamically selected clusterheads and gateway nodes connect clusters. The ITF network discussion in Ephremides et al. [Ephremides+ 1987] is a comprehensive description of the design methodology used, including techniques for eliminating the hidden terminal problem, as well as network initialization and clustering.

The ITF network was initially designed only for data, but the recently completed Navy Data/Voice Integration ATD fulfilled many of the concepts described in Ephremides et al. [Ephremides+ 1987]. A UHF demand-assigned multiple access (DAMA) satellite communications capability for linking a remote Navy task force to shore facilities was also integrated into the packet radio network. The final phase of this three-phase ATD demonstrated Internet services such as interactive voice, voice conferencing, whiteboarding, e-mail, file and image transfers, and web-browsing applications over a six-node network combining HF and UHF satellite communications links [Baker 1997].

Air Force
The U.S. Air Force Research Laboratory in Rome, New York, in partnership with DARPA, explored the use of the packet radio network concept to provide communications between ground stations through a network of aircraft. The program also explored enhancements to address the challenge of partitioned networks, in which a single packet radio network separates into disjoint networks that can communicate only through the use of another network. The goal was to provide a survivable command and control capability. This concept was demonstrated in the Strategic Command and Control Communications (C3) experiment in 1985 [Frankel 1986].

2.2.4 Other Efforts in MANET

Interest in packet radio networks was not limited to the United States. In the United Kingdom, the Royal Signals and Radar Establishment (RSRE) developed a packet radio network based on a narrow-band combat net radio [Davies+ 1987]. As with the U.S. Army SINCGARS overlay, the packet radio network concept utilized by the British involved overlaying a network on existing radio technology through the addition of control processors.

Another application of packet radio network concepts was explored in the DARPA Multiple Satellite System (MSS) program [Binder+ 1987].

The goal was to establish a packet radio network using a large number of LEO satellites, thereby creating a dynamic mesh of nodes with downlinks to users. A design study was completed on the effort, but it was concluded that satellite and related technology was not sufficiently mature to pursue the concept further. The MSS program and recent commercial mobile communications satellite initiatives, such as Iridium, have many similarities.

By the late 1980s, many of the concepts of packet radio networking had been demonstrated in a variety of DoD programs. Concurrently, packet radio concepts were being explored in the amateur and commercial sector. Amateur radio was used as the underlying connectivity to support packet communications and to create an amateur packet radio network [Karn+ 1985]. Commercial applications of the technology were also being explored [Leiner+ 1987b], but widespread application to support mobile users was inhibited by the state of the art in low-cost, low-power, small-size radio and microprocessor technology. The LPR was an improvement over earlier designs, but it was not adequate to provide the kind of form factor and battery life required to support a ground mobile user. This was to change dramatically with the microsystems revolution of the late early 1980s and early 1990s.

2.3 THE PRESENT

The growth of the Internet infrastructure and the microcomputer revolution have made the initial packet radio network ideas both more applicable and feasible. The January 1987 *Proceedings of the IEEE Special Issue, Packet Radio Networks* [Leiner+ 1987c][2] documents some of the foundational accomplishments in this area. This section will discuss how these early ideas are currently being applied and enhanced to take advantage of the advances in the supporting technologies. However, before proceeding to the discussion of current MANET work, it is interesting to consider what has and hasn't changed in the state of the art since the early work.

Packet switching techniques, such as asynchronous transfer mode (ATM) and the Internet Protocol (IP), are widely accepted. Therefore, a MANET must be able to interact with the dominant protocols of the existing infrastructure, whether or not it will actually use them or their variants.

There have been significant increases in the computational capability and in the memory storage (Moore's Law) of the microcomputers used

---

[2]A review of the January 1987 *Proceedings of the IEEE Special Issue, Packet Radio Networks* is suggested for readers who are interested in a deeper exploration of MANET.

for compression and signal processing. However, the data rates of wireless communications devices have not experienced anywhere near the exponential growth in data rates of fiber optic cable, although the form factors of wireless communications devices, such as handheld cellular phones, are much smaller than a decade ago. It is a safe assumption for the foreseeable future that the data rate and bit error rate for wireless communications will be several orders of magnitude behind those for the state-of-the-art wired media, especially if the wireless user is moving.

The use of spread spectrum is no longer confined to military users who operate in low probability of interception/detection (LPI/D) modes. The use of some form of spread spectrum is now considered a wise decision for multipath and co-channel interference mitigation. In the commercial cellular standard IS-95, the motivation for using the DS form of spread spectrum is to increase the capacity of the cellular system by allowing dynamic sharing of the channel. Both DS and FH modes of operation are contained in the IEEE 802.11 standard for wireless local area networks (LANs) to meet power spectrum density requirements.

User expectations have risen with the proliferation of wireless technology. Users will soon expect the same connectivity available in an office environment to be available on demand in handheld devices, through either the cellular infrastructure or emerging commercial mobile communications satellites.

In the midst of all these changes, the laws of physics and chemistry are constants: Frequencies above roughly 100 MHz will rarely propagate beyond LOS, and the speed of light will not exceed roughly 3×10^8 m/s. Moreover, the energy storage capabilities of batteries have increased only gradually over the last few decades.

The issue of spectrum availability has both positive and negative aspects. The ISM and UNII bands at 800 MHz, 2.4 GHz, and 5 GHz are now available for use and have created new opportunities for commercial development. However, it is difficult for commercial or military users to gain access to significant amounts of contiguous bandwidth. In fact, the military has lost access to spectrum that has been auctioned off to the commercial sector. The inability to occupy a contiguous portion of the spectrum that is sufficiently wideband reduces some of the advantages of using direct-sequence (DS) waveforms to mitigate multipath.

In this section we consider four areas of current MANET activity: the U.S. Army's Task Force XXI (TF XXI) Advanced Warfighting Experiment (AWE), which built a tactical internet (TI); the U.S. Navy and Marines' Extending the Littoral Battlespace (ELB) Advanced Concept Technology Demonstration (ACTD); the DARPA Global Mobile (GloMo) Information Systems program; and the Internet Engineering Task Force (IETF) MANET Working Group (WG).

2.3.1 Tactical Internet

Embodying many of the basic attributes of a MANET, the U.S. Army's March 1997 TF XXI AWE may be the largest-scale implementation (comprising thousands of nodes) of a mobile, wireless, multihop packet radio network. In the TI, nodes consist of both vehicular and man-packed radios that were already in the government inventory—primarily Enhanced Position-Location Reporting Systems (EPLRSs) and Single Channel Ground-Airborne Radio Systems, running modified commercial Internet protocols. Originally designed for robust geolocation but now used for data connectivity, EPLRS is a direct-sequence spread-spectrum, time-division multiple-access radio capable of transmitting data at tens of kilobits per second. The decision to use commercial protocols as a basis in the TI and in all future DoD communications systems is mandated by the Joint Technical Architecture (JTA) [JTA 1997]. The JTA is the DoD network "building code" to which future communications systems must adhere. The SINCGARS packet overlay technology has been discussed; however, technology from the DARPA packet radio programs also improved EPLRS by eliminating the requirement for a central network control station to manage the EPLRS network [Sass 1999].

The TI was a success and allowed the Army to demonstrate important doctrinal and operational concepts. However, it reinforced the fact that existing commercial protocols specifically developed for the fixed, wired infrastructure must be appropriately modified before they are used in the mobile, wireless environment. The JTA has contributed greatly to the improved interoperability of the vast majority of the DoD communications infrastructure. However, protocols, such as the Open Shortest Path First (OSPF) standard, which uses periodic hello messages to determine network connectivity, were never designed be used in an environment in which the network topology can change rapidly and in which nodes are connected by low data rate, high bit error rate links. Thus, the resulting network settling times using OSPF were long [Strater+ 1996].

2.3.2 ELB

The purpose of the April 1999 Extending the Littoral Battlespace Advanced Concept Technology Demonstration was to demonstrate the feasibility of Marine Corps warfighting concepts that require over-the-horizon (OTH) communications from ships at sea to Marines on land via an aerial relay. The physical layer for the MANET of the ELB ACTD was a commercial wireless local area network (WLAN) product, Lucent's WaveLAN, and the VRC-99A, a direct-sequence spread-spectrum radio descended from the DARPA LPR. WaveLAN was used to connect to an access point on a terrestrial or airborne relay, and VRC-99As were used as the mobile backbone to connect the terrestrial or airborne routers. While the number of nodes in the network, approximately 20, was small compared to that in the TF XXI AWE, the ELB ACTD was successful in demonstrating the use of aerial relays for connecting users beyond LOS.

The ELB ACTD set very aggressive cost and performance goals for MANET technology. WaveLAN and the VRC-99A were selected primarily to reduce system cost by utilizing existing commercial or military equipment, respectively. However, WaveLAN required several modifications, such as the addition of an external power amplifier and the increase in certain time-out settings, to operate at the extended ranges involved. The sum of these modifications reduced much of the advantage of using existing commercial equipment. In addition, the ability of nodes to roam seamlessly throughout the network was limited. The second phase of the ELB ACTD is targeting these areas for improvement [Althouse 1999].

2.3.3 GloMo

The widespread implementation of Internet and Web technology provided incentive to both commercial and defense sectors to extend the global information infrastructure into the mobile wireless environment. One DoD response to these changes was the initiation of the DARPA Global Mobile (GloMo) Information Systems program in 1994 [Leiner+ 1996], which has just recently concluded.

The goal of the GloMo program [Ruth 1998] was "to make the mobile, wireless environment a first-class citizen in the defense information infrastructure by providing user friendly connectivity and access to services for mobile users." It aimed to provide office-environment, Ethernet-type multimedia (voice, video, images, etc.) connectivity any time, anywhere, in handheld devices, not just in devices mounted on platforms moving in the air or over water or land. The GloMo program had the following five thrusts [Leiner+ 1996]:

1. Infrastructure design, such as computer-aided design tools
2. Untethered nodes that provide low-cost, low-power wireless access with sufficient processing power to support sophisticated network management algorithms
3. Network protocols and algorithms with robust architectures that can be rapidly deployed
4. End-to-end networking in heterogeneous environments
5. Mobile applications that adapt to varying network connectivity and quality of service (QoS)

Figure 2.3. Flat Network Architecture

GloMo pursued a number of networking approaches for MANET, including the Wireless Internet Gateways (WINGs) project of the University of California at Santa Cruz and the Multimedia Mobile Wireless Network (MMWN) project of GTE Internetworking (formerly Bolt Beranek & Newman, BBN). The goal of WINGs [Garcia-Luna-Aceves 1997] was to design and demonstrate seamless operation between a MANET and the Internet without treating the MANET as an opaque sub-network that uses an intranet routing protocol below IP for packet forwarding. WINGs uses a flat (peer-to-peer) network architecture (Figure 2.3). Several prototype versions were demonstrated within the GloMo program.

MMWN is based on a hierarchical network architecture (Figure 2.4) that has its roots in the SURAN program [Ramanathan+ 1998; see also this book's Chapter 4]. It uses a modular system of link and network layer algorithms to support distributed, realtime multimedia applications in a MANET. MMWN has three components: clustering techniques; location management; and virtual circuit setup and repair. It is currently being demonstrated as part of the GloMo program, and philosophically similar techniques are being applied in the Near-Term Digital Radio (NTDR) program currently under development.

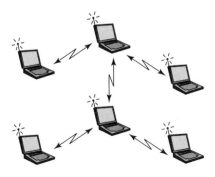

Figure 2.4. Hierarchical Network Architecture

2.3.4 IETF MANET Working Group

One focal point for recent interest in MANET is the Internet Engineering Task Force MANET Working Group (IETF MANET WG). The activities of an IETF WG may not appear to be relevant to the military, but the DoD mandate to use open standards [JTA 1997] has made it critical to participate in standards groups such as the IETF. Many of the commercial protocols developed for the fixed, wired infrastructure rarely translate well to the mobile, wireless regime. Because future DoD communications systems must comply with the JTA, the best way to ensure the existence of network protocols that operate effectively in military environments is for the DoD to be actively involved in the development of standards for commercial protocols that eventually become part of the JTA.

While the original motivation for MANET was military needs, its non-military applications have grown substantially since the mid-1980s when military-based applications were the focus for most of the effort in packet radio networks [Leiner+ 1987c]. Police, fire and rescue, disaster relief, robotics, space, distributed sensors, and impromptu team communications are a few possible applications of MANET technology.

The near-term goal of the MANET WG is to "standardize an inter-domain unicast routing protocol which provides one or more modes of operation, each mode specialized for efficient operation in a given mobile networking 'context,' where a context is a predefined set of network characteristics" [Macker+ 1998a]. There are nearly a dozen candidate routing protocols currently being discussed within the MANET WG for achieving this goal [Macker+ 1998b].

2.4 THE FUTURE

In our discussion of the future of MANET, we consider the prospects for commercial and DoD applications and comment on some areas of further research.

2.4.1 Commercial Applications

The formation of the IETF MANET WG is a signal that the commercial marketplace is considering MANET applications, but it is not yet clear what final form this technology will take. For example, there is an ad hoc mode within the IEEE 802.11 standard, but this standard does not include a multihop relaying capability. The increase in wireless data rates, as evolving in satellite and cellular systems as well as in unique systems such as Metricom's Ricochet (*http://www.metricom.com*), may make the mobile wireless Internet much more attractive to users, both military and commercial.

It remains to be seen if these markets for MANET technology will be large enough to alter the existing commercial paradigm of cellular (one-hop) connectivity to the wired infrastructure. In this section, we describe one vision of a potential mass-market application of MANET.

Imagine a utopian view of the future in which people and machines are nodes on the global MANET. A global MANET using unlicensed spectrum will free users of the fixed infrastructure (and the control of the telecommunications conglomerates), thereby bypassing the cellular and wired infrastructure in the same way that Internet telephony has the potential to bypass long-distance phone companies. The price to the user will be the initial cost of the MANET device and the electricity used when operating or recharging batteries (and, of course, the inevitable software and hardware upgrades). In this imagined global MANET there will be no billing for service. Because user cooperation is necessary to obtain the dense mesh of users required for sufficient connectivity, there may be a charge to the owner of a device who does not participate in the network sufficiently and a good-behavior credit given to the user who does. With widespread use of MANET devices, users' cost will decrease, as has occurred with computers and consumer electronics. The DoD will benefit greatly from the availability of open MANET standards and low-cost MANET equipment, if such commercial equipment adequately addresses specific military needs.

Along with the regulatory hurdles involving access to spectrum and the many legal issues that need to be resolved with the companies owning the existing communications infrastructure, there remain many technical obstacles to overcome. For example, will MANET users cooperate with each other by forwarding data packets in a timely and fair manner? That is, will a user share his radio device by forwarding another user's data packets without unfairly delaying those data packets to transmit his own? Forwarding other users' data packets is of concern because this action reduces the available battery power of a user's radio device, which may result in an inability to send and receive the user's own data packets at a future time. Consider the analogy of driving a car on a public road and participating in a MANET. Automobile drivers cooperate and behave (most of the time) by driving at the speed limit, obeying traffic signals, and so forth, because there are established rules and consequences. But how can a MANET be patrolled to encourage good behavior (participating in the MANET by forwarding data packets promptly) and to prevent malicious users from reducing network efficiency? The military has a corporate structure that, for the most part, can enforce good behavior of authorized users, but such a structure does not exist in a heterogeneous, commercial environment.

Another issue that must be resolved is whether or not other group members can be trusted to forward data packets. How is a user to be prevented from eavesdropping on data packets belonging to other users that are being routed through her node? Encryption can be used to protect the actual data, but there are situations in which the initial sender may not want other users who are forwarding her data packet to know where it is going and who sent it. Knowledge of the source and destination might assist a malicious user in identifying which data packets to copy for possible decryption over a period of time. This issue can be a concern even in military environments because information can be classified at different levels. In such a case, how does an unclassified node route classified data packets? Routing data packets securely through other users who may not be trustworthy is a problem that must be solved before commercial uses of MANET become possible.

While numerous issues remain unexplored, the overriding obstacle for commercial use of MANET may be the lack of a "killer app" for mobile wireless users. For example, the Internet existed for many years running e-mail and file transfers essentially in the same way it does now. It did not begin the rapid growth it is currently experiencing until the introduction of the Web and Internet browser technology. Situational awareness (SA) and command and control (C2) messages show the potential to be killer apps for the military, but what killer app will move MANET technology into the commercial mass market? Given the modest gains of the mobile wireless data market using the cellular infrastructure in the last few years, it is not certain that e-mail, file transfers, or the Web will be the killer apps for mobile wireless data.

2.4.2 DoD

MANET technology is critical to achieving information dominance as described in DoD visions of the future. However, the current cost of equipping every vehicle and soldier as a MANET node is prohibitive. The military is attempting to leverage commercial-off-the-shelf (COTS) technology to reduce the cost. Unfortunately, as previously described, technologies for the commercial environment do not always function acceptably in the dynamic military environment. The key to fielding affordable MANET technology will be developing military-unique components only when necessary and leveraging COTS products as building blocks whenever possible.

As previously mentioned, the NTDR now entering the DoD's inventory implements many of the technologies, such as link clustering, developed during the SURAN program [Ruppe+ 1997]. The future generation of adaptive, multiband, multimode radios—the Joint Tactical Radio System (JTRS)—will offer improved flexibility over half-duplex, single-channel radios at higher layers of the system because of the ability to simultaneously transmit and receive on different bands using different waveforms.

Although airborne relays were not used in the TI, there are other DoD programs, such as the Navy and Marines' ELB ACTD, that are exploring the use of airborne relays to provide mobile infrastructure via a backbone in the sky as an alternative to the terrestrial backbone used in the TI.

2.4.3 Open Research Issues

Along with overarching issues, such as security and energy consumption, there are a host of unresolved research issues related to the realization of a global MANET. In a world dominated by packet switching technologies, such as ATM and IP, and by the ubiquitous nature of cellular phones, the advances in MANET technology that are needed may seem incremental by comparison. However, fundamental MANET problems remain unsolved. A major research topic derives not from the MANET itself but rather from the interaction of such networks with the global information infrastructure. As mentioned earlier, the Internet was originally motivated by a desire to tie together disparate networks into a seamless computer communications infrastructure. This was accomplished by making minimal assumptions about the component networks, asking only that they be able to deliver a packet on a best-effort basis. As the fiber optic plant grew, data rates of long-haul and local lines increased. Concurrently, as the power of the PC grew, so grew the services demanded of the Internet.

Many of the recent Internet efforts have been aimed at increasing the delivered bandwidth and quality of service to the end user. In this process, assumptions have been made about the underlying infrastructure, many of which are not appropriate for the mobile wireless environment. For example, the Transport Control Protocol (TCP) backs off on packet transmissions when a packet is lost or delayed beyond the acknowledgment time-out period, assuming that the packet was dropped by a congested router. A lost packet in a mobile environment is most likely due to bit errors caused by fluctuations in received signal level. In this case, the appropriate response on an end-to-end basis is different from that of a congested router. The research challenge, then, is to develop appropriate adaptive techniques that can deal with the peculiarities of both the wired and wireless environments.

MANET modeling and simulation are at present incomplete and difficult tasks. Existing tools do not realistically and cleanly blend the physical and MAC layers with the data link and network layers. Computer-aided design (CAD) tools that run simulations within a reasonable time are needed that accurately incorporate channel effects at the physical layer and multiple access interference (MAI) at the MAC layer in large-scale networks (thousands of nodes).

Distributed techniques for sensing and adapting to the dynamics in the network topology (e.g., using link-state or distance-vector techniques if the network topology is fairly static and active or flooding techniques if the network topology is highly dynamic) have the potential to increase network efficiency. However, such techniques are problematic without any centralized controller to prevent network instability in that different nodes in various portions of that network can sense dissimilar local conditions and adopt incompatible modes of operation. For the military, there may be ways to determine the network state a priori. That is, if the battle is about to begin the network should be configured for highly dynamic operation, but if the battle is over the network may operate more efficiently if it functions more as a static network [Corson 1998].

Techniques for efficiently searching the network and creating routes to the intended receiver may benefit from location information derived from global positioning system (GPS) satellites [Herring 1996]. Cellular networks use historical usage information about a user to page the user in his home area, roaming area, last-known location, and so on, before issuing a global page. A MANET could use information about a user's location to search first in a given geographic direction to increase the search speed and reduce network overhead. This technique could be used in military settings because the general geographic location of a user is often known; thus, the search for that user could proceed first in that direction (e.g., search to the west behind friendly lines).

New technologies at the physical layer hold near-term promise for increasing the reliability of the wireless channel. Multiuser detection techniques may finally be close to eliminating the loss in performance resulting from the near/far problem associated with DS code division multiple access (CDMA) without the use of centralized power control as utilized in commercial cellular phone systems [Verdu 1998]. With the move to higher frequencies, adaptive antenna arrays are approaching a form factor that can be integrated into each node so that routing and beam pointing are coordinated. This has the effect of reducing MAI and increasing the data rate or reducing the bit error rate. In the longer term, ultra-wideband (impulse radio) techniques [Scholtz+ 1998] may be able to offer nearly simultaneous transmit and receive capability at the same frequency. This will result in a full-duplex communications link that has the potential to operate outside channelized bandwidth restrictions by being FCC Part 15 compliant.

2.5 CONCLUSION

The present flurry of activity in the area of MANET is part of a continuum of activity begun in the early 1970s. MANET has a rich DoD history and a bright future for commercial and military applications. For the military to be able to take full advantage of this emerging technology and build and deploy MANETs to respond to its needs, it is essential that commercial wireless networking products be leveraged. As the MANET community moves forward, developing approaches that both leverage commercial products and satisfy the military need for rapidly deployable and survivable ad hoc networks is perhaps the key challenge.

Acknowledgments

The authors are grateful to Paul Sass of the Mitre Corporation, formerly with the U.S. Army Communications-Electronics Command (CECOM) Research, Development, and Engineering Center (RDEC) in Ft. Monmouth, New Jersey, and to Joseph Macker of the U.S. Naval Research Laboratory (NRL) in Washington, D.C., for reviewing early versions of this chapter and providing many helpful comments that greatly improved the historical and technical accuracy and completeness of the content.

References

[Althouse 1999] E. Althouse. *Extending the Littoral Battlespace (ELB)*. Advanced Concept Technology Demonstration (ACTD), NATO Information Systems Technology Panel Symposium on Tactical Mobile Communications, June 1999.

[Baker 1997] D. Baker. Data/Voice Communication over a Multihop, Mobile, High-Frequency Network. In *Proceedings of the IEEE Military Communications Conference (MILCOM '97)*, November 1997.

[Binder+ 1987] R. Binder, S. Huffman, I. Gurantz, and P. Vena. Crosslink Architectures for a Multiple Satellite System. *Proceedings of the IEEE* 75(1):75–82, January 1987.

[Corson 1998] M.S. Corson. *Thoughts on the Future of Mobile Ad Hoc Networking*. U.S. Army Research Office Strategy Planning Workshop, January 1998.

[Davies+ 1987] B. Davies and T. Davies. The Application of Packet Switching Techniques to Combat Net Radio. *Proceedings of the IEEE* 75(1):43–55, January 1987.

[Ephremides+ 1987] A. Ephremides, J. E. Wieselthier, and D. J. Baker. A Design Concept for Reliable Mobile Radio Networks with Frequency Hopping Signaling. *Proceedings of the IEEE* 75(1):56–73, January 1987.

[Fifer+ 1987] W. Fifer and F. Bruno. The Low-Cost Packet Radio. *Proceedings of the IEEE* 75(1):33–42, January 1987.

[Fischer+ 1987] J. Fischer, J. Cafarella, D. Arsenault, G. Flynn, and C. Bouman. Wide-Band Packet Radio Technology. *Proceedings of the IEEE* 75(1):100–115, January 1987.

[Frankel 1986] M. Frankel. Tactical C3 for the Ground Forces. In *Telecommunications and Processing for Military Command and Control: An Architecture for the 21st Century*, AFCEA International Press, Washington, DC, 1986.

[Garcia-Luna-Aceves 1997] J.J. Garcia-Luna-Aceves. Wireless Internet Gateways (WINGS). In *Proceedings of the IEEE Military Communications Conference (MILCOM '97)*, November 1997.

[Herring 1996] T.A. Herring. The Global Positioning Systems. *Scientific American* 274(2):44–50, February 1996.

[Jacobs+ 1978] I. Jacobs, R. Binder, and E. Hoversten. General Purpose Packet Satellite Networks. *Proceedings of the IEEE* 66(11):1448–1467, November 1978.

[JTA 1997] *Joint Technical Architecture, Version 5.0,* September 1997.

[Jubin+ 1987] J. Jubin and J. Tornow. The DARPA Packet Radio Network Protocols. *Proceedings of the IEEE* 75(1):21–32, January 1987.

[Kahn+ 1978] R. Kahn et al. Advances in Packet Radio Technology. *Proceedings of the IEEE* 66:1468–1496, November 1978.

[Karn+ 1985] P. Karn, H. Price, and R. Diersing. Packet Radio in the Amateur Service. *IEEE Journal on Selected Areas of Communications* SAC-3(3):431–439, May 1985.

[Ko+ 1998] Y. Ko and N.H. Vaidya. Location-Aided Routing (LAR) in Mobile Ad Hoc Networks. In *Proceedings of the Fifth ACM/IEEE International Conference on Mobile Computing and Networking (MOBICOM '98),* August 1998.

[Leiner+ 1986] B. Leiner, T. Klein, and B. Graff. Tactical C3 for the Ground Forces. In *Data Distribution in a Tactical Environment,* AFCEA International Press, Washington, DC, 1986.

[Leiner+ 1987a] B. Leiner, D. Nielson, and F. Tobagi. Issues in Packet Radio Network Design. *Proceedings of the IEEE (Special Issue, Packet Radio Networks)* 75(1):6–20, January 1987.

[Leiner+ 1987b] B. Leiner, D. Nielson, and F. Tobagi. Scanning the Issue. *Proceedings of the IEEE* 75(1):3–5, January 1987.

[Leiner+ 1987c] B. Leiner, D. Nielson, and F. Tobagi (eds.). *Proceedings of the IEEE (Special Issue, Packet Radio Networks)* 75(1), January 1987.

[Leiner+ 1996] B. Leiner, R. Ruth, and A.R. Sastry. Goals and Challenges of the DARPA GloMo Program. *IEEE Personal Communications,* 34–43, December 1996.

[Leiner+ 1997] B. Leiner et al. The Past and Future History of the Internet. *Communications of the ACM* 40(2):102–108, February 1997.

[Macker+ 1998a] J. Macker and M.S. Corson. Mobile Ad Hoc Networking and the IETF. *ACM Mobile Computing and Communication Review* 2(1):9–14, January 1998.

[Macker+ 1998b] J. Macker and M.S. Corson. Mobile Ad Hoc Networking and the IETF. *ACM Mobile Computing and Communication Review* 2(2):9–12, April 1998.

[Ramanathan+ 1998] R. Ramanathan and M. Steenstrup. Hierarchically-Organized, Multihop Mobile Wireless Networks for Quality-of-Service Support. *ACM/Baltzer Mobile Networks and Applications Journal* 3(1):101–119, January 1998.

[Ruppe+ 1997] R. Ruppe, S. Griswald, P. Walsh, and R. Martin. Near Term Digital Radio (NTDR) System. In *Proceedings of the IEEE Military Communications Conference (MILCOM '97),* November 1997.

[Ruth 1998] R. Ruth. *Global Mobile Information Systems Program Overview*, July 1998.

[Sass 1999] P. Sass. Communications Networks for the Force XXI Digitized Battlefield. *ACM/Baltzer Mobile Networks and Applications Journal (Special Issue, Mobile Ad Hoc Networking)* 4, October 1999.

[Scholtz+ 1998] R. Scholtz and M. Win. Impulse Radio: How It Works. *IEEE Communications Letter* 2(2):36–38, February 1998.

[Shacham+ 1987] N. Shacham and J. Westcott. Future Directions in Packet Radio Architectures and Protocols. *Proceedings of the IEEE* 75(1):83–99, January 1987.

[Strater+ 1996] J. Strater and B. Wollman. *OSPF Modeling and Test Results and Recommendations*. Mitre technical report 96W0000017, Xerox Office Products Division, March 1996.

[Tobagi 1987] F. Tobagi. Modeling and Performance Analysis of Multihop Packet Radio Networks. *Proceedings of the IEEE* 75(1):135–155, January 1987.

[Verdu 1998] S. Verdu. *Multiuser Detection*. Cambridge University Press, New York, 1998.

3

DSDV
Routing over a
Multihop Wireless
Network of Mobile
Computers

Charles E. Perkins
IBM Research

Pravin Bhagwat
University of Maryland

Abstract

An *ad hoc* network is the cooperative engagement of a collection of mobile nodes without the required intervention of any centralized access point. In this chapter we present a design for the operation of such ad hoc networks. The basic idea of the design is to operate each mobile node as a specialized router, which periodically advertises its view of the interconnection topology with other mobile nodes within the network. This amounts to a new sort of routing protocol. We have investigated modifications to the basic Bellman-Ford [Bertsekas+ 1987] routing mechanisms, as specified by the Routing Information Protocol (RIP) [Malkin 1993], making it suitable for a dynamic and self-starting network mechanism as is required by users wishing to utilize ad hoc networks. Our modifications address some of the previous objections to the use of Bellman-Ford, related to the poor looping properties of such algorithms in the face of broken links and the resulting time-dependent nature of the interconnection topology describing the links between the mobile nodes. Finally, we describe the ways in which the basic network-layer routing can be modified to provide MAC-layer support for ad hoc networks.

Note: From *Mobile Computing,* Imielinski, T., and Korth, H. F. (eds.), pp. 183–206— Chapter 6 by C. E. Perkins and P. Bhagwat. Norwood, Mass.: Kluwer, 1996. Copyright © Kluwer Publishing. Used with permission.

3.1 INTRODUCTION

Recently there has been tremendous growth in the sales of laptop and portable computers. These smaller computers, despite their size, can be equipped with hundreds of megabytes of disk storage, high-resolution color displays, pointing devices, and wireless communications adapters. Moreover, since many of these small (in size only) computers operate for hours with battery power, users are free to move about at their convenience without being constrained by wires.

This is a revolutionary development in personal computing. Battery-powered, untethered computers are likely to become a pervasive part of our computing infrastructure. As mobile computers become handy, for whatever purposes, sharing information between them will become a natural requirement. Currently such sharing is made difficult by the need for users to perform administrative tasks and set up static, bidirectional links between their computers. However, if the wireless communications systems in the mobile computers support a broadcast mechanism, much more flexible and useful ways of sharing information can be imagined. For instance, any number of people could conceivably enter a conference room and agree to support communications links between themselves, without necessarily engaging the services of existing equipment in the room (i.e., without requiring any existing communications infrastructure). Thus, one of our primary motivations is to allow the construction of temporary networks with no wires and no administrative intervention required. In this chapter, such an interconnection between mobile computers will be called an *ad hoc* network, in conformance with current usage within the IEEE 802.11 subcommittee [IEEE 1997].

Ad hoc networks differ significantly from existing networks. First, the topology of interconnections may be quite dynamic. Second, most users will not wish to perform any administrative actions to set up such a network. To provide service in the most general situation, we do not assume that every computer is within communication range of every other computer. This lack of complete connectivity would certainly be a reasonable characteristic of, say, a population of mobile computers in a large room that rely on infrared transceivers to effect their data communications.

From a graph theoretic point of view, an ad hoc network is a graph, $G(N, E(t))$, which is formed by denoting each of the N mobile hosts by a node and drawing an edge between two nodes if they are in direct communication range of each other. The set of edges, $E(t)$, so formed is a function of time and keeps changing as nodes in the ad hoc network move around. The topology defined by such a network can be very arbitrary, as there are no constraints on where mobiles can be located with respect to each other.

Routing protocols for existing networks [Malkin 1993, McQuillan+ 1980, Schwartz+ 1980] have not been designed specifically to provide the kind of self-starting behavior needed for ad hoc networks. Most protocols exhibit their least desirable behavior when presented with a highly dynamic interconnection topology. Although we thought that mobile computers could naturally be modeled as *routers,* it was also clear that existing routing protocols would place too heavy a computational burden on each one. Moreover, the convergence characteristics of existing routing protocols did not seem good enough to fit the needs of ad hoc networks. Lastly, the wireless medium differs in important ways from wired media, which requires that we make modifications to whichever routing protocol we might choose to experiment with. For instance, mobile computers may well have only a single network interface adapter, whereas most existing routers have network interfaces to connect two separate networks together. Because we had to make many changes anyway, we decided to follow our ad hoc network model as far as we could. We ended up with a substantially new approach to the classic distance-vector routing.

3.2 OVERVIEW OF ROUTING METHODS

In our environment, the problem of routing is essentially the distributed version of the shortest-path problem [Schwartz+ 1980]. Each node in the network maintains for each destination a preferred neighbor (a *next hop*). Each data packet contains a destination node identifier in its header. When a node receives a data packet, it forwards the packet to the preferred neighbor for its destination. The forwarding process continues until the packet reaches its destination. The manner in which route tables are constructed, maintained, and updated differs from one routing method to another. Popular routing methods, however, attempt to achieve the common objective of routing packets along the optimal path. The next-hop routing methods can be categorized as two primary classes: *link-state* and *distance-vector*.

3.2.1 Link-State

The link-state approach is closer to the centralized version of the shortest-path computation method. Each node maintains a view of the network topology with a cost for each link. To keep these views consistent, each node periodically broadcasts the link costs of its outgoing links to all other nodes using a protocol such as flooding. As a node receives this information, it updates its view of the network topology and applies a shortest-path algorithm to choose its next hop for each destination. Some of the information about the link costs at any particular node can be incorrect because of long propagation delays, a partitioned network, and so forth. Such inconsistent views of network topologies might lead to formation of routing loops. These loops, however, are short-lived, because they disappear in the time it takes a message to traverse the diameter of the network [McQuillan+ 1980].

3.2.2 Distance-Vector

In traditional distance-vector algorithms, every node i maintains, for each destination x, a set of distances $\{d_{ij}(x)\}$ for each node j that is a neighbor of i. Node i treats neighbor k as a next hop for a packet destined for x if $d_{ik}(x)$ equals $min_j\{d_{ij}(x)\}$. The succession of next hops chosen in this manner leads to x along the shortest path. To keep the distance estimates up to date, each node monitors the cost of its outgoing links and periodically broadcasts, to all of its neighbors, its current estimate of the shortest distance to every other node in the network.

The distance-vector algorithm just described is the classical Distributed Bellman-Ford (DBF) algorithm [Bertsekas+ 1987]. Compared to link-state algorithms, it is computationally more efficient, is easier to implement, and requires much less storage space. However, it is well known that this algorithm can cause the formation of both short-lived and long-lived loops [Cheng+ 1989]. The primary cause for formation of routing loops is that nodes choose their next hops in a completely distributed fashion on the basis of information that may be stale and therefore incorrect. Almost all proposed modifications to the DBF algorithm [Jaffe+ 1982, Garcia-Luna-Aceves 1989, Merlin+ 1979] eliminate the looping problem by forcing all nodes in the network to participate in some form of internodal coordination protocol. Such internodal coordination might be effective when topological changes are rare. However, within an ad hoc mobile environment, enforcing any internodal coordination mechanism will be difficult because of the rapidly changing topology of the underlying routing network.

Simplicity is one of the primary attributes that make any one routing protocol preferred over others for implementation within operational networks. The Routing Information Protocol (RIP) [Malkin 1993] is a well-known example. Despite the *counting-to-infinity* problem, it has proven to be very successful within small internetworks. The usefulness of RIP within an ad hoc environment, however, is limited, as it was not designed to handle rapid topological changes. Furthermore, the techniques of *split-horizon* and *poisoned-reverse* [Malkin 1993] are not useful within the wireless environment for devices that have a single network interface to a restricted broadcast transmission medium. For these reasons, our design goal has been a routing method for ad hoc networks that preserves the simplicity of RIP yet at the same time avoids the looping problem. Our approach is to tag each route table entry with a sequence number so that nodes can quickly distinguish stale routes from the new ones and thus avoid formation of routing loops.

3.3 DESTINATION-SEQUENCED DISTANCE-VECTOR PROTOCOL

Consider a collection of mobile computers, which may be far from any base station, that can exchange data along changing and arbitrary paths of interconnection. The computers must also exchange control messages so that all computers in the collection have a (possibly multihop) path along which data can be exchanged. The solution must remain compatible with operation in cases where a base station is available. By the methods outlined in this chapter, not only will we see routing as solving the problems associated with ad hoc networks, but we will also describe ways to perform such routing functions at layer 2, which traditionally has not been utilized as a protocol level for routing.

3.3.1 Protocol Overview

Packets are transmitted between the nodes of the network using route tables stored at each node. Each route table, at each of the nodes, lists all available destinations and the number of hops to each. Each route table entry is tagged with a sequence number that is originated by the destination node. To maintain the consistency of route tables in a dynamically varying topology, each node periodically transmits updates, doing so immediately when significant new information is available. Since we do not assume that the mobile hosts are maintaining any sort of time synchronization, we also make no assumption about the phase relationship of the update periods between the mobile hosts. These packets indicate which nodes are accessible from each node and the number of hops necessary to reach them, following traditional distance-vector routing algorithms. It is not the purpose of this chapter to propose any new metrics for route selection other than the freshness of the sequence numbers associated with the route; cost or other metrics might easily replace the number of hops in other implementations. We permit packets to be transmitted containing either layer-2 (MAC) addresses or layer-3 (network) addresses.

Routing information is advertised by broadcasting or multicasting the packets that are transmitted periodically and incrementally as topological changes are detected—for instance, when nodes move within the network. Data is also kept about the length of time between the arrival of the *first* and the arrival of the *best* route for each particular destination. On the basis of this data, a decision may be made to delay advertising routes that are about to change, thus damping fluctuations of the route tables. The advertisement of possibly unstable routes is delayed to reduce the number of rebroadcasts of possible route entries that normally arrive with the same sequence number.

3.3.2 Route Advertisements

The DSDV protocol requires each mobile node to advertise, to each of its current neighbors, its own route table (for instance, by broadcasting its entries). The entries in this list may change fairly dynamically over time, so the advertisement must be made often enough to ensure that every mobile computer can almost always locate every other mobile computer in the collection. In addition, each mobile computer agrees to relay data packets to other computers upon request. This agreement places a premium on the ability to determine the shortest number of hops for a route to a destination; we want to avoid disturbing mobile hosts unnecessarily if they are in sleep mode. In this way a mobile computer may exchange data with any other mobile computer in the group even if the target of the data is not within range for direct communication. If the notification about other mobile computers that are accessible from any particular computer in the collection is done at layer 2, DSDV will work with whatever higher-layer (e.g., network layer) protocol might be in use.[1]

All the computers interoperating to create data paths between themselves broadcast the necessary data periodically, say, once every few seconds. In a wireless medium, it is important to keep in mind that broadcasts are limited in range by the physical characteristics of the medium, in ways that are difficult to characterize precisely. This is different from the situation with wired media, which usually have a much more clearly defined range of reception.

3.3.3 Route Table Entry Structure

The data broadcast by each mobile computer will contain its new sequence number and the following information for each new route:

- The destination's address
- The number of hops required to reach the destination
- The sequence number of the information received regarding that destination, as originally stamped by the destination

Within the headers of the packet, the transmitted route tables will also contain the hardware address and (if appropriate) the network address of the mobile computer transmitting them. The route tables will also include

---

[1]But, see Chapter 1, Section 1.1.2, regarding problems with address resolution.

a sequence number created by the transmitter. Routes with more recent sequence numbers are always preferred as the basis for forwarding decisions, but they are not necessarily advertised. Of the paths with the same sequence number, those with the smallest metric will be used. By the natural way in which the route tables are propagated, the sequence number is sent to all mobile computers, which may each decide to maintain a routing entry for that originating mobile computer.

Routes received in broadcasts are also advertised by the receiver when it subsequently broadcasts its routing information; the receiver adds an increment to the metric before advertising the route, as incoming packets will require one more hop to reach the destination (namely, the hop from the transmitter to the receiver). Again, we do not explicitly consider here the changes required to use metrics that do not use the hop count to the destination.

Wireless media differ from traditional wired networks because asymmetries produced by one-way "links" are more prevalent. Receiving a packet from a neighbor therefore does not indicate the existence of a single-hop data path back to that neighbor across the wireless medium. To avoid problems caused by such one-way links, no mobile node may insert routing information received from a neighbor unless that neighbor shows that it can receive packets from the mobile node. Thus, our routing algorithms effectively use only links that are bidirectional.

One of the most important parameters to be chosen is the time between broadcasting the routing information packets. However, when any new or substantially modified route information is received by a mobile node, the new information will be retransmitted soon (subject to constraints imposed for damping route fluctuations), effecting the most rapid as possible dissemination of routing information among all of the cooperating mobile nodes. This quick rebroadcast introduces a new requirement for our protocols to converge as soon as possible. It would be calamitous if the movement of a mobile node caused a storm of broadcasts, degrading the availability of the wireless medium.

3.3.4 Responding to Topology Changes

Mobile nodes cause broken links as they move from place to place. The broken link may be detected by the layer-2 protocol, or it may be inferred if no broadcasts have been received for a while from a former neighbor. A broken link is described by a metric of ∞ (i.e., any value greater than the maximum allowed metric). When a link to a next hop has broken, any route through that next hop is immediately assigned an ∞ metric and an updated sequence number. Since this qualifies as a substantial route change, such modified routes are immediately disclosed in a broadcast routing information packet. Building information to describe broken links is the only situation in which the sequence number is generated by any mobile node other than the destination mobile node. Sequence numbers generated to indicate ∞ hops to a destination will be one greater than the last sequence number received from the destination. When a node receives an ∞ metric, and it has an equal or later sequence number with a finite metric, it triggers a route update broadcast to disseminate the important news about that destination. In this way routes containing any finite metric will supersede routes generated with the ∞ metric.

In a very large population of mobile nodes, adjustments will likely be needed for the time between broadcasts of the routing information packets. To reduce the amount of information carried in these packets, two types will be defined. One, called a *full dump,* will carry all of the available routing information. The other, called an *incremental,* will carry only information changed since the last full dump. By design, an incremental routing update should fit in one network protocol data unit (NPDU). The full dump will most likely require multiple NPDUs, even for relatively small populations of mobile nodes. Full dumps can be transmitted relatively infrequently when no movement of mobile nodes is occurring. When movement becomes frequent and the size of an incremental approaches the size of a NPDU, a full dump can be scheduled so that the next incremental will be smaller. It is expected that mobile nodes will implement some means for determining which route changes are significant enough to be sent out with each incremental advertisement. For instance, when a stabilized route shows a different metric for some destination, that is likely to constitute a significant change that needs to be advertised after stabilization. If a new sequence number for a route is received but the metric stays the same, that is unlikely to constitute a significant change.

3.3.5 Route Selection Criteria

When a mobile node receives new routing information (usually in an incremental packet as just described), that information is compared to the information already available from previous routing information packets. Any route with a more recent sequence number is used; routes with older sequence numbers are discarded. A route with a sequence number equal to an existing route is chosen if it has a "better" metric, and the existing route is discarded or stored as less preferable. The metrics for routes chosen from the newly received broadcast information are each incremented by one hop. Newly recorded routes are scheduled for immediate advertisement to the current mobile node's neighbors. Routes that show a more recent sequence number may be scheduled for advertisement at a later time, which time depends on the average settling time for routes to the particular destination under consideration.

Timing skews between the various mobile nodes are expected. The broadcasts of routing information by the mobile nodes are to be regarded as somewhat asynchronous events, even though some regularity is expected. In such a population of independently transmitting agents, some fluctuation can develop using the preceding procedures for updating routes. It may turn out that a particular mobile node receives new routing information in a pattern that causes it to consistently change routes from one next hop to another, even when the destination mobile node has not moved. This happens because there are two ways for new routes to be chosen: They might have a later sequence number, or they might have a better metric. Conceivably, a mobile node can always receive two routes to the same destination, with a newer sequence number, one after another (via different neighbors), but it always gets the route with the worse metric first. Unless care is taken, this will lead to a continuing burst of new route transmittals upon every new sequence number from that destination. Each new metric is propagated to every mobile host in the neighborhood, which propagates to its neighbors, and so on.

One solution is to delay the advertisement of such routes when a mobile node can determine that a route with a better metric is likely to show up soon. The route with the later sequence number must be available for use, but it does not have to be advertised immediately unless it is a route to a previously unreachable destination. Thus, there will be two route tables kept at each mobile node—one for use with forwarding packets and another to be advertised via incremental routing information packets. To determine the probability of imminent arrival of routing information showing a better metric, the mobile node has to keep a history of the weighted average time that routes to a particular destination fluctuate until the route with the best metric is received. Received route updates with infinite metrics are not included in this computation of the settling time for route updates. We hope that such a procedure will allow us to predict how long to wait before advertising new routes.

3.3.6 Operating DSDV at Layer 2

The addresses stored in the route tables will correspond to the layer at which the DSDV ad hoc networking protocol is operated. That is, operation at layer 3 will use network layer addresses for the next hop and destination addresses; operation at layer 2 will use layer-2 medium access control (MAC) addresses.

Using MAC addresses for the forwarding table introduces a new requirement, however. The difficulty is that layer-3 network protocols provide communication based on network addresses, and a way must be provided to resolve these layer-3 addresses into MAC addresses. Otherwise, a broadcast address resolution mechanism would be needed, and a corresponding loss of bandwidth in the wireless medium would be observed whenever the resolution mechanisms were utilized. This loss could be substantial because such mechanisms would require broadcasts and retransmitted broadcasts by every mobile node in the ad hoc network. Thus, unless special care is taken, every address resolution might produce a glitch in the normal operation of the network, which may well be noticeable to any active users.

The solution proposed here, for operation at layer 2, is to include layer-3 protocol information along with the layer-2 information. Each destination host would advertise which layer-3 protocols it supports, and each mobile node advertising reachability to that destination would include, along with the advertisement, the information about the layer-3 protocols supported at that destination. This information would have to be transmitted only when it changes, which occurs rarely. Changes would be transmitted as part of each incremental dump. Since each mobile node could support several layer-3 protocols (and many will), this list would have to be variable in length.

3.3.7 Extending Base Station Coverage

Mobile computers will frequently be used in conjunction with base stations, which allow them to exchange data with other computers connected to the wired network. By participating in the DSDV protocol, base stations can extend their coverage beyond the range imposed by their wireless transmitters. When a base station participates in DSDV, it is shown as a default route in the tables transmitted by a mobile node. In this way, mobile nodes within range of a base station can cooperate to effectively extend the base station range to serve other nodes out of that range, as long as those other mobile nodes are close to one of the mobile nodes that are within range.

3.4 EXAMPLES OF DSDV IN OPERATION

Consider MH_4 in Figure 3.1. Table 3.1 shows a possible structure of the forwarding table maintained at MH_4. Suppose that the address[2] of each mobile node is represented as MH_i. Suppose further that all sequence numbers are denoted SNNN_MH_i, where MH_i specifies the computer that created the sequence number and SNNN is a sequence number value. Also suppose that there are entries for all other mobile nodes, with sequence numbers SNNN_MH_i, before MH_1 moves away from MH_2. The install time field helps determine when to delete stale routes. With our protocol, the deletion

---

[2]If DSDV is operated at level 2, MH_i denotes the MAC address; otherwise, it denotes a level-3 address.

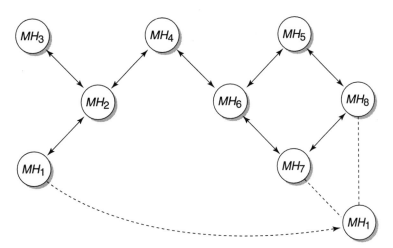

Figure 3.1. Movement in an Ad Hoc Network

Table 3.1. MH_4 Forwarding Table

Destination	Next Hop	Metric	Sequence Number	Install	Stable_Data
MH_1	MH_2	2	S406_MH_1	T001_MH_4	Ptr1_MH_1
MH_2	MH_2	1	S128_MH_2	T001_MH_4	Ptr1_MH_2
MH_3	MH_2	2	S564_MH_3	T001_MH_4	Ptr1_MH_3
MH_4	MH_4	0	S710_MH_4	T001_MH_4	Ptr1_MH_4
MH_5	MH_6	2	S392_MH_5	T002_MH_4	Ptr1_MH_5
MH_6	MH_6	1	S076_MH_6	T001_MH_4	Ptr1_MH_6
MH_7	MH_6	2	S128_MH_7	T002_MH_4	Ptr1_MH_7
MH_8	MH_6	3	S050_MH_8	T002_MH_4	Ptr1_MH_8

of stale routes should rarely occur, as the detection of link breakages should propagate through the ad hoc network immediately. Nevertheless, we monitor for the existence of stale routes and take appropriate action.

From Table 3.1, we can surmise, for instance, that all of the computers become available to MH_4 at about the same time because, for most of them, its Install_Time is about the same. Ptr1_MH_i will all be pointers to null structures because there are no routes in Figure 3.1 that are likely to be superseded or to compete with other possible routes to any particular destination.

Table 3.2 shows the structure of the advertised route table of MH_4.

Now suppose that MH_1 moves into the general vicinity of MH_8 and MH_7 and away from the others (especially MH_2). The new internal forwarding tables at MH_4 might then appear as shown in Table 3.3.

Table 3.2. MH_4 Advertised Route Table

Destination	Metric	Sequence Number
MH_1	2	$S406\_MH_1$
MH_2	1	$S128\_MH_2$
MH_3	2	$S564\_MH_3$
MH_4	0	$S710\_MH_4$
MH_5	2	$S392\_MH_5$
MH_6	1	$S076\_MH_6$
MH_7	2	$S128\_MH_7$
MH_8	3	$S050\_MH_8$

Table 3.3. MH_4 Forwarding Table (Updated)

Destination	Next Hop	Metric	Sequence Number	Install	Stable_Data
MH$_1$	**MH$_6$**	**3**	**$S516\_MH_1$**	**$T810\_MH_4$**	$Ptr1\_MH_1$
MH_2	MH_2	1	$S238\_MH_2$	$T001\_MH_4$	$Ptr1\_MH_2$
MH_3	MH_2	2	$S674\_MH_3$	$T001\_MH_4$	$Ptr1\_MH_3$
MH_4	MH_4	0	$S820\_MH_4$	$T001\_MH_4$	$Ptr1\_MH_4$
MH_5	MH_6	2	$S502\_MH_5$	$T002\_MH_4$	$Ptr1\_MH_5$
MH_6	MH_6	1	$S186\_MH_6$	$T001\_MH_4$	$Ptr1\_MH_6$
MH_7	MH_6	2	$S238\_MH_7$	$T002\_MH_4$	$Ptr1\_MH_7$
MH_8	MH_6	3	$S160\_MH_8$	$T002\_MH_4$	$Ptr1\_MH_8$

Only the entry for MH_1 shows a new metric, but in the intervening time many new sequence number entries have been received. The first entry thus must be advertised in subsequent incremental routing information updates until the next full dump occurs. When MH_1 moves into the vicinity of MH_8 and MH_7, it triggers an immediate incremental routing information update, which is then broadcast to MH_6. MH_6, having determined that significant new routing information has been received, also triggers an immediate update, which carries along the new routing information for MH_1. MH_4, upon receiving this information, then broadcasts it at every interval until the next full routing information dump. At MH_4, the incremental advertised routing update has the form shown in Table 3.4.

In this advertisement, the information for MH_4 comes first, since it is doing the advertisement. The information for MH_1 comes next, not because it has a lower address but because MH_1 is the only one that has any significant route changes affecting it. As a general rule, routes with changed

Table 3.4. MH_4 Advertised Table (Updated)

Destination	Metric	Sequence Number
MH_4	0	S820_MH_4
MH_1	3	S516_MH_1
MH_2	1	S238_MH_2
MH_3	2	S674_MH_3
MH_5	2	S502_MH_5
MH_6	1	S186_MH_6
MH_7	2	S238_MH_7
MH_8	3	S160_MH_8

metrics are first included in each incremental packet. The remaining space is used to include those routes whose sequence numbers have changed.

In this example, one node has changed its routing information, as it is in a new location. All nodes have recently transmitted new sequence numbers. If there were too many updated sequence numbers to fit in a single packet, only the ones that fit would be transmitted, selected with a view to fairly transmitting them in their turn over several incremental update intervals. There is no such required format for the transmission of full routing information packets. As many packets as needed are used, and all available information is transmitted. The frequency of transmitting full updates is reduced if the volume of data begins to consume a significant fraction of the available capacity of the medium.

3.4.1 Damping Fluctuations

This section describes how the settling time table is used to prevent fluctuations of route table entry advertisements. The general problem arises because route updates are selected according to one of the following criteria:

- Routes are always preferred if the sequence numbers are newer.
- Routes are preferred if the sequence numbers are the same and yet the metric is better.

To see the problem, suppose that two routes with identical sequence numbers are received by a mobile node but in the wrong order. In other words, suppose that MH_4 receives the higher-metric next hop first and soon after gets another next hop with a lower metric but the same sequence number. This can happen when there are many mobile nodes, all transmitting their updates irregularly. Alternatively, if the mobile hosts are acting

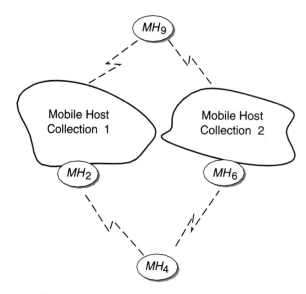

Figure 3.2. Receiving Fluctuating Routes

independently and with markedly different transmission intervals, the situation can occur with correspondingly fewer hosts. Suppose that, in any event, Figure 3.2 has enough mobile nodes to cause the problem, in two separate collections both connected to a common destination MH_9 but with no other mobile nodes in common. Suppose further that all mobile nodes are transmitting updates approximately every 15 seconds, that mobile node MH_2 has a route to MH_9 with 12 hops, and that mobile node MH_6 has a route to MH_9 with 11 hops. Moreover, suppose that the routing information update from MH_2 arrives at MH_4 approximately 10 seconds before the routing information update from MH_6. This might occur every time a new sequence number is issued from mobile node MH_9. In fact, the time differential can be significant if any mobile node in collection 2 begins to issue its sequence number updates in multiple incremental update intervals, as happens, for instance, when there are too many hosts with new sequence number updates for all of them to fit within a single incremental packet update. In general, the larger the number of hops, the larger the differentials between delivery of the updates that can be expected in Figure 3.2.

The settling time data is stored in a table with the following fields, keyed by the first field:

- Destination address
- Last settling time
- Average settling time

The settling time is calculated by maintaining, for each destination, a running, weighted average over the most recent updates of the routes.

Suppose that a new routing information update arrives at MH_4, and the sequence number in the new entry is newer than the sequence number in the currently used entry but has a worse (i.e., higher) metric. Then MH_4 must use the new entry in making subsequent forwarding decisions. However, MH_4 does not have to advertise the new route immediately and can consult its route settling time table to decide how long to wait before advertising. The average settling time is used for this determination. For instance, MH_4 may decide to delay (Average Settling_Time $\times$ 2) before advertising a route.

This can be quite beneficial because if the possibly unstable route were advertised immediately, the effects would ripple through the network; this bad effect would probably be repeated every time mobile node MH_9's sequence number updates rippled through the ad hoc network. On the other hand, if a link via mobile node MH_6 actually does break, the advertisement of a route via MH_2 should proceed immediately. To achieve this when there is a history of fluctuations at mobile node MH_4, the link breakage should be detected fast enough so that an intermediate host in collection 2 discovers the problem and begins a triggered incremental update showing an ∞ metric for the path to mobile node MH_9. Routes with an ∞ metric are required to be advertised by this protocol without delay.

To bias the damping mechanism in favor of recent events, the most recent measurement of the settling time of a particular route must be counted with a higher weighting factor than that for less recent measurements. And, importantly, a parameter must be selected that indicates how long a route has to remain stable before it is counted as actually stable. This amounts to specifying a maximum value for the settling time for the destination in the settling time table. Any route more stable than this maximum value will cause a triggered update if it is ever replaced by another route with a different next hop or metric.

When a new routing update is received from a neighbor, at the same time that the updates are applied to the table, processing also occurs to delete stale entries. Stale entries are defined as those for which no update has been applied within the last few update periods. Each neighbor is expected to send regular updates; when no updates are received for a while, the receiver may make the determination that the corresponding computer is no longer a neighbor. When that occurs, any route using that computer as a next hop should be deleted, including the route indicating that computer as the actual (formerly neighboring) destination. Increasing the number of update periods before entries are determined would result in more stale routing entries but would also allow for more transmission errors. Transmission errors are likely to occur when a CSMA-type broadcast medium is used, as may well be the case for many wireless implementations. When the link breaks, an ∞ metric route should be advertised for it as well as for the routes that depend on it.

Additional data fields, other than those stated before, might be transmitted as part of each entry in the route tables that are broadcast by each participating computer (mobile or base station). These fields may depend, for instance, on higher-level protocols or other protocols according to the operation of layer 2. For instance, to enable correct ARP operation, each route table entry must also contain an association between the Internet Protocol (IP) address and the destination's MAC address. This also enables an intermediate computer, when serving a routing function for its neighbors, to issue proxy ARP replies instead of routing ARP broadcasts around. However, if packet forwarding is based on MAC addresses, such techniques ought to be unnecessary. And, if forwarding is based on IP addresses, no ARP is strictly necessary as long as neighboring nodes keep track of associations gleaned from route table broadcasts. Note also that layer-3 operation violates the normal subnet model of operation, as even if two mobile nodes share the same subnet address there is no guarantee that they will be directly connected—in other words, within range of each other. Even so, this is compatible with the model of operation offered by the Mobile IP Working Group of the IETF [Perkins 1994, Perkins 1996].[3]

The new routing algorithm was developed to enable the creation of ad hoc networks, which are specifically targeted to the operation of mobile computers. However, both the routing algorithm and the ad hoc network can be beneficially used in situations that do not include mobile computers. For instance, the routing algorithm can be applied in any situation in which reduced memory requirements are desired (compared to link-state routing algorithms), and an ad hoc network can be applied to wired as well as wireless mobile computers. In general, then, we provide a new destination-sequenced routing algorithm, and this algorithm is supplemented by a technique for damping fluctuations.

3.5 PROPERTIES OF THE DSDV PROTOCOL

At all instances, the DSDV protocol guarantees loop-free paths to each destination. To see why this property holds, consider a collection of N mobile hosts forming an instance of an ad hoc-style network. Further, assume that the system is in steady state; that is, the routing tables of all nodes have already converged to the actual shortest paths. At this instant, the next

---

[3]Note that this paragraph was originally written well before Mobile IP was promoted as a proposed standard.

node indicators to each destination induce a tree rooted at that destination. Thus, the route tables of all nodes in the network can be collectively visualized as forming N trees, one rooted at each destination. In the following discussion, we will focus our attention on one specific destination x and follow the changes occurring on the directed graph $G(x)$ defined by nodes i and arcs $(i, p_i(x))$, where $p_i(x)$ denotes the next hop for destination x at node i. Operation of the DSDV algorithm ensures that at every instant $G(x)$ is loop-free or, equivalently, is a set of disjoint directed trees. Each such tree is rooted either at x or at a node whose next hop is nil. Because this property holds with respect to each destination x, all paths induced by the route tables of the DSDV algorithm are indeed loop-free at all instants.

Starting from a loop-free state, a loop may potentially form each time node i changes its next hop. Two cases should be considered. In the first case, when node i detects that the link to its next hop is broken, the node resets $p_i(x)$ to nil. Clearly, this action cannot form a loop involving i. In the second case, node i receives, from one of its neighbors, k, a route to x, with sequence number $s_k(x)$ and metric m, which is selected to replace the current route it has through $p_i(x)$. Let $s_i(x)$ denote the value of the sequence number stored at node i and let $d_i(x)$ denote the distance estimate from i to x just prior to receiving a route from k. Node i will change its next hop from $p_i(x)$ to k only if either of the following two situations occurs.

1. The new route contains a newer sequence number; that is, $s_k(x) > s_i(x)$.
2. The sequence number $s_k(x)$ is the same as $s_i(x)$, but the new route offers a shorter path to x; that is, $m < d_i(x)$.

In the first case, by choosing k as its new next hop, node i cannot close a loop. This can be easily deduced from the following observation. Node i propagates sequence number $s_i(x)$ to its neighbors only after receiving it from its current next hop. Therefore, the sequence number value stored at the next hop is always greater than or equal to the value stored at i. Starting from node i, if we follow the chain of next-hop pointers, the sequence number values stored at visited nodes form a nondecreasing sequence. Now suppose that node i forms a loop by choosing k as its next hop. This implies that $s_k(x) \leq s_i(x)$. But this contradicts our initial assumption that $s_k(x) > s_i(x)$. Hence, loop formation cannot occur if nodes use newer sequence numbers to pick routes.

The loop-free property holds in the second scenario because of a theorem proved by Jaffe and Moss [Jaffe+ 1982], which states that in the presence of static or decreasing link weights distance-vector algorithms always maintain loop-free paths.

3.6 COMPARISON WITH OTHER METHODS

Table 3.5 presents a quick summary of some of the main features of a few chosen routing protocols. The chosen set, although small, is representative of the routing techniques most commonly employed in operational data networks. Except for the link-state approach, all routing methods shown in the table are a variant of the basic distance-vector approach. The comparison criteria reflect some of the most desirable features that a routing algorithm should possess for it to be useful in a dynamic ad hoc environment. In wireless media, communication bandwidth is the most precious and scarce resource. The formation of any kind of routing loops is therefore, highly undesirable. In the case of infrared LANs that employ a pure CSMA protocol, looping packets not only consume the communication bandwidth but can further degrade performance by causing more collisions in the medium. A common technique employed for loop prevention is what we call *internodal coordination,* whereby strong constraints on the ordering of the updates among nodes is imposed. The resulting internode protocols tend to be complex. Furthermore, their update coordination may restrict a node's ability to obtain alternate paths quickly in an environment in which topology changes are relatively frequent. The last criterion used for comparison is the space requirement of the routing method. Nodes in an ad hoc network may be battery powered laptops, or even handheld notebooks, which do not have the kind of memory that backbone routers are expected to have. Therefore, economy of space is important.

The primary concern with a DBF algorithm [Bertsekas+ 1987] in an ad hoc environment is its susceptibility to forming routing loops and the counting-to-infinity problem. RIP [Malkin 1993], which is very similar to

Table 3.5. Comparison of Various Routing Methods

Routing Method	Looping	Internodal Coordination	Space Complexity
Bellman-Ford	s/l	–	$O(nd)$
Link-State	s	–	$O(n+e)$
Loop-Free BF*	s	–	$O(nd)$
RIP	s/l	–	$O(n)$
Merlin Segall	Loop-free	Required	$O(nd)$
Jaffe Moss	Loop-free	Required	$O(nd)$
DSDV	Loop-free	–	$O(n)$

s—short-term loop, l—long-term loop, n—number of nodes, d—maximum degree of a node.

*See [Cheng+ 1989].

DBF, also suffers from this problem. Unlike DBF, RIP keeps track of only the best route to each destination, which results in some space saving at no extra performance hit. It also employs techniques known as *split-horizon* and *poisoned-reverse* to avoid a ping-pong style of looping, but these techniques are not powerful enough to avoid loops involving more than two hops. The primary cause of loop formation in DBF algorithms is that nodes make uncoordinated modifications to their route tables on the basis of information that could be incorrect. This problem is alleviated by employing an internodal coordination mechanism as proposed by Merlin and Segall [Merlin+ 1979]. A similar technique, but with better convergence results, is developed by Jaffe and Moss [Jaffe+ 1982]. However, we do not know of any operational routing protocols that employ these complex coordination methods to achieve loop freedom, which leads us to the conclusion that the usefulness of such complex methods, from a practical point of view, is diminished.

Link-state algorithms [McQuillan+ 1980] are also free of the counting-to-infinity problem. However, they need to maintain the up-to-date version of the entire network topology at every node, which may constitute excessive storage and communication overhead in a highly dynamic network. Besides, link-state algorithms proposed or implemented to date do not eliminate the creation of temporary routing loops.

It is evident that within an ad hoc environment the design tradeoffs and the constraints under which a routing method has to operate are quite different. The proposed DSDV approach offers a very attractive combination of desirable features. Its memory requirement is a very moderate $O(n)$. It guarantees loop-free paths at all instants, and it does so without requiring nodes to participate in any complex update coordination protocol. The worst-case convergence behavior of the DSDV protocol is not optimal, but in the average case it is expected that convergence will be quite rapid.

3.7 FUTURE WORK

Many parameters of interest control the behavior of DSDV—for instance, the frequency of broadcast, the frequency of full route table dumps versus incremental notifications, and the percentage change in the routing metric that triggers an immediate broadcast of new routing information. By performing simulations, we hope to discover optimal values for many of these parameters for large populations of mobile computers.

Our original goals did not include making any changes to the idea of using the number of hops as the sole metric for making route table selections. We ended up designing a method to combat fluctuations in route tables at the mobile nodes, which can be caused by information arriving faster over a path that has more hops. However, it may well be the case that such paths are preferable just because they are faster, even if more mobile computers are involved in the creation of the path. We would like to consider how to improve the routing metric by taking into account a more sophisticated cost function that includes the effects of time and cost as well as the number of hops.

The DSDV approach relies on periodic exchange of routing information among all participating nodes. An alternative is to design a system that performs route discovery on a need-to-know basis. For devices operating on limited battery power, this may be an important design consideration.[4]

A pure on-demand system operates in two phases: *route discovery* and *route maintenance*. A source starts the first phase by broadcasting a route discovery (RD) packet in the network. These packets are relayed by all participating nodes to their respective neighbors. As an RD packet travels from a source to various destinations, it automatically causes formation of *reverse paths* from visited nodes to the source. To set up a reverse path, a node is only required to record the address of the neighbor from which it receives the first copy of the RD packet; any duplicates received thereafter are discarded. When the RD packet arrives at the destination, a reply is generated and forwarded along the reverse path. By a mechanism similar to reverse-path setup, *forward route* entries are initialized as the reply packet travels toward the source. Nodes not lying on the path between source/destination pairs eventually time out their reverse path routing entries. Once the path setup is complete, the route maintenance phase takes over. The second phase is responsible for maintaining paths between active source/destination pairs in the face of topological changes.

3.8 SUMMARY

Providing convenient connectivity for mobile computers in ad hoc networks is a challenge that is only now being met. DSDV models the mobile computers as routers cooperating to forward packets to each other as needed. We believe that this approach makes good use of the properties of the wireless broadcast medium. It can be utilized either at the network layer (layer 3) or below the network layer but still above the MAC layer software in layer 2. In the latter case certain additional information should be included along with the route tables for the most convenient and efficient operation. The information in the route tables is similar to that found in route tables with today's distance-vector (Bellman-Ford) algorithms, but it

---

[4]Such systems are described in several other chapters; specifically, AODV (Chapter 5) may be viewed as an on-demand modification of DSDV.

includes a sequence number as well as settling time data useful for damping out fluctuations in route table updates.

All sequence numbers are generated by the destination computer in each route table entry, except in cases when a link has been broken. Such a case is described by an ∞ metric; it is easily distinguishable, as no ∞ metric will ever be generated along the tree of intermediate nodes receiving updates originating from the destination. By the natural operation of the protocol, the metric chosen to represent broken links will be superseded as soon as possible by real routes propagated from the newly located destination. Any newly propagated routes will necessarily use a metric less than what was used to indicate the broken link. This allows real route data to quickly supersede temporary link outages when a mobile computer moves from one place to another.

We have borrowed the existing mechanism of triggered updates to make sure that pertinent route table changes can be propagated throughout the population of mobile hosts as quickly as possible whenever any topology changes are noticed. This includes movement from place to place as well as the disappearance of a mobile host from the interconnect topology (perhaps as a result of turning off its power).

To combat problems arising with large populations of mobile hosts, which can cause route updates to be received in an order delaying the best metrics until after poorer metric routes are received, we have separated the route tables into two distinct structures. The actual routing is according to information kept in the internal route table, but this information is not always advertised immediately upon receipt. We have defined a mechanism whereby routes are not advertised until it is likely, on the basis of history, that they are stable. This measurement of the settling time for each route is biased toward the most recent measurements for the purpose of computing an average.

We have found that mobile computers, modeled as routers, can effectively cooperate to build ad hoc networks. We hope to explore further the necessary application-level support needed to automatically enable use of the network-layer route capabilities to provide simple access to conferencing and workplace tools for collaboration and information sharing.

References

[Bertsekas+ 1987] D. Bertsekas and R. Gallager. *Data Networks*. Prentice-Hall, Englewood Cliffs, N.J., 1987, 297–333.

[Cheng+ 1989] C. Cheng, R. Riley, S.P.R. Kumar, and J.J. Garcia-Luna-Aceves. A Loop-Free Bellman-Ford Routing Protocol without Bouncing Effect. In *Proceedings of ACM SIGCOMM '89*, September 1989, 224–237.

[Garcia-Luna-Aceves 1989] J.J. Garcia-Luna-Aceves. A Unified Approach to Loop-Free Routing Using Distance Vectors or Link States. In *Proceedings of ACM SIGCOMM '89,* September 1989, 212–223.

[IEEE 1997] IEEE Computer Society LAN MAN Standards Committee. *Wireless LAN Medium Access Control (MAC) and Physical Layer (PHY) Specifications, IEEE Standard 802.11-97.* The Institute of Electrical and Electronics Engineers, New York, 1997.

[Jaffe+ 1982] J.M. Jaffe and F. Moss. A Responsive Distributed Routing Algorithm for Computer Networks. *IEEE Transactions on Communications* COM-30:1758–1762, July 1982.

[Malkin 1993] G. Malkin. RIP Version 2—Carrying Additional Information. RFC 1388 (proposed standard), Internet Engineering Task Force, January 1993.

[McQuillan+ 1980] J.M. McQuillan, I. Richer, and E.C. Rosen. The New Routing Algorithm for the ARPANET. *IEEE Transactions on Communications* COM-28(5):711–719, May 1980.

[Merlin+ 1979] P.M. Merlin and A. Segall. A Failsafe Distributed Routing Protocol. *IEEE Transactions on Communications* COM-27:1280–1287, September 1979.

[Perkins 1994] C. Perkins. Mobile IP as Seen by the IETF. *Connexions,* March 1994, 2–20.

[Perkins 1996] C. Perkins. IP Mobility Support. RFC 2002 (proposed standard), Internet Engineering Task Force, October 1996.

[Schwartz+ 1980] M. Schwartz and T. Stern. Routing Techniques Used in Computer Communication Networks. *IEEE Transactions on Communications* COM-28: 539–552, April 1980.

4

Cluster-Based Networks

Martha Steenstrup
Bolt Beranek & Newman

A communications network, whether fixed wireline or mobile wireless, is a dynamic entity whose state may change frequently in ways that cannot be accurately predicted. To meet performance goals prescribed for user traffic, a network must be able to adapt its behavior to accommodate changes in its intrinsic properties (e.g., connectivity, capacity, and offered load). Ideally, the control functions that govern the network's performance should meet two objectives.

- To respond rapidly and correctly when adapting the network's behavior to current network state.
- To minimize consumption of the network's transmission, processing, and storage resources both during and as a result of the adaptation process.

These objectives, however, are competing, not complementary, and hence much of the work on network control has focused on the tradeoff between accuracy and efficiency.

In a network, control functions are performed with respect to a *control structure* that is superimposed on the physical network of nodes and links and that consists of a set of controllers together with their spheres of influence. Establishment of a control structure for a fixed network is usually an integral part of the network design process and hence the responsibility of network managers. Boundaries of control are often drawn along administrative lines, and the number and placement of controllers is selected to improve their accessibility and to limit the load on each. Thus, a network manager may tailor a control structure to meet specific performance goals given a particular network topology and traffic pattern. This approach, however, is impractical for mobile networks with constantly changing connectivity and for large networks with commensurately large numbers of parameters to configure. These types of networks are better served by a self-organizing control structure, which the nodes, in cooperation, build and maintain. Self-organizing control structures increase network availability, reduce delay in responding to changes in network state, and reduce the probability of configuration errors.

An appropriate choice of network control structure and algorithms for organizing and using this structure depends on the control functions to be performed, the size of the network, and the expected frequency and magnitude of changes in network state. For example, a control structure for routing that provides a high degree of accuracy and robustness is isomorphic to the physical structure of the network, such that each node independently performs the routing functions on the basis of state information obtained for the entire network. This type of control structure, while appropriate for small networks that experience infrequent state changes, may be infeasible for large dynamic networks because of the quantity of resources required to handle state information and to execute control decisions.

Cluster-based control structures promote more efficient use of resources in controlling large dynamic networks. With cluster-based control, the physical network is transformed into a virtual network of interconnected node clusters. Each cluster has one or more controllers acting on its behalf to make control decisions for cluster members and, in some cases, to construct and distribute representations of cluster state for use outside of the cluster.

In this chapter, we present and compare several different cluster-based control structures and associated control algorithms that have been proposed for use in large dynamic networks. We investigate the applicability of these structures and algorithms to ad hoc networks in particular, concentrating on the routing functions. In ad hoc networks, cluster-based control structures contribute to improved efficiency of resource use by creating contexts for:

- Managing wireless transmissions among multiple nodes to reduce channel contention.
- Forming routing backbones to reduce network diameter.
- Abstracting network state information to reduce its quantity and variability.

The nature of the control functions to be performed influences both the control structure and the algorithms for organizing and using this structure, as we discuss in the following sections.

4.1 CLUSTERING FOR TRANSMISSION MANAGEMENT

Broadcasting in a shared wireless medium may result in multiple nodes receiving a transmission destined for a single node and, ultimately, in multiple transmissions mutually interfering at a single node. Nodes can reduce the chances of interference by separating transmissions in time, space, frequency, or spreading code. By coordinating this separation instead of acting independently, nodes can further reduce the chances of interference and hence increase network throughput. The cluster-based control structure described below and designed specifically for use in ad hoc networks provides a natural organization of network nodes that simplifies coordination of transmissions among neighboring nodes.

4.1.1 Link-Cluster Architecture

The *link-clustered architecture* [Baker+ 1981a, Baker+ 1981b, Ephremides+ 1987] is a network control structure that reduces interference in a multiple-access broadcast environment by forming distinct clusters of nodes in which transmissions can be scheduled in a contention-free manner. Transmissions in adjoining clusters can be isolated through spread-spectrum multiple access [Chiang 1996; Gerla+ 1995; Lin+ 1995; Lin+ 1997], by using different (and preferably orthogonal) spreading codes in each such cluster. With the link-clustered architecture, nodes autonomously organize themselves into interconnected clusters whose union of members is all network nodes. Each cluster contains a *clusterhead,* one or more *gateways,* and zero or more *ordinary nodes* that are neither clusterheads nor gateways, as shown in Figure 4.1. The clusterhead schedules transmissions and allocates resources within the clusters. For example, it might issue tokens to potential transmitters, emit busy tones when a transmission is in progress, or assign slots to specific transmitters and sessions. Gateways connect adjacent clusters. A gateway may directly connect two clusters by acting as a member of both, or it may indirectly connect two clusters by acting as a member of one and forming a link to a member of the other. Hence, the link-clustered architecture accommodates both overlapping and disjoint clusters.

With the link-clustered architecture, all cluster members are within one hop of the clusterhead and hence within two hops of each other. This arrangement provides low-delay paths between cluster members that may communicate frequently, and it places clusterheads in the ideal locations to coordinate transmissions among their cluster members. Clusterheads are distinct from gateways; hence, those for different clusters are separated by

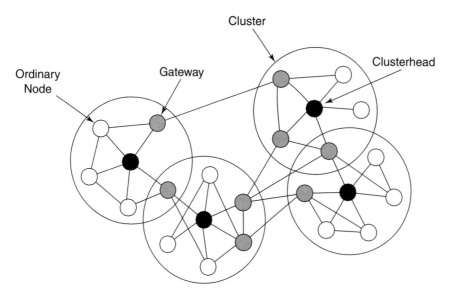

Figure 4.1. The Link-Clustered Architecture

at least two hops. To establish a link-clustered control structure over a physical network, the nodes

1. Discover neighbors to which they have bidirectional connectivity by broadcasting a list of those neighbors they can hear and by receiving broadcasts from neighbors.
2. Elect clusterheads and form clusters.
3. Agree on gateways between clusters.

Clusterheads

At least two clusterhead election algorithms have been proposed for the link-clustered architecture: *identifier-based clustering* [Baker+ 1981a, Baker+ 1981b, Ephremides+ 1987] and *connectivity-based clustering* [Gerla+ 1995, Parekh 1985]. Each admits both a centralized and a distributed implementation. With the centralized version, the node with the lowest- or highest-numbered identifier (identifier-based clustering) or with the largest number of neighbors (connectivity-based clustering) is chosen as a clusterhead for the cluster containing that node and its one-hop neighbors. (For connectivity-based clustering, ties are broken by selecting as the clusterhead the node with the lowest- or highest-numbered identifier.) All nodes in the cluster thus defined are excluded from further consideration, and the process of clusterhead selection and cluster formation repeats with the remaining nodes in the network until all nodes are contained within some cluster.

With the distributed version of identifier-based clustering, a node elects itself as a clusterhead if it has the lowest- or highest-numbered identifier in its neighborhood. Otherwise, it elects the bidirectionally connected neighbor with the lowest- or highest-numbered identifier unless that node has relinquished clusterhead status to another node. With the distributed version of connectivity-based clustering, a node becomes a clusterhead if it is the most highly connected of all of its *uncovered* neighbors. Any node that has not yet elected its clusterhead is said to be uncovered. If a node has already elected another node as its clusterhead, it cannot become a clusterhead itself. Clusterhead ties are resolved according to lowest- or highest-numbered node identifiers.

The clustering algorithms described by Lin and Gerla [Lin+ 1995, Lin+ 1997] are variants of identifier-based and connectivity-based clustering, respectively, that always form disjoint clusters. In both cases, clusterheads are used only as aids in cluster formation and not as coordinators of intracluster transmissions. Instead, transmission scheduling is distributed over the nodes in the cluster using, for example, a round-robin slotting schedule with contention only for unused slots.

Gateways

Any node with links to more than one cluster is a candidate gateway connecting these clusters. If the node has two clusterheads as neighbors, it is a candidate gateway connecting two overlapping clusters. If the node has one clusterhead as a neighbor and can reach a second clusterhead in two hops, it is a candidate gateway linked to a candidate gateway in another cluster, which together connect two disjoint clusters. Figure 4.1 illustrates both overlapping and disjoint clusters. Conferring gateway status on all candidates increases the chances that the clusters will remain connected, even if some connectivity between individual gateways is lost. Nevertheless, most of the schemes built around the link-clustered architecture (e.g., [Ephremides+ 1987, Gerla+ 1995]) attempt to ensure that only a single gateway or gateway pair connects two clusters even if multiple candidates exist. For overlapping clusters, the gateway selected is the one with the highest- or lowest-numbered identifier. For disjoint clusters, the two gateways selected are the linked pair in which one member has the highest- or lowest-numbered identifier among all candidates connecting the two clusters. Unambiguous selection of a single gateway pair joining two clusters may require advertisement of node identifiers beyond one-hop neighbors.

Node Mobility

As nodes move about the network, cluster membership must be updated accordingly to ensure proper scheduling of transmissions. To maximize availability of communications, all nodes must be capable of executing the clusterhead and gateway functions if elected to do so. The clustering algorithms described by Baker, Ephremides, Wieselthier, Gerla, and Tsai [Baker+ 1981a, Baker+ 1981b, Ephremides+ 1987, Gerla+ 1995] do not merely adjust but actually recompute cluster membership and clusterhead and gateway status whenever a node moves into or out of a cluster. When using the cluster recomputation approach, a node's clusterhead status is likely to change more frequently with connectivity-based clustering than with identifier-based clustering, as loss of a neighbor may reduce the node's connectivity such that it is no longer the most highly connected. Thus, in the presence of mobile nodes identifier-based clustering results in a more stable link-clustered architecture than connectivity-based clustering can achieve.

The *least cluster change* algorithm [Chiang 1996] reduces the number of changes in clusterhead status required after node movement. Specifically, a change in clusterhead status occurs only if two clusterheads move within range of each other, in which case one of the two nodes relinquishes its role as clusterhead, or if a non-clusterhead node moves out of range of any other node, in which case it becomes a clusterhead for its own cluster. The least cluster change algorithm may be used in conjunction with either of the identifier-based or connectivity-based clustering algorithms. Lin and Gerla [Lin+ 1995, Lin+ 1997] propose cluster maintenance schemes designed to minimize the number of changes in the set of existing clusters as nodes move. These schemes do not recluster after each movement, but instead make small adjustments to cluster membership as necessary. Significant changes in cluster membership occur only when the most highly connected node in a cluster moves.

Routing

The link-clustered architecture provides a natural routing backbone consisting of clusterheads and gateways and the links between them. Constraining all traffic to traverse clusterheads, however, may reduce both the throughput and the robustness of the network: Clusterheads as points of traffic concentration may become congested, and each clusterhead may become a single point of failure for communication across its cluster. For these reasons, many of the routing algorithms proposed for use in networks organized according to the link-clustered architecture do not use these clusters as their routing control structure (e.g., [Gerla+ 1995, Lin+ 1997]). Instead, they treat the set of nodes and links as a nonclustered multihop network in which each node distributes and collects routing information and generates and selects routes. Thus, neither intracluster nor intercluster routing requires clusterhead traversal. With the link-clustered architecture, clusters exist primarily to define regions for transmission management and secondarily to form a routing backbone.

4.2 CLUSTERING FOR BACKBONE FORMATION

In any network, the delay incurred by a packet at each hop is a function of the processing and queueing delays at the transmitting node and the transmission (including medium access) and propagation delays over the link. Thus, in a multihop network reducing the number of hops in a route may significantly reduce the end-to-end delays experienced by packets traversing the route. Routing backbones consisting of small numbers of long-range links are frequently employed to provide low-delay, high-speed connectivity between distant nodes in large networks. Fultz [Fultz 1972] appears to have been the first to propose the use of routing backbones, recommending the organization of any large network into a set of national, regional, and local subnetworks according to the geographic coverage of these subnetworks.

In multihop wireless networks, the need for reduced route length is even greater than in wireline networks because of the larger delays likely to be experienced at each hop. These delays include

- Medium access delay resulting from contention for the shared channel.
- Transmission delay resulting from increased packet size for error-control or direct-sequence spread-spectrum coding.
- Retransmission delay resulting from link layer Automatic Repeat Request (ARQ) protocols for reliability over error-prone links.
- Radio-dependent delay such as that incurred when switching between transmission and reception modes.

In a wireless network, reduced-hop backbone topologies can be formed by expanding the transmission range of some or all of the nodes. Increasing a node's transmission range by increasing its transmission power enables direct communication with a more distant node, but it may also increase interference because the node's transmissions will be received at higher power and by a larger number of nodes. Thus, care must be exercised to isolate (usually by frequency) local transmissions within a cluster from distant transmissions along the backbone. In the next sections, we describe two different approaches, specifically designed for use in ad hoc networks, that employ cluster-based formation of and access to routing backbones, which connect distant nodes via a small number of hops without causing excessive interference.

4.2.1 Near-Term Digital Radio Network

The Near-Term Digital Radio (NTDR) networking algorithms have been designed to support mobile tactical communications [Zavgren 1997]. Unlike

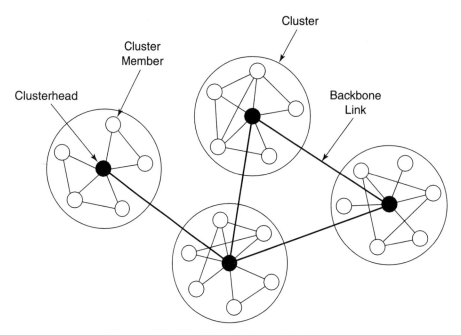

Figure 4.2. The NTDR Network Architecture

most of the approaches we describe in this chapter, they have actually been deployed in large tactical radio networks. NTDR produces a set of clusters, each containing a clusterhead, which when linked together form a routing backbone, as shown in Figure 4.2. The NTDR clustering architecture resembles the link-clustered architecture in that both comprise a single level of clusters, each composed of nodes within one hop of a clusterhead. However, it also differs substantially in the following respects. The NTDR architecture restricts direct intercluster communication to clusterheads only; hence, the clusterheads function as the gateways. Furthermore, a cluster cannot be treated as an arbitrary multihop network; neighboring nodes within one hop of each other can communicate directly, but all other intracluster communication must traverse the clusterhead.

The NTDR clustering scheme was specifically designed to cope with the frequent node movements and outages expected in a tactical network. While each clusterhead may represent a single point of failure in a sparsely connected backbone, nodes compensate for this weakness by being aggressive in attempting to maintain the routing backbone and access to it. All nodes are capable of quickly becoming clusterheads should the need arise as node interconnectivity changes. Each node keeps track of the neighbors with which it has bidirectional connectivity by receiving and periodically broadcasting *beacons*. All beacons contain the medium access control (MAC) address of the issuing node and the lowest-numbered MAC address among all nodes reachable from the issuing node. This latter piece of information is used in detecting network partitions and is called a *partition identifier*. A clusterhead's beacon also contains

- The clusterhead's organizational affiliation.
- The list of cluster members.
- The quality of the link from each member as measured by the clusterhead.
- The clusterhead's transmit power level.

This information is used by nodes receiving the beacon to determine whether to affiliate with the clusterhead.

To isolate intercluster from intracluster transmissions, each clusterhead communicates on two different frequencies, one assigned to all clusterheads and one assigned to all members of its cluster. With the exception of the clusterhead, the transmission range of the cluster members is kept small to limit interference and to enable spatial reuse of frequencies among distant clusters.

Clusterheads

An NTDR node elects itself as clusterhead if it does not detect any other clusterheads in its vicinity or if it detects that it can heal a network partition. The clusterhead election procedure does not use node properties, such as degree or identifier, to determine clusterhead status. Instead, a node becomes a clusterhead if it does not receive beacons from any clusterhead or if it receives beacons advertising two different partition identifiers.

Multiple nodes may independently detect and react to network partitioning and clusterhead disappearance resulting from changes in node interconnectivity. Thus, the NTDR clustering algorithm includes the following two mechanisms to limit the number of nodes that simultaneously attempt to become clusterheads following initial network deployment or subsequent node movements.

- Each node that detects one of the two conditions for becoming a clusterhead waits a short random time interval and then retests the condition; only if the condition remains true following the waiting period does the node assume the role of clusterhead.
- Each new clusterhead immediately issues beacons in quick succession proclaiming its status.

Superfluous clusterheads may appear, and so there exists a means to eliminate them. Specifically, a node can relinquish its role as clusterhead if doing so will not partition the network and if all cluster members can join other clusters. To limit the number of nodes that simultaneously relinquish their roles as clusterheads, however, the NTDR clustering algorithm has been designed so that checks for clusterhead relinquishment are staggered randomly among nodes over time. Nevertheless, in a highly mobile network, where there are likely to be continual changes in node interconnectivity, nodes may oscillate between clusterhead and nonclusterhead status.

Cluster Affiliation

Cluster affiliation involves both the clusterhead and the prospective cluster member. A node seeking cluster affiliation prefers clusters such that

- Both it and the clusterhead belong to the same organization.
- The signal from the clusterhead is transmitted at low power but received at high strength.
- The resulting cluster size is relatively small.

The clusterhead has the right to refuse an affiliation request from a node, but once it negotiates an affiliation it distributes its updated cluster membership to all other clusterheads. This update not only informs all clusterheads of the node's current location with respect to the set of clusters, to aid them in computing routes to the node; it also alerts the node's previous clusterhead to the fact that the node now has a new affiliation. A cluster member remains affiliated with its chosen clusterhead until one of the following events occurs, at which time it seeks an alternate affiliation:

- The clusterhead relinquishes its role.
- The clusterhead's beacons no longer list the member, or they indicate that the quality of the link to the clusterhead has become unacceptably poor.
- The received signal strength from the clusterhead is unacceptably low.

Routing

In the NTDR network, the clusterheads share responsibility for maintaining the routing backbone and hence monitor and distribute among themselves information about changes that occur in the backbone. Each clusterhead generates membership information pertaining to its cluster and link-state information pertaining to its links to neighboring clusterheads. It floods this information over the backbone and computes routes to other network nodes on the basis of it. The link state includes a "resistance" metric, similar to that described by Pursley and Russell [Pursley+ 1993], that is a measure of the interference likely to be encountered by future transmissions over the link. Clusterheads compute least-resistance routes to destinations, using

Dijkstra's shortest-path-first (SPF) algorithm [Dijkstra 1959], and they establish forwarding information based on them. Specifically, a clusterhead maintains information about the next hop to use for each destination, based on knowledge of the destination's currently affiliated clusterhead and the least-resistance route to it.

Whenever a clusterhead detects a state change that may affect routing in the backbone (e.g., a change in cluster membership or in the value of the metric on the link to a neighboring clusterhead), it immediately floods the updated state information to all clusterheads in the network, which can then recompute new routes reflecting this state change. In large and highly mobile networks, there are likely to be frequent changes in cluster membership as well as in connectivity between neighboring clusters, as such connectivity is determined by a single link between clusterheads. Thus, wide distribution of state updates may result in unacceptable behavior in such networks because the high volume of update traffic is likely to saturate the network's transmission capacity.

4.2.2 Virtual Subnet Architecture

The *virtual subnet architecture* [Sharony 1996] employs not one but a set of several disjoint routing backbones to provide fault-tolerant connectivity and load balancing in a multihop mobile wireless network. Initially, the network is partitioned into a set of disjoint clusters, which are termed *physical subnets* and are based on node locality. Members of different physical subnets are clustered together to form *virtual subnets,* each of which ideally spans all physical subnets and is used to provide communication paths among distant nodes. Each member of a virtual subnet is assumed to be able to adjust its transmission power to maintain connectivity with other members located in neighboring physical subnets. This assumption is reasonable provided that neighboring physical subnets remain in close proximity. Neighboring physical subnets and all virtual subnets are assigned different frequencies for communication to reduce interference. Both the maximum number, P, of physical subnets and the maximum number, Q, of virtual subnets in the network are predetermined. Formation of subnet clusters and assignment of subnet frequencies may be computed offline and subsequently configured into the network, or they may be computed by distributed procedures executed by the nodes within the network.

Each node is a member of exactly one physical subnet and zero or more virtual subnets, as shown in Figure 4.3. Under most circumstances, a node is a member of exactly one virtual subnet, but it might be permitted to belong to multiple virtual subnets if it communicates frequently with those subnets' members. A node's address within this cluster-based control structure uniquely identifies both its physical and virtual subnet affiliations. An

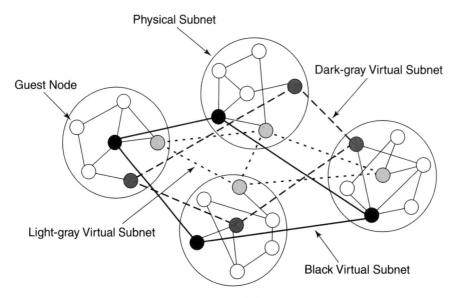

Figure 4.3. The Virtual Subnet Architecture

address comprises a prefix representing the physical subnet and a suffix representing the virtual subnet. Any node that is a member of multiple virtual subnets possesses multiple address suffixes and hence multiple addresses.

Note that here, as well as elsewhere in this chapter, we use the word "address" to denote the location of a node with respect to the cluster-based control structure under discussion. Nodes may possess additional addresses that relate to other control structures in which they participate. For example, in addition to its bipartite physical-virtual address within the virtual subnet architecture, a node may also be associated with one or more IP addresses if it is a member of an IP-based internetwork, but these IP addresses are not used for routing within the physical and virtual subnets.

The virtual subnet architecture presents a framework for organizing and using multiple overlaid routing backbones in an ad hoc network. However, it does not provide any particular algorithms for subnet clustering and frequency assignment, for distributing addressing and routing information, for requesting and obtaining destination addresses, or for computing routes and forwarding packets. One would need to specify a complete set of networking algorithms compatible with this architecture before it could be realized in an actual ad hoc network.

Node Mobility

After moving from one geographical location to another, a node may no longer be within range of any other member of its physical subnet and thus must join a different physical subnet to remain connected to the network. If there are no proximate physical subnets, the node remains isolated from the rest of the network. Joining a new physical subnet almost always necessitates joining a new virtual subnet as well. If there are proximate physical subnets, the node attempts to join one whose quota, Q, of virtual subnet affiliations has not yet been filled. In this case, the node affiliates with the physical subnet and one of the available virtual subnets. If all proximate physical subnets have filled their quotas of virtual subnet affiliations, the node affiliates with one of these physical subnets as a "guest" and may later also affiliate with a virtual subnet if one becomes available when another node leaves the physical subnet.

After formation of an affiliation with a physical subnet, the node acquires a new address; the prefix reflects the new physical subnet affiliation, and the suffix reflects either the new virtual subnet affiliation or the guest identity. The node subsequently announces its new address to all members of its new physical and virtual subnets. Note, however, that a node that is a guest member of a physical subnet currently has no virtual subnet affiliation and hence does not distribute its new address in any virtual subnet.

A source node wishing to communicate with a destination node must determine the destination's address. First, the source distributes an address query within its physical subnet, using a globally unique location-invariant identifier for the destination. The destination's address will be returned to the source, provided that the destination is currently affiliated with a virtual subnet represented by some member of the source's physical subnet. If the source is unsuccessful in obtaining the destination's address from any node within its physical subnet, it distributes the address query within its virtual subnet(s). In this case, the destination's address will be returned to the source, provided that the destination is currently affiliated with a physical subnet represented by some member of one of the source's virtual subnets. Note that the address for any destination that is a guest within some physical subnet can be obtained via this second type of query.

Routing

Within the virtual subnet architecture, each node has access to multiple routes that connect it to every other node in the network, via the set of distinct virtual subnets that interconnect the physical subnets. Such natural route diversity increases a source's ability to efficiently and quickly obtain an alternate route to a destination, and hence to maintain an existing session, as nodes move and connectivity changes within the network.

Two strategies have been suggested for exploiting the multiple forwarding choices available in a network organized according to the virtual subnet architecture. Using the first strategy, which we refer to as *direct routing*, the source forwards packets to the destination solely on the basis of the source and destination addresses. It uses the physical and virtual subnet components of the source and destination addresses to select the next hop, physical or virtual. Specifically, the source begins by searching for a node, x, that is a member of both the source's physical subnet and the destination's virtual subnet. Provided that such an x exists, the source forwards packets toward the destination via x. The packets travel within the source's physical subnet from the source to x and within the destination's virtual subnet from x to the destination, as shown in Figure 4.4(a). If, however, the destination is a guest within a physical subnet, no such x exists. In this case, the source uses its virtual subnet when forwarding packets toward the destination. The packets travel within the source's virtual subnet from the source to a node, y, that is a member of both the source's virtual subnet and the destination's physical subnet and within the destination's physical subnet from y to the destination, as shown in Figure 4.4(b).

This simple routing strategy works well assuming two things: that each physical subnet contains a member of each virtual subnet and that no subnet, physical or virtual, is partitioned. In the presence of highly mobile nodes, however, these two assumptions are unlikely to hold, and a more robust routing strategy is required. The second strategy, termed *long-path*

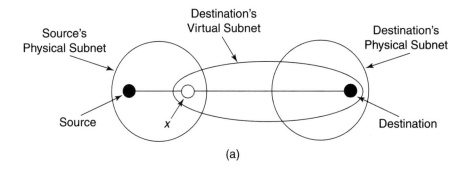

(a)

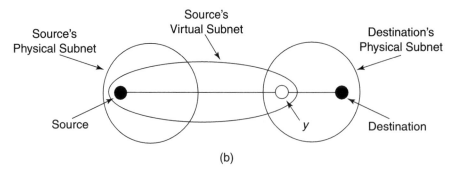

(b)

Figure 4.4. Direct Routing

routing, randomly distributes the routes selected over the space of possible routes, thus helping the network to accommodate partitioned subnets and to balance traffic load among nodes. Using this strategy, the source chooses at random one of the (at most Q) virtual subnets represented within its physical subnet. Provided that the source is not a member of the chosen virtual subnet, it forwards packets toward the destination via a node, u, that is a member of both the chosen virtual subnet and the source's physical subnet. From u, the packets travel within the chosen virtual subnet to a node, v, in the destination's physical subnet and from v to the destination, as shown in Figure 4.5(a).

On the other hand, if the source is a member of the chosen virtual subnet, it chooses at random one of the (at most $P - 1$) physical subnets that is distinct from its own and represented within its virtual subnet. The source then forwards packets toward the destination via the chosen physical subnet. The packets travel from the source to a node, w, that is a member of both the source's virtual subnet and the chosen physical subnet. From

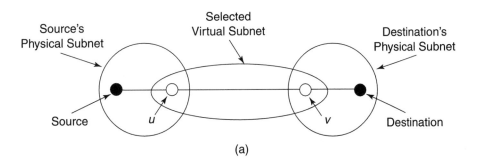

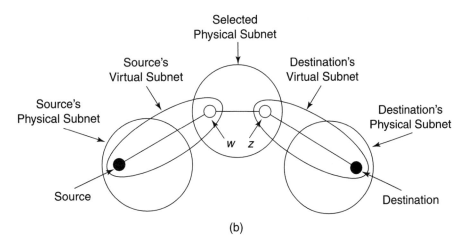

Figure 4.5. Long-Path Routing

w, the packets travel within the chosen physical subnet to a node, z, in the destination's virtual subnet and from z to the destination, as shown in Figure 4.5(b).

Long-path routing produces at most $Q + P - 1$ different routes (distinguished at the granularity of subnets, not nodes) from a source to a destination, provided that each subnet is connected. When subnets partition, intermediate nodes along a route may also need to make random selections of next-hop subnets to route around such partitions, thus increasing the number of potential route choices. Consider the example illustrated in Figure 4.5(a), and suppose that u can no longer reach v within the chosen virtual subnet. Now u randomly selects a physical subnet represented within the chosen virtual subnet, just as the source does in the example illustrated in Figure 4.5(b). In the worst case, the process of random subnet selection may be invoked at each physical–virtual and virtual–physical juncture along the route, and routes may become very long. Nodes can reduce route lengths by making available more information about their interconnectivity and by using this information during route selection. For example, if nodes have available information about which subnets are partitioned, they can adopt a routing strategy that is a combination of the two described before. Specifically, nodes can invoke direct routing preferentially and invoke long-path routing only when they encounter a partitioned subnet. These and other routing strategies remain to be explored in more detail in the context of the virtual subnet architecture.

4.3 CLUSTERING FOR ROUTING EFFICIENCY

The network control functions rely on accurate information about the current state of the network in order to choose actions that will cause the network to achieve the desired performance goals. Events that affect the structure or loading of the network (e.g., failure of a node or injection of users' traffic) as well as the control applied in response to such events (e.g., rerouting or dropping of packets) may cause changes in network state. To detect and respond to changes in network state, controllers sense local state and may collect state information from and distribute it to other controllers in the network. Network state information may include, but is not limited to, location and interconnectivity of assets and availability of and demand for services.

In mobile wireless networks, and in ad hoc networks in particular, network state changes tend to be greater in frequency and magnitude than in fixed wireline networks because of the increased number of factors causing such changes. Node movements affect both node interconnectivity and link quality. Moreover, wireless links are a limited and highly volatile resource even when nodes are stationary. Radio signal propagation is sensitive to a number of environmental factors, including distance between nodes, number and power of transmissions within reception range, external noise, weather, terrain, and vegetation. Consequently, radio signals commonly experience path loss, interference, and fading, causing errors in and loss of wireless transmissions, and thus constraining the available capacity of wireless links. Furthermore, small changes in the environment may result in large changes in radio signal propagation and consequently large variations in wireless link capacity.

Controllers consume storage, transmission, and processing resources in the network whenever they record, report on, and react to changes in network state. They need not respond to every state change, however, as many such changes have neither significant nor global ramifications for network performance. Small changes are likely to induce commensurately small perturbations in network behavior, and those occurring in one part of a network may have little or no effect on the behavior of the network's distant parts. Furthermore, in a highly dynamic network, the interval between successive state changes may be shorter than the response delay of the controllers, and the resulting control decisions will lag behind the current state. Thus, unconditional widespread reaction to and dissemination of information about each change in network state may be superfluous, ineffective, wasteful, and even counterproductive. Appropriate sensitivity for a network controller depends on the particular control function to be performed, the resources available, the volatility of network state, and the anticipated magnitude and extent of the consequences of a state change.

The inherently dynamic nature of ad hoc networks poses challenges for the design of effective yet efficient network control algorithms and their ancillary state representation and distribution techniques. In this section, we focus on the routing functions, and we describe how hierarchical cluster-based control structures can significantly reduce the overhead costs imposed by routing without unduly sacrificing the quality of the routes produced. While many of these routing techniques were originally designed for fixed networks, all are applicable (with some modification) to mobile networks. We now present an in-depth discussion of hierarchical routing, followed by a brief discussion of formation and maintenance of cluster-based routing structures.

4.3.1 Hierarchical Routing

The concept of using hierarchical cluster-based control structures as a means of containing routing costs in large networks has existed for at least 25 years and was introduced by McQuillan [McQuillan 1974]. To obtain the control structure, a network consisting of N nodes is organized into an m-level

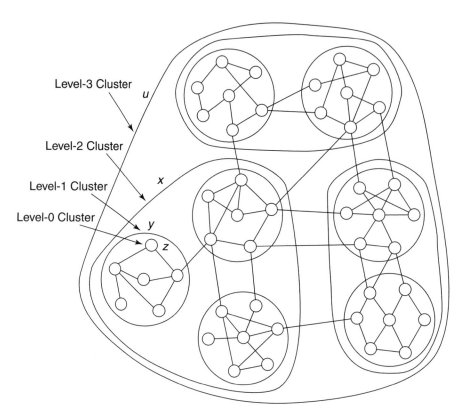

Figure 4.6. The Nested Cluster Architecture

hierarchy of nested clusters of nodes, as shown in Figure 4.6, such that all level-i clusters are disjoint for $0 \leq i \leq m$. Each node is a level-0 cluster. These are grouped into level-1 clusters that in turn are grouped into level-2 clusters, and so on, such that eventually all level-$(m-1)$ clusters are grouped into a single level-m cluster containing all nodes. (Node clustering algorithms are treated separately in Section 4.3.) The resulting structure of nested clusters encourages a natural assignment of hierarchical addresses to nodes. Each node acquires an address relative to its position in the clustering hierarchy. This address is expressed in terms of ancestral clusters, specifically as the concatenation of the labels of the level-$(m-1)$ through level-0 clusters that contain the node. The label of the single level-m cluster is omitted from a node's address, as it is common to all node addresses. For example, with respect to the clustering hierarchy depicted in Figure 4.6, the address of the node z is $x.y.z$ with u as the implicit prefix.

All of the hierarchical routing schemes discussed in this section rely on an underlying control structure consisting of nested clusters. Moreover, all but one of these routing schemes is described here in the context of a nested clustering hierarchy in which each pair of clusters is disjoint unless one is an ancestor of the other. This disjointness criterion is not a constraint imposed by the routing schemes, but is a means to simplify the presentation. Each of these routing schemes can operate correctly in the presence of overlapping nonancestral clusters, and one scheme (described at the end of the subsection on quasi-hierarchical routing) actually requires that proximate clusters have some common members.

In a mobile network, cluster overlap is often desirable. Enabling a node to hold simultaneous membership in multiple clusters, and hence maintain multiple addresses, allows it to remain reachable when it moves between clusters and when an ancestral cluster partitions. Furthermore, for some hierarchical routing schemes (such as the hybrid described later in this section), the average route length can be modestly reduced, as shown by Garcia-Luna-Accves [Garcia-Luna-Aceves+ 1985], by redrawing the boundaries of disjoint clusters so that neighboring level-1 clusters overlap at one or more nodes. Cluster overlap may occur not only within a single clustering hierarchy but also between multiple clustering hierarchies imposed over the same set of nodes. When two level-1 clusters, a_1 and b_1 (contained in the same hierarchy or in different hierarchies), overlap, each of their level-i ancestral clusters, a_i and b_i, must also overlap such that $a_1 \cap b_1 \subseteq a_i \cap b_i$ for $i \geq 1$. Thus, a node that is a member of two level-1 clusters must maintain state information about twice as many clusters, in the worst case, as a node that is a member of a single level-1 cluster must maintain.

Garcia-Luna-Aceves, Lauer, and Shacham [Garcia-Luna-Aceves+ 1985, Lauer 1995, Shacham 1984, Shacham 1985] further consider the costs and benefits of cluster overlap as they apply to routing in mobile networks. Each recommends that level-1 clusters within a single hierarchy be allowed to overlap. In the terminology of Garcia-Luna-Aceves and Shacham, nonidentical level-i ancestral clusters of overlapping level-1 clusters are said to be "disjoint" because the overlap does not affect routing at level i for $i > 1$. Lauer restricts cluster overlap so that a node may be a member of at most two level-1 clusters [Lauer 1995]. In fact, the overlap is allowed to persist only for the time it takes a node to move from one cluster to another; the node relinquishes its membership in the former cluster as soon as it has advertised its membership in the new one. Shacham suggests that each node start out as a member of at least two level-1 clusters, which implies careful construction of the initial clustering hierarchy. In an earlier publication [Shacham 1984], he considers the use of cluster overlap between multiple distinct hierarchies, each of which is composed of disjoint level-i clusters, for $i \geq 0$. In this case, each node is a member of each of n different hierarchies, and hence the amount of network resources required to distribute, process, and store routing information is n times that required for a single hierarchy.

While the use of overlapping clusters can significantly reduce the number and duration of interruptions in communications with mobile nodes, it is an expensive approach not only for the nodes that lie within the intersection of two level-1 clusters but for all network nodes. The amount of node addressing information that must be distributed and maintained in the network is proportional to the number of addresses per node, and each node in the network acquires one address corresponding to each of its level-1 parent clusters. Route selection is complicated by such factors as determining when to use which node address in order to maximize reachability during node movement. Cluster formation and maintenance are complicated by constraints on the amount of cluster overlapping permitted or required. Before implementing a hierarchical network control structure that accommodates overlapping clusters, one must carefully weigh the advantages and disadvantages according to the environment in which it will be used.

Given a hierarchical control structure consisting of nested clusters of nodes, network controllers acting on behalf of clusters can obtain and represent network state information at multiple levels of granularity. Controllers within a cluster have access to detailed information about the connectivity and services currently available within that cluster and hence can exercise fine-grained control. They also construct and present to controllers outside of the cluster a single abstract representation of the cluster, which subsumes the details visible within it. By representing state information at the granularity of its cluster, a controller can reduce both the amount of information required to represent the state of the cluster and the number of intracluster state changes that are visible external to the cluster. Abstraction of network state, however, may result in loss of information and hence may reduce the accuracy of any control decisions that are based on this abstracted state. In fact, much of the work on hierarchical cluster-based control structures for routing (e.g., [Awerbuch+ 1998a, Kamoun+ 1979]) has focused on characterizing the tradeoff in granularity of state information and quality of routes generated.

We use the term *cluster representative* for a network controller that acts on behalf of a cluster to generate and distribute routing information for it. The loss of a cluster representative implies the loss of up-to-date routing information for that cluster, potentially causing reachability problems for nodes attempting to contact destinations that lie within it. Thus, with most hierarchical routing schemes, multiple nodes within a cluster are capable of quickly assuming the role of cluster representative should the need arise. In packet forwarding, however, cluster representatives play no key role; hence, the loss of a cluster representative is no different from the loss of any other node in the cluster.

Specific hierarchical cluster-based routing schemes differ in their treatment of state information with respect to abstraction, dissemination, and route generation. They also differ in the location and number of controllers performing these functions. Classification of a routing scheme as *quasi-hierarchical* or *strict-hierarchical,* as defined by Lauer [Lauer 1986], is one of the more useful distinctions that can be drawn. With the information provided by quasi-hierarchical routing, each node learns the next node to use in order to reach each level-i cluster within its level-$(i+1)$ ancestral cluster. With the information provided by strict-hierarchical routing, each node learns the next level-i cluster to use in order to reach each level-i cluster within its level-$(i+1)$ ancestral cluster. It also learns which level-i clusters lie on the boundary of its level-$(i+1)$ cluster and to which neighboring clusters each such boundary cluster is directly linked.

We further elaborate on this distinction with the following example. Suppose that c_k is the lowest-level cluster containing both the source and the destination of a session. Figure 4.7 illustrates this example with $k = 3$. With quasi-hierarchical routing, a packet is routed directly from the source, s_0, to the boundary of d_{k-1}, the level-$(k-1)$ cluster of the destination, d_0. From there, the packet is routed directly to the boundary of d_{k-2}, d_0's level-$(k-2)$ cluster, and so on, until finally being routed directly from the boundary of d_1 to d_0. With strict-hierarchical routing, a packet is routed indirectly from s_0 to the boundary of s_{k-1}, s_0's level-$(k-1)$ cluster, as follows. First, the packet is routed directly from s_0 to the boundary of s_1,

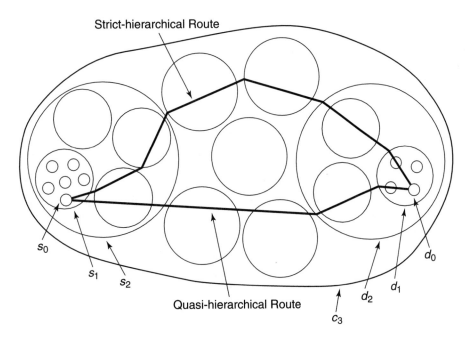

Figure 4.7. Quasi-hierarchical Routing versus Strict-hierarchical Routing

s_0's level-1 cluster. From there, it is routed through level-1 clusters in s_2, s_0's level-2 cluster, until it reaches the boundary of s_2, and so on, until it reaches the boundary of s_{k-1}. Once at the boundary of s_{k-1}, the packet is routed through level-$(k-1)$ clusters in c_k to the boundary of d_{k-1}. From there, the packet is routed through level-$(k-2)$ clusters in d_{k-1} to reach the boundary of d_{k-2}, and so on, until finally being routed directly from the boundary of d_1 to d_0.

Quasi-hierarchical Routing

Most of the hierarchical cluster-based routing schemes fall into the quasi-hierarchical category, including the original version proposed [McQuillan 1974] as well as its many variants discussed next. Furthermore, almost all of these quasi-hierarchical routing schemes are derivatives of the *distance-vector* routing approach [Ford+ 1962]. Most were originally designed for use in fixed wireline networks, but can be readily adapted for use in mobile wireless networks.

In the context of a clustering hierarchy, the objective of distance-vector routing is to determine the next hop on the minimum-cost route from a node to each level-i cluster within the node's level-$(i+1)$ cluster, for $0 \le i < m$. A cluster representative advertises, to nodes outside of its cluster, an abstracted cost for reaching destinations within the cluster. The advertised cost represents the abstracted cost from the cluster representative to any node in the cluster. With *closest entry routing* [Kleinrock+ 1977], this abstracted cost is zero; with *overall best routing* [Kleinrock+ 1977], this abstracted cost is computed as the average of the costs from the cluster representative to all nodes within the cluster. Thus, no detailed information about routing inside of the cluster is distributed outside of the cluster.

Nodes update forwarding information and propagate cost advertisements about clusters as follows. Let x and y be two nodes that share a direct link and hence are neighbors. Suppose that x and y belong to the same level-$(j+1)$ ancestral cluster but to different level-j clusters. Whenever x receives from a neighbor, z, a new cost advertisement for a level-i cluster, c, contained in x's level-$(i+1)$ cluster, for any $0 \le i < m$, x determines whether it needs to update its forwarding information for c and whether it needs to distribute a new cost advertisement for c to its neighbors. There are two separate cases to consider with respect to updating the forwarding table at x.

1. If c is not an ancestral cluster of x, x compares the cost currently stored in its forwarding table entry for c to the sum of the cost to c in the advertisement received from z and the cost of the link from x to z. Provided that the former cost exceeds the latter summed cost, x updates

its forwarding information for c, replacing the currently stored cost with the newly computed latter cost and replacing the currently stored next-hop node with z. It also updates the cost advertisement for c accordingly and determines the set of neighbors to which it will distribute this advertisement. Otherwise, x takes no further action as a result of receiving the cost advertisement from z.

2. If c is an ancestral cluster of x, x makes no adjustments to its forwarding information for c and does not update the cost advertisement for c. However, it does determine the set of neighbors to which it will distribute this cost advertisement.

Before distributing to y the cost advertisement for c, x must check that the following two conditions are true: (1) $i \geq j$, with i and j as defined above, to prevent propagation of detailed routing information about a cluster's descendant clusters outside of that cluster; and (2) the next hop contained in x's forwarding table entry for c is not equal to y to help avoid formation of routing loops.

This quasi-hierarchical routing scheme reduces the amount of routing information received and forwarding information retained by each node from $O(N)$ for a nonhierarchical control structure to $O(mC_{max})$ for an m-level hierarchical control structure of nested clusters, where C_{max} is the maximum number, over all i, of level-i clusters contained within a level-$(i + 1)$ cluster. Note that if each level-i cluster contains the same number of level-$(i - 1)$ clusters, for $0 < i \leq m$, the amount of forwarding information at each node equals $mN^{1/m}$. For large values of m and arbitrary sources and destinations, this quasi-hierarchical routing scheme may yield routes whose costs are significantly larger than those of the true minimum-cost paths. In practice, however, clustering hierarchies are constructed with only a few levels, and hence differences in the costs of the generated routes and the true minimum-cost paths tend to be small. Kamoun and Kleinrock [Kamoun 1976, Kamoun+ 1979, Kleinrock+ 1977] provide an extensive analysis of the performance of this quasi-hierarchical routing scheme. The principal results characterizing the size of the forwarding tables and the optimality of the routes selected are as follows:

- The number of entries in a node's forwarding table is minimized when the number of level-i clusters in each level-$(i + 1)$ cluster equals e and when the number of levels in the clustering hierarchy equals $\ln N$, in which case the forwarding table contains $e \ln N$ entries.
- For any arbitrary source and destination, the difference in lengths between the route produced by quasi-hierarchical routing and the

true minimum-hop path tends to zero as $N \to \infty$, under the following ideal assumptions:

1. All level-i clusters contain the same number of level-$(i-1)$ clusters, for $0 < i \leq m$.
2. Each level-i cluster contains the minimum-hop path between any two nodes resident in that cluster.
3. The diameter of any level-i cluster does not exceed $bn^v - c$, where n is the number of nodes in the cluster, $0 \leq v \leq 1$ indicates the connectivity of the cluster, and b, c are positive parameters.

In practice, clusters are usually permitted to contain tens to hundreds of members and are not restricted to the two or three members required to achieve the minimum forwarding table size. Thus, m is usually much less than $\ln N$ and in fact may be quite small even for large N. Results presented by Kamoun [Kamoun 1976] indicate that, for $m \leq 4$, substantial reductions in forwarding table size are realized with only a modest increase in route length over the true minimum. Similar results presented by Lauer [Lauer 1986] were obtained for randomly generated networks containing up to 200 nodes and three levels of clustering. Kamoun provides additional performance results for quasi-hierarchical routing, characterizing the impact of route length and volume of distributed routing information on the delay and throughput experienced by user traffic [Kamoun+ 1979]. These results are valid within the context of the three ideal assumptions and these two arguably unrealistic assumptions: that all links have equal capacity and that traffic rates between any two nodes are identical.

Minimum-Cost Paths   The evidence just discussed suggests that the average cost of the routes produced by quasi-hierarchical routing tends to exceed the average cost of the corresponding minimum-cost paths by only a small amount. Nevertheless, quasi-hierarchical routing schemes are not guaranteed to provide near-minimum-cost routes. To understand the magnitude of the worst-case discrepancy between the costs of quasi-hierarchical routes and true minimum-cost paths, consider the following example in which cost is expressed in terms of node hops.

Suppose that d_{i+1}, a level-$(i+1)$ cluster, is the lowest-level ancestral cluster of both the source and destination nodes, s_0 and d_0, respectively, and that d_i is a level-i ancestral cluster of d_0 but not of s_0. Quasi-hierarchical routing yields, for each node within d_{i+1}, the minimum-hop route from that node to d_i. Once a packet sent by s_0 reaches a node on the boundary of d_i, termed a *border node*, that border node has a forwarding entry for the minimum-hop route to d_{i-1}, d_0's level-$(i-1)$ cluster, but this route does not necessarily coincide with the minimum-hop path to d_0 unless $i = 1$. Thus, while each of the routes to successively lower-level clusters in d_i is a minimum-hop path, the routes' concatenation is not necessarily a minimum-hop path from the border node of d_i to d_0. Furthermore, even if this border node did know the minimum-hop route from itself to d_0, the concatenation of the minimum-hop path from s_0 to the border node of d_i and the minimum-hop path from that border node to d_0, is not necessarily the minimum-hop path from s_0 to d_0. In the worst case, for a given source and destination the length of the route produced by quasi-hierarchical routing may exceed the length of the true minimum-hop path by a factor of $2^m - 1$, as shown by Baratz and Hagouel [Baratz+ 1986, Hagouel 1983].

Baratz [Baratz+ 1986] proposes a modification to closest entry routing, which enables any source node to obtain the minimum-cost route to any destination node. This approach is applicable to a clustering hierarchy of arbitrary depth, but for simplicity we describe it in the context of a two-level hierarchy. The source begins by determining the minimum-cost route to each border node of the destination's level-1 cluster, using closest entry routing. Next, the source queries each of these border nodes for the cost of its minimum-cost route to the destination. Ultimately, the source computes the minimum-cost route from itself to the destination by determining the *critical border node* for the destination's cluster. The critical border node is the one for which the sum of the costs of the minimum-cost routes from the source to itself and from itself to the destination is the minimum over all border nodes of the destination's cluster.

The ability to compute true minimum-cost routes between arbitrary sources and destinations comes at the cost of queries to and responses from all border nodes of a destination's cluster. For this reason, Baratz [Baratz+ 1986] recommends this approach for use in the context of virtual circuit forwarding, where the query-response cost for the route can be amortized over all packets in the session. This quasi-hierarchical routing scheme can be generalized to an arbitrary m-level hierarchy by recursion of the query-response step for each lower-level ancestral cluster of the destination node. In the worst case, the number of queries necessary to determine the minimum-cost route to the destination is $O(B^m)$, where B is the maximum number of border nodes for any cluster. Thus, this true minimum-cost approach may be impractical for networks with many border nodes per cluster or many levels in the clustering hierarchy.

Link-State Routing   All of the quasi-hierarchical routing schemes discussed thus far are based on the distance-vector routing approach. We now describe a quasi-hierarchical routing scheme [Ramamoorthy+ 1983, Tsai+ 1989], depicted in Figure 4.8, that is based on the *link-state* routing approach [McQuillan+ 1980]. Although this scheme is proposed for use within a two-level hierarchy and described as such next, it can easily be generalized for use within an arbitrary m-level hierarchy.

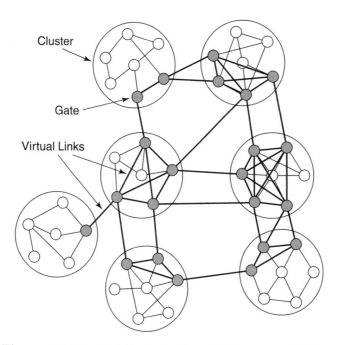

Figure 4.8. The Link-State Routing Architecture with Gates

With this scheme, nodes generate, distribute, and use hierarchical link-state routing information as follows. Each node within a level-1 cluster floods, to all other nodes within the cluster, its link-state information expressed in the form of link costs to its neighboring nodes. Thus, all nodes within the cluster obtain sufficient information to generate minimum-cost routes, via Dijkstra's SPF algorithm [Dijkstra 1959], to all other nodes within that cluster, assuming no partitioning of the cluster. Each node on the boundary of a cluster, termed a *gate,* uses intracluster link-state information to compute the minimum-cost route to every other gate for the cluster. A gate then constructs link-state information in the form of costs over *virtual links* to "neighboring" gates both within the same cluster and in adjacent clusters connected to the gate via direct links. The gate floods this link-state information to all other gates in all level-1 clusters. Thus, all gates in the network have sufficient information to generate minimum-cost routes to all other gates, and hence to all other clusters, in the network. In addition, each gate floods to nodes within its cluster its notion of the minimum cost to all other clusters. By combining this intercluster cost information with the intracluster link-state information, a node within a cluster can determine the next hop on the minimum-cost route to any destination cluster. The route to the destination node, however, is not necessarily a minimum-cost path because, unlike the scheme just discussed, there is no means for the source to discover the minimum-cost routes connecting gates of the destination's cluster to the destination node.

Hybrid Schemes   Lauer describes how the distance-vector and link-state quasi-hierarchical routing schemes discussed before can be applied individually and in combination for routing in large tactical packet radio networks [Lauer 1986, Lauer 1995], specifically those conceived under the DARPA survivable adaptive networks (SURAN) program [Shacham+ 1987]. In the SURAN context, the routing control structure consists of a three-level hierarchy of nodes, clusters, and *superclusters,* as shown in Figure 4.11, but the routing schemes proposed can be generalized to an arbitrary m-level hierarchy. Two quasi-hierarchical routing schemes were suggested for SURAN. The first scheme is simply an application of distance-vector routing, in the form of either closest entry routing or overall best routing, within the SURAN clustering hierarchy.

The second scheme is a hybrid of distance-vector and link-state routing. Each node ultimately uses distance-vector routing to determine the next hop on the minimum-cost route to each destination, but for destinations outside of its cluster the distance-vector routing information is in part derived from link-state information exchanged between clusters and superclusters. Border nodes for clusters (or superclusters) within a supercluster (or network) exchange, via flooding, cluster (or supercluster) interconnectivity information in the form of link states. With this information, a border node for a cluster (or supercluster) can compute the minimum-cost route to any cluster (or supercluster) within its supercluster (or network). Supercluster border nodes flood this cost information to border nodes for component clusters, thus enabling cluster border nodes to compute minimum-cost routes to superclusters. Cluster border nodes in turn inject this cost information for clusters and superclusters into the distance-vector information distributed among cluster members, ultimately enabling a cluster member to determine the minimum-cost route to any other cluster member, to any cluster within the ancestral supercluster, and to any supercluster.

Routing via Focal Nodes   Both of the quasi-hierarchical routing schemes described next enlist certain nodes to serve as focal points for routing. In particular, these focal nodes help to guide nodes in making forwarding decisions for a packet as it travels from source to destination, by serving as subgoals to be attained along the way. We note, however, that both of these routing schemes enable nodes to choose more direct routes when available. Thus, the subgoals specified for a destination need not be attained by packets traveling from source to destination, and hence the associated focal nodes are seldom visited by such packets.

Regional Node Routing   With *regional node routing* [Garcia-Luna-Aceves 1988], each level-k cluster, termed a *k-region,* contains one (or more) k-*regional nodes,* with the exception of the top-level m-region, which does not contain any m-regional nodes. A node is both a 0-region as well as a 0-regional node, and a k-regional node is also an i-regional node for each i-region in which it resides, for $0 \leq i \leq k$. Moreover, each k-regional node is affiliated with one $(k + 1)$-regional node in its ancestral $(k + 1)$ region. Thus, a node can be distinguished by its chain of affiliations among regional nodes, implying a natural addressing scheme as follows. A node's address is expressed as the concatenation of pairs of region and regional node labels for its ancestral regions, in descending order, followed by the node's own label, as shown in Figure 4.9. Although regional node routing specifies one address per node, there is nothing to preclude a k-regional node from affiliating with multiple $(k + 1)$-regional nodes, if they exist; hence, a node may acquire multiple addresses.

Each k-regional node distributes distance-vector routing information that propagates throughout the node's $(k + 1)$-region but no further. This implies that each node within a k-region learns the next-hop node on the minimum-cost route to each k-regional node contained within the ancestral $(k + 1)$-region; it also implies that all nodes in a k-region learn the next

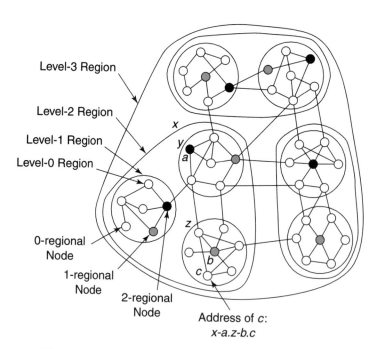

Figure 4.9. The Regional Node Routing Architecture

hop on the minimum-cost route to each $(k-1)$-regional node contained in a descendant $(k-1)$-region, assuming no partitioning of any region. Thus, a node's forwarding table contains entries pertaining to regional nodes at multiple levels.

To forward a packet toward its destination, a source first consults its forwarding table to find an entry for a reachable regional node whose address has the longest match with the destination's address contained in the packet. If no entries result in any match, the source discards the packet. Otherwise, when multiple entries result in a longest match, the source selects the entry whose corresponding route cost is lowest, choosing at random among multiple entries with the lowest route cost. The source then includes the address of the selected regional node, r, in the packet; subsequent nodes will use this address in making forwarding decisions as described below. At this point, the source forwards the packet to the next-hop node indicated in the forwarding table entry for r.

Each subsequent node, x, that receives the packet performs the same steps as the source does, plus the following additional steps. To select a forwarding table entry for an appropriate regional node, r', x uses information about the regional node, r, whose address appears in the packet. If r is a member of the set, F, of regional nodes that have entries in x's forwarding table and that exhibit longest address matches with and lowest-cost routes to the destination, then x selects $r' = r$ and forwards the packet to the next-hop node indicated by the forwarding table entry for r. If r is not a member of F, x selects r' in exactly the same manner as the source selects r. Provided that the address match between r' and the destination is at least as long as the address match between r and the destination, x replaces the address of r with that of r' in the packet before forwarding the packet to the next-hop node indicated by the forwarding table entry for r'. Otherwise, if the destination address match with r' is shorter than that with r, or if no r' can be found, x discards the packet.

This forwarding strategy, executed by each node, uses information about routes to regional nodes to guide packets toward their destinations. As a packet travels from source to destination, however, it may visit few if any of these regional nodes, the exception being the destination node itself, which is a 0-regional node. Provided that there are no partitioned regions, this procedure ensures that a packet will make progress toward its destination at each receiving node. The route produced is not necessarily minimum cost, but it is comparable to that produced by closest entry routing. When a region does partition, the forwarding procedure offers a means of maintaining reachability with the destination, yet it discourages packets from circulating aimlessly in a network in which regions partition frequently. Specifically, as long as there exists a route to an alternate regional node that is at least as close, in terms of regional ancestry, as the current but now unreachable regional node, the packet will be forwarded toward the destination. Thus, regional node routing improves node reachability in a dynamic network by providing a simple means of selecting alternate routes to a destination.

Landmark Routing   With *landmark routing* [Tsuchiya 1988], each level-i *landmark*, x, defines a level-i cluster consisting of all nodes that are within a *radius* of $r_i(x)$ node hops from x, where $0 < r_i(x) \le r_i$ and r_i is the maximum radius permitted for a level-i cluster. Each level-m landmark has a radius that is at least as large as the diameter of the network, and thus each level-m cluster covers the entire network. Every node is a level-0 landmark. For $0 \le i < m$, more than one level-i landmark is also a level-$(i+1)$ landmark, and for each such landmark, y, $r_{i+1}(y) > r_i(y)$.

Each node x employs distance-vector routing to distribute its cost advertisements throughout its level-j cluster, where j is the highest level at which x acts as a landmark. To constrain propagation of its advertisement to members of its level-j cluster, x includes in the advertisement a hop count equal to the cluster radius, $r_j(x)$. Each node that receives the advertisement for x computes its own cost to x and decrements the hop count. Only if the decremented hop count is still greater than 0 will the recipient node further distribute the advertisement, with the route cost and hop count information set to the new values it has computed. Thus, all nodes within $r_j(x)$ hops of x learn the minimum-cost route to x and the next-hop node on that route. Furthermore, each node learns how to reach all level-m landmarks. With this information, each node builds a forwarding table in which each entry refers to a landmark and indicate the cost of and the next-hop node on the minimum-cost route to that landmark.

The landmarks and associated clusters form the cluster-based control structure for landmark routing, termed the *landmark hierarchy.* In the landmark hierarchy, the relationship among clusters is entirely different from that of any of the other hierarchical control structures we describe in this chapter. At level 0, any two clusters associated with neighboring nodes must overlap, as $r_0(x) > 0$ for any node, x. At level m, all clusters must overlap because each level-m cluster covers the whole network. At intermediate levels, however, cluster overlap may, but need not, occur.

Each node must be able to acquire at least one address within the landmark hierarchy. A node's address is expressed as the concatenation of landmark labels in descending order of level, such that the relationship among the specified landmarks satisfies the following two conditions, for $1 \le i \le m$:

1. The level-i landmark lies within the cluster defined by the level-$(i-1)$ landmark.

2. The level-0 landmark lies within the cluster defined by each level-i landmark.

The first condition ensures that, for the landmarks specified in a destination address, the level-i landmark knows how to reach the level-$(i-1)$ landmark. The second condition ensures that a node can obtain enough landmark information to discover its own address. Tsuchiya offers no procedure for address discovery [Tsuchiya 1988], but we do note that address discovery requires that a node obtain enough information from all reachable landmarks to determine if any subset of them satisfies the above two conditions for an address. Examples of two landmark hierarchies, both of which satisfy the conditions for valid addressing, are shown in Figures 4.10(a) and (b).

Landmarks specified in the destination address for a packet are seldom actually visited, and in some cases landmarks may never even be used to

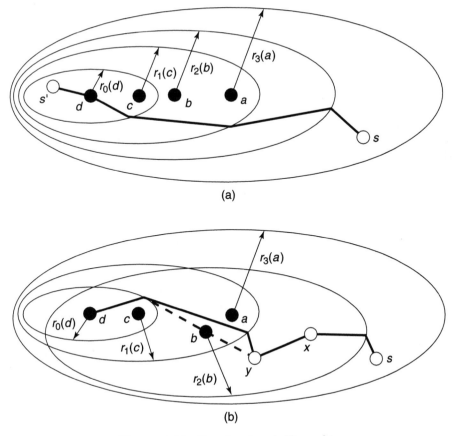

(a)

(b)

Figure 4.10. Two Landmark Hierarchies

make forwarding decisions, depending on the relative locations of source and destination. To forward a packet toward its destination, a node consults its forwarding table to find an entry for one of the landmarks specified in the destination address. If no entries correspond to any of the specified landmarks, the node discards the packet. Otherwise, when a node finds an entry for more than one landmark, it chooses the entry corresponding to the lowest level among those landmarks. Refer to Figure 4.10(a) for the following example. Sources s and s' both wish to communicate with the destination d, whose address is $a_3.b_2.c_1.d_0$ (subscripts indicate the levels of the landmarks). The minimum-cost route from s' to landmark a traverses d's cluster, whereas the minimum-cost route from s to a does not. Hence, once a packet sent by s' to d using landmark a reaches a node in d's cluster, that node can forward the packet to d directly; landmarks b and c are never used. Packets sent by s to d, however, make use of all of the landmarks in d's address.

This forwarding procedure also permits a node to make a forwarding decision according to a landmark that is at a higher level than that of the landmark used by the previous node. Refer to Figure 4.10(b) for the following example. Source s wishes to communicate with destination d, whose address is $a_3.b_2.c_1.d_0$. Nodes x and y lie within the cluster defined by landmark b and hence use this landmark when forwarding packets to d. Suppose that y is x's next hop to d and that as x forwards a packet to y bound for d, b becomes unreachable from y. As the higher-level landmark, a, is still reachable from y, y uses this landmark in forwarding the packet to d. On the way to a, the packet enters c's cluster, and from there it can be routed using the landmarks c and then d. This forwarding strategy is more lenient than that of regional node routing; thus, it increases the chance that destinations remain reachable in a dynamic network, but it also increases the risk of packets indefinitely meandering in a network in which landmarks may often become unreachable.

Strict-hierarchical Routing

Strict-hierarchical routing schemes, while traditionally not as popular as their quasi-hierarchical counterparts for fixed wireline networks, have become a favored approach in mobile wireless networks because they are more robust in the presence of changes in network state. This robustness comes at the expense of increased route costs and packet forwarding overhead compared to those resulting from quasi-hierarchical routing. Nevertheless, in a highly dynamic network, the benefits of strict-hierarchical routing usually outweigh the disadvantages, as we discuss next.

With strict-hierarchical routing, a representative of a level-i cluster, c, assembles routing information pertaining to c. In doing so it computes the cluster cost (i.e., the cost of traversing c), ascertains whether c lies on the boundary of its level-$(i+1)$ cluster, and if so determines to which neighboring level-j clusters, where $j \geq i+1$, c is directly linked. Note that $j = i+1$ if the neighboring cluster is contained within c's level-$(i+2)$ cluster and that $j = k > i+1$ if c is also on the boundary of a higher-level ancestral cluster, where k is the highest level of such ancestral clusters. The representative of c distributes this routing information (employing either the distance-vector or the link-state approach) to the representatives of all other level-i clusters within its level-$(i+1)$ cluster. Using routing information similarly obtained from other clusters, c's representative computes the minimum-cost routes and next-hop clusters (at the granularity of level-i clusters) from c to any other level-i cluster within its level-$(i+1)$ cluster; it also learns which level-i clusters lie on the boundary of its level-$(i+1)$ cluster and the neighboring clusters to which they are directly linked. Subsequently, the representative of c distributes the route cost and next-hop cluster information together with the cluster boundary information to all nodes within c. Each node thus learns the next-hop level-i cluster on the minimum-cost route (at the granularity of level-i clusters) to each level-i cluster within its level-$(i+1)$ cluster. It also learns the set of level-i clusters that lie on the boundary of its level-$(i+1)$ cluster and the neighboring clusters to which each of these is directly linked.

At a general level, the forwarding tables produced by quasi-hierarchical routing and strict-hierarchical routing are identical in terms of the number and type of entries. The next-hop forwarding table at a node, x, includes an entry for each level-i cluster, c', contained in x's level-$(i + 1)$ cluster, for $0 \leq i < m$, which indicates the next hop on the minimum-cost route to c'. When forwarding a packet from a source to a destination, a node determines the longest match between the destination's address and the cluster entries in its forwarding table, and it forwards the packet according to the matching entry. Closer inspection of forwarding table contents and the routes on which they are based, however, reveals two key differences between quasi-hierarchical routing and strict-hierarchical routing with respect to forwarding information.

The first difference concerns the number of forwarding table entries a node must consult to determine the next-hop node to a destination. With quasi-hierarchical routing, the next hop to c' stored in the forwarding table is always a node (i.e., a level-0 cluster) that is a neighbor of x. With strict-hierarchical routing, the next hop to c' stored in the forwarding table is always a cluster at level $j \leq i$, as explained below. Note that for an entry for c' to appear in x's forwarding table, c' and x's level-i cluster, c, must be siblings within x's level-$(i + 1)$ cluster. If c' and c are nonneighboring siblings, the next hop to c' is a level-i cluster that is a neighbor of c. If c'

and c are neighboring siblings, the next hop to c' is a level-j cluster, where $0 \le j < i$, that lies on the boundary of c and contains at least one node, y, with a direct link to c'. In this case, j is the highest level at which the ancestral clusters of x and y differ.

With quasi-hierarchical routing, a node can determine the next-hop node to any destination using a single forwarding table entry, whereas with strict-hierarchical routing, a node may have to consult up to $2m-1$ forwarding table entries to determine the next-hop node to a destination. We note, however, that this additional per-packet overhead of multiple forwarding table consultations performed by each node along a route is modest as long as m remains small, which is likely in practice, as we previously discussed. Moreover, many strict-hierarchical routing schemes do not produce a strict m-level forwarding table. Two of the routing schemes discussed below collapse forwarding information for all clusters at level $i \ge 1$ into forwarding information at level 1, so that a node's forwarding table contains the next-hop node to each destination in the node's level-1 cluster, the next-hop node to each neighboring level-1 cluster, and the next-hop level-1 cluster to any level-i cluster, for $1 \le i < m$, contained in the node's level-$(i+1)$ cluster. Thus, determining the next-hop node to any destination requires consultation of at most three forwarding table entries, independent of the size of m.

The second difference concerns the costs of the routes from which the forwarding entries are derived. With quasi-hierarchical routing, the cost to reach the level-i cluster, c', from x is always the true minimum cost because it is computed as the sum of individual link costs. With strict-hierarchical routing, the cost to reach c' from x is computed as the sum of the individual cluster costs over all level-i clusters in the route from c to c'. In some versions of strict-hierarchical routing, this cost may be refined to separately capture the costs of the routes from x's level-j cluster to the boundary of x's level-$(j+1)$ cluster, for $0 \le j < i$, and the cost of the route from the boundary of c to c'. In any case, a portion of the cost to reach c' from x is computed on the basis of higher-level cluster costs and not link costs. The cost of traveling across a cluster between two different neighboring clusters may be expressed in a variety of ways, as discussed toward the end of this section. For example, cluster cost might be expressed simply as 1, indicating only that the cluster directly connects the two neighboring clusters, or it might be expressed as the average delay from the boundary of one neighboring cluster to the boundary of the other, averaged over all such transcluster paths. Depending on the fidelity of the abstraction of cluster cost to the actual transcluster costs, the sequence of clusters composing the selected route might not contain the true minimum-cost path; even if it did, there might be a large discrepancy between the computed cost of the route and the true minimum cost.

Strict-hierarchical routing is likely to yield higher-cost routes than quasi-hierarchical routing yields because it does not necessarily provide [Lauer 1986, Lauer 1995] the true minimum-cost route from a source node to the boundary of the destination cluster. Coarser-granularity cluster costs provide less information about the true link-based costs encountered along routes, but they are less susceptible to change when individual link costs change. With quasi-hierarchical routing, whenever the cost of a link changes it affects the costs of all routes using that link. The nodes at the end of that link must advertise the corresponding cost changes, and minimum-cost routes must be recomputed. Thus, strict-hierarchical routing is likely to cause a significant reduction in the amount of routing information distributed throughout the network because cost updates resulting from changes in individual links are usually confined to level-1 clusters. In fact, Lauer [Lauer 1986] gives analytical results that show more than an order of magnitude reduction in the number of cost advertisements with strict-hierarchical routing in a 1,000-node network with three levels in the clustering hierarchy. He also gives simulation results comparing route lengths achieved with strict-hierarchical, quasi-hierarchical, and nonhierarchical routing in networks containing up to 200 nodes with at most three levels of clustering [Lauer 1986]. These results show that, on average, routes produced by strict-hierarchical routing are longer than those produced by quasi-hierarchical routing, which in turn are longer than those produced by nonhierarchical routing. However, the differences in the average route lengths among the three routing schemes is less than a single hop.

A Prototypical Scheme   Previously, we discussed the several variants of quasi-hierarchical routing proposed for use in SURAN packet radio networks [Lauer 1986, Lauer 1995]. The following strict-hierarchical routing scheme, however, ultimately emerged as the approach of choice because of route stability in the presence of dynamically changing nodes and links. Each node uses distance-vector routing to determine the minimum-cost routes and next-hop nodes to all nodes within its cluster and to all neighboring clusters within its supercluster. As shown in Figure 4.11, one node within each cluster (or supercluster) acts as a clusterhead (or superclusterhead) that is responsible for generating and distributing routing information about the cluster (or supercluster) to all other clusters (or superclusters) within the same supercluster (or network). Every superclusterhead is also a clusterhead for some component cluster of the supercluster.

Routing information at the level of clusters and superclusters is represented in terms of link states. Each clusterhead (or super-clusterhead) determines the connectivity and cost to each neighboring clusterhead (or

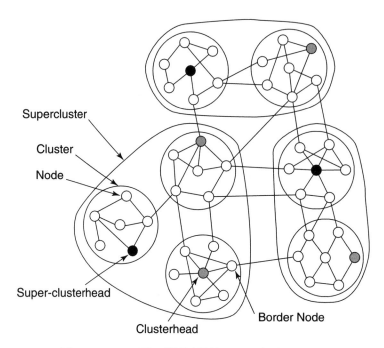

Figure 4.11. The SURAN Routing Architecture

super-clusterhead), which might not be within its supercluster. It then floods this link-state information to all clusterheads (or super-clusterheads) in its supercluster (or network). Suggested costs from one clusterhead (or super-clusterhead) to a neighboring one include the number of node hops to the neighboring clusterhead (or super-clusterhead), the number of cluster hops to the neighboring super-clusterhead, and the value 1 to indicate inter(super)cluster connectivity only.

Using the link-state information received from other clusterheads, a clusterhead employs Dijkstra's SPF algorithm [Dijkstra 1959] to compute the minimum-cost route (in terms of cluster costs) and next-hop cluster to each cluster in its supercluster and to each neighboring supercluster in the network. Similarly, using the link-state information received from other super-clusterheads, each super-clusterhead computes the minimum-cost route (in terms of supercluster costs) and next-hop supercluster to each supercluster in the network. Note that although clusterheads and super-clusterheads generate link-state information and compute routes, they play no central role in packet forwarding.

Each super-clusterhead distributes, to all clusterheads for its supercluster's component clusters, information concerning the next-hop supercluster to any supercluster in the network. Each clusterhead combines the information received from its super-clusterhead with its own information concerning the next-hop cluster to any neighboring supercluster, to obtain the next-hop cluster to any supercluster in the network. Thus, the clusterhead learns the next-hop cluster to any cluster in its supercluster and to any supercluster in the network. Each clusterhead distributes this information to all nodes within its cluster. Ultimately, each node learns the next-hop node on the minimum-cost route to any other node in its cluster and to any neighboring cluster, as well as the next-hop cluster on the minimum-cost route (in terms of clusters and superclusters) to any other cluster in its supercluster and to any other supercluster in the network.

A Hybrid Scheme   Shacham and Klemba [Shacham 1985, Shacham+ 1984] propose a strict-hierarchical routing scheme for use in large, tactical packet radio networks, as envisioned by the DARPA PRNet program [Kahn+ 1978]. This routing scheme is strict-hierarchical in terms of the granularity of forwarding table entries, but it is also quasi-hierarchical in terms of the granularity and propagation of routing information.

Each node participates in distance-vector routing to determine the minimum-cost route and corresponding next hop to each node in its level-1 cluster and add to discover the *boundary nodes* of that level-1 cluster and their connectivity to neighboring clusters. Within a level-1 cluster, route cost is expressed in terms of the number of node hops, and the next hop is a neighboring node. Routing outside of a node's level-1 cluster is accomplished with information provided by *global routing nodes*. Each level-1 cluster contains a global routing node, as shown in Figure 4.12, that participates in distance-vector routing to determine the minimum-cost route (in terms of level-1 clusters) and next hop (in terms of global routing nodes) to each level-i cluster contained in the level-1 cluster's level-$(i + 1)$ ancestral cluster, for $0 < i < m$. Global routing nodes, like (super)clusterheads and regional nodes, distribute routing information but do not serve any key role in packet forwarding.

Playing the role of cluster representatives, global routing nodes execute the quasi-hierarchical routing procedure described at the beginning of this chapter but with the following differences.

- Route cost is expressed in terms of the number of level-1 cluster hops, which implies the following cost-updating rules. When a node, x, updates its cost to a cluster on the basis of a cost advertisement received directly from a neighboring node, z, x considers the cost from itself to z to be equal to zero. When a global routing node, g, updates its cost to a cluster on the basis of a cost advertisement received indirectly from a global routing node, g', in a neighboring level-1 cluster, g considers the cost from itself to g' to be equal to 1.

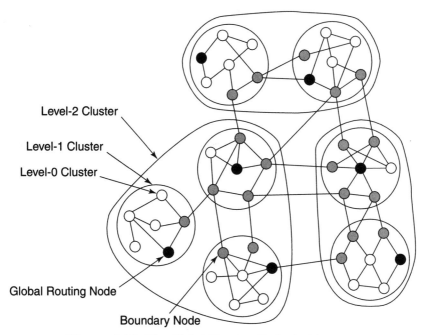

Level-2 Cluster

Level-1 Cluster

Level-0 Cluster

Global Routing Node

Boundary Node

Figure 4.12. The Global Routing Node Architecture

- The next hop to a destination cluster is neither a neighboring node nor cluster but a global routing node in the neighboring level-1 cluster.

With the routing information provided from inside and outside its level-1 cluster, each node constructs a forwarding table with entries as follows. For each destination within the node's level-1 cluster, the entry includes the cost of the minimum-hop route (in terms of node hops) and the next-hop node along that route. For each level-i destination cluster contained in the node's level-$(i + 1)$ cluster, for $0 < i < m$, the entry includes the cost of the minimum-hop route (in terms of level-1 cluster hops), the next-hop global routing node along that route, and the next-hop boundary node (for the node's level-1 cluster) toward that global routing node. Thus, to determine the next-hop node to a level-i destination cluster, a node first consults the forwarding table to determine the next-hop boundary node toward the destination and then consults the forwarding table again to determine the next-hop node toward that boundary node. In a dynamic network, this routing scheme is less robust than the SURAN scheme described previously because changes in connectivity between neighboring level-1 clusters are visible to all nodes in the network, not just to those nodes in the ancestral level-2 cluster.

Link-State Routing   The two strict-hierarchical routing schemes described below have been designed primarily to provide quality-of-service routing in large dynamic networks; hence, both exhibit common features as follows.

- Nodes represent and distribute routing information according to the link-state approach, at all levels of the clustering hierarchy. In the context of quality-of-service provision, link-state routing is superior to distance-vector routing because it enables nodes to gather more information about the state of individual clusters and hence to tailor individual routes to the service needs of specific sessions.
- Nodes select routes with the objective of satisfying individual users' service requests given the constraints imposed by the current state of the network, and they forward packets as directed by the sources.

Destination-based packet forwarding, employed by all of the other hierarchical routing schemes discussed in this section (with the exception of the minimum-cost path approach described early on), is not sufficient in the context of quality-of-service provision. To ensure that each packet of a session follows a route consistent with the session's service needs, each node that receives the packet must have information about the source and destination addresses as well as about the services requested by the source or, equivalently, information about the route selected by the source. Source-directed forwarding, in the form of either a route carried in the packet or a virtual circuit established for the session, provides an efficient means for a node to determine a next hop that is consistent with the service desired for the packet's session. The choice of a source-directed forwarding method depends on the expected number of packets in the session. For sessions consisting of many packets, virtual-circuit forwarding is preferable because the per-packet forwarding overhead is small; moreover, the cost of establishing the virtual circuit can be amortized over all session packets.

Note that even if quality of service (QoS) is not a consideration, source-directed forwarding is still preferable to destination-based forwarding in a large highly dynamic network. The reason is that some nodes that are supposed to receive a particular link-state update might not actually receive the update because of changes in node reachability during update propagation. As a result, different nodes may have different and possibly even inconsistent views of network state. Correct operation of destination-based forwarding relies on different nodes making consistent forwarding decisions for a given packet, but it cannot be assured if update receipt cannot be guaranteed. Source-directed forwarding, however, ensures that different nodes make forwarding decisions consistent with the route selected by the source and hence increase the chances of successful packet delivery. Moreover, source-directed forwarding usually results in significantly smaller forwarding tables than does destination-based forwarding. With explicit-route forwarding, a node does not even need to maintain a forwarding table, as all forwarding directives are supplied by the packets themselves. With virtual-circuit forwarding, the size of a node's forwarding table is directly proportional to the number of virtual circuits in which it participates, which is usually much smaller than the number of destinations for which it has received routing information. With destination-based forwarding, however, the size of a node's forwarding table is directly proportional to the number of destinations for which it has received routing information and hence knows how to reach; moreover, a node is likely to make use of only a small percentage of these forwarding table entries.

MMWN   Ramanathan [Ramanathan+ 1998] presents a strict-hierarchical routing scheme designed specifically for multimedia support in large mobile wireless networks—henceforth referred to as *MMWN*. The nested-cluster architecture for MMWN, illustrated in Figure 4.13, is a generalization of the nested-cluster architecture introduced at the beginning of Section 4.3.1

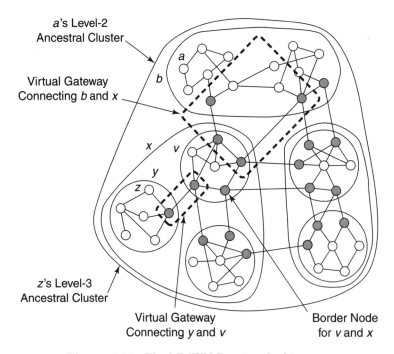

Figure 4.13. The MMWN Routing Architecture

and is assumed by all hierarchical routing schemes thus far discussed. Each node is a level-0 cluster, but two distinct nodes may have different numbers of ancestral clusters. Thus, a cluster may be associated with multiple levels in the clustering hierarchy, and the height of the clustering hierarchy is expressed as the maximum level associated with the single cluster that contains all others. Two clusters are considered to be siblings, even if they appear at different levels in the clustering hierarchy, provided that they both share the same parent cluster. Sibling clusters may form a connecting *virtual gateway* provided that a direct link exists between at least one pair of border nodes, one in each cluster. A virtual gateway consists of the border nodes in each of the two clusters together with their connecting links. Two virtual gateways attached to a cluster form the endpoints of a *virtual link* across that cluster.

Each cluster contains at least one *QoS manager* that generates abstracted link-state information for the cluster and distributes this information to other clusters. Link-state information pertaining to a cluster includes the connectivity and services available across the cluster and to neighboring clusters; it is expressed in terms of service characteristics (e.g., delay, throughput, loss rate) of virtual links and virtual gateways, as described in more detail later in this section. A QoS manager for a cluster floods the cluster's link-state updates to all nodes within the parent cluster. Thus, if no node reachability problems occur during update propagation, each node ultimately receives link-state information for each child cluster within its level-$(i + 1)$ ancestral cluster, for $i \geq 0$.

Using this link-state information, a node attempts to generate routes that are consistent with both the users' service requests and the network's current capabilities. The problem of generating routes that meet multiple cost constraints is NP-complete, for most choices of costs, specifically those such that the cost of a link makes a positive contribution to the cost of the route. Note, however, that for some choices of costs, there do exist polynomial-time algorithms for solving multiconstraint routing problems. For example, that a route exists with a hop count of not more than h and a throughput of not less than t, between a given source and destination, can be determined using a breadth-first search with a test for constraint satisfaction when considering whether to add a link to a route. If, however, we replace throughput (for which the cost of the route is the minimum of the cost of the component links) with delay (for which the cost of the route is the sum of the costs of the component links) and further constrain route delay to be no more than d, the routing problem becomes NP-complete. When applied to this modified problem, breadth-first search is no longer guaranteed to find a route that satisfies the cost constraints, even when such a route exists. We provide an example of this behavior using the network pictured in Figure 4.14.

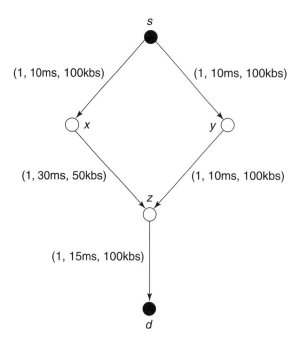

Figure 4.14. Multiconstraint Route Selection

Suppose that the problem is to find two routes between a source, s, and a destination, d, each with no more than five hops. Furthermore, suppose that one route should provide no more than 50 msec of delay and that the other should provide no less than 100 Kbytes/sec throughput. In Figure 4.14, each triple is the vector of link costs whose components represent hop count, delay in milliseconds, and throughput in kilobytes per second, respectively. Assume that during the breadth-first search beginning at s, the next hops from x are examined before those from y. With respect to construction of a route that meets the throughput constraint, the link from x to z is examined, is found to fail to meet the throughput constraint, and is hence not added to the route. The link from y to z is examined next, is found to meet the throughput constraint, and is subsequently added to the route. Ultimately, the route constructed from s to d passes through y and has cost vector (3,35,100), which meets the hop count and throughput constraints specified. With respect to construction of a route that meets the delay constraint, the link from x to z is examined, is found to yield a route that meets the delay constraint, and is hence added to the route. The link from y to z is examined next and is also found to meet the delay constraint, but because there is already a satisfactory route to z through x, the route through y is ignored. When the link from z to d is examined, however, the route from s through x to d is found to have cost vector (3,55,100), which meets the hop count constraint but not the delay constraint. A satisfactory route from s through y to d, with cost vector (3,35,100), does exist but cannot be found by simple breadth-first search.

The MMWN route selection algorithm executed by each node allows the node to trade off the costs of generating multiconstraint routes with the benefits of obtaining routes that meet the users' specified service constraints. This route selection algorithm is an iterative variant of Dijkstra's SPF algorithm [Dijkstra 1959]. In the MMWN context, a single SPF search is of complexity $O(V + C \log_2 C)$, where V is the number of virtual gateways and $C \approx mN^{1/m}$ is the number of clusters represented in a node's link-state database. Each session indicates, among its specified service constraints, the most important constraint to be satisfied. The source node then uses the cost defined by this constraint to guide the SPF search, eliminating from consideration any cluster or virtual gateway that would result in a partial route that fails to meet at least one of the cost constraints. During the search, the node saves all partial routes that meet all of the cost constraints. Thus, if the initial SPF search fails to yield a satisfactory route, the source can initiate a secondary SPF, using the stored partial routes as a starting point. The source may execute multiple SPF searches to find a suitable route depending on how important it is that the route meet the session's service constraints.

We now return to the example of constructing a route that meets the specified hop count and delay constraints, as pictured in Figure 4.14. Suppose that the SPF search is based on hop count and not delay. Both partial routes to z will be saved because each meets the hop count and delay constraints, but now suppose that the route through x to z is the one that is expanded to d. This route meets the hop count constraint but fails to meet the delay constraint. If s elects to perform a second SPF search using the remaining partial routes, the route to z through y will be expanded to d, resulting in a route that meets both the hop count and delay constraints.

Each route as specified by the source node is expressed in terms of the sequence of clusters through which it passes. Consider the lowest-level ancestral cluster, c, of the source that is also an ancestral cluster of the destination. Let j be the level of c with respect to the source and k be the level of c with respect to the destination. The route to the destination as specified by the source contains:

- The sequence of clusters connecting the source's level-i cluster to the boundary of its level-$(i + 1)$ cluster, for $0 \leq i < j - 1$, where the clusters in each sequence are siblings within the source's level-$(i + 1)$ cluster.
- The sequence of sibling clusters, within c, connecting the source's level-$(j - 1)$ cluster to the destination's level-$(k - 1)$ cluster.

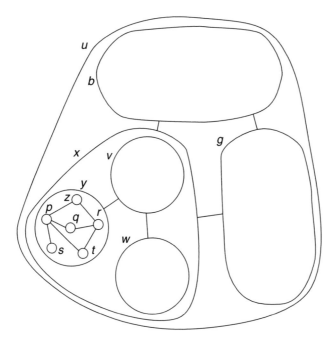

Figure 4.15. Link-State Information Maintained by Node s

Thus, the granularity of the route specification decreases as the distance to the destination (in terms of cluster levels) increases.

Consider the link-state information maintained by a source, s, as shown in Figure 4.15. To reach the destination, d, whose address is, say, $g.h.d$, the source might generate the following route:

$$x.y.s \rightarrow x.y.p \rightarrow x.y.q \rightarrow x.y.r \rightarrow x.y \rightarrow x.v \rightarrow x \rightarrow b \rightarrow g \rightarrow g.h.d$$

This route is sufficient to get a packet from the source to the node $x.y.r$ on the border of $x.y$. Acting as a member of the virtual gateway to $x.v$, $x.y.r$ must then decide the next hop into $x.v$. Once the packet reaches the border of $x.v$, the receiving node refines the source's route by generating a route that specifies the successive hops across $x.v$, which are unknown to s. Such refinements are performed by border nodes all along the way from s to d.

With MMWN routing, packets may be forwarded according to a route carried in the packet or according to a virtual circuit established along a route. MMWN accommodates point-to-multipoint sessions and hence point-to-multipoint virtual circuits. (The multipoint-specific features of MMWN are discussed elsewhere [Steenstrup 1999].) Moreover, it accommodates multiple end-to-end virtual circuits per session, for sessions demanding high throughput or reliability. In the former case, the routes are chosen so that they collectively provide the requested throughput; different packets are forwarded along different virtual circuits. In the latter case, the routes are chosen to be maximally disjoint; the additional virtual circuits may act as standbys in case the primary one fails, or a packet may be forwarded along all virtual circuits for maximum reliability.

For multipacket sessions, virtual circuit forwarding is more efficient than explicit-route forwarding, as it avoids the overhead of transmitting and refining the route for each packet of the session. Each end-to-end virtual circuit actually consists of multiple lower-level virtual circuits, one for each virtual link and virtual gateway traversed. The lowest-level virtual circuit(s) connecting to the source (or to a destination) do not traverse an entire level-1 virtual link; instead, they traverse a sequence of nodes and links from the source to the boundary of the source's level-1 cluster (or from the boundary of the destination's level-1 cluster to the destination). To reduce the cost of establishing a virtual circuit for a session, nodes attempt to build higher-level virtual circuits by concatenating pre-existing lower-level virtual circuits provided that the lower-level virtual circuits offer the services needed. Thus, multiple higher-level virtual circuits may be multiplexed over a single lower-level virtual circuit. Each node is an active participant in the following types of virtual circuit:

- Each level-0 virtual circuit for which it is a component node.
- Each level-i virtual circuit, where $i > 0$, for which it is a source or a destination.
- Each level-$(i + 1)$ virtual circuit, where $i \geq 0$, multiplexed on top of a level-i virtual circuit for which it is a source or destination.

For virtual circuit forwarding, each packet carries a dynamic stack of virtual circuit identifiers, which are pushed and popped as the packet moves between level-i and level-$(i + 1)$ virtual circuits when traveling from source to destination.

If reachability is lost between a pair of successive nodes, x and y, in a virtual circuit, the upstream node, x, attempts to make a local repair of the virtual circuit, thus minimizing the network resources required for repair as well as the time during which the source and destination are disconnected. Lowest-level virtual circuits may be repaired by one of three procedures, described in detail by Ramanathan [Ramanathan+ 1998]: *Handoff*, which does not increase and may even decrease the route length; *local reroute*, which increases the route length by at most a prespecified amount; and *end reroute*, which may increase, decrease, or leave unchanged the route length. The first two procedures seek to repair the level-0 virtual circuit by finding a route segment that can be established from x to the node, z, that is immediately downstream from y on the virtual circuit. The third procedure searches for a route segment from x to the destination node of the virtual circuit. If the level-0 virtual circuit cannot be repaired, the connectivity of higher-level virtual circuits multiplexed onto this virtual circuit will be affected. Higher-level virtual circuits can be repaired using end reroute only because the component nodes normally do not have knowledge of specific downstream nodes. Note, however, that in the best case repairing a single lower-level virtual circuit may transparently repair all higher-level virtual circuits multiplexed onto it, thus reducing the cost of virtual circuit repair.

Nimrod   A strict-hierarchical routing scheme, henceforth referred to as Nimrod, has been proposed [Castineyra+ 1994, Steenstrup 1996], designed primarily for use in large dynamic networks, such as the Internet, in which the dynamism is a result not of node movement but of addition and removal of nodes and failure of links. The Nimrod routing scheme, a generalization of IDPR [Steenstrup 1994], is a precursor to the MMWN routing scheme but differs from it in several respects, discussed below, many of which are a result of the fact that nodes are assumed to be stationary in the Nimrod context.

   With Nimrod routing, each cluster contains one or more representatives that generate and distribute link-state updates on behalf of that cluster. These link-state updates are an abstract representation of cluster interconnectivity and services, based on link-state updates received from child clusters. Each cluster also contains one or more *route agents* that generate routes on behalf of nodes within that cluster; level-0 clusters, however, contain no level-0 route agents.

   A cluster representative distributes a cluster's link-state updates to all representatives and route agents for the parent cluster. Thus, within a cluster each representative and route agent automatically receives them from all child clusters, but does not automatically receive them from any other descendant or ancestral clusters. This significantly reduces not only the transmission load of distributing link-state updates but also the amount of link-state information that must be stored and used in route generation. In fact, at the minimum a route agent need only maintain $C \approx N^{1/m}$ entries in its link-state database, one for each of the child clusters of the cluster on whose behalf it acts. Without additional link-state information, the route agents for a cluster are limited to constructing routes within that cluster, at the granularity of the child clusters, and must rely on route agents in other clusters to complete the route to the destination. Route agents, however, may also request additional link-state information from representatives of any cluster in the network and hence may obtain sufficient information to compute routes to any destinations in the network at any granularity of clusters. The cost of maintaining and using large link-state databases thus falls predominantly to those route agents that wish to compute fine-granularity routes and not to the network at large.

To obtain a route to a destination node, a source node begins by placing a request to a route agent, r_1, acting on behalf of its level-1 cluster. Each node must therefore have sufficient information to reach at least one route agent for its level-1 ancestral cluster [Steenstrup 1996]. Once r_1 receives a route request, it uses the source and destination addresses to determine the source's lowest-level ancestral cluster that also contains the destination. Let j be the level of that cluster with respect to the source, and let k be the level of that cluster with respect to the destination. With Nimrod, one or more of the following three procedures may be employed to build a route to a destination.

Route concatenation   With this technique, r_1 concatenates routes obtained from route agents for the source's level-i clusters, for $0 < i \leq j$, to build a route to the destination's level-$(k - 1)$ cluster. First, r_1 requests from a route agent, r_j, for the source's level-j cluster, a route from the source's level-$(j - 1)$ cluster to the destination's level-$(k - 1)$ cluster. Next, r_1 requests from a route agent, r_{j-1}, for the source's level-$(j - 1)$ cluster, a route from the source's level-$(j - 2)$ cluster to a sibling cluster that is on the boundary of the source's level-$(j - 1)$ cluster and directly connected to the next cluster listed in the route obtained from the route agent for the level-j cluster. Repeating this procedure at each lower level, r_1 obtains from each r_i, for $0 < i \leq j$, a segment of the source–destination route traversing the source's level-i cluster, computing the route segment in the source's level-1 cluster itself. By concatenating these segments, r_1 forms a route from the source to the destination's level-$(k - 1)$ cluster. In fact, this route is identical to the route r_1 would have produced if it had had access to link-state information for all of the sibling clusters in each of the source's ancestral clusters, as in MMWN.

Thus, a packet can be routed from the source to the destination's level-$(k - 1)$ cluster. Once the packet reaches this cluster, successive portions of the route through each of the destination's level-i descendant clusters, for $k > i > 1$, are filled in by route agents for those clusters as follows. When the packet reaches the boundary of the destination's level-i cluster, that node requests a route to the boundary of the destination's level-$(i - 1)$ cluster, from a route agent, r'_i, for the level-i cluster. Once the packet reaches the boundary of the destination's level-1 cluster, that node requests a route to the destination, from a route agent, r'_1, for that cluster.

Single-level routes   With this technique, each r_i, for $0 < i \leq k$, computes only the portion of the source–destination route that lies entirely within the source's level-i cluster. Beginning at the source's level-1 cluster, if $j = 1$, r_1 computes the entire route from source to destination provided that the level-1 cluster is not partitioned; if $j > 1$, r_1 computes the route to the boundary of the source's level-1 cluster. Successive portions of the route through each of the source's level-i clusters, for $1 < i < j$, are filled in by route agents for those clusters as follows. When the packet reaches the boundary of the source's level-i cluster, the recipient node requests a route to the boundary of the parent cluster, from a route agent, r_{i+1}, for the parent cluster. Once the packet reaches the boundary of the source's level-$(j - 1)$ cluster, that node requests a route to the sibling cluster containing the destination, placing a query to a route agent, r_j, for the source's level-j cluster. As with the route concatenation technique, once the packet reaches the destination's level-$(k - 1)$ cluster, successive portions of the route are supplied by the route agents for the destination's level-i clusters, for $k > i \geq 1$.

This routing technique reduces the amount of link-state information that a route agent must maintain to construct its routes. There is, however, a penalty for permitting route agents to maintain link-state information for only a single level of cluster, and that is the potential for packets to traverse longer and generally higher-cost routes than if multilevel link-state information were available for route computation. With its minimal amount of link-state information, a route agent is unable to determine which exit point to the next higher-level cluster will ultimately result in the lowest-cost route to the destination's level-$(k - 1)$ cluster, and hence it may select an exit point that results in a higher-cost route.

Fine-granularity routing With this technique, r_1 can retain complete control over the route from source to destination by obtaining link-state information from representatives of any clusters in the network and computing the entire source–destination route based on it. When r_1 receives a route request from a source, it first examines its own link-state information to determine whether it should collect link-state information from other clusters before computing the route. First, r_1 makes sure that it has link-state information for all of the sibling clusters in each of the source's ancestral clusters. Information about all child clusters is available with a single request to the representative of the parent cluster. Note that link-state information for ancestral clusters above level j may be required for route computation if the level-j cluster is partitioned. Additionally, r_1 may request link-state information for the sibling clusters of the destination's level-i clusters, for $k > i > 0$. Moreover, r_1 is able to obtain link-state information about any descendant cluster of any cluster for which it already has link-state information. Usually, r_1 makes such detailed requests if the link-state information advertised for a cluster is inconclusive concerning the specifics of the services available within the cluster. Thus, r_1 can compute a true minimum-cost route (in terms of nodes and links) from source to destination, but may need to acquire and use a large quantity of link-state information to do so.

Route agents cache link-state information obtained automatically from representatives of child clusters and on demand from representatives of other clusters. They also cache the routes they compute or obtain on demand from other route agents. Caching increases the storage requirements at the route agents, but significantly reduces the costs of generating routes, which includes computation of routes, transmission of routing information (link states and routes), and delay in obtaining routes. The Nimrod routing design assumes that route agents have ample storage resources and that the frequency of state changes perceived for level-i clusters, $i > 0$, is low enough that cache entries do not become stale quickly. While abstraction of cluster state helps to lower the frequency of intracluster state changes perceived outside of a cluster, cached routing information is likely to go out of date rapidly in highly mobile networks. Thus, in MMWN routes are not cached; only link states, which are updated and distributed whenever state changes occur, are cached.

With Nimrod, as with MMWN, packets may be forwarded according to a route carried in the packet or according to a virtual circuit established along a route. The route specification supplied by a route agent and ultimately used in packet forwarding is likely to include only a subset of the clusters on the route. In fact, this specification may be a reduction of the route actually computed by the route agent, containing only those clusters that must be traversed to meet the session's service constraints. Such partially specified routes not only reduce packet overhead but also provide flexibility in defining portions of the route, thus enabling intermediate nodes to fill in and refine the route on the basis of the most recent information about their clusters. This flexibility is particularly useful in dynamic networks in which cluster state may change frequently.

Abstraction of Cluster State Hierarchical cluster-based control structures offer the opportunity to significantly reduce the quantity of network state information—particularly routing information—that must be distributed, processed, and stored throughout a network. To realize such reductions, however, a hierarchical routing scheme must be able to represent the state of a cluster in an abstracted form that hides the details of connectivity and services offered within the cluster. A desirable abstraction presents a reduced version of the cluster's state information yet captures the cluster's features with sufficient fidelity so that there are only minor discrepancies between the qualities of service advertised for the cluster and those actually provided to packets. Constructing a reasonable abstraction for a cluster with wide-ranging or frequently changing characteristics requires trading off size and fidelity of the abstraction.

In the context of link-state hierarchical routing, several abstraction techniques have been proposed for capturing the dimensions of connectivity, services, and time in the representation of cluster state. The resulting abstractions range in size from $O(SA)$ to $O(SA^2)$ for a single cluster, c, where S is the number of distinct service parameters relevant within c and A is the number of neighboring clusters—each such neighbor is a sibling cluster of c or of an ancestor of c. All of these abstractions, however, share the feature that the connectivity and services for c are expressed relative to c's neighboring clusters, which are entry points to and exit points from c. Note that multiple border nodes for c may be connected to a single neighboring cluster.

For c, the connectivity to an adjacent cluster, termed an *adjacency*, and the connectivity across c between two adjacent clusters are each represented as a single abstract entity (e.g., the virtual gateways and virtual links of the MMWN architecture). Most of the state information available for building an abstraction for c is itself in an abstract form, specifically the set of abstractions for c's child clusters. The exceptions are the adjacencies whose abstract representations are built from the characteristics of the component nodes and links. While building higher-level abstractions from lower-level abstractions simplifies the abstraction procedure at any given level in the clustering hierarchy, it also increases the probability that important aspects of network state will be lost during the abstraction procedure and thus fail to appear in the state representations for higher-level clusters. Note that the Nimrod routing scheme offers a means to reclaim this lost information by enabling route agents to request and collect link-state information from clusters at any level and location within the clustering hierarchy.

The proposed abstractions for cluster state representation cover a wide range in terms of the granularity of state information provided. For each representation, connectivity is represented by a graph consisting of *logical nodes* and *logical links*, each of which possesses associated service attributes. Below, we provide several examples of abstractions of cluster state, as illustrated in Figure 4.16, but many other variations exist. Awerbuch [Awerbuch+ 1998a] and Lee [Lee 1995] compare the advantages and disadvantages of several of these abstractions, with the former providing simulation results for randomly generated networks. All but one of the following abstractions can be represented by a graph with $O(A)$ logical nodes and $O(A)$ logical links.

The most compact of these abstractions represents a cluster's state with an undirected *hub-spoke* graph consisting of a single logical node and associated vector of service costs and one logical link for each adjacent cluster with a single vector of service costs that applies to the set of all logical links. This simple abstraction, however, cannot capture different service costs for different adjacencies, for different transcluster service costs depending on the entry and exit adjacencies, or for direction-dependent service costs (i.e., from versus to an adjacent cluster). If this abstraction

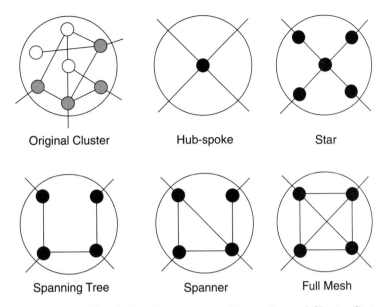

Figure 4.16. Graphs for Representing Abstractions of Cluster State

is extended so that each logical link has its own vector of service costs, it can then capture some of the differences in the service costs of different adjacencies and different transcluster routes. The undirected graph must be further extended to become a directed graph if direction-dependent service costs are to be captured.

Additional flexibility in discrimination of service costs is possible if a more complicated graph is adopted for a cluster's state abstraction. A *star* graph, consisting of a single central logical node and one logical link to each logical node representing an adjacency, permits isolation of adjacency service costs and transcluster service costs. This graph may be undirected or directed, to capture direction-dependent service costs, and it may have service cost vectors per set of logical links or per logical link, to capture neighbor-dependent service costs.

The final three examples of cluster state abstractions are all subgraphs of the complete graph over the set of logical nodes representing adjacencies. Each of these subgraphs may be directed or undirected and may have service cost vectors per logical link or per set of logical links, depending on the representation in the original complete graph from which the subgraph is derived. The first of these subgraphs is a *spanning tree* that might be generated in a number of ways (e.g., at random or so as to minimize one of the service costs). The second of these subgraphs is a *spanner,* that is, a subgraph whose nodes are identical to the nodes in the original graph but whose links are a proper subset of the links in the original graph. Althofer et al. [Althofer+ 1993] present an algorithm for constructing a spanner of *stretch t* requiring $O(A^{1+1/t})$ links, such that between any two nodes the cost of the minimum-cost path is at most t times greater in the spanner than in the original graph from which it was derived. Awerbuch and Shavitt [Awerbuch+ 1998b] present an algorithm for constructing an undirected spanner from a complete directed graph, G, over the logical nodes representing adjacencies, with the following properties. The spanner includes $O(A)$ links, each of which has *distortion* of $O(\sqrt{\rho}A)$, where $\rho = \max\{\rho_{x,y}\}$ over all $x, y \in G$ and $\rho_{x,y} = w(x, y)/w(y, x)$, the ratio of the directional logical link costs between logical nodes x and y in G.

The third of these subgraphs is the complete, or *full-mesh*, graph over the logical nodes representing the adjacencies. In its most detailed form, this is a directed graph whose logical links and nodes each have an associated service cost vector. Use of this abstraction for hierarchical routing is often discouraged because of the potentially large size of the abstraction for clusters with many neighbors; the graph has $O(A)$ logical nodes but $O(A^2)$ logical links. We note, however, that when this graph exhibits similar service cost vectors for different logical links, the representation can be collapsed so that a single service cost vector applies to a set of logical links. In fact, in the best case, this abstraction reduces to the most compact one, namely the hub-spoke graph. Elsewhere [Steenstrup 1994] cluster state is represented in terms of a complete directed graph over the logical nodes representing adjacencies, but is provided with a means for aggregating, whenever possible, directed logical links into undirected ones, logical node–link pairs into logical links, and multiple service vectors into a single vector. This enables compact yet flexible abstraction of cluster state.

The components of a service cost vector for a particular logical node or logical link are computed on the basis of the characteristics of the set of underlying routes represented by that logical node or link, which are expressed in terms of quality of and restrictions on access to services. These service costs may be configured values that are independent of network state, or they may be dynamic values that change with network state. Each component of a service cost vector specifies a single value that is intended to be representative of a route subsumed by the logical node or logical link. Examples from Steenstrup's Internet draft [Steenstrup 1996] include

- The "optimistic" value (e.g., minimum delay over all routes)
- The "pessimistic" value (e.g., maximum delay over all routes)
- The mean value (e.g., average delay over all routes)
- A measure of variation among values (e.g., variance, range delimited by optimistic and pessimistic values)
- Some combination of these

These abstractions capture the wide range of services offered over different routes and at different times within a cluster.

For calculating service cost vectors in networks in which cluster state is time varying, we offer the following example procedure, developed for the MMWN routing described previously. A cluster's QoS manager computes the value of each component of the service cost vector for a logical node or a logical link as the recency-weighted mean and deviation from the mean of the values for all routes thus far selected for carrying traffic over the logical node or the logical link. With recency weighting, more recently selected routes are given larger weights in the average, $avg(t+1) = sample$ $(t+1) + \alpha(avg(t) - sample(t+1))$, $0 \leq \alpha \leq 1$. Such statistical descriptions of the service costs, based on recently selected routes, provide a reasonable estimate of the services that will be available to a session. If, however, no traffic has yet been forwarded over the logical node or the logical link, the service cost vector is assembled as follows. The QoS manager computes minimum-cost routes for each of the service costs and forms the service cost vector based on the "optimistic" values derived from these routes.

4.3.2 Clustering

Formation and maintenance of a cluster-based control structure requires algorithms for initially clustering nodes and for adjusting clusters as nodes join, leave, or move within the network. In this section we describe several algorithms for building the initial clustering hierarchy and for restructuring the hierarchy as network connectivity changes.

Building a Clustering Hierarchy
In a communications network, a clustering algorithm must produce clusters such that each is connected. It may also strive to attain other objectives such as

1. Minimizing the amount of routing information that must be distributed, processed, and stored by each node
2. Maximizing the connectivity within each cluster
3. Localizing high-intensity traffic within a cluster
4. Localizing highly variable traffic within a cluster
5. Minimizing the number of intercluster links
6. Maximizing the stability of intercluster links
7. Minimizing the difference between the hierarchical route and the true optimal route (with respect to some cost) for each pair of nodes

Furthermore, the clustering algorithm may be subject to constraints such as the following:

1. Upper and lower limits on the number of child clusters within each cluster

2. An upper limit on the diameter of each cluster in terms of child
   clusters
3. All clusters containing the same number of child clusters

Fixed Networks Many combinations of the objectives and constraints
just listed result in a clustering problem that is NP-complete. Moreover,
some objectives and constraints may conflict, and in such cases one may
choose to relax constraints to achieve a clustering that is closer to the
objective. For fixed networks, one has the luxury of computing clustering
hierarchies offline where sufficient processing power and time can be applied
to achieve those that are arbitrarily close to the objective. Examples of
offline clustering algorithms include the following.

Kleinrock and Kamoon present clustering as an integral part of the network design problem and propose solutions that minimize the computational cost of the design [Kleinrock+ 1980].

Muralidhar and Sundareshan characterize and solve the clustering
problem as a 0-1 programming problem, which attempts to maximize
the sum of the ratio of traffic variability over hop count for all pairs
of nodes, subject to a constraint on the maximum amount of routing
information that can be stored at a cluster controller. The cluster controller is selected as the node with the highest degree in the cluster,
thus tending to reduce the delay in communicating with the other cluster members [Muralidhar+ 1986].

Krishnan et al. describe a clustering problem in which the objective is to
produce connected clusters, such that the intercluster cost is minimized
(objectives 3 and 4 can each be expressed in terms of this general objective) and each cluster satisfies constraint 1. An interative approach
to solving this clustering problem is presented. The algorithm achieves
reasonable clusterings in polynomial time by using variations of several simple heuristics that have been effectively applied to conventional
graph partitioning problems [Krishnan+ 1999].

Ramamoorthy et al. propose several clustering algorithms, satisfying different combinations of objective 5 and constraints 1 and 2. The following
algorithm limits the maximum size of a cluster and, incidentally, tends
to produce "rounded" rather than "elongated" clusters. Initially, a node
is selected as cluster leader. Proceeding in a breadth-first fashion out
from the leader, the algorithm adds nodes to the cluster until the cluster
size limit is attained. A new cluster is formed by selecting a leader and
applying the above algorithm. Candidates for cluster leader are those
nodes that surround the most recently formed cluster and are not yet
members of any cluster. If there are no such nodes surrounding the most

recently formed cluster, the second most recently formed cluster is considered, and so on, until an appropriate cluster leader is found or all nodes are members of some cluster. To form parent clusters over a set of existing clusters, each existing cluster is collapsed into a single logical node and links between two such clusters are collapsed into a single logical link. Then the above clustering algorithm is applied to the graph of logical nodes and links [Ramamoorthy+ 1987].

Miyao et al. propose a clustering algorithm that, when given a network and a pre-existing set of cluster controllers, constructs a set of clusters such that each one contains at most one controller and each node belongs to the same cluster as that of the nearest controller. For each controller, a shortest-path spanning tree rooted at the controller is constructed. A node is affiliated with a set of cluster controllers, such that for each candidate the route from the controller to the node is shortest, thus enuring that each node will belong to at least one cluster. To ensure that each node will belong to exactly one cluster and that that cluster will be connected, a single candidate is chosen from the set, such that the route from the controller to the node includes only nodes in the cluster [Miyao+ 1986].

Tsuchiya outlines an algorithm for constructing a landmark hierarchy. Each node begins as a level-0 landmark and advertises itself to all nodes within r_0 hops. If a node receives an advertisement from a level-1 landmark, it acquires the label of that landmark as the level-1 portion of its address and shrinks its radius to fit within the level-1 cluster. If the node receives no advertisements from any level-1 landmark, it executes an election algorithm with all other level-0 landmarks from which it has received advertisements, in order to designate a level-1 landmark. This procedure is repeated at each level to form the entire hierarchy. The result exhibits cluster nesting (a constraint not demanded by landmark routing), such that all level-i clusters whose nodes have the same level-$(i + 1)$ landmark are contained within the level-$(i + 1)$ cluster defined by that landmark [Tsuchiya 1988].

Ramamoorthy et al. provide an algorithm for generating overlapping clustering hierarchies of the form suggested by Shacham [Shacham 1984], where in each hierarchy sibling clusters are disjoint. The first clustering hierarchy is generated by any suitable algorithm and used in generating the second clustering hierarchy as follows. First, each intercluster link between level-1 clusters (and the link's associated endpoint nodes) in the first hierarchy is collapsed into a single logical node. Second, the clustering algorithm is rerun with this set of nodes and logical nodes. Third, the logical nodes are expanded into their original links and endpoint nodes. The resultant second hierarchy is guaranteed to exhibit nontrivial cluster overlap with the first hierarchy at each level i, for $i > 0$ [Ramamoorthy+ 1987].

Mobile Networks   In a mobile network, the initial clustering hierarchy may be constructed offline provided that the initial relationships among nodes are known. In ad hoc networks, this condition is unlikely to be true. Thus, many of the hierarchical routing schemes proposed for mobile networks also include online clustering algorithms that can be performed by the network nodes. To limit the computational requirements for clustering at each node, the clustering problems to be solved are usually simpler (in terms of objectives and constraints) than those for fixed networks. Two examples of clustering algorithms designed specifically for mobile networks are discussed below. For both algorithms, the sole objective is to produce connected clusters. The second algorithm also attempts to satisfy constraints on cluster size and volatility of intercluster links.

Lauer outlines a clustering algorithm for SURAN-style networks. Nodes cooperate to elect clusterheads and super-clusterheads (no specific election algorithm is given, however). Each node then affiliates itself with the closest clusterhead, and all nodes affiliated with a given clusterhead form a cluster. Each clusterhead affiliates itself with a super-clusterhead, thus affiliating all cluster members with the same super-clusterhead. All nodes affiliated with a given super-clusterhead form a supercluster [Lauer 1986].

Ramanathan and Steenstrup give a clustering algorithm for MMWN-style networks, which for simplicity we describe for a two-level clustering hierarchy. The algorithm uses link-state information distributed among network nodes and recursive bisection to produce connected level-1 clusters that obey both upper and lower bounds on size. A single node, the *cluster leader,* performs the clustering. The cluster leader is the node with the lowest-numbered identifier in a group of mutually reachable nodes, but each node is capable of assuming the role of cluster leader if necessary. To begin, the cluster leader selects two "seed" nodes and performs a bisection of the initial large cluster. The following heuristic for choosing seeds helps to ensure that they are well separated and hence encourages the formation of balanced clusters. First, a node is chosen at random; then a second node at maximum hop count from the first is chosen; finally, a third node at maximum hop count from the second is chosen. The second and third nodes become the seeds for two clusters.

To form each cluster, the cluster leader alternates between clusters, attempting to add to a cluster another node that is not yet a member of any cluster and is adjacent to a node in that cluster, until each node is a member of one of the two clusters. If the size of either cluster exceeds the specified upper bound, the cluster leader for that cluster bisects the cluster using the above algorithm. This procedure is repeated until all clusters are within the prescribed size limit. Within each cluster, the leader informs the component nodes of the identity of the cluster of which they are members; a cluster's identity corresponds to the identity of the cluster leader. Nodes with intercluster links attempt to form virtual gateways with other clusters. Each virtual gateway consists of at least one intercluster link and preferably more to help maintain connectivity between clusters in the presence of node movements and failures. Higher-level clusters may be formed using the same approach but with clusters collapsed into logical nodes prior to clustering [Ramanathan+ 1998].

Routing, Clustering, and Abstraction Hierarchical cluster-based control structures force a tight coupling among routing, clustering, and abstraction. The choice of algorithm for any one of these functions affects the output of that function, which forms an important part of the input for the other two functions. For example, the choice of clustering algorithm determines which nodes are clustered together, which in turn determines the connectivity and services that can be provided by each cluster and hence what state information can be abstracted for use by routing. On the other hand, the choice of abstraction and routing algorithms influences the clusterings possible. The abstraction algorithm determines the representation of cluster state, which in turn may influence the formation of higher-level clusters if the clustering algorithm tends to group together similar lower-level clusters. The routing algorithm determines which routes are selected, which in turn affects traffic load in the network, and thus may affect the formation of clusters based on criteria such as traffic localization. Moreover, in a dynamic network routes, clusters, and abstracted cluster states are constantly undergoing modification according to detected changes in network state. Determining which combination of routing, clustering, and abstraction algorithms is most appropriate for a particular network, exhibiting both low overhead and a high probability of finding routes that meet users' service requirements and conform to the network's service limitations, is a topic for further research.

Restructuring a Clustering Hierarchy

In an ad hoc network, where nodes may be in constant motion, the initial clustering hierarchy must be adjusted to accommodate time-varying changes in connectivity. While an entire reclustering could be performed whenever a node moves, in a highly dynamic network it is likely to be not only prohibitively expensive, in terms of computational resources, but also unnecessary. Instead, algorithms for locally adjusting the clustering hierarchy in response to node movements are preferable because they can quickly modify cluster membership while consuming few resources. As an example, we provide the techniques for maintaining the clustering hierarchy for MMWN.

Cluster leaders split their clusters and merge them with others, in an effort to keep them within the prescribed upper and lower bounds on size, as nodes move among clusters. Periodically, each cluster leader determines the number of child clusters within its cluster on the basis of received link-state information. If this number exceeds the prescribed upper bound on cluster size, the cluster leader splits the cluster in two, using the recursive bisection technique described previously. If, however, this number is less than the prescribed lower bound, the cluster leader attempts to merge its cluster with a neighboring cluster in order to form a cluster of acceptable size. The selected neighboring cluster must be small enough that its size after merging does not exceed the upper bound.

Node movement or failure may result in a cluster *partition,* that is, a loss of connectivity such that at least two nodes in the cluster can no longer communicate via a route that lies entirely within that cluster. In each of the subclusters created by the partition, the node with the lowest-numbered identifier assumes the role of subcluster leader and determines the size of the subcluster. If the subcluster is smaller than the prescribed lower bound, the leader attempts to merge it into a neighboring cluster. Undersized subclusters that have been unable to merge with neighboring clusters and subclusters of acceptable size must be recognized and treated as independent entities for the purpose of routing. There are two basic approaches to routing in the presence of such subclusters. The first requires nodes in subclusters to acquire new addresses [Ramanathan+ 1998]; the second permits nodes in subclusters to retain their addresses in terms of the original nonpartitioned cluster [Steenstrup 1994, Steenstrup 1996]. The choice of approach depends on the expected frequency of cluster partitions and on the expected number and size of the resulting subclusters. Descriptions of these two approaches follow. Perlman provides a detailed discussion of these and other solutions to the network partition problem [Perlman 1985].

1. Each subcluster becomes a separate new cluster labeled by its leader and advertises its own link-state updates. All nodes within this cluster acquire new addresses that reflect their cluster membership.

2. Each subcluster operates as a separate cluster from the perspective of routing, but nodes within a subcluster retain their addresses with respect to the original nonpartitioned cluster. Specifically, a subcluster advertises its own link-state updates, which bear the identity of the original cluster and are further distinguished by the identity of the subcluster leader. Identification of subclusters enables the route generation procedure to differentiate among the subclusters. Route generation, however, is complicated by the fact that nodes retain addresses with respect to the original nonpartitioned cluster. To ensure selection of a route connecting a source with a destination located within one of the subclusters, routes must be generated from the source to each distinct subcluster. The reason is that the source cannot readily determine in which subcluster the destination resides unless the source and destination happen to reside in the same subcluster. Moreover, for some forwarding schemes copies of a packet for the destination must be sent down all such routes to ensure that one copy reaches that destination.

Location Management

When a node moves to another cluster, it acquires an address that reflects its new location with respect to the clustering hierarchy. In fact, as discussed previously, a node may be allowed to hold simultaneous membership in multiple clusters to help it maintain reachability as it moves. The mapping between a node's identity and address must be maintained by nodes within the network such that a source can determine the address of any destination in the network. The term *location management* refers to the set of procedures for maintaining this mapping for each node and for providing this mapping information on request. A location manager *updates* address mappings in the location database as nodes move, *finds* the mapping for a node in the location database, and *pages* a portion of the network for the address of a node when the mapping in the database is stale.

Lauer discusses two approaches to distributing the contents of the location database throughout a hierarchical cluster-based control structure for mobile networks [Lauer 1988].

1. The network contains a set of redundant top-level location managers such that each location manager maintains the address mapping for each node in the network. With this approach, updating costs are high, since each change of address for each node must be reported to all location managers. Finding costs are low, however, since only a single query to a location manager is required to obtain an address mapping.

2. The network contains a set of local location managers, one per cluster, such that each location manager maintains only the address mappings for nodes within its cluster. When a source requests the address of a destination, the address query propagates from a lowest-level location manager to successively higher-level location managers until it reaches one that can respond to the query or until a page is deemed necessary (i.e., the highest-level location manager has no address mapping for the destination in its location database). With this approach, updating costs are low because a node need only distribute its location updates to location managers in its ancestral clusters. Finding costs are high, however, since an address query may have to propagate through many levels of location managers before it can be answered.

With either of these approaches, paging costs are high because each page must be distributed to all nodes in the network. Nevertheless, costs can be kept low provided that, for each of its address changes, a node immediately updates all relevant location managers. Lauer also discusses the advantages and disadvantages of enabling location managers to cache the address mappings obtained during finding and paging [Lauer 1988].

MMWN provides location management based on a variation of the second approach described in the preceding list. With MMWN, the costs of updating and paging may be traded off node by node on the basis of a node's *call-to-mobility ratio* (i.e., the frequency of sessions requiring its participation versus the frequency of its movement). Each node is assigned a *roaming level, j*, according to its call-to-mobility ratio, which defines a *roaming cluster* that is a level-j ancestral cluster of the node. The node distributes its location updates to location managers only if it moves outside of its current roaming cluster. Thus, if the node moves among descendant clusters of its current roaming cluster, it does not distribute a location update. Paging may therefore be required to determine the node's current location within its roaming cluster. For mobile nodes that rarely communicate with other nodes, there is no need to update the address mapping on every movement, so the roaming level may be set high. For mobile nodes that communicate frequently with other nodes, there is a need to keep the address mapping up to date in the location database, so the roaming level should be set low.

Each cluster contains at least one location manager that aids sources in determining the addresses of destinations with which they wish to communicate. When a node moves outside of its current roaming cluster, it sends a location update to each location manager in its level-1 cluster, one of which in turn sends a location update to each location manager in its level-2 cluster, and so on, up to the location manager in its level-k cluster, where k is the level of the lowest common cluster in which the movement occurred. When a source wishes to communicate with a destination, it requests the destination's address from a location manager, x, in its level-1 cluster. If x has no address mapping for the destination, it requests the address from a location manager in its parent cluster, and so on, up the hierarchy until the address query reaches a location manager with an address mapping for the destination. The address query then descends down the clustering hierarchy through location managers until it reaches a location manager in the destination's last-known level-1 cluster. If the destination is no longer within that cluster, that location manager pages the destination's entire roaming cluster for the destination's address mapping. Once that location manager obtains the address for the destination, it sends the address directly to x, which gives the address to the source.

4.4 CONCLUSION

In this chapter, we discussed how cluster-based control structures for large dynamic networks naturally lend themselves to managing a shared transmission medium, constructing routing backbones and building abstractions of network state, and thus how they can have a major impact on network efficiency and ultimately performance. Although the concept of cluster-based network control has existed for almost thirty years, it has yet to be realized to its fullest extent in any communications network. Only a few of the many examples of cluster-based control structures described in this chapter have thus far been deployed and exercised in full-scale networks. The remainder have been assessed through mathematical modeling, simulation, or limited experimentation in small laboratory test networks.

Ad hoc networks possess two properties that make them ideal candidates for cluster-based control: mobile nodes, which may cause frequent changes in network connectivity; and wireless links, which have shared access, are susceptible to large and frequent fluctuations in quality, and may induce significant per-hop delays. With the resurgence of multihop mobile wireless networking, now referred to as ad hoc networking, we expect renewed interest in the study and application of cluster-based control structures as a primary means of improving the performance of these networks through reduced sensitivity to small changes in state and through localized control in response to significant changes in state.

Acknowledgment
The preparation of this chapter was funded in part by the Defense Advanced Research Projects Agency (DARPA) under contract DABT63-96-C-0100.

References

[Althofer+ 1993] I. Althofer, G. Das, D. Dopkin, D. Joseph, and J. Soares, On Sparse Spanners of Weighted Graphs. *Discrete and Computational Geometry* 3(1):81–100, 1993.

[ATM 1996] ATM Forum Technical Committee. *Private Network–Network Interface Specification (PNNI), Version 1.0,* March 1996.

[Awerbuch+ 1998a] B. Awerbuch, Y. Du, B. Khan, and Y. Shavitt. Routing through Teranode Networks with Topology Aggregation. In *Proceedings of ISCC '98*, June 1998.

[Awerbuch+ 1998b] B. Awerbuch and Y. Shavitt. Topology Aggregation for Directed Graphs. In *Proceedings of ISCC '98*, June 1998.

[Baker+ 1981a] D.J. Baker and A. Ephremides. A Distributed Algorithm for Organizing Mobile Radio Telecommunication Networks. In *Proceedings of the Second International Conference on Distributed Computer Systems*, April 1981, 476–483.

[Baker+ 1981b] D.J. Baker and A. Ephremides. The Architectural Organization of a Mobile Radio Network via a Distributed Algorithm. *IEEE Transactions on Communications* COM-29(11):1694–1701, November 1981.

[Baratz+ 1986] A.E. Baratz and J.M. Jaffe. Establishing Virtual Circuits in Large Computer Networks. *Computer Networks and ISDN Systems* 12:27–37, 1986.

[Castineyra+ 1994] I. Castineyra, J.N. Chiappa, and M. Steenstrup. The Nimrod Routing Architecture. RFC 1992, December 1994.

[Chiang 1996] C.-C. Chiang. Routing in Clustered Multihop, Mobile Wireless Networks. In *Proceedings of ICOIN 11*, 1996.

[Dijkstra 1959] E.W. Dijkstra. A Note on Two Problems in Connection with Graphs. *Numerische Math.* 1:269–271, 1959.

[Ephremides+ 1987] A. Ephremides, J.E. Wieselthier, and D.J. Baker. A Design Concept for Reliable Mobile Radio Networks with Frequency Hopping Signaling. *Proceedings of the IEEE* 75(1):56–73, January 1987.

[Ford+ 1962] L.R. Ford, Jr., and D. R. Fulkerson. *Flows in Networks*. Princeton University Press, Princeton, N.J., 1962.

[Fultz 1972] G.L. Fultz. *Adaptive Routing Techniques for Message Switching Computer-Communication Networks*. Ph.D. thesis, University of California at Los Angeles, July 1972.

[Garcia-Luna-Aceves 1988] J.J. Garcia-Luna-Aceves. Routing Management in Very Large-Scale Networks. *Future Generations Computer Systems* 4:81–93, 1988.

[Garcia-Luna-Aceves+ 1985] J.J. Garcia-Luna-Aceves and N. Shacham. Analysis of Routing Strategies for Packet Radio Networks. In *Proceedings of IEEE INFOCOM '85*, March 1985, 292–302.

[Gerla+ 1995] M. Gerla and J.T.-C. Tsai. Multicluster, Mobile, Multimedia Radio Network. *Wireless Networks* 1(3):255–265, October 1995.

[Hagouel 1983] J. Hagouel. *Issues in Routing for Large and Dynamic Networks*. Ph.D. thesis, Columbia University, New York, May 1983.

[Kahn+ 1978] R.E. Kahn, S.A. Gronmeyer, J. Burchfiel, and R.C. Kunzelman. Advances in Packet Radio Technology. *Proceedings of the IEEE* 66(11):1468–1496, November 1978.

[Kamoun 1976] F. Kamoun. *Design Considerations for Large Computer Communication Networks*. Ph.D. thesis, University of California at Los Angeles, 1976.

[Kamoun+ 1979] F. Kamoun and L. Kleinrock. Stochastic Performance Evaluation of Hierarchical Routing for Large Networks. *Computer Networks* 3(5):337–353, 1979.

[Kleinrock+ 1977] L. Kleinrock and F. Kamoun. Hierarchical Routing for Large Networks: Performance Evaluation and Optimization. *Computer Networks* 1(1):155–174, 1977.

[Kleinrock+ 1980] L. Kleinrock and F. Kamoun. Optimal Clustering Structures for Hierarchical Topological Design of Large Computer Networks. *Networks* 10(3):221–248, Fall 1980.

[Krishnan+ 1999] R. Krishnan, R. Ramanathan, and M. Steenstrup. Optimization Algorithms for Large Self-Structuring Networks. In *Proceedings of IEEE INFOCOM '99,* March 1999, 71–78.

[Lauer 1986] G.S. Lauer. Hierarchical Routing Design for SURAN. In *Proceedings of IEEE ICC '86,* June 1986, 93–102.

[Lauer 1988] G.S. Lauer. Address Servers in Hierarchical Networks. In *Proceedings of IEEE ICC '88,* June 1988, 443–451.

[Lauer 1995] G.S. Lauer. Packet-Radio Routing. In *Routing in Communications Networks,* M. Steenstrup, ed., Prentice-Hall, Englewood Cliffs, N.J., 1995.

[Lee 1995] W.C. Lee. Topology Aggregation in Hierarchical Routing in ATM Networks. *ACM SIGCOMM '95 Corporate Communications Review* 25(2):82–92, 1995.

[Lin+ 1995] C.R. Lin and M. Gerla. Multimedia Transport in Multihop Dynamic Packet Radio Networks. In *IEEE ICNP* (November):209–216, 1995.

[Lin+ 1997] C.R. Lin and M. Gerla. Adaptive Clustering for Mobile Wireless Networks. *IEEE Journal on Selected Areas of Communications* 15(7):1265–1275, September 1997.

[McQuillan 1974] J. McQuillan. *Adaptive Routing Algorithms for Distributed Computer Networks.* Bolt Beranek & Newman report 2831, May 1974.

[McQuillan+ 1980] J. McQuillan, I. Richer, and E. Rosen. The New Routing Algorithm for the ARPANET. *IEEE Transactions on Communications,* COM-28:711–719, May 1980.

[Miyao+ 1986] J. Miyao, K. Ishida, T. Kikuno, and N. Yoshida. Network Clustering Algorithm in Large Computer Networks. In *Proceedings of the Nineteenth Hawaii International Conference on System Sciences,* 321–329, 1986.

[Muralidhar+ 1986] K.H. Muralidhar and M.K. Sundareshan. On the Decomposition of Large Communication Networks for Hierarchical Control Implementation. *IEEE Transactions on Communications* COM-34(10):985–987, October 1986.

[Parekh 1985] A.K. Parekh. Selecting Routers in Ad-Hoc Wireless Networks. In *Proceedings of the SBT/IEEE International Telecommunications Symposium,* August 1994.

[Perlman 1985] R. Perlman. Hierarchical Networks and the Subnetwork Partition Problem. *Computer Networks and ISDN Systems* 9:297–303, 1985.

[Pursley+ 1993] M.B. Pursley and H.B. Russell. Routing in Frequency-Hop Packet Radio Networks with Partial-Band Jamming. *IEEE Transactions on Communications* COM-41(7):1117–1124, July 1993.

[Ramamoorthy+ 1983] C. Ramamoorthy and W.-T. Tsai. An Adaptive Hierarchical Routing Algorithm. In *Proceedings of IEEE COMPSAC '83,* November 1983, 93–104.

[Ramamoorthy+ 1987] C.V. Ramamoorthy, A. Bhide, and J. Srivastava. Reliable Clustering Techniques for Large, Mobile Packet Radio Networks. In *Proceedings of IEEE INFOCOM '87,* March 1987, 218–226.

[Ramanathan+ 1998] R. Ramanathan and M. Steenstrup. Hierarchically-Organized, Multihop Mobile Wireless Networks for Quality-of-Service Support. *ACM/Baltzer Mobile Networks and Applications Journal* 3(1):101–119, January 1998.

[Shacham 1984] N. Shacham. Organization of Dynamic Radio Networks by Overlapping Clusters: Architecture Considerations and Optimization. In *Performance '84,* December 1984, 435–447.

[Shacham 1985] N. Shacham. Hierarchical Routing in Large, Dynamic Ground Radio Networks. In *Proceedings of the Eighteenth Hawaii International Conference on System Sciences,* 1985, 292–301.

[Shacham+ 1984] N. Shacham and K. Klemba. An Architecture for Large Packet Radio Networks and Some Implementation Considerations. In *SRNTN 11,* SRI International, February 1984.

[Shacham+ 1987] N. Shacham and J. Westcott. Future Directions in Packet Radio Architectures and Protocols. *Proceedings of the IEEE* 75(1):83–99, January 1987.

[Sharony 1996] J. Sharony. An Architecture for Mobile Radio Networks with Dynamically Changing Topology Using Virtual Subnets. *ACM Mobile Networks and Applications* (MONET) 1(1):75–86, August 1996.

[Steenstrup 1994] M. Steenstrup. IDPR: An Approach to Policy Routing in Large Diverse Internetworks. *Journal of High Speed Networks* 3(1):81–105, 1994.

[Steenstrup 1996] M. Steenstrup. *A Perspective on Nimrod Functionality.* IETF working Internet draft, 1996 (work in progress).

[Steenstrup 1999] M.E. Steenstrup. Dynamic Multipoint Virtual Circuits for Multimedia Traffic in Multihop Mobile Wireless Networks. In *Proceedings of IEEE WCNC '99,* September 1999, 1016–1020.

[Tsai+ 1989] W.T. Tsai, C.V. Ramamoorthy, W.K. Tsai, and O. Nishiguchi. An Adaptive Hierarchical Routing Protocol. *IEEE Transactions on Communications* 38(8):1059–1075, August 1989.

[Tsuchiya 1988] P.F. Tsuchiya. The Landmark Hierarchy: A New Hierarchy for Routing in Very Large Networks. In *Proceedings of ACM SIGCOMM '88,* August 1988, 35–42.

[Zavgren 1997] J. Zavgren. NTDR Mobility Management Protocols and Procedures. In *Proceedings of the IEEE Military Communications Conference (MILCOM '97),* November 1997.

DSR
The Dynamic Source Routing Protocol for Multihop Wireless Ad Hoc Networks

David B. Johnson
Department of Computer Science
Rice University

David A. Maltz, Josh Broch
Carnegie-Mellon University

Abstract

The *Dynamic Source Routing* protocol (DSR) is a simple and efficient routing protocol designed specifically for use in multihop wireless ad hoc networks of mobile nodes. DSR allows the network to be completely self-organizing and self-configuring, without the need for any existing network infrastructure or administration. The protocol is composed of the two mechanisms of *Route Discovery* and *Route Maintenance,* which work together to allow nodes to discover and maintain *source routes* to arbitrary destinations in the ad hoc network. The use of source routing allows packet routing to be trivially loop free, avoids the need for up-to-date routing information in the intermediate nodes through which packets are forwarded, and allows nodes that are forwarding or overhearing packets to cache the routing information in them for their own future use. All aspects of the protocol operate entirely *on demand,* allowing the routing packet overhead of DSR to scale *automatically* to only that needed to react to changes in the routes currently in use. We have evaluated the operation of DSR through detailed simulation on a variety of movement and communication patterns and through implementation and significant experimentation in a physical outdoor ad hoc networking testbed we have constructed in Pittsburgh, and we have demonstrated the excellent performance of the protocol. In this chapter, we describe the design of DSR and provide a summary of some of our simulation and testbed implementation results for it.

The *Dynamic Source Routing* protocol [Johnson 1994, Johnson+ 1996a, Broch+ 1999a] is a simple and efficient routing protocol designed specifically for use in multihop wireless ad hoc networks of mobile nodes. Using DSR, the network is completely self-organizing and self-configuring, requiring no existing network infrastructure or administration. Network nodes (computers) cooperate to forward packets for each other to allow communication over multiple "hops" between nodes not directly within wireless transmission range of one another. As nodes in the network move about or join or leave the network, and as wireless transmission conditions such as sources of interference change, all routing is automatically determined and maintained by DSR. Because the number or sequence of intermediate hops needed to reach any destination may change at any time, the resulting network topology may be quite rich and rapidly changing.

DSR allows nodes to dynamically discover a *source route* across multiple network hops to any destination in the ad hoc network. Each data packet sent then carries in its header the complete, ordered list of nodes through which the packet must pass, allowing packet routing to be trivially loop free and avoiding the need for up-to-date routing information in the intermediate nodes through which the packet is forwarded. With the inclusion of this source route in the header of each data packet, other nodes forwarding or overhearing any of the packets may also easily cache this routing information for future use.

This work is a part of the Monarch Project at Carnegie-Mellon University [Johnson+ 1996b, Monarch], which is a long-term study that is developing networking protocols and protocol interfaces to allow truly seamless wireless and mobile networking. The Monarch Project is named in reference to the migratory behavior of the monarch butterfly; it can also be considered as an acronym for "*Mo*bile *N*etworking *Arch*itectures." The scope of our research includes protocol design, implementation, performance evaluation, and usage-based validation, roughly ranging from portions of the ISO data link layer (layer 2) through part of the presentation layer (layer 6).

In designing DSR, we sought to create a routing protocol that has very low overhead yet is able to react quickly to changes in the network, providing highly reactive service to help ensure successful delivery of data packets in spite of node movement or other changes in network conditions. On the basis of our evaluations of DSR and other protocols to date, through detailed simulation and testbed implementation, we believe this goal has been well met [Johnson+ 1996a, Broch+ 1998, Maltz+ 1999a, Maltz+ 1999b]. In particular, in our detailed simulation comparison of routing protocols for ad hoc networks [Broch+ 1998], DSR outperformed the other protocols that we studied, and recent results by Johansson et al. [Johansson+ 1999] have shown generally similar results. The protocol specification for DSR has also been submitted to the Internet Engineering Task Force (IETF), the principal protocol standards development body for the Internet, and is currently one of the protocols under consideration in the IETF Mobile Ad Hoc Networks (MANET) Working Group for adoption as an Internet standard for IP routing in ad hoc networks [MANET].

This chapter describes the design of the DSR protocol and provides a summary of some of our current simulation and testbed implementation results for it. Section 5.1 discusses our assumptions in the design. In Section 5.2, we present the design of the protocol and describe its resulting important properties. In particular, we describe the design of the two mechanisms that make up the operation of DSR: *Route Discovery* and *Route Maintenance*. We also discuss the use of DSR in supporting heterogeneous networks and interconnecting to the Internet, and we describe the current support present in DSR for routing of multicast packets in ad hoc networks. Section 5.3 summarizes some of our simulation results for DSR and describes a physical outdoor ad hoc network testbed we have built in Pittsburgh for DSR experiments. Finally, we discuss related work in Section 5.4 and present conclusions in Section 5.5.

5.1 ASSUMPTIONS

We assume that all nodes wishing to communicate with other nodes within the ad hoc network are willing to participate fully in the network protocols. In particular, each participating node should be willing to forward packets for other nodes.

We refer to the minimum number of hops necessary for a packet to travel from any node located at one extreme edge of the ad hoc network to any node located at the opposite extreme as the *diameter* of the network. We assume that the diameter will often be small (perhaps 5 or 10 hops), but it may often be greater than 1.

Packets may be lost or corrupted in transmission on the wireless network. A node receiving a corrupted packet can detect the error and discard the packet.

Nodes within the ad hoc network may move at any time without notice and may even move continuously, but we assume that the speed with which nodes move is moderate with respect to the packet transmission latency and wireless transmission range of the underlying network hardware. In particular, DSR can support very rapid rates of arbitrary node mobility, but we assume that nodes do not continuously move so rapidly as to make the flooding of every individual data packet the only possible routing protocol.

We assume that nodes may enable *promiscuous* receive mode on their wireless network interface hardware, causing the hardware to deliver every received packet to the network driver software without filtering based on link layer destination address. Although we do not require this facility, it is, for example, common in current LAN hardware for broadcast media, including wireless, and some of our optimizations can take advantage of its availability. Use of promiscuous mode does increase the software overhead on the CPU, but we believe that wireless network speeds are more the inherent limiting factor to performance in current and future systems; we also believe that portions of the protocol are suitable for implementation directly within a programmable network interface unit to avoid this overhead on the CPU [Johnson+ 1996a]. Use of promiscuous mode may also increase the power consumption of the network interface hardware, depending on the design of the receiver hardware. In such cases, DSR can easily be used without the optimizations that depend on promiscuous receive mode or can be programmed to switch the interface into promiscuous mode only periodically.

At times, wireless communication between any pair of nodes may not work equally well in both directions, perhaps because of differing antenna or propagation patterns or sources of interference around the two nodes [Bantz+ 1994, Lauer 1995]. That is, wireless communications between each pair of nodes will in many cases be able to operate *bidirectionally,* but at times the wireless link between two nodes may be only *unidirectional,* allowing one node to successfully send packets to the other while no communication is possible in the reverse direction. Although many routing protocols operate correctly only over bidirectional links, DSR can successfully discover and forward packets over paths that contain unidirectional links. Some medium access control (MAC) protocols, however, such as MACA [Karn 1990], MACAW [Bharghavan+ 1994], or IEEE 802.11 [IEEE 1997], limit unicast data packet transmission to bidirectional links because of the required bidirectional exchange of RTS and CTS packets in these protocols and because of the link level acknowledgment feature in IEEE 802.11. When used on top of MAC protocols such as these, DSR can take advantage of additional optimizations, such as the route reversal optimization described below.

Each node selects a *single* IP address by which it will be known in the ad hoc network. Although a single node may have many different physical network interfaces, which in a typical IP network each have a different IP address, we require each node to select one of these and to use only that address when participating in the DSR protocol. This allows each node to be recognized by all other nodes in the ad hoc network as a single entity regardless of which network interface the other nodes use to communicate with it. In keeping with the terminology used by Mobile IP [Johnson 1995], we refer to the address by which each mobile node is known in the ad hoc network as its *home address,* as this is typically the one that the node uses while connected to its home network (rather than while away, being a member of the ad hoc network). Each node's home address may be assigned by any mechanism (e.g., static assignment or use of DHCP for dynamic assignment [Droms 1997]), although the method of such assignment is outside the scope of the DSR protocol.

5.2 DSR PROTOCOL DESCRIPTION—OVERVIEW AND IMPORTANT PROPERTIES

The DSR protocol is composed of two mechanisms that work together to allow the discovery and maintenance of source routes in the ad hoc network:

- *Route Discovery,* by which a node **S** wishing to send a packet to a destination node **D** obtains a source route to **D**. Route Discovery is used only when **S** attempts to send a packet to **D** and does not already know a route to it.
- *Route Maintenance,* by which node **S**, while using a source route to **D**, is able to detect, if the network topology has changed such that it can no longer use its route to **D** because a link along the route no longer works. When Route Maintenance indicates that a source route is broken, **S** can attempt to use any other route to **D** it happens to know, or it can invoke Route Discovery again to find a new route. Route Maintenance is used only when **S** is actually sending packets to **D**.

Route Discovery and Route Maintenance each operate entirely *on demand.* In particular, DSR, unlike other protocols, requires *no* periodic packets of *any kind* at *any level* within the network. For example, it does not use any periodic routing advertisement, link status sensing, or neighbor detection packets; nor does it rely on these functions from any underlying protocols in the network. This entirely on-demand behavior and lack of periodic activity allow the number of overhead packets caused by DSR to scale down to *zero* when all nodes are approximately stationary with respect to each other and all routes needed for current communication have already been discovered. As nodes begin to move more or as communication patterns change, the routing packet overhead of DSR *automatically* scales to only that needed to track the routes currently in use.

In response to a single Route Discovery (as well as through routing information from other packets' overheard), a node may learn and cache multiple routes to any destination. This allows the reaction to routing changes to be much more rapid because a node with multiple routes to a destination can try another cached route if the one it has been using fails. This caching of multiple routes also avoids the overhead incurred by performing a new Route Discovery each time a route in use breaks.

Route Discovery and Route Maintenance are designed to allow unidirectional links and asymmetric routes to be easily supported. In particular, as noted in Section 5.1, in wireless networks it is possible that a link between two nodes may not work equally well in both directions because of differing antenna or propagation patterns or sources of interference. DSR allows such unidirectional links to be used when necessary, improving overall performance and network connectivity in the system.

DSR also supports internetworking between different types of wireless networks, allowing a source route to be composed of hops over a combination of any network types available [Broch+ 1999b]. For example, some nodes in the ad hoc network may have only short-range radios while other nodes may have both short-range and long-range radios; the combination of these nodes can be considered by DSR as a single ad hoc network. In addition, the routing of DSR has been integrated into standard Internet routing, where a "gateway" node connected to the Internet also participates in the ad hoc network routing protocols; it has also been integrated into Mobile IP routing, where such a gateway node also serves the role of a Mobile IP foreign agent [Johnson 1995].

5.2.1 DSR Route Discovery

When some node **S** originates a new packet destined for some node **D**, it places in the header of the packet a *source route* giving the sequence of hops that the packet should follow. Normally, **S** obtains a suitable source route by searching its *Route Cache* of routes previously learned, but if no route is found in its cache it initiates the Route Discovery protocol to find a new route to **D** dynamically. In this case, we call **S** the *initiator* and **D** the *target* of the Route Discovery.

Figure 5.1 illustrates an example Route Discovery, in which node **A** is attempting to discover a route to node **E**. To initiate the Route Discovery, **A** transmits a ROUTE REQUEST message as a single local broadcast packet, which is received by (approximately) all nodes currently within wireless

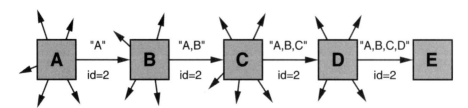

Figure 5.1. Route Discovery Example with Node **A** as the Initiator and Node **E** as the Target

transmission range of **A.** Each ROUTE REQUEST message identifies the initiator and target of the Route Discovery and also contains a unique *request ID,* determined by the initiator of the REQUEST. Each ROUTE REQUEST also contains a record listing the address of each intermediate node through which this particular copy of the ROUTE REQUEST message has been forwarded. This route record is initialized to an empty list by the initiator of the Route Discovery.

When another node receives a ROUTE REQUEST, if it is the target of the Route Discovery it returns a ROUTE REPLY message to the Route Discovery initiator, giving a copy of the accumulated route record from the ROUTE REQUEST; when the initiator receives this ROUTE REPLY, it caches this route in its Route Cache for use in sending subsequent packets to this destination. Otherwise, if the node receiving the ROUTE REQUEST recently saw another ROUTE REQUEST message from this initiator bearing this same request ID, or if it finds that its own address is already listed in the route record in the ROUTE REQUEST message, it discards the REQUEST. If not, this node appends its own address to the route record in the ROUTE REQUEST message and propagates it by transmitting it as a local broadcast packet (with the same request ID).

In returning the ROUTE REPLY to the Route Discovery initiator, such as node **E** replying to **A** in Figure 5.1, node **E** typically examines its own Route Cache for a route back to **A** and, if found, uses it for the source route for delivery of the packet containing the ROUTE REPLY. Otherwise, **E** may perform its own Route Discovery for target node **A**, but to avoid possible infinite recursion of Route Discoveries it must piggyback this ROUTE REPLY on its own ROUTE REQUEST message for **A**. It is also possible to piggyback other small data packets, such as a TCP SYN packet [Postel 1981b], on a ROUTE REQUEST using this same mechanism. Node **E** can also simply reverse the sequence of hops in the route record that it is trying to send in the ROUTE REPLY and use this as the source route on the packet carrying the ROUTE REPLY itself. For MAC protocols such as IEEE 802.11 that require a bidirectional frame exchange as part of the MAC protocol [IEEE 1997], this route reversal is preferred as it avoids the overhead of a possible second Route Discovery and it tests the discovered route to ensure that it is bidirectional before the Route Discovery initiator begins using it. However, this technique will prevent the discovery of routes using unidirectional links. In wireless environments where the use of unidirectional links is permitted, such routes may in some cases be more efficient than those with only bidirectional links, or they may be the only way to achieve connectivity to the target node.

When initiating a Route Discovery, the sending node saves a copy of the original packet in a local buffer called the *Send Buffer.* The Send Buffer contains a copy of each packet that cannot be transmitted by this node because it does not yet have a source route to the packet's destination. Each packet in the Send Buffer is stamped with the time that it was placed there and is discarded after residing in the Send Buffer for some time-out period; if necessary to prevent the Send Buffer from overflowing, a FIFO or other replacement strategy can be used to evict packets before they expire.

While a packet remains in the Send Buffer, the node should occasionally initiate a new Route Discovery for the packet's destination address. However, the node must limit the rate at which such new Route Discoveries for the same address are initiated because it is possible that the destination node is not currently reachable. In particular, because of the limited wireless transmission range and the movement of the nodes in the network, the network may at times become partitioned, meaning that there is currently no sequence of nodes through which a packet can be forwarded to reach the destination. Depending on the movement pattern and the density of nodes in the network, such network partitions may be either rare or common.

If a new Route Discovery was initiated for each packet sent by a node in such a situation, a large number of unproductive ROUTE REQUEST packets will be propagated throughout the subset of the ad hoc network reachable from this node. To reduce such overhead, we use exponential backoff to limit the rate at which new Route Discoveries may be initiated by any node for the same target. If the node attempts to send additional data packets to this same node more frequently than this limit allows, the subsequent packets should be buffered in the Send Buffer until a ROUTE REPLY is received, but the node must not initiate a new Route Discovery until the minimum allowable interval between new Route Discoveries for this target has been reached. This limitation on the maximum rate of Route Discoveries for the same target is similar to the mechanism required by Internet nodes to limit the rate at which ARP requests are sent for any single target IP address [Braden 1989].

5.2.2 DSR Route Maintenance

When originating or forwarding a packet using a source route, each node transmitting the packet is responsible for confirming that the packet has been received by the next hop along the source route; the packet is re-transmitted (up to a maximum number of attempts) until this confirmation of receipt is received. For example, in the situation illustrated in Figure 5.2, node **A** has originated a packet for **E** using a source route through intermediate nodes **B**, **C**, and **D**. In this case, node **A** is responsible for receipt of the packet at **B**, node **B** is responsible for receipt at **C**, node **C** is responsible for receipt at **D**, and finally node **D** is responsible for receipt at **E**. This confirmation of receipt may in many cases be provided at no cost to DSR, either as an existing standard part of the MAC

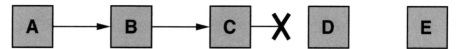

Figure 5.2. Route Maintenance Example Node **C** is unable to forward
a packet from **A** to **E** over its link to the next hop, **D**.

protocol in use (such as the link level acknowledgment frame defined by
IEEE 802.11 [IEEE 1997]) or by a *passive acknowledgment* [Jubin+ 1987]
(in which, for example, **B** confirms receipt at **C** by overhearing **C** transmit the packet to forward it on to **D**). If neither of these confirmation
mechanisms is available, the node transmitting the packet may set a bit
in the packet's header to request that a DSR-specific software acknowledgment be returned by the next hop; this software acknowledgment will
normally be transmitted directly to the sending node, but, if the link between these two nodes is unidirectional, it may travel over a different,
multihop path.

If the packet is retransmitted by some hop the maximum number of
times and no receipt confirmation is received, this node returns a ROUTE
ERROR message to the original sender of the packet, identifying the link
over which the packet could not be forwarded. For example, in Figure 5.2,
if **C** is unable to deliver the packet to the next hop **D**, **C** returns a ROUTE
ERROR to **A**, stating that the link from **C** to **D** is currently "broken." Node
A then removes this broken link from its cache, and any retransmission of
the original packet is a function for upper-layer protocols such as TCP. For
sending such a retransmission or other packets to this same destination **E**, if
A has in its Route Cache another route to **E** (for example, from additional
ROUTE REPLYs from its earlier Route Discovery or from having overheard
sufficient routing information from other packets), it can send the packet
using the new route immediately. Otherwise, it may perform a new Route
Discovery for this target (subject to the exponential backoff described in
Section 5.2.1).

5.2.3 Additional Route Discovery Features

Caching Overheard Routing Information
A node forwarding or otherwise overhearing any packet may add the routing information from that packet to its own Route Cache. In particular,
the source route used in a data packet, the accumulated route record in a
ROUTE REQUEST, or the route being returned in a ROUTE REPLY may
all be cached by any node. Routing information from any of these packets
received may be cached whether the packet was addressed to this node, sent
to a broadcast (or multicast) MAC address, or received while the node's
network interface was in promiscuous mode.

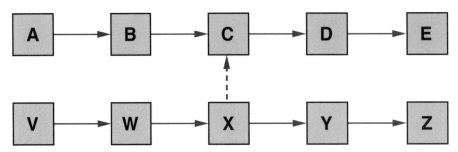

Figure 5.3. Limitations on Caching Overheard Routing Information
Node **C** is forwarding to **E** and overhears packets from **X**.

However, one limitation on caching of such overheard routing information is the possible presence of unidirectional links in the ad hoc network (Section 5.1). For example, Figure 5.3 illustrates a situation in which node **A** is using a source route to communicate with node **E**. As node **C** forwards a data packet along the route from **A** to **E**, it can always add to its cache the presence of the "forward" direction links, which it learns from the headers of these packets, from itself to **D** and from **D** to **E**. However, the "reverse" direction of the links identified in the packet headers, from **C** back to **B** and from **B** to **A**, may not work because these links might be unidirectional. If **C** knows that the links are in fact bidirectional—for example, because of the MAC protocol in use—it can cache them but otherwise should not.

Likewise, node **V** in Figure 5.3 is using a different source route to communicate with node **Z**. If node **C** overhears node **X** transmitting a data packet to forward it to **Y** (from **V**), **C** should consider whether or not the links involved can be known to be bidirectional before caching them. If the link from **X** to **C** (over which this data packet was received) can be known to be bidirectional, **C** can cache the link from itself to **X**, the link from **X** to **Y**, and the link from **Y** to **Z**. If all links can be assumed to be bidirectional, **C** can also cache the links from **X** to **W** and from **W** to **V**. Similar considerations apply to the routing information that might be learned from forwarded or otherwise overheard ROUTE REQUEST or ROUTE REPLY packets.

Replying to Route Requests Using Cached Routes
A node receiving a ROUTE REQUEST for which it is not the target searches its own Route Cache for a route to the REQUEST target. If a route is found, the node generally returns a ROUTE REPLY to the initiator itself rather than forwarding the ROUTE REQUEST. In the ROUTE REPLY, it sets the route record to list the sequence of hops over which this copy of the ROUTE REQUEST was forwarded to it, concatenated with its own idea of the route from itself to the target from its Route Cache.

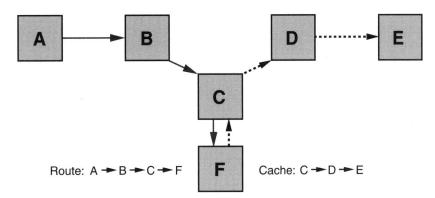

Route: A → B → C → F   Cache: C → D → E

Figure 5.4. A Possible Duplication of Route Hops Avoided by the Route Discovery Limitation on Replying to ROUTE REQUESTS from the Route Cache

However, before transmitting a ROUTE REPLY packet that was generated using information from its Route Cache in this way, a node must verify that the resulting route being returned in the ROUTE REPLY, after this concatenation, contains no duplicate nodes listed in the route record. For example, Figure 5.4 illustrates a case in which a ROUTE REQUEST for target **E** has been received by node **F** and node **F** already has in its Route Cache a route from itself to **E**. The concatenation of the accumulated route from the ROUTE REQUEST and the cached route from **F**'s Route Cache includes a duplicate node in passing from **C** to **F** and back to **C**.

Node **F** in this case *could* attempt to edit the route to eliminate the duplication, resulting in a route from **A** to **B** to **C** to **D** and on to **E**, but in this case node **F** is not on the route that it returned in its own ROUTE REPLY. DSR Route Discovery prohibits node **F** from returning such a ROUTE REPLY from its cache for two reasons. First, this limitation increases the probability that the resulting route is valid because **F** in this case should have received a ROUTE ERROR if the route had stopped working. Second, this limitation means that a ROUTE ERROR traversing the route is very likely to pass through any node that sent the ROUTE REPLY for the route (including **F**), which helps to ensure that stale data is removed from caches (such as at **F**) in a timely manner. Otherwise, the next Route Discovery initiated by **A** might also be contaminated by a ROUTE REPLY from **F** containing the same stale route. If the ROUTE REQUEST does not meet these restrictions, the node (**F** in this example) discards the ROUTE REQUEST rather than replying to or propagating it.

Preventing Route Reply Storms
The ability of nodes to reply to a ROUTE REQUEST on the basis of information in their Route Caches, as described in the previous section, can

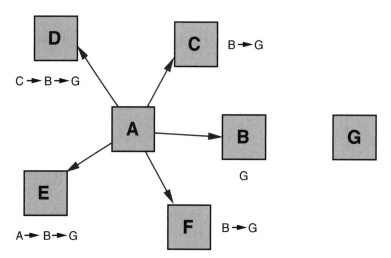

Figure 5.5. A ROUTE REPLY Storm

result in a possible ROUTE REPLY "storm" in some cases. In particular, if a node broadcasts a ROUTE REQUEST for a target node for which the node's neighbors have a route in their Route Caches, each neighbor may attempt to send a ROUTE REPLY, thereby wasting bandwidth and possibly increasing the number of network collisions in the area.

For example, in the situation shown in Figure 5.5, nodes **B**, **C**, **D**, **E**, and **F** all receive **A**'s ROUTE REQUEST for target **G**, and each has the indicated route cached for this target. Normally, they all attempt to reply from their own Route Caches and all send their REPLYs at about the same time because they all received the broadcast ROUTE REQUEST at about the same time. Such simultaneous replies from different nodes all receiving the ROUTE REQUEST may create packet collisions among some or all of these REPLYS and may cause local congestion in the wireless network. In addition, it is often the case that the different replies indicate routes of different lengths, as shown in this example.

If a node can put its network interface into promiscuous receive mode, it should delay sending its own ROUTE REPLY for a short period and listen to see if the initiating node begins using a shorter route first. That is, this node should delay sending its own ROUTE REPLY for a random period $d = H \times (h - 1 + r)$, where h is the length in number of network hops for the route to be returned in this node's ROUTE REPLY, r is a random number between 0 and 1, and H is a small constant delay (at least twice the maximum wireless link propagation delay) to be introduced per hop. This delay effectively randomizes the time at which each node sends its ROUTE REPLY; all nodes sending ROUTE REPLYs giving routes of length less than h send their REPLYs before this node, and all nodes sending ROUTE REPLYs giving routes of length greater than h send their REPLYs after this node. Within the delay period, this node promiscuously receives all packets, looking for data packets from the initiator of this Route Discovery destined for the target of the Discovery. If such a data packet received by this node during the delay period uses a source route of length less than or equal to h, the node may infer that the initiator of the Route Discovery has already received a ROUTE REPLY giving an equally good or better route. In this case, this node cancels its delay timer and does *not* send its ROUTE REPLY for this Route Discovery.

Route Request Hop Limits

Each ROUTE REQUEST message contains a "hop limit" that may be used to limit the number of intermediate nodes allowed to forward that copy of the ROUTE REQUEST. As the REQUEST is forwarded, this limit is decremented, and the REQUEST packet is discarded if the limit reaches zero before finding the target. We use this mechanism to send a *nonpropagating* ROUTE REQUEST (i.e., with hop limit 0) as an inexpensive method of determining if the target is currently a neighbor of the initiator or if a neighbor node has a route to the target cached (effectively using the neighbor's cache as an extension of the initiator's own cache). If no ROUTE REPLY is received after a short time-out, a *propagating* ROUTE REQUEST (i.e., with no hop limit) is sent.

We have also considered using this mechanism to implement an *expanding ring* search for the target [Johnson+ 1996a]. For example, a node can send an initial nonpropagating ROUTE REQUEST as described above; if no ROUTE REPLY is received for it, the node can initiate another ROUTE REQUEST with a hop limit of 1. For each ROUTE REQUEST initiated, if no ROUTE REPLY is received for it, the node can double the hop limit used on the previous attempt to progressively explore for the target node without allowing the ROUTE REQUEST to propagate over the entire network. However, this expanding ring search approach can increase the average latency of Route Discovery, as multiple Discovery attempts and time-outs may be needed before a route to the target node is found.

5.2.4 Additional Route Maintenance Features

Packet Salvaging

After sending a ROUTE ERROR message as part of Route Maintenance, as described in Section 5.2.2, a node may attempt to *salvage* the data packet that caused the ROUTE ERROR rather than discard it. To salvage a packet, the node sending a ROUTE ERROR searches its own Route Cache for a route from itself to the destination of the packet causing the ERROR.

If such a route is found, the node may salvage the packet after returning the ROUTE ERROR, by replacing the original source route on the packet with the route from its Route Cache. It then forwards the packet to the next node indicated along this source route. For example, in Figure 5.2, if node **C** has another route cached to node **E**, it can salvage the packet by applying this route to it rather than discard it.

When salvaged in this way, the packet is also marked as having been salvaged to prevent a single packet being salvaged multiple times. Otherwise, it is possible for the packet to enter a routing loop as different nodes repeatedly salvage it and replace the source route on it with routes to each other. An alternative salvaging mechanism that we have considered is to replace only the unused suffix of the original route (the portion in advance of this node) with the new route from this node's Route Cache, forming a new route whose prefix is the original route and whose suffix is the route from the Cache. In this case, the normal rules for avoiding the listing of duplicate nodes in a source route are sufficient to avoid routing loops. However, this mechanism prevents the new route from "backtracking" from this node to an earlier node already traversed by this packet and then being forwarded along a different remaining sequence of hops to the destination. Our current salvaging mechanism allows backtracking but prevents a packet from being salvaged more than once.

Automatic Route Shortening

Source routes may be automatically shortened if one or more of their intermediate hops become unnecessary. This mechanism of automatically shortening routes is somewhat similar to the use of passive acknowledgments. In particular, if a node is able to overhear a packet carrying a source route (e.g., by operating its network interface in promiscuous receive mode), it examines the route's unused portion. If this node is not the intended next hop for the packet but is named in the later unused portion of the packet's source route, it can infer that the intermediate nodes before itself in the source route are no longer needed. Figure 5.6 illustrates an example in which node **C** has overheard a data packet being transmitted from **A** to **B** for later forwarding to **C**; the arrow pointing to one node in the source route

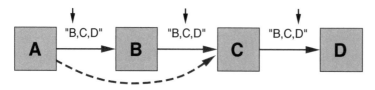

Figure 5.6. An Example of Automatic Route Shortening

in each packet indicates the intended next receiver of the packet along the route.

In this case, this node (**C**) returns a *gratuitous* ROUTE REPLY message to the original sender of the packet (**A**). The ROUTE REPLY gives the shorter route as the concatenation of the portion of the original source route up through the node that transmitted the overheard packet plus the suffix of the original source route beginning with the node returning the gratuitous ROUTE REPLY. In this example, the route returned in the gratuitous ROUTE REPLY message sent from **C** to **A** gives the new route as the sequence of hops from **A** to **C** to **D**.

Increased Spreading of Route Error Messages

When a source node receives a ROUTE ERROR for a data packet that it originated, it propagates it to its neighbors by piggybacking it on its next ROUTE REQUEST. In this way, stale information in the caches of nodes around this source node will not generate ROUTE REPLYs that contain the same invalid link for which this source node received the ROUTE ERROR.

For example, in the situation shown in Figure 5.2, node **A** learns from the ROUTE ERROR message from **C** that the link from **C** to **D** is currently broken. It thus removes this link from its own Route Cache and initiates a new Route Discovery (if it doesn't have another route to **E** in its Route Cache). On the ROUTE REQUEST packet initiating this Route Discovery, node **A** piggybacks a copy of this ROUTE ERROR message, ensuring that it spreads well to other nodes and guaranteeing that any ROUTE REPLY that it receives (including those from other nodes' Route Caches) in response to this ROUTE REQUEST does not contain a route that assumes the existence of this broken link.

We have also considered, but not simulated, a further improvement to Route Maintenance in which a node that receives a ROUTE ERROR, such as **A** in Figure 5.4, forwards it along the same source route that resulted in it. This will almost guarantee that the ROUTE ERROR reaches the node that generated the ROUTE REPLY containing the broken link, which prevents that node from contaminating a future Route Discovery with the same broken link.

Caching Negative Information

In some cases, DSR can potentially benefit from nodes caching "negative" information in their Route Caches. For example, in Figure 5.2, if node **A** caches the fact that the link from **C** to **D** is currently broken (rather than simply removing this hop from its Route Cache), it can guarantee that no ROUTE REPLY that utilizes this broken link, which it receives in response to its new Route Discovery, will be accepted. A short expiration period must be placed on this negative cached information because, while this entry is in its Route Cache, **A** will otherwise refuse to allow this link in its cache even if this link begins working again.

Another case in which caching negative information in a node's Route Cache might be useful is one in which a link is providing highly variable service, sometimes working correctly but often not. This situation can occur, for example, when the link is near the limit of the sending node's wireless transmission range and there are significant sources of interference (e.g., multipath) near the receiving node on this link. In this case, by caching the negative information that this link is broken, a node can avoid adding this problematic link back to its Route Cache during the brief periods in which it is working correctly.

We have not included this caching of negative information in our simulations or implementation of DSR, although we have found situations in our testbed implementation (Section 5.3.2) where it could improve the performance of Route Discovery [Maltz+ 1999b]. A challenge in implementing the caching of negative information that we are researching is the difficulty of picking a suitable expiration period for such cache entries.

5.2.5 Support for Heterogeneous Networks and Mobile IP

In configuring and deploying an ad hoc network, in many cases all nodes will be equipped with the same type of wireless network interfaces, allowing simple routing between nodes over arbitrary sequences of network hops. However, a more flexible configuration might be to also equip a subset of the nodes with a second network interface consisting of a longer-range (and thus generally lower-speed) wireless network interface. For example, in a military setting a group of soldiers might use short-range radios to communicate among themselves while relaying through truck-mounted higher-power radios to communicate with other groups.

This general type of network configuration is the ad hoc equivalent of wireless *overlay networks* [Katz+ 1996]. Because of the high degree of locality likely to be present among directly cooperating nodes communicating with each other, such a network configuration allows high-speed communication among such cooperating nodes and at the same time allows communication with other nodes further away without requiring very large numbers of network hops. The longer-range radios might also allow gaps between different groups of nodes to be spanned, reducing the probability of network partition. A simple example of such an ad hoc network configuration is shown in Figure 5.7, where nodes **A**, **B**, and **C** each have both short-range and long-range radio interfaces and all other nodes in the ad hoc network have only short-range interfaces. Node **X** is using a source route to node **Y** that employs a sequence of both short-range and long-range hops.

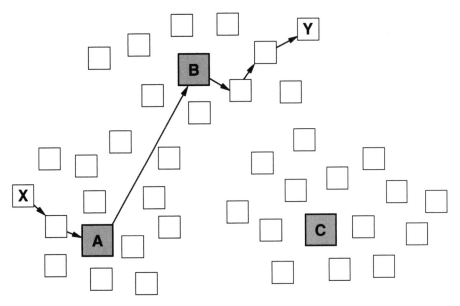

Figure 5.7. A Heterogeneous Ad Hoc Network

Use of Interface Indices in DSR

DSR supports automatic, seamless routing in these (see Figure 5.7) and other heterogeneous configurations through its logical addressing model [Broch+ 1999b]. Using conventional IP addressing, each ad hoc network node configures a different IP address for its possibly many individual network interfaces, but, as noted in Section 5.1, each node using DSR chooses *one* of these as its *home address* to use for all communication while in the ad hoc network. This use of a single IP address per node gives DSR the ability to treat the overall network as single routing domain. To then distinguish between the different network interfaces on a node, each node independently assigns a locally unique *interface index* to each of its own network interfaces.

The interface index for any network interface on a node is an *opaque* value assigned by the node itself. The particular value chosen must be unique among the network interfaces on that individual node, but it need have no other significance and need not be coordinated with any other nodes in the choice of their own interface indices. On many operating systems, a unique value to identify each network interface is already available and can be used for this purpose; for example, the `if_index` field in the `ifnet` structure for a network interface in BSD UNIX-based networking stacks [Wright+ 1995] can be used directly by a node for the interface index for that network interface.

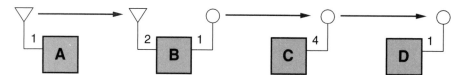

Figure 5.8. An Ad Hoc Network of Nodes with Heterogeneous Network Interfaces

As an example, Figure 5.8 illustrates a simple ad hoc network of four nodes, in which node **A** is using one type of network interface (represented by the triangles), node **C** and node **D** are using a different type (represented by the circles), and node **B** is configured with both types and can forward packets between the two. The number labeling each network interface indicates the interface index chosen by the interface's corresponding node. Because the interface indices are chosen independently by each node, it is possible, for example, that nodes **B** and **D** each choose index 1 for their circle network interfaces but that node **C** chooses index 4.

The interface index is used as part of each hop in each source route discovered and used by DSR. Specifically, a path through the ad hoc network from a source node $\mathbf{N}_0$ to a destination node $\mathbf{N}_m$ is fully represented as a series of hops $\mathbf{N}_0/i_0 \rightarrow \mathbf{N}_1/i_1 \rightarrow \mathbf{N}_2/i_2 \rightarrow \ldots \rightarrow \mathbf{N}_m$, where $\mathbf{N}_k/i_k$ indicates that node $\mathbf{N}_k$ must transmit the packet using its network interface i_k in order to deliver the packet over the next hop to node $\mathbf{N}_{k+1}$.

In forwarding a ROUTE REQUEST, a node adds to the route record in it not only its own address (Section 5.2.1) but also the interface index of its own network interface on which it forwards the packet. To allow the reversing of a sequence of hops for a reverse route back to the originating node (when, for example, the existence of bidirectional links can be assumed on the basis of the underlying MAC protocol), the node forwarding the ROUTE REQUEST may also add to the route record in it the interface index of its own network interface on which it *received* the ROUTE REQUEST packet. For example, the source route shown in Figure 5.8 is $\mathbf{A}/1 \rightarrow \mathbf{B}/1 \rightarrow \mathbf{C}/4 \rightarrow \mathbf{D}$. The corresponding reversed route is $\mathbf{D}/1 \rightarrow \mathbf{C}/4 \rightarrow \mathbf{B}/2 \rightarrow \mathbf{A}$. The interface indices to represent a route are carried in the ROUTE REQUEST, the ROUTE REPLY, and the source route in the headers of the data packets.

Internet Interconnection and Mobile IP

DSR supports the seamless interoperation between an ad hoc network and the Internet, allowing packets to be routed transparently from the ad hoc network to nodes in the Internet and from the Internet to nodes in the ad hoc network [Broch+ 1999b]. To enable this interoperation, one node (or more) in the ad hoc network must be connected to the Internet, such that it participates in the ad hoc network through DSR and also participates in the Internet through standard IP routing. We call such a node a *gateway* between the ad hoc network and the Internet. In this way, DSR allows the coverage range around a wireless Internet base station, for example, to be dynamically enlarged through multiple "hops" between nodes through the ad hoc network. It is also possible for such a gateway node to operate as a Mobile IP home agent or foreign agent [Johnson 1995], allowing nodes to visit the ad hoc network as a Mobile IP foreign network and allowing nodes whose home network is the ad hoc network to visit other networks using Mobile IP.

This Internet interconnection is implemented through two special reserved interface index values, used by gateway nodes to identify their interconnection to the Internet. If the node has a separate physical network interface other than the network interface(s) that it uses for participation in the ad hoc network, by which it connects to the Internet, the reserved interface index is used to identify that interface. However, it is also possible for a node to use a single network interface both for ad hoc network participation and for Internet connection through standard IP routing. In this case, the reserved interface index identifies the logically separate functionality of this interface for its Internet connection, and the node uses another (locally assigned) interface index value to identify this interface in its separate logical participation in the ad hoc network.

If the gateway node is acting as a Mobile IP home agent or foreign agent (termed a *mobility agent*) on this network interface, it uses the reserved interface index value `IF_INDEX_MA`. Otherwise, the gateway node uses the reserved value `IF_INDEX_ROUTER`. The distinction between the reserved index values for mobility agents and for routers allows mobility agents to advertise their existence (as needed for Mobile IP) at no cost. A node in the ad hoc network that processes a routing header listing the interface index `IF_INDEX_MA` can then send a unicast Mobile IP AGENT SOLICITATION [Perkins 1996] to the corresponding address in the routing header to obtain complete information about the Mobile IP services provided.

In processing a received ROUTE REQUEST, a gateway node generates a ROUTE REPLY, giving its reserved interface index value, if it believes that it may be able to reach the target node through its Internet connection. Thus, the originator of the Route Discovery may receive REPLYs both from the gateway and from the node itself if the node is present in the ad hoc network. When later sending packets to this destination, the sender should prefer cached routes that do not traverse a hop with an interface index of `IF_INDEX_MA` or `IF_INDEX_ROUTER`, as these will favor routes that lead directly to the destination node within the ad hoc network.

5.2.6 Multicast Routing with DSR

DSR does not currently support true multicast routing, but it does support an approximation that is sufficient in many network contexts. Through an extension of the Route Discovery mechanism, DSR supports the controlled flooding of a data packet to all nodes in the ad hoc network that are within some specified number of hops of the originator. These nodes may then apply destination address filtering (e.g., in software) to limit the packet to those nodes subscribed to the packet's indicated multicast destination address. Even though this mechanism does not support pruning of the broadcast tree to conserve network resources, it can be used to distribute information to all nodes in the ad hoc network subscribed to the destination multicast address. This mechanism may also be useful for sending application-level packets to all nodes in a limited range around the sender.

In this form of multicasting, an application on a DSR node sends a packet to a multicast destination address and DSR piggybacks the data from the packet inside a ROUTE REQUEST targeted at the multicast address. The normal ROUTE REQUEST propagation scheme described in Section 5.2.1 results in this packet being efficiently distributed to all nodes in the network within the specified hop count (TTL) of the originator. After forwarding the packet as defined for Route Discovery, each receiving node then individually examines its destination address and discards the packet if it is destined for a multicast address to which this node is not subscribed.

5.2.7 Location of DSR Functions in the ISO Network Reference Model

In our design of DSR, we had to determine the layer within the protocol hierarchy at which to implement ad hoc network routing. We considered two options: the *link layer* (ISO layer 2) and the *network layer* (ISO layer 3). Originally, we opted for the link layer for several reasons:

• Pragmatically, running the DSR protocol at the link layer maximizes the number of mobile nodes that can participate in ad hoc networks. For example, the protocol can route equally well between IPv4 [Postel 1981a], IPv6 [Deering+ 1998], and IPX [Turner 1990] nodes.

• Historically [Johnson 1994, Johnson+ 1996a], as described more fully in Section 5.4, DSR grew from our contemplation of a multihop propagating version of the Internet Address Resolution Protocol (ARP) [Plummer 1982] as well as from the routing mechanism used in IEEE 802 source routing bridges [Perlman 1992]. These are layer-2 protocols.

• Technically, we designed DSR to be simple enough to be implemented directly in the firmware inside wireless network interface cards [Johnson 1994, Johnson+ 1996a], well below the layer-3 software within a mobile node. We see great potential in this for DSR running inside a cloud of mobile nodes around a fixed base station, where it would transparently extend the coverage range to these nodes. Mobile nodes that would otherwise be unable to communicate with the base station because of factors such as distance, fading, or local interference could then reach the base station through their peers.

Ultimately, however, we decided to specify [Broch+ 1999a] and to implement [Maltz+ 1999b] DSR as a layer-3 protocol because this is the only layer at which we could realistically support nodes with multiple network interfaces of different types, as described in Section 5.2.5.

5.3 DSR EVALUATION

This section summarizes some of our experiences in evaluating DSR through detailed studies using discrete event simulation and through implementation and actual operation and experience with the protocol in an ad hoc networking testbed environment. Complete details of this evaluation can be found in other publications [Broch+ 1998, Maltz+ 1999a, Maltz+ 1999b].

5.3.1 Simulation Summary

Our simulation environment consists of a set of wireless and mobile networking extensions that we created [Broch+ 1998]. Based on the publicly available *ns-2* network simulator from the University of California at Berkeley and the VINT Project [Fall+ 1997], these extensions provide a detailed model of the physical and link layer behavior of a wireless network and allow arbitrary movement of nodes within it. At the physical layer, we provide realistic modeling of factors such as free space and ground reflection propagation, transmission power, antenna gain, receiver sensitivity, propagation delay, carrier sense, and capture effect [Rappaport 1996]. At the link layer, we model the complete Distributed Coordination Function (DCF) MAC protocol of the IEEE 802.11 wireless LAN protocol standard [IEEE 1997], along with the standard Internet ARP [Plummer 1982]. These wireless and mobile networking extensions are available from the Carnegie-Mellon University Monarch Project web pages [Monarch] and have been widely used by other researchers; a version has also been adopted as a part of the standard VINT release of *ns-2*.

We conducted a number of simulation studies with this environment, analyzing the behavior and performance of DSR and comparing it to other proposed routing protocols for ad hoc networks [Broch+ 1998, Maltz+ 1999a]. Here we summarize only some of the basic results that indicate DSR's excellent performance. All simulations were run in ad hoc networks of

50 mobile nodes moving according to the *random waypoint* mobility model [Johnson+ 1996a] within a flat rectangular (1500 m × 300 m) area; all simulations were run for 15 minutes (900 seconds) of simulated time. Data traffic was generated using constant bit rate (CBR) UDP traffic sources, with either 10, 20, or 30 mobile nodes acting as traffic sources generating 4 packets/second each. We show here the results for 20 sources, although the results for 10 and 30 sources are similar. All movement and application layer communication were generated in advance and captured in a *scenario file*, allowing us to rerun DSR or other ad hoc network routing protocols on the *identical* workloads. The physical radio characteristics of each mobile node's network interface, such as antenna gain, transmit power, and receiver sensitivity, were chosen to approximate the Lucent WaveLAN [Tuch 1993] direct sequence spread-spectrum radio.

In the random waypoint mobility model [Johnson+ 1996a], each mobile node begins at a random location and and moves independently during the simulation. It remains stationary for a specified period that we call the *pause time* and then moves in a straight line to some new randomly chosen location at a randomly chosen speed up to some maximum speed. Once it reaches that new location, the node again remains stationary for the pause time and then chooses a new random location to proceed to at some new randomly chosen speed; it continues to repeat this behavior throughout the simulation run. We have found that this model can produce large amounts of relative node movement and network topology change, and thus it provides a good movement model with which to stress DSR or any other ad hoc network routing protocol.

Figure 5.9 summarizes the performance of DSR as a function of pause time for two different maximum node movement speeds: Figures 5.9(a) and (b) show the performance for 1 meter/second (about 2 miles/hour), and Figures 5.9(c) and (d) show the performance for 20 meters/second (about 45 miles/hour). For the two respective node movement speeds, the packet delivery ratio—see Figures 5.9(a) and (c)—is the overall percentage of the UDP data packets originated by nodes that were successfully delivered by DSR, and the routing overhead—see Figures 5.9(b) and (d)—is the number of routing overhead packets generated by DSR to achieve this level of data packet delivery. Each point in the graphs represents the average of 10 random movement and communication scenarios for the given pause time. At a pause time of 0 (on the left of each graph), all nodes in the network are in constant motion; as the pause time increases from left to right, the average node movement rate in the network decreases. At a pause time of 900 (on the right of each graph), all nodes are stationary because each simulation was run for 900 simulated seconds of operation of the ad hoc network. The vertical scales on the graphs for 1 meter/second and for 20 meters/second differ in order to make the detail visible.

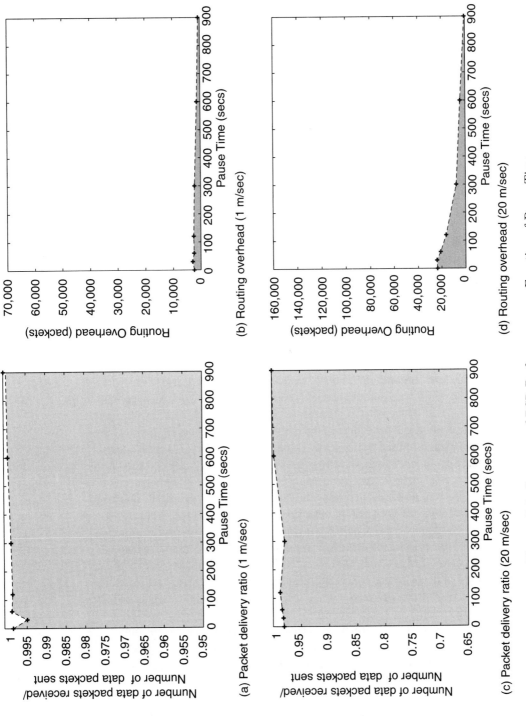

Figure 5.9. Summary of DSR Performance as a Function of Pause Time

At both movement speeds, DSR delivers almost all data packets, regardless of pause time, with the packet delivery ratio rising to equal 100% at pause time 900 (a stationary network). Similarly, at all pause times routing overhead is low—essentially 0 at pause time 900, rising only slowly as pause time decreases (as the average node mobility rate in the network increases). At the lower movement speed of 1 meter/second, DSR is able to deliver greater than 99.5% of all packets, with most cases delivering greater than 99.8%; the slight decrease at pause time 30 is due to the random generation of the scenarios that we used in the simulations. At the higher movement speed of 20 meters/second, DSR is able to deliver greater than 98% of all packets, even at pause time 0.

5.3.2 DSR Implementation and Testbed Summary

To study the behavior of DSR in a real network, we have implemented DSR in the FreeBSD version of UNIX [FreeBSD] and have experimented with this implementation extensively in an outdoor testbed constructed in Pittsburgh, where Carnegie-Mellon University is located [Maltz+ 1999b]. This has allowed us to experience the full variability and dynamics of real radio propagation, to evaluate user perceptions of applications running over the protocols, and to confirm the results from our simulations.

All of the code implementing DSR resides in the kernel in a module that straddles the IP layer. Conceptually, however, DSR can be thought of as a virtual network interface (*dsr0*) residing below the IP layer. Like other protocol implementation efforts that have used virtual interfaces to hide mobility from the normal network stack [Cheshire+ 1996], the *dsr0* interface accepts packets from the normal IP stack just as any other network interface does, but uses its own mechanisms to arrange for their delivery via the actual physical network interfaces.

To allow multiple types of DSR information to be combined in a single packet, and to allow DSR information to be piggybacked on existing packets, we used a packet format modeled after the *extension header* and *option* format used by IPv6 [Deering+ 1998, Hinden 1996]. In particular, ROUTE REQUESTs, ROUTE REPLYs, and ROUTE ERRORs are each encoded as an option within either a hop-by-hop or an end-to-end extension header, and a DSR source route on a packet is encoded as a separate extension header.

We have experimented extensively with this implementation of DSR in our actual ad hoc networking testbed [Maltz+ 1999b]. Over a period of four months between December 1998 and March 1999, we operated this ad hoc networking testbed daily. Figure 5.10 shows a map of the testbed site and illustrates the layout of the nodes and the mobility in the network. We describe here the movement and communication behavior that we utilized for many of our experiments.

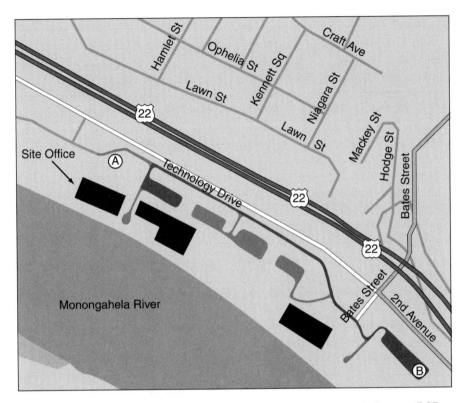

Figure 5.10. Map of the Carnegie-Mellon University Monarch Project DSR Ad Hoc Networking Testbed Site

The testbed consisted of five mobile nodes implemented as cars driving at about 25 MPH (about 10 meters/second), plus two stationary nodes (labeled **A** and **B** in Figure 5.10) separated by a distance of about 700 meters (typically about three radio hops). The mobile node cars moved continuously in a loop along a path starting in the rectangular parking area near **A** (in front of the Site Office building and the building next to it) and then along the shaded roadway to the parking area at **B**; then they turned there and returned to the first parking area, and repeated this route. All cars typically moved along this loop, in nearly constant motion, throughout a run of the testbed. As the cars moved, the route between the two stationary nodes **A** and **B** constantly changed, as did the route between any car and any other car as the cars moved relative to one another. The area used for the testbed was open to general vehicle traffic and had several stop signs, so the actual speed of each node also varied over time, just as it would in any real, deployed network. All of the routes within the ad hoc network were dynamically found and maintained through our DSR ad hoc network routing protocol.

In each car, a laptop computer implemented the DSR routing protocol, served as an endpoint in different higher-layer protocol connections and applications, and allowed local logging of network events on its hard disk. The wireless network interfaces used to form the ad hoc network were WaveLAN PCMCIA PC card radios, operating at 900 MHz, from Lucent Technologies [Tuch 1993]. Each car was also outfitted with a highly accurate global positioning system (GPS) receiver operating in real time kinematic (RTK) mode, providing each node with its own current position to centimeter-level accuracy. During different runs of the testbed, we were thus able to have each mobile node log its own current GPS position as well as the source, destination, and contents of each packet sent or received, along with all significant DSR state transition events. To facilitate additional position logging, the sender's current GPS position was piggybacked on each packet sent, which was logged along with the data of the packet on receipt. The signal strength and signal quality for each received packet (as reported by the WaveLAN hardware) were also logged. Logging this data allowed us to determine whether the protocol was working as intended and helped us diagnose any problems encountered. We have begun attempting to use this data to help with a detailed validation of our simulation models and results [Johnson 1999].

In operating the testbed [Maltz+ 1999b], we experimented with a wide variety of simultaneous data traffic types and network loads, including bulk file transfer, telnet, constant bit rate UDP streams similar to voice or video loading the network, and realtime position and status reporting packets. All realtime GPS "correction" data, required for the RTK GPS operation, was also sent once per second to each node over the ad hoc network from a GPS reference station located on top of the Site Office building shown in the map in Figure 5.10. This system was successfully demonstrated in February and March 1999 to a number of the sponsors and partners in our research, including the DARPA Global Mobile Information Systems Program (GloMo), Lucent Technologies, Bell Atlantic Mobile, and Caterpillar Corporation. In these demonstrations, the mobile node cars were in constant motion, as described above, with the network successfully carrying a large volume of all of these types of traffic. The demonstrations also included interconnection of the ad hoc network to the Internet and integration with Mobile IP, as described in Section 5.2.3.

5.4 RELATED WORK

Research on routing in multihop wireless ad hoc networks dates back at least to 1973, when the U.S. Defense Advanced Research Projects Agency

(DARPA) began the Packet Radio Network (PRNet) project [Jubin+ 1987]. PRNet and its successor, the Survivable Adaptive Networks (SURAN) project [Lauer 1995], generated a substantial number of fundamental results in this area. With the increasing capabilities and decreasing costs of small, portable computers—such as laptops and personal digital assistants (PDAs)—and with the increasing availability of inexpensive wireless network interface devices—such as wireless LAN interfaces packaged as PCMCIA PC cards—a growing number of other research projects in ad hoc networking have developed, some of which are described in other chapters of this book. In our discussion of related work here, we concentrate on research specifically related to the DSR protocol.

The initial design of DSR, including our basic Route Maintenance and Route Discovery mechanisms, was first published in December 1994, with significant additional design details and initial simulation results published in early 1996 [Johnson 1994, Johnson+ 1996a]. As noted at the beginning of this chapter, the design specification for DSR has also been submitted to the IETF MANET (Mobile Ad Hoc Networks) Working Group to help in their efforts to standardize a protocol for routing IP packets in an ad hoc network [Broch+ 1999a, MANET].

The original motivation in the design of DSR came from the ARP [Plummer 1982] used in the TCP/IP suite of protocols in the Internet. ARP is used on Ethernets and other types of networks to find the link layer MAC address of a node on the same subnet as the sender. A node sending a packet to a local IP address, for which it does not yet have the MAC address cached, broadcasts an ARP REQUEST packet on the local subnet link, giving the IP address of the node it is looking for. That node responds with an ARP REPLY packet, giving its MAC address, and all other nodes ignore the REQUEST. If all nodes in an ad hoc network are within wireless transmission range of each other, this is the only routing protocol needed for the ad hoc network. DSR extends this basic ARP behavior by allowing the REQUEST packet (the ROUTE REQUEST rather than an ARP REQUEST) to be propagated multiple hops away through forwarding by neighbor nodes, with the ultimate ROUTE REPLY being returned over multiple hops back to the initiator of the REQUEST.

DSR's nonpropagating ROUTE REQUEST packets are indeed quite similar to the basic ARP REQUEST behavior, except that a mobile node may answer the ROUTE REQUEST from its cache, whereas ARP REQUESTs are normally answered only by the target node itself. With ARP, in cases in which several LANs have been bridged together, the bridge may run "proxy" ARP [Postel 1984], which allows it to answer an ARP REQUEST on behalf of another node (behind the bridge). In this sense, our nonpropagating ROUTE REQUESTs are also similar to proxy ARP; they expand the effective size of a single node's Route Cache by allowing it to make cheap use of the caches of neighboring nodes to reduce the need for propagating ROUTE REQUESTs. Our original implementation of DSR in 1997 also was structured as an extension of ARP, integrated into the existing ARP implementation in the FreeBSD UNIX kernel [FreeBSD] using an extension of the ARP REQUEST and ARP REPLY packet formats. As described in Sections 5.2.5 and 5.3.2, however, we ultimately decided to operate DSR at the network layer rather than at the link layer to allow routing between different heterogeneous networks all forming a single ad hoc network.

DSR is also similar in approach to the source routing discovery mechanism used in the IEEE 802 SRT bridge standard [Perlman 1992]; related mechanisms have also been used in other systems, including FLIP [Kaashoek+ 1993] and SDRP [Estrin+ 1995]. In particular, our ROUTE REQUEST packet serves essentially the same role in Route Discovery as an "all paths explorer" packet does in IEEE 802 source routing bridges. However, in wired networks a bridge can copy such an explorer packet from one network interface onto each of its other interfaces (i.e., to each other link to which this bridge is attached) and be sure that the explorer packet will flood the network in an orderly and complete way. DSR, however, must operate in a wireless ad hoc network, in which nodes forward packets on the same wireless network interface on which they receive them, making such a flood more difficult to implement efficiently. DSR also contains many optimizations designed specifically for the problem of routing in multihop wireless ad hoc networks, and it defines the new Route Maintenance mechanism to quickly and efficiently detect broken links between nodes, allowing alternate routing paths to be taken or new paths to be discovered.

The amateur radio community has worked extensively with routing in wireless networks of (sometimes) mobile hosts [Karn+ 1985], having held an annual packet radio computer networking conference sponsored by the American Radio Relay League (ARRL) since 1981. Amateur packet radio networking originally used only source routing with explicit source routes constructed by the user, although some had considered the possibility of a more dynamic source routing scheme [Garbee 1987]. A system known as NET/ROM was also developed to allow the routing decisions to be automated, using a form of distance vector routing protocol rather than source routing [Frank 1988, Geier+ 1990]. NET/ROM also allows updating of its routing table based on the source address information in the headers of packets that it receives.

Recently, a number of other protocols have been structured around mechanisms similar to the Route Discovery and Route Maintenance mechanisms in DSR. For example, the Signal Stability-Based Adaptive (SSA) routing protocol [Dube+ 1997] and the Associativity-Based Routing (ABR) protocol [Toh 1996] discover routes on demand in a way similar to Route Discovery in DSR, but they attempt to select only long-lived links between nodes where possible; favoring long-lived links helps avoid routes breaking soon after they are discovered but may result in use of routes over a greater number of hops rather than over the shortest routes available. ABR also adds overhead for periodic beacon packets required to monitor link stability. The Ad Hoc On-Demand Distance Vector (AODV) routing protocol [Perkins+ 1999] uses mechanisms similar to DSR's Route Discovery and Route Maintenance, but it uses them to create hop-by-hop routes rather than source routes, as is done in DSR; this use of hop-by-hop routes avoids the source routing header overhead of DSR but prevents or makes difficult many of DSR's route caching and other Route Discovery optimizations and prevents AODV from supporting unidirectional links between nodes. The Zone Routing Protocol (ZRP) [Haas 1997, Haas+ 1998] defines a "routing zone" around each individual node, with a periodic (proactive) protocol such as distance-vector or link-state for routing within a zone and an on-demand protocol such as DSR for routing between zones; the use of routing zones reduces some of the overhead of the Route Discovery procedure, as in DSR, but adds the overhead of maintaining zone membership and routing information within each zone. ZRP may also fail at times to successfully deliver packets with highly mobile nodes because within a zone it does not utilize on-demand operation.

Finally, DSR has been used as a basis for further work by other researchers, including suggested improvements to the Route Discovery mechanism. For example, Ko and Vaidya [Ko+ 1998] proposed an optimization to Route Discovery, known as location-aided routing (LAR), that uses knowledge of the physical (geographical) location of the target node of the Route Discovery (e.g., from GPS) to narrow the area of the network over which the ROUTE REQUEST packets must be propagated. Castañeda and Das [Castañeda+ 1999] have proposed a similar Route Discovery optimization that uses only logical (topological), not physical, location information and thus does not require access to GPS. Holland and Vaidya [Holland+ 1999] recently studied the behavior of TCP in ad hoc networks above the routing layer, using DSR as a routing protocol; their work added explicit interaction between TCP and the Route Discovery and Route Maintenance mechanisms to allow TCP to correctly react to a route failure rather than treat it as network congestion, and to allow it to restart sending as soon as a new route to the destination is discovered.

5.5 CONCLUSION

The Dynamic Source Routing protocol provides excellent performance for routing in multihop wireless ad hoc networks. As shown in our detailed simulation studies and in our implementation of the protocol in a real ad hoc network of cars driving and routing among themselves, DSR has very low routing overhead and is able to correctly deliver almost all originated data packets, even with continuous, rapid motion of all nodes in the network.

A key reason for this good performance is that DSR operates *entirely* on demand [Johnson 1994], with *no* periodic activity of *any kind* required at *any level* within the network. For example, DSR does not use any periodic routing advertisement, link status sensing, or neighbor detection packets; nor does it rely on these functions from any underlying protocols in the network. This entirely on-demand behavior and the lack of periodic activity allow the number of routing overhead packets caused by DSR to scale to *zero,* when all nodes are approximately stationary with respect to each other and all routes needed for current communication have already been discovered. As nodes begin to move more or as communication patterns change, the routing packet overhead of DSR *automatically* scales to only that needed to track the routes currently in use.

In this chapter, we described the principle mechanisms of *Route Discovery* and *Route Maintenance* used by DSR, and we showed how they enable wireless mobile nodes to automatically form a completely self-organizing and self-configuring network among themselves. Our current work in the Monarch Project at Carnegie-Mellon University includes further improvements to DSR performance—for example, scaling to very large networks—and the addition of new features such as multicast routing and adaptive quality of service reservations and resource management. Our goal is to create an integrated set of protocols that allow mobile computers, and the applications running on them and communicating with them, to make the most efficient use of the best available network connections at any time, seamlessly. DSR is an important component of such a system.

Acknowledgments

The research described in this chapter has been carried out as part of the Monarch Project at Carnegie-Mellon University, whose team members include Josh Broch, Yih-Chun Hu, Jorjeta Jetcheva, David B. Johnson, Qifa Ke, and David A. Maltz (*http://www.monarch.cs.com.edu*). This work was supported in part by the National Science Foundation (NSF) under CAREER Award NCR-9502725, by the Air Force Materiel Command under DARPA contract number F19628-96-C-0061, and by Caterpillar Corporation. David Maltz was also supported under an Intel Graduate Fellowship and an IBM Cooperative Fellowship. The views and conclusions contained here are those of the authors and should not be interpreted as necessarily representing the official policies or endorsements, either express or implied, of the editor, the publisher, NSF, AFMC, DARPA, Caterpillar, Intel, IBM, Carnegie-Mellon University, or the U.S. government.

References

[Bantz+ 1994] D.F. Bantz and F.J. Bauchot. Wireless LAN Design Alternatives. *IEEE Network* 8(2):43–53, March/April 1994.

[Bharghavan+ 1994] V. Bharghavan, A. Demers, S. Shenker, and L. Zhang. MACAW: A Media Access Protocol for Wireless LANs. In *Proceedings of ACM SIGCOMM '94*, August 1994, 212–225.

[Braden 1989] R.T. Braden, ed. Requirements for Internet Hosts — Communication Layers. RFC 1122, October 1989.

[Broch+ 1998] J. Broch, D.A. Maltz, D.B. Johnson, Y.-C. Hu, and J. Jetcheva. A Performance Comparison of Multi-Hop Wireless Ad Hoc Network Routing Protocols. In *Proceedings of the Fourth Annual ACM/IEEE International Conference on Mobile Computing and Networking (MOBICOM '98)*, October 1998, 85–97.

[Broch+ 1999a] J. Broch, D.B. Johnson, and D.A. Maltz. *The Dynamic Source Routing Protocol for Mobile Ad Hoc Networks*. Internet draft (draft-ietf-manet-dsr-03.txt), October 1999 (work in progress).

[Broch+ 1999b] J. Broch, D.A. Maltz, and D.B. Johnson. Supporting Hierarchy and Heterogeneous Interfaces in Multi-Hop Wireless Ad Hoc Networks. In *Proceedings of the Fourth International Symposium on Parallel Architectures, Algorithms and Networks (ISPAN '99), Workshop on Mobile Computing*, June 1999, 310–315.

[Castañeda+ 1999] R. Castañeda and S.R. Das. Query Localization Techniques for On-Demand Routing Protocols in Ad Hoc Networks. In *Proceedings of the Fifth Annual ACM/IEEE International Conference on Mobile Computing and Networking (MOBICOM '99)*, August 1999.

[Cheshire+ 1996] S. Cheshire and M. Baker. Internet Mobility 4x4. In *Proceedings of ACM SIGCOMM '96*, August 1996, 318–329.

[Deering+ 1998] S.E. Deering and R.M. Hinden. Internet Protocol, Version 6 (IPv6) Specification. RFC 2460, December 1998.

[Droms 1997] R. Droms. Dynamic Host Configuration Protocol. RFC 2131, March 1997.

[Dube+ 1997] R. Dube, C.D. Rais, K.-Y. Wang, and S.K. Tripathi. Signal Stability-Based Adaptive Routing (SSA) for Ad Hoc Mobile Networks. *IEEE Personal Communications* 4(1):36–45, February 1997.

[Estrin+ 1995] D. Estrin, D. Zappala, T. Li, Y. Rekhter, and K. Varadhan. *Source Demand Routing: Packet Format and Forwarding Version 1*. Internet draft, January 1995 (work in progress).

[Fall+ 1997] K. Fall and K. Varadhan, eds. *ns Notes and Documentation*. The VINT Project, University of California at Berkeley, Laurence Berkeley Laboratory, University of Southern California Information Sciences Institute, and Xerox PARC, November 1997 (available from *http://www-mash.cs.berkeley.edu/ns/*).

[Frank 1988] D.M. Frank. Transmission of IP Datagrams over NET/ROM Networks. In *Proceedings of the ARRL Amateur Radio Seventh Computer Networking Conference*, October 1988, 65–70.

[FreeBSD] *FreeBSD Project.* FreeBSD Home Page (available at *http://www. freebsd.org/*).

[Garbee 1987] B. Garbee. Thoughts on the Issues of Address Resolution and Routing in Amateur Packet Radio TCP/IP Networks. In *Proceedings of the ARRL Amateur Radio Sixth Computer Networking Conference*, August 1987, 56–58.

[Geier+ 1990] J. Geier, M. DeSimio, and B. Welsh. Network Routing Techniques and Their Relevance to Packet Radio Networks. In *Proceedings of the ARRL/ CRRL Amateur Radio Ninth Computer Networking Conference*, September 1990, 105–117.

[Haas 1997] Z.J. Haas. A New Routing Protocol for the Reconfigurable Wireless Networks. In *Proceedings of the Sixth International Conference on Universal Personal Communications*, October 1997, 562–566.

[Haas+ 1998] Z.J. Haas and M.R. Pearlman. The Performance of Query Control Schemes for the Zone Routing Protocol. In *Proceedings of ACM SIGCOMM '98*, September 1998, 167–177.

[Hinden 1996] R.M. Hinden. IP Next Generation Overview. *Communications of the ACM* 39(6):61–71, June 1996.

[Holland+ 1999] G. Holland and N. Vaidya. Analysis of TCP Performance over Mobile Ad Hoc Networks. In *Proceedings of the Fifth Annual ACM/IEEE International Conference on Mobile Computing and Networking (MOBICOM '99)*, August 1999, 219–230.

[IEEE 1997] IEEE Computer Society LAN MAN Standards Committee. *Wireless LAN Medium Access Control (MAC) and Physical Layer (PHY) Specifications, IEEE Standard 802.11-1997*. The Institute of Electrical and Electronics Engineers, New York, 1997.

[Johansson+ 1999] P. Johansson, T. Larsson, N. Hedman, B. Mielczarek, and M. Degermark. Routing Protocols for Mobile Ad-Hoc Networks—A Comparative Performance Analysis. In *Proceedings of the Fifth Annual ACM/IEEE International Conference on Mobile Computing and Networking (MOBICOM '99)*, August 1999.

[Johnson 1994] D.B. Johnson. Routing in Ad Hoc Networks of Mobile Hosts. In *Proceedings of the IEEE Workshop on Mobile Computing Systems and Applications*, December 1994, 158–163.

[Johnson 1995] D.B. Johnson. Scalable Support for Transparent Mobile Host Internetworking. *Wireless Networks* 1(3):311–321, October 1995.

[Johnson 1999] D.B. Johnson. Validation of Wireless and Mobile Network Models and Simulation. In *Proceedings of the DARPA/NIST Workshop on Validation of Large Scale Network Models and Simulation*, May 1999.

[Johnson+ 1996a] D.B. Johnson and D.A. Maltz. Dynamic Source Routing in Ad Hoc Wireless Networks. In *Mobile Computing*, T. Imielinski and H. Korth, eds., Kluwer Academic Publishers, Norwell, Mass., 1996, 153–181.

[Johnson+ 1996b] D.B. Johnson and D.A. Maltz. Protocols for Adaptive Wireless and Mobile Networking. *IEEE Personal Communications* 3(1):34–42, February 1996.

[Jubin+ 1987] J. Jubin and J.D. Tornow. The DARPA Packet Radio Network Protocols. *Proceedings of the IEEE* 75(1):21–32, January 1987.

[Kaashoek+ 1993] M.F. Kaashoek, R. van Renesse, H. van Staveren, and A.S. Tanenbaum. FLIP: An Internetwork Protocol for Supporting Distributed Systems. *ACM Transactions on Computer Systems* 11(1):73–106, February 1993.

[Karn+ 1985] P.R. Karn, H.E. Price, and R.J. Diersing. Packet Radio in the Amateur Service. *IEEE Journal on Selected Areas of Communications* SAC-3(3):431–439, May 1985.

[Karn 1990] P. Karn. MACA—A New Channel Access Method for Packet Radio. In *Proceedings of the ARRL/CRRL Amateur Radio Ninth Computer Networking Conference*, September 1990, 134–140.

[Katz+ 1996] R.H. Katz and E.A. Brewer. The Case for Wireless Overlay Networks. In *Proceedings of the SPIE Multimedia and Networking Conference (MMNC '96)*, January 1996.

[Ko+ 1998] Y.-B. Ko and N. Vaidya. Location-Aided Routing (LAR) in Mobile Ad Hoc Networks. In *Proceedings of the Fourth Annual ACM/IEEE International Conference on Mobile Computing and Networking (MOBICOM '98)*, October 1998, 66–75.

[Lauer 1995] G. S. Lauer. Packet-Radio Routing. In *Routing in Communications Networks*, M. Steenstrup, ed., Prentice-Hall, Englewood Cliffs, N.J., 1995, 351–396.

[Maltz+ 1999a] D.A. Maltz, J. Broch, J. Jetcheva, and D.B. Johnson. The Effects of On-Demand Behavior in Routing Protocols for Multi-Hop Wireless Ad Hoc Networks. *IEEE Journal on Selected Areas of Communications* 17(8):1439–1453, August 1999.

[Maltz+ 1999b] D.A. Maltz, J. Broch, and D.B. Johnson. *Experiences Designing and Building a Multi-Hop Wireless Ad Hoc Network Testbed*. Technical report CMU-CS-99-116, School of Computer Science, Carnegie-Mellon University, Pittsburgh, March 1999.

[MANET] IETF MANET Working Group. *Mobile Ad Hoc Networks (MANET)* (Working Group Charter available at *http://www.ietf.org/html.charters/manet-charter.html*).

[Monarch] Carnegie-Mellon University Monarch Project. CMU Monarch Project Home Page (available at *http://www.monarch.cs.cmu.edu/*).

[Perkins 1996] C. Perkins, ed. IP Mobility Support. RFC 2002 (proposed standard), October 1996.

[Perkins+ 1999] C. Perkins and E.M. Royer. Ad Hoc On-Demand Distance Vector Routing. In *Proceedings of the Second Annual IEEE Workshop on Mobile Computing Systems and Applications*, February 1999, 90–100.

[Perlman 1992] R. Perlman. *Interconnections: Bridges and Routers.* Addison-Wesley, Reading, Mass., 1992.

[Plummer 1982] D.C. Plummer. An Ethernet Address Resolution Protocol: Or Converting Network Protocol Addresses to 48-bit Ethernet Addresses for Transmission on Ethernet Hardware. RFC 826, November 1982.

[Postel 1981a] J.B. Postel, ed. Internet Protocol. RFC 791, September 1981.

[Postel 1981b] J.B. Postel, ed. Transmission Control Protocol. RFC 793, September 1981.

[Postel 1984] J.B. Postel. Multi-LAN Address Resolution. RFC 925, October 1984.

[Rappaport 1996] T.S. Rappaport. *Wireless Communications: Principles and Practice.* Prentice-Hall, Englewood Cliffs, N.J., 1996.

[Toh 1996] C.-K. Toh. A Novel Distributed Routing Protocol to Support Ad-Hoc Mobile Computing. In *Proceedings of the 1996 IEEE Fifteenth Annual International Phoenix Conference on Computers and Communications*, March 1996, 480–486.

[Tuch 1993] B. Tuch. Development of WaveLAN, an ISM Band Wireless LAN. *AT&T Technical Journal* 72(4):27–33, July/August 1993.

[Turner 1990] P. Turner. NetWare Communications Processes. *NetWare Application Notes,* Novell Research, September 1990, 25–91.

[Wright+ 1995] G.R. Wright and W.R. Stevens. *TCP/IP Illustrated, Volume 2: The Implementation.* Addison-Wesley, Reading, Mass., 1995.

6

The Ad Hoc On-Demand Distance-Vector Protocol

Charles E. Perkins
Nokia Research Center

Elizabeth M. Royer
University of California at Santa Barbara

The Ad Hoc On-Demand Distance-Vector (AODV) routing protocol provides quick and efficient route establishment between nodes desiring communication and AODV was designed specifically for ad hoc wireless networks, it provides communication between mobile nodes with minimal control overhead and minimal route acquisition latency.

The initial design of AODV was undertaken after our experience with the Destination-Sequenced Distance-Vector (DSDV) routing algorithm [Perkins+ 1994]. Its goal is to reduce the need for system-wide broadcasts to the furthest extent possible. DSDV issues broadcasts to announce every change in the overall connectivity of the ad hoc network. Every time that two nodes enter communication range of each other, they become neighbors and change the network topology. This triggers a broadcast of the new connectivity information to the rest of the nodes in the ad hoc network. Similarly, when two neighboring nodes drift out of direct communication range, the link break causes a broadcast-triggered update.

With AODV, it is no longer required that such changes initiate system-wide broadcasts. In fact, if the link status does not affect ongoing communication or multicast tree maintenance, no broadcast occurs. This localizes the effects caused by local movements. In DSDV, local movements have global effects. In AODV, the only nonlocal effects result from a distant source trying to use a broken link. The triggered broadcast in DSDV is replaced by more careful bookkeeping that identifies the one or more nodes that had been using the broken link. Only those nodes have to be informed of the link's changed status. In the frequent case that a link was idle, no such indication is sent.

AODV has other minimalist features in addition to drastically reducing the number of broadcasts resulting from a link break. Whenever a route is available between source and destination, AODV does not add any over-head to the packets carrying the data. Whenever routes are not used, they are expired and consequently discarded, which reduces the effects of stale routes as well as the need for route maintenance for unused routes. Careful route aging is difficult to manage in the absence of other timing information, such as how long a link might be expected to remain operational. Never-theless, our simulations have shown that it is advantageous to age routes. AODV also minimizes the number of routes between any active source and destination.

Interesting designs have been proposed that allow multiple routes to be used whenever they are collected during a route discovery phase. While this approach has promise, we observe three possible difficulties:

- It is nontrivial to simultaneously manage the aging process for multiple routes between the same source/destination pair.
- If an alternate route is taken after a primary route has gone stale, it might be difficult to know whether the alternate route is still valid.
- Careful bookkeeping is required ensure that two seemingly different routes do not actually utilize the same broken link.

Because it is still too early to know how great a benefit may be re-alized from the use of multiple routes, we have decided to avoid them in our attempt to minimize latency in the common case. AODV's use of a single route to unicast destination amounts to a tradeoff in favor of reduced latency at the possible expense of an increased number of route finding broadcasts. We look forward to experiments that may quantify the benefits of this tradeoff.

Another feature distinguishing AODV from DSDV and other ad hoc protocols is its integrated handling of multicast routing. By modeling the multicast routing problem as an extension of AODV's distance-vector algo-rithm, we can apply protocol improvements to both unicast and multicast at the same time. Many of the design parameters and protocol variations are of similar importance to both situations. Routes to particular nodes within the multicast tree can be used for unicast routes as well if those nodes turn out to be destinations for unicast traffic. A sequence number for each multicast route is also used to prevent loops during the construction of multicast trees. The unification in the handling of multicast traffic comes without the need to degrade the minimalist approach that AODV offers for unicast packet routing.

In this chapter, the design and protocol details for AODV are fully described. The following section summarizes the basic design goals and properties that have guided AODV's evolution for the last six years. Then, AODV's building of routes between sources and unicast destinations is detailed. After a description of unicast route establishment, the details and description of the additional operations needed to handle multicast route establishment are given.

Next, various simulation results are presented. These results indicate that the design goals for minimizing control traffic and overhead, while still offering efficient and useful route establisment for unicast and multicast routing, have been achieved. Finally, we offer ideas for future work and draw conclusions about the protocol.

6.1 AODV PROPERTIES

AODV does not attempt to maintain routes from every node to every other node in the network. Routes are discovered on an *as-needed* basis and are maintained only as long as they are necessary. AODV is loop free at all times, even while repairing broken links [Perkins+ 1999]. This loop freedom is accomplished through the use of sequence numbers. Every node maintains its own monotonically increasing sequence number, which it increases each time it learns of a change in the topology of its neighborhood. This sequence number ensures that the most recent route is selected whenever route discovery is executed. In addition, each multicast group has its own sequence number, which is maintained by the multicast group leader.

AODV is able to provide unicast, multicast, and broadcast communication ability. Combining all three communication forms in a single protocol has numerous advantages. A protocol that offers both unicast and multicast communication can be streamlined so that route information obtained when searching for a multicast route can also increase unicast routing knowledge and vice versa. In a mobile environment, any reduction in control overhead is a significant advantage. Offering all three types of communication in a single protocol simplifies coding. Lastly, it is expected that continued improvements to the basic algorithm (e.g., for quality of service (QoS) applications, for client–server discovery, or for utilizing asymmetric routing paths) will benefit both unicast and multicast data transmission.

AODV currently utilizes only symmetric links between neighboring nodes, but otherwise does not depend specifically on particular aspects of the physical medium across which packets are disseminated. AODV is capable of operating on both wired and wireless media, although it is designed specifically for the wireless domain.

Route tables are used by AODV to store pertinent routing information. AODV utilizes both a route table (for unicast routes) and a multicast route table (for multicast routes). The route table is used to store the destination and next-hop IP addresses as well as the destination sequence number. Additionally, for each destination the node maintains a list of *precursor nodes,* which route through it in order to reach the destination. This list is maintained for the purpose of route maintenance if the link breaks, as described in Section 6.2.4. Also associated with each route table entry is a lifetime, which is updated whenever a route is used. If a route has not been used within its lifetime, it is expired. This is because a route that is not being used is also not being maintained, and so nodes along the route are likely to have moved, making the route invalid.

The multicast route table includes fields that are similar to the route table except that each multicast route table entry may have more than one next-hop associated with it. Each next-hop entry in the multicast route table has an Activated flag and a direction. The Activated flag is set when the next hop is selected to be added to the multicast tree. Only after the route is activated can it be used to forward multicast data packets. The direction is relative to the multicast group leader, where upstream is toward the leader and downstream is away from it.

AODV is able to maintain both unicast and multicast routes even for nodes in constant movement. It also provides for the quick deletion of invalid routes through the use of a special route error message (Section 6.2.4). AODV responds to topological changes that affect active routes in a quick and timely manner. It builds routes with only a small amount of overhead from routing control messages and no additional network overhead. AODV requires nodes to maintain only next-hop routing information, thereby decreasing the storage requirement at each of the mobile nodes. Finally, AODV does not place any additional overhead on data packets because it does not utilize source routing.

6.2 UNICAST ROUTE ESTABLISHMENT

In this section, the algorithms used by AODV for establishing unicast routes are described.

Route discovery with AODV is purely on demand and follows a route request/route reply discovery cycle. Requests are sent using a Route Request (RREQ) message. Information enabling the creation of a route is sent back in a Route Reply (RREP) message.

The basic outline of the route discovery process is as follows:

1. When a node needs a route to a destination, it broadcasts a RREQ.
2. Any node with a current route to that destination (including the destination itself) can unicast a RREP back to the source node.
3. Route information is maintained by each node in its route table.
4. Information obtained through RREQ and RREP messages is kept with other routing information in the route table.

5. Sequence numbers are used to eliminate stale routes.

6. Routes with old sequence numbers are aged out of the system.

The following sections explain these actions in more detail. We first describe the broadcast route discovery algorithm and then the unicast Route Reply message.

6.2.1 Route Discovery

When a node wishes to send a packet to some destination node, it checks its route table to determine whether it has a current route to that node. If so, it forwards the packet to the appropriate next hop toward the destination. However, if the node does not have a valid route to the destination, it must initiate a *route discovery* process. To begin such a process, the node (call it the source) creates a RREQ packet. This packet contains the source node's IP address and current sequence number as well as the destination's IP address and last known sequence number. The RREQ also contains a broadcast ID, which is incremented each time the source node initiates a RREQ. In this way, the broadcast ID and the IP address of the source node form a unique identifier for the RREQ. After creating the RREQ, the source node broadcasts the packet and then sets a timer to wait for a reply.

When a node receives a RREQ, it first checks whether it has seen it before by noting the source IP address and broadcast ID pair. Each node maintains a record of the source IP address/broadcast ID for each RREQ it receives, for a specified length of time. If it has already seen a RREQ with the same IP address/broadcast ID pair, it silently discards the packet. Otherwise, it records this information and then processes the packet.

To process the RREQ, the node sets up a *reverse route* entry for the source node in its route table. This reverse route entry contains the source node's IP address and sequence number as well as the number of hops to the source node and the IP address of the neighbor from which the RREQ was received (i.e., the next hop toward the source node from the node processing the RREQ). In this way, the node knows how to forward a RREP to the source if one is received later. Figure 6.1 indicates the propagation of RREQs across the network as well as the formation of the reverse route entries at each of the network nodes. Associated with the reverse route entry is a lifetime. If this route entry is not used within the specified lifetime, the route information is deleted to prevent stale routing information from lingering in the route table.

To respond to the RREQ, the node must have an unexpired entry for the destination in its route table. Furthermore, the sequence number associated with that destination must be at least as great as that indicated in the RREQ. This prevents the formation of routing loops by ensuring that

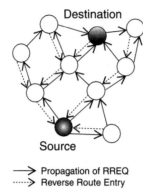

Destination

Source

→ Propagation of RREQ
····> Reverse Route Entry

Figure 6.1. Propagation of RREQ throughout the Network

the route returned is never old enough to point to a previous intermediate node. Otherwise, the previous node would have responded to the RREQ. If the node is able to satisfy these two requirements, it responds by unicasting a RREP back to the source, as described in Section 6.2.3. If it is unable to satisfy the RREQ, it increments the RREQ's hop count and then broadcasts the packet to its neighbors. Naturally, the destination node is always able to respond to the RREQ.

If the RREQ is lost, the source node is allowed to retry the broadcast route discovery mechanism. After **rreq_retries** additional attempts, it is required to notify the application that the destination is unreachable. Simulations have shown that the optimal value for **rreq_retries** is 2 [Perkins+ 1999].

6.2.2 Expanding Ring Search

Each time a node initiates route discovery for some new destination, it must broadcast a RREQ across the network. For a small network, the impact of this flooding is minimal. However, for a large network the impact may become increasingly detrimental. To control network-wide broadcasts of RREQs, the source node should use an expanding ring search technique, which allows a search of increasingly larger areas of the network if a route to the destination is not found. To use the expanding ring search, the source node sets the Time to Live (TTL) value of the RREQ to an initial **ttl_start** value. If no reply is received within the discovery period, the next RREQ is broadcast with a TTL value increased by an increment value. This process of increasing the TTL value continues until a threshold value is reached, beyond which the RREQ is broadcast across the entire network up to **rreq_retries** more times.

When a new route is established, the distance to the destination is recorded in the route table. If route discovery must be initiated to this same destination later, the initial TTL value for the new RREQ is set to this distance plus the increment value. In this way the source node can first search the area where the destination was last seen or to which it is likely to have moved. The expanding ring search then continues as previously described.

6.2.3 Forward Path Setup

When a node determines that it has a route current enough to respond to the RREQ, it creates a RREP. For the purposes of replying to a RREQ, any route with a sequence number not smaller than that indicated in the RREQ is deemed current enough. The RREP sent in response to the RREQ contains the IP address of both the source and destination. If the destination node is responding, it places its current sequence number in the packet, initializes the hop count to zero, and places the length of time this route is valid in the RREP's Lifetime field. However, if an intermediate node is responding, it places its record of the destination's sequence number in the packet, sets the hop count equal to its distance from the destination, and calculates the amount of time for which its route table entry for the destination will still be valid. It then unicasts the RREP toward the source node, using the node from which it received the RREQ as the next hop.

When an intermediate node receives the RREP, it sets up a *forward path* entry to the destination in its route table. This forward path entry contains the IP address of the destination, the IP address of the neighbor from which the RREP arrived, and the hop count, or distance, to the destination. To obtain its distance to the destination, the node increments the value in the Hop Count field by 1. Also associated with this entry is a lifetime, which is set to the lifetime contained in the RREP. Each time the route is used, its associated lifetime is updated. If the route is not used within the specified lifetime, it is deleted. After processing the RREP, the node forwards it toward the source. Figure 6.2 indicates the path of a RREP from the destination to the source node.

It is likely that a node will receive a RREP for a given destination from more than one neighbor. In this case, it forwards the first RREP it receives and forwards a later RREP only if that RREP contains a greater destination sequence number or a smaller hop count. Otherwise, the node discards the packet. This decreases the number of RREPs propagating toward the source while ensuring the most up-to-date and quickest routing information. The source node can begin data transmission as soon as the first RREP is received and can later update its routing information if it discovers a better route.

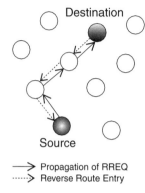

Figure 6.2. Route Determination from Source to Destination

6.2.4 Route Maintenance

Once a route has been discovered for a given source/destination pair, it is maintained as long as needed by the source node. Movement of nodes within the ad hoc network affects only the routes containing those nodes; such a path is called an *active path*. Movement not along an active path does not trigger any protocol action. If the source node moves during an active session, it can reinitiate route discovery to establish a new route to the destination. When either the destination or some intermediate node moves, however, a Route Error (RERR) message is sent to the affected source nodes. This RERR is initiated by the node upstream of the break (i.e., closer to the source nodes). It lists each of the destinations that are now unreachable because of the loss of the link. If the node upstream of the break has one or more nodes listed as a precursor node for the destination (implying that one or more nodes route through it in order to reach the destination), it broadcasts the RERR to these neighbors. When the neighbors receive the RERR, they mark their route to the destination as invalid by setting the distance to the destination equal to infinity and in turn propagate the RERR to their precursor nodes, if any such nodes are listed for the destinations in their route tables. When a source node receives the RERR, it can reinitate route discovery if the route is still needed.

Figure 6.3 illustrates the route maintenance procedure. In Figure 6.3(a), the original path from the source to the destination is through nodes 1, 2, and 3. Node 3 then moves to location 3′, causing a break in connectivity with node 2. Node 2 notices this break and send a RERR to node 1. Node 1 marks this route as invalid and then forwards the RERR to the source. On receiving the RERR, the source node determines that it still needs the route, and so it reinitiates route discovery. Figure 6.3(b) shows the new route found through node 4.

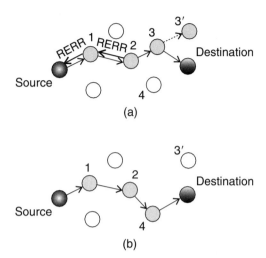

Figure 6.3. Route Maintenance

Route entries with an ∞ metric are not immediately deleted because they contain useful routing information with a recent destination timestamp. Instead, they expire in roughly the same amount of time as do reverse routes formed during route discovery. We believe that whenever current route information is generated in a particular region of the ad hoc network, it is too valuable to be discarded. Discarding current route information, even of the negative variety, is especially to be avoided for algorithms that depend on local repair mechanisms for reducing system-wide broadcasts.

If a node receives a data packet destined for a node for which it does not have an active route, it creates a RERR message for the destination node. It then broadcasts the RERR as previously described. In this way, the node without the route that is receiving the data packets can inform its upstream neighbor that it should stop sending the data packets, and the data packets are not sent indefinitely into a black hole.

6.2.5 Local Connectivity Management

Neighborhood information is obtained from broadcasts sent by neighboring nodes. Each time a node receives a broadcast from a given neighbor, it updates the Lifetime field associated with that neighbor in its route table. If there is no entry for that neighbor already in the table, the node creates one. In the event that a node has not broadcast anything within the last `hello_interval`, it can broadcast a Hello packet to inform its neighbors that it is still in the vicinity. The `hello_interval` is the maximum amount of time that can transpire before the node broadcasts a Hello packet—

generally set to 1 second. The Hello message is a special unsolicited RREP that contains the node's IP address and current sequence number. It is prevented from being rebroadcast outside the neighborhood of the node because it contains a TTL value of 1. The failure to receive any transmissions from a neighbor in the time defined by the periodic transmission of several Hello messages is an indication that the local connectivity has changed and that the route information for this neighbor should be updated.

Hello messages are incorporated into AODV so that the protocol need not rely on an underlying protocol, such as IEEE 802.11 [IEEE 1994], for connectivity information. If a MAC layer protocol capable of providing feedback information about unreachable next hops is run under AODV, the Hello messages need not be used.

6.2.6 Actions after Reboot

A node participating in the ad hoc network must take certain actions after reboot, as it will have lost its prior sequence number as well as its last known sequence numbers for various other destinations. Additionally, neighboring nodes may be using this node as an active next hop, which can create routing loops. To prevent this possibility, each node on reboot waits for `delete_period`, during which it does not respond to any routing packets. However, if it receives a data packet, it broadcasts a RERR, as described in Section 6.2.4, and resets the waiting timer (lifetime) to expire after the current time plus `delete_period`.

It can be shown that, by the time the rebooted node comes out of the waiting phase and becomes an active router again, none of its neighbors will still be using it as an active next hop. Its own sequence number is updated once it receives a RREQ from any other node, as the RREQ always carries the maximum destination sequence number seen en route.

6.3 MULTICAST ROUTE ESTABLISHMENT

Multicast route discovery follows directly from unicast route discovery in that it utilizes the same two message types (RREQ and RREP) for the route request/route reply discovery cycle. Multicast group membership is dynamic; nodes are able to join and leave the group at any time. As nodes join the group, a bidirectional multicast tree composed of group members and nodes used to connect them is created. Each multicast group has associated with it a multicast group leader. That node is responsible for maintaining the multicast group sequence number and is in no way a central point of failure.

6.3.1 Route Discovery

Multicast route discovery begins either when a node wishes to join a multicast group or when it has data to send to a multicast group and does not have a current route to it. This source node creates a RREQ with destination address set to the IP address of the multicast group and that contains the group's last known sequence number. The node indicates in the RREQ whether it wishes to join the multicast group (through a *Join* flag). It then broadcasts the RREQ to its neighbors.

If the RREQ is a join request, only a node that is a member of the desired multicast tree (i.e., a router for the group) may respond. Otherwise, any node with a current route to the multicast group may reply. If a node receives a join RREQ for a multicast group of which it is not a member, or if it receives a RREQ and does not have a route to that group, it creates a reverse route entry to the source and then broadcasts the RREQ to its neighbors. Figure 6.4(a) shows the propagation of a join RREQ.

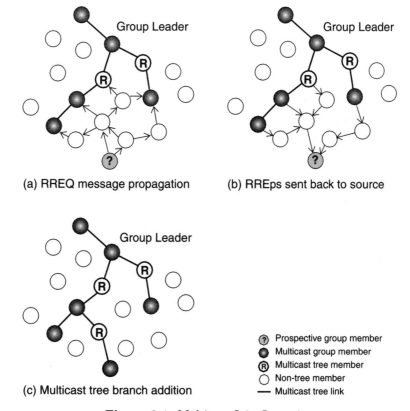

Figure 6.4. Multicast Join Operation

The source node waits the length of the discovery period to receive a reply. If it does not receive a reply within that time, it rebroadcasts its request with the broadcast ID increased by 1. It continues to do this until it either receives a reply or sends the RREQ rreq_retries additional times. If no reply is received after this maximum number of broadcasts, it can be assumed that no other group members exist in the connected portion of the network. If the node was attempting to join the group, it becomes that group's leader.

When a node receives a join RREQ for a multicast group, it adds an unactivated entry for the source node in its multicast route table. Each next-hop entry in the multicast route table has an associated Actived flag. If this flag is false, the node does not forward any data packets for the multicast group along that link. Only after the link is enabled can it be used to send data packets.

6.3.2 Forward Path Setup

If a node receives a join RREQ for a multicast group, it may reply if it is a router for the multicast group's tree and if its recorded sequence number for the multicast group is at least as great as that contained in the RREQ. Naturally, the group leader can always reply to a join RREQ for its multicast group. The responding node updates its multicast route table by placing the requesting node's next-hop information in the table and then generates a RREP. The node unicasts the RREP back to the node indicated in the RREQ. Figure 6.4(b) illustrates the path of the RREPs to the source node.

As nodes along the path to the source node receive the RREP, they set up a forward path entry for the multicast group in their multicast route table by adding the node from which they received the RREP as a next hop. Then they increment the Hop Count field and forward the RREP to the next node.

6.3.3 Multicast Route Activation/Deactivation

The source node must wait the length of the route discovery interval before using the route. If the request is to join the tree, the RREPs set up potential branches. The selected path to the tree must be explicitly activated at the end of the discovery interval so that one of these paths may be grafted onto the tree. Similarly, RREPs for a nonjoin request set up paths to the multicast tree. Because multicast data packets may be sent as broadcast traffic, neighboring nodes that forward RREPs to the source node all have routes to the multicast tree. When a multicast data packet is transmitted, each of these neighboring nodes can rebroadcast the packet, resulting in an inefficient use of bandwidth. Hence, only one of these paths must be selected for data packet forwarding.

During the discovery interval, the source node keeps track of the route with the greatest multicast group sequence number and the smallest hop count to the multicast tree. At the end of the discovery interval, it activates that route by unicasting a *multicast activation* (MACT) message to its selected next hop and by setting the Activated flag for that entry in its multicast route table. Once the next hop receives this message, it activates the route and, if it was not the originator of the RREP, then sends its own MACT message to *its* next hop. This continues until the originator of the RREP is reached. At that point, the new path to the multicast tree has been determined. For a join request this branch has been successfully added to the multicast tree and can be used for forwarding data packets to the new multicast group member. Figure 6.4(c) illustrates a multicast tree branch addition created in this manner.

The MACT message is also used when a node wishes to revoke its member status and leave the multicast group. If a leaf node wishes to leave the group, it may do so and then prune itself from the tree. If a nonleaf node decides to leave the group, it may, but it must not prune itself from the tree. Doing so would leave the tree partitioned, so it must continue to serve as a router for the tree.

A leaf node that wishes to revoke its member status unicasts a MACT message with the Prune flag set to its next hop. It then deletes the multicast group information from its multicast route table. When the next hop receives the prune message, it deletes the next-hop information for the sending node. If the deletion of this next-hop entry makes this node a leaf, and if the node is not a multicast group member, it may similarly prune itself from the tree by unicasting a prune message to its next hop. Otherwise, if it is still not a leaf node or if it is a member of the multicast group, it does not prune itself from the tree.

Figure 6.5 illustrates the removal of a multicast group member from the multicast tree. In Figure 6.5(a), node A decides to leave the group and sends its upstream neighbor, node B, a MACT message with a set Prune flag. When node B receives the MACT message and deletes node A from its list of next hops, it discovers that it is now a leaf node itself. Because it is a router for the tree and not a group member, it in turn sends a MACT message to its next hop. Figure 6.5(b) shows the multicast tree after the prune.

6.3.4 Multicast Tree Maintanence

The multicast tree must be maintained for the lifetime of the multicast group. Because the network nodes are likely to be moving, continual topological changes in the network are possible. This causes breaks in the links on the multicast tree. Unlike in the unicast scenario, however, a link break

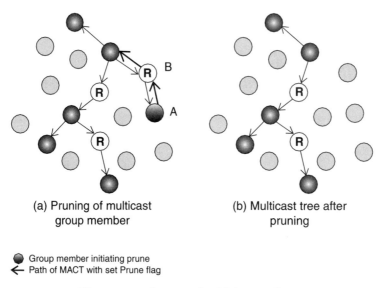

       (a) Pruning of multicast   (b) Multicast tree after
            group member   pruning

⬤ Group member initiating prune
← Path of MACT with set Prune flag

Figure 6.5. Leaving the Multicast Group

necessarily triggers route reconstruction because the multicast group members must remain connected during the group's lifetime. Stated another way, each multicast link requires ongoing route maintenance to ensure that other multicast tree members are always reachable; a unicast destination does not need to be reachable unless another node is currently sending packets to it. Multicast tree maintenance takes two forms: repairing a broken tree branch following a link break, and reconnecting the tree after a network partition.

Link Breaks

Nodes may notice a link break on the multicast tree in one of two ways. If no data packets have been sent recently, a node must receive a broadcast from each of its next hops at every `hello_interval`. This broadcast can be a RREQ, a GRPH (Group Hello—see next section), a multicast data packet, or a Hello message. A Hello message is a form of unsolicited RREP, with a TTL of 1, as described in Section 6.2.5. If a node has not broadcast anything within the last `hello_interval`, it must broadcast a Hello so that its next hops on the multicast tree know that it is still within transmission radius. Failure to receive any broadcasts from a next hop on the multicast tree for

$$\texttt{hello\_life} = (1 + \texttt{allowed\_hello\_loss}) * \texttt{hello\_interval}$$

indicates that the next hop is out of transmission range and so the link must be repaired.

When a link break occurs, the node *downstream* of the break (i.e., the node that is farther from the multicast group leader) is responsible for repairing it. This distinction is made because if nodes on both sides of the break try to repair the link, they may establish different paths and thus form a loop. The downstream node initiates the repair by broadcasting a join RREQ for the multicast group which includes an Extension field indicating the sending node's distance from the group leader. Only nodes on the multicast tree that are at least this close to the multicast group leader may reply to the RREQ. This prevents nodes on the same side of the break as the initiating node from responding, thereby ensuring that a new route to the group leader is found.

Because the node with which the initiating node lost contact is likely to still be nearby, the initial TTL of the RREQ is set to a small value. In this way, the effects of the link break can be localized. If no RREP is received within the local discovery period, all successive RREQs are broadcast across the network. Any node can respond to a RREQ by sending a RREP as long as it satisfies the following conditions:

- It is a part of the multicast tree.
- It has a fresh enough multicast group sequence number.
- Its hop count to the multicast group leader is smaller than that indicated by the extension field of the RREQ.

Forward path setup and subsequent route deletions occur as described in Sections 6.3.2 and 6.3.3. In Figure 6.6(a), the node indicated as downstream initiates the repair by broadcasting the RREQ. In this example, it sets the extension Hop Count field to 2 because it is two hops from the group leader.

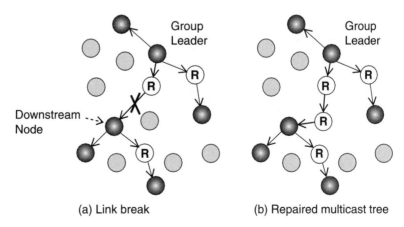

(a) Link break   (b) Repaired multicast tree

Figure 6.6. Repair of a Broken Tree Link

At the end of the discovery period, the node selects its next hop and unicasts a MACT message to it to activate the link, as described in Section 6.3.3. Because the node was repairing a tree break, it is possible that it is now a different distance from the group leader than it was before the break. If this is the case, it must inform its downstream next hops of their new distance from the group leader by broadcasting a MACT message with the Update flag set and the Hop Count field set to the node's new distance. This Update flag indicates that multicast tree nodes should update their distance. If these nodes have downstream next hops, they must send them a MACT message with a set Update flag, and so on. The Hop Count field is incremented by 1 each time the packet is received. Figure 6.6(b) illustrates the multicast tree after the repair has been completed.

When a link breaks, it is possible that the tree will be repaired through different intermediate nodes. Hence, if the node upstream of the break is not a group member, and if the loss of that link causes it to become a leaf node, it sets a prune timer to wait for the link to be repaired. This `prune_timeout` should be larger than the route discovery time so as to give the link time to be repaired. If, when this timer expires, the node has not received a MACT message selecting it to be a part of the repaired tree branch, it prunes itself from the tree by sending a MACT with a set Prune flag to its next hop, as described in Section 6.3.3.

The expanding ring search described in Section 6.2.2 may also be applied to breaks in the multicast tree. The initial TTL should be set to some small value because it is likely that the two nodes that lost contact are still in relative proximity of each other. If the link is not reestablished, the TTL may be increased by some increment until either the link is repaired or the threshold is reached, as previously described.

If the node initiating the repair does not receive a RREP after `rreq_retries` additional attempts, it can be assumed that the network has become partitioned and that at this time the tree cannot be repaired. Because this side of the partition is then left without a group leader, a new leader must be selected and can be in a number of ways. If the node attempting to repair the link is itself a group member, it becomes the group leader. Otherwise, if the loss of the link has made it a leaf node, the node sends a prune message to its next hop and prunes itself from the tree. The next hop, on receiving the prune message, notes that the message came from its upstream link. If this node is a group member, it becomes the new group leader. Otherwise, it proceeds as the previous node proceeded.

If the node initiating the repair is not a group member, and if it has more than one downstream link, it cannot prune itself from the tree because doing so would leave the tree partitioned. Instead, the node selects one of its next hops and unicasts a MACT message with a set *Group Leader* flag that indicates that the next group member to receive the message should become the group leader. If the next hop is a group member, it becomes the group leader. Otherwise, it selects one of its downstream hops and unicasts to it a MACT message with a set Group Leader flag. This process continues until a group member receives the MACT message and becomes the group leader.

However the new group leader is selected, there are now two group leaders for the multicast group.

Reconnecting Partitioned Trees

After a network partition, topological changes in the network can reconnect two network components. A multicast tree member from one partition will know that it has new connectivity to another partition if it receives a *Group Hello* (GRPH) message for the multicast group that contains group leader information different from its own records. For this purpose, the GRPH message is periodically broadcast by the multicast group leader across the network. It contains the IP address of the group leader and the IP address and current sequence number of the multicast group for which it is the group leader. If a group leader receives a GRPH message for a multicast group of which it is a leader, and if the group leader information contained in that message indicates that a different node is the group leader, then by implication two partitions of the same multicast tree are now within communication range of each other. A repair of the multicast tree must take place, initiated by the group leader with the lower IP address. This distinction is made so that only one group leader attempts to repair the tree, thereby avoiding the potential for forming loops.

The group leader with the lower IP address (GL_1) *unicasts* a RREQ to the other group leader (GL_2) using the node from which it received the GRPH message as the next hop. This RREQ has a *Repair* flag that indicates special handling. It also contains GL_1's record of the multicast group sequence number. If any nodes on GL_2's tree receive the RREQ, they must forward it along a branch of the multicast tree toward GL_2. This enables the two trees to be connected without any loops being formed. When GL_2 receives the RREQ, it takes the larger of its record of the multicast group sequence number and that indicated in the RREQ; it then increments this value by 1 and unicasts a RREP back to GL_1. This RREP also has the Repair flag set. As nodes receive this message, they add the next-hop entry to their multicast route table and activate it. If any node on GL_1's multicast tree receives the RREP as it travels back to GL_1, it must forward it along the multicast tree toward GL_1. The node also reverses the link directions in its multicast route table to indicate that the node from which it received the RREP is now the upstream link and that the next hop toward GL_1 is now a downstream link. When GL_1 receives the RREP, the tree is reconnected. Figure 6.7 illustrates a tree reconnected in this manner.

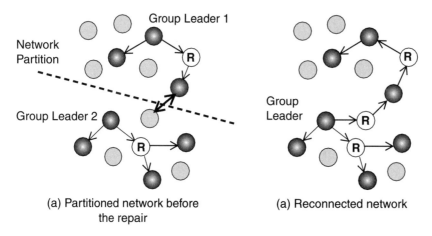

Figure 6.7. Merge of Partitioned Multicast Trees

6.3.5 Actions after Reboot

A node participating in the multicast tree that reboots (or restarts the routing daemon) might lose all of its multicast tree information. Upon reboot, a node should broadcast a MACT message with a set *Reboot* flag to inform neighboring nodes of the loss. Because the rebooted node does not know whether it was previously a member of the multicast tree, it should broadcast this packet unconditionally when it begins routing. When a node on the multicast tree receives the reboot MACT message, it checks whether this message came from one of its next hops on the multicast tree. If so, one of two situations exists.

If the reboot MACT came from a downstream link, the node deletes that link from its list of next hops and sets a prune timer according to the guidelines in Section 6.3.4. If the reboot MACT came from a node's upstream link, it must rebuild the tree branch as also indicated in that section.

6.4 BROADCAST

AODV specifies behavior for transmitting broadcasts. When a node wishes to generate a broadcast, it sends the broadcast packet to the well-known broadcast address 255.255.255.255.

Every node maintains a list of those broadcast packets that have already been received and retransmitted. This list contains the source IP address and the 16-bit IP `ident` value from the IP header of each broadcast packet it receives. It stores these values for `broadcast_record_time`.

When a node receives a packet broadcast to address 255.255.255.255, it notes the source IP address, the IP `ident` value, and the fragment effect of the packet's IP header. It then checks its broadcast list entries to determine whether the packet has already been received and thus whether it has already been retransmitted. If there is no such matching entry, the node processes and retransmits the broadcast packet. If there is such an entry, the node silently discards the packet.

6.5 SIMULATIONS

Numerous simulations of AODV have been performed using the GloMoSim [Bajaj+ 1997] simulation package. The simulations described in this section all use a model environment like GloMoSim. The mobility model used in each of the simulations is known as random direction [Royer+ 2000]. In each simulation, nodes are initially placed randomly within a predefined $L \times L$ area. Each node then chooses a random direction between 0 and 360 degrees and a speed from some predefined range; it then proceeds in that direction at that speed. Once the node reaches the boundary of the room, it chooses a period of time to remain stationary (again from some predefined range). At the end of this "pause time," the node chooses a new direction, this time between 0 and 180 degrees, adjusted relative to the wall of the room on which the node is located. The node then resumes movement at a newly selected speed. This process repeats throughout the simulation, causing continuous changes in the topology of the underlying network.

The MAC layer protocol used in the simulations is the IEEE standard 802.11 Distributed Coordination Function (DCF) [IEEE 1994]. This standard uses request-to-send (RTS) and clear-to-send (CTS) control packets for unicast data transmissions between neighboring nodes. A node wishing to unicast a data packet to its neighbor broadcasts a short RTS control packet. When its neighbor receives the packet, it responds with a CTS packet. Once the source node receives the CTS, it transmits the data packet. After receiving this unicast data packet, the destination then sends an acknowledgment (ACK) to the source, signifying reception. The use of the RTS and CTS control packets reduces the potential for the hidden terminal problem [Tobagi+ 1975]. Broadcast data packets and RTS control packets are sent using the unslotted Carrier Sense Multiple Access protocol with Collision Avoidance (CSMA/CA) [IEEE 1994]. When a node wishes to broadcast a packet, it first senses the channel. If it does not detect an ongoing transmission, it broadcasts its packet. If it does detect a transmission, it calculates a backoff time to wait before trying the transmission again. Broadcast packets are not acknowledged.

The data rate for the simulations is 2 Mb/second, and the data packet size is 64 bytes. The propagation model used is known as free space

[Rappaport 1996] with threshold cutoff included in the GloMoSim simulation package. The free space model has a power signal attenuation of $1/d^2$, where d is the distance between nodes. The radio model used also has capture capability, whereby it can lock on to a strong signal in the face of other signal interference and still receive the packet. Other interfering packets with weaker signal strength are dropped.

Simulations of both unicast and multicast operation of the protocol have been performed. Each class of simulation is run for node movement speeds between 0 meters/sec and 10 meters/sec for unicast and 0 meters/sec and 5 meters/sec for multicast. For each movement speed, ten simulation runs are completed, each of which has a different initial network configuration. The results of these simulations are averaged together to produce the resulting graphs. Each simulation models 300 seconds of real time.

6.5.1 Unicast Simulations

The unicast simulations have been performed using four networks of 50, 100, 250, and 500 nodes, respectively. Sessions are created between randomly chosen sources and destinations throughout the simulation. Once a session is begun, data packets are sent at a rate of four packets per second until either the simulation ends or the maximum number of packets for that session is reached. Twenty such data sessions are created during the simulations. If at any time a route to the destination cannot be found after `rreq_retries` + 1 attempts, the session is aborted. The interconnection pattern of an ad hoc network is determined in part by the communication range (R_{max}). For the simulations described here, R_{max} is held constant at 250 meters. The room sizes for the different numbers of nodes are shown in Table 6.1. They were chosen so that the node density is approximately constant in the different simulations (Figure 6.8).

The primary objective of these simulations is to show that AODV can find routes quickly and accurately and can maintain them as long as they are needed. To evaluate AODV's performance, a variety of results are examined.

Figure 6.9 shows the achieved packet delivery ratio for each of the different-sized networks. The packet delivery ratio is similar to throughput in that it represents the number of data packets received compared to

Table 6.1. Room Sizes for Network Simulations

Number of Nodes	50	100	250	500
Room Size	$1{,}000 \times 1{,}000$ meters^2	$1{,}500 \times 1{,}500$ meters^2	$2{,}400 \times 2{,}400$ meters^2	$3{,}450 \times 3{,}450$ meters^2

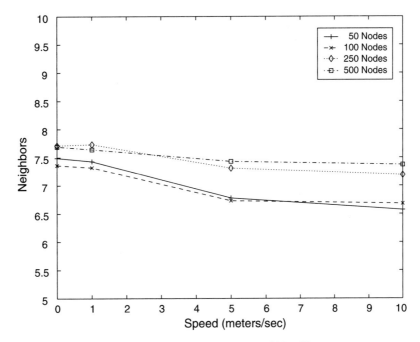

Figure 6.8. Average Number of Neighbors

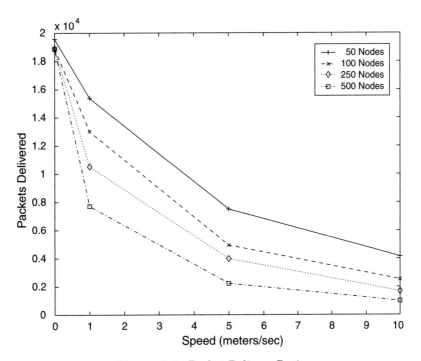

Figure 6.9. Packet Delivery Ratio

number sent. Because nodes are frequently moving and routes between nodes break, the ratio is not likely to be 100%. AODV does not retransmit data packets that are lost because of node movement and hence does not guarantee packet delivery. However, it does find good routes for IP's best-effort delivery, and the packet delivery ratio is high. The graph in Figure 6.9 shows that for stationary networks the ratio is approximately constant across the different-sized networks. As node mobility increases, however, the number of deliverable packets decreases at a more rapid rate for the large networks than for the small. This is due to the longer path lengths required to maintain connectivity between sources and destinations in the larger networks, as will be shown in a later figure.

Figure 6.10 represents the amount of overhead in terms of RREQ, RREP, and RERR messages sent. The simulations presented do not utilize the expanding ring search described in Section 6.2.2. Each RREQ is broadcast across the entire network, so there are a large number of RREPs generated, specifically in the larger-sized networks. The expanding ring search significantly reduces this number.

To show that AODV finds routes in a timely manner, route acquisition latency is examined. It is computed by noting the simulation time when an initial RREQ is broadcast for a given destination and then noting the time

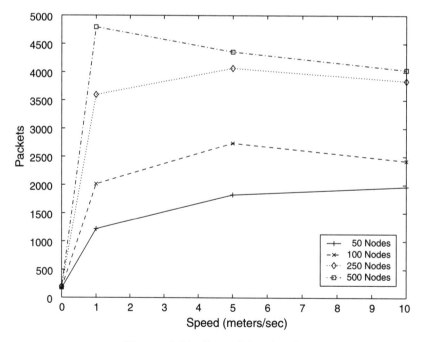

Figure 6.10. Control Overhead

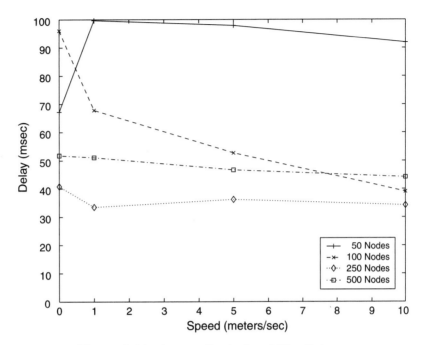

Figure 6.11. Average Route Acquisition Latency

when the first RREP is received at the source. For successive RREQ retries
for the same route, the start time for the route is held at the time at which
the first RREQ is sent. If a route to a destination is never found, this time
lapse is not taken into account in the computation. Figure 6.11 represents
the average route acquisition latency for the simulations. It indicates that
there is no significant difference between the different network sizes and
mobility levels. The delay is more a factor of the network topologies and
the queueing delays experienced at the individual nodes. In all cases, routes
can be discovered with minimal delay.

Figure 6.12 shows the average path length of discovered routes. Because
the node density is kept nearly constant, the nodes in the larger networks
occupy a greater area and hence more hops are needed to connect a given
source/destination pair.

To further verify that the longer paths result in more link breaks, the
number of route repairs per simulation is shown in Figure 6.13. An interesting phenomenon occurs here. For low mobilities, the larger networks
require more route repairs because of the longer path, but once a certain
mobility threshold is reached the repairs in the larger networks are actually fewer than those in the smaller networks. This indicates that the
long path/high mobility combination makes routing extremely difficult—

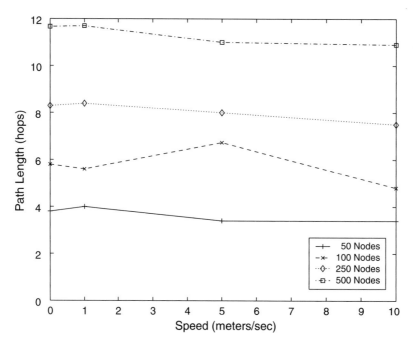

Figure 6.12. Average Path Length

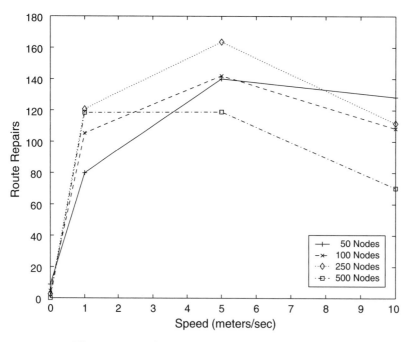

Figure 6.13. Average Number of Route Repairs

so difficult, in fact, that sessions are likely to be aborted because of the inability to acquire a route that is stable enough to send data packets across it. The route must be stable between the time that the RREQ is transmitted and the time that the RREP is received at the source, so that the RREP can be successfully routed back to the source. For long path lengths and high mobilities, the probability of a route break during route discovery becomes so high that eventually routes cannot be maintained and the session must be terminated.

6.5.2 Multicast Simulations

As with unicast, it is important to verify the correct operation of the AODV multicast protocol as well as to evaluate the amount of overhead created by it and its efficiency in delivering data packets to the multicast group members. To this end, simulations of 50- and 100-node networks are modeled with the unicast respective room sizes. Four different node mobilities are modeled: 0 meters/sec, 1 meters/sec, 3 meters/sec, and 5 meters/sec. Again, each parameter combination is run for ten initial configurations, and the results are averaged to produce the graphs.

In the following simulations, there is one multicast group that nodes can join. Ten randomly selected nodes join the group at the beginning of the simulation and remain members for the duration. Once all ten have joined the group, one begins sending data packets to the rest of the group and continues to do so until the simulation ends. Data packets are 64 bytes and are sent at a rate of four per second.

To evaluate the performance of the protocol, the packet delivery ratio is examined. To achieve a 100% ratio, each member of the multicast group must receive every data packet that is transmitted by the source. Hence, each transmission is in effect multiplied by ten to account for the ten group members, and then each time a group member receives a data packet the received packet count is incremented. Because multicast traffic is transmitted locally by broadcast, the next hop may fail to receive the transmission, unlike the unicast case. There is no MAC layer feedback to determine whether the next hop has moved out of range, and there is the possibility of collision because of the packet being broadcast. As in unicast, when a link break occurs packets are dropped until the link is repaired. Because of these characteristics, and because of the multitude of links that must be maintained across the multicast tree, the packet delivery ratio is not likely to be 100%.

Figure 6.14 illustrates the achieved packet delivery ratio for the simulations. For zero mobility, the number of received data packets is between 95% and 100%. Packet delivery of 100% is not achieved for zero mobility because of the possibility of collisions. As the speed of node movement increases, the packet delivery ratio decreases as it becomes more and more

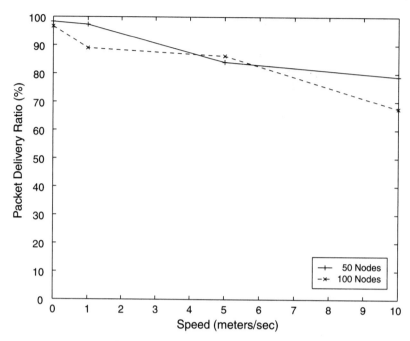

Figure 6.14. Packet Delivery Ratio

difficult to maintain the multicast tree links. For slow node mobilities, however, the protocol performs well, achieving between 87% and 97% packet delivery. As node movement increases, the smaller network outperforms the larger network by an increasingly greater margin.

Before examining the specific characteristics of the different networks, the amount of control overhead generated is studied. Figure 6.15 represents the total number of control packets generated per simulation. This number is found by summing the RREQ, RREP, MACT, GRPH, and Hello messages transmitted during the simulation. As stated in Section 6.3.4, Hello messages are needed to monitor the status of multicast tree links. The two networks have similar amounts of control traffic for the stationary networks. As mobility increases, however, the number of control messages needed to maintain the 100-node network increases at a much greater rate than that needed by the 50-node network. This is due to the greater number of links maintained on the multicast tree in the 100-node network because of the larger network area. Again, as node mobility increases, the number of control messages also increases because the need to repair multicast tree branches is more frequent.

Figures 6.16 and 6.17 give a breakdown of the control messages generated for the 50- and 100-node networks, respectively. The number of Hello

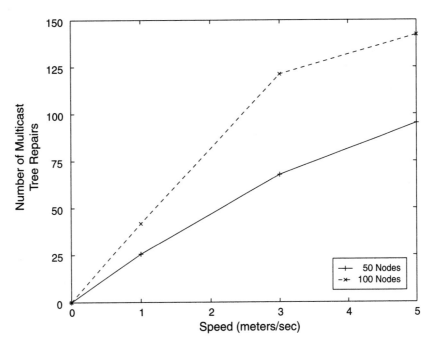

Figure 6.15. Total Control Overhead

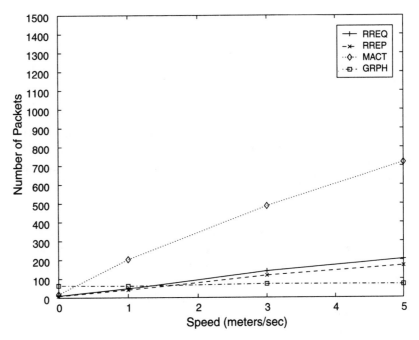

Figure 6.16. Control Overhead in a 50-Node Network

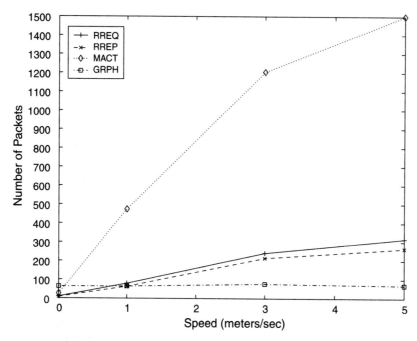

Figure 6.17. Control Overhead in a 100-Node Network

messages is not shown. The figures show that the MACT messages clearly dominate the control traffic, particularly for higher mobilities. The GRPHs are sent periodically and are not affected by the movement speed. The number of RREQs and RREPs sent increase as node movement increases but by a much smaller percentage than that for the number of MACTs. A breakdown of the MACT message overhead is shown in Figures 6.18 and 6.19. The MACT link activations and updates are the dominant forms of MACT traffic sent. The number of prune messages is minimal and there are no GRPLDR (Group Leader) messages sent because of the infrequent partitioning of the multicast tree in these scenarios.

To understand why the speed of the nodes has such an effect on the packet delivery ratio and the amount of control overhead, it is necessary to examine some other results from the simulations. Figure 6.20 shows the number of repairs needed for the multicast tree. As node movement increases, more and more repairs are needed to keep the tree intact. The 100-node network requires more repairs than the 50-node network because of its larger size. Figure 6.21 shows that the average distance from a group member to the group leader in the 100-node network is a hop or two greater than that in the 50-node network. Because of the additional length of the

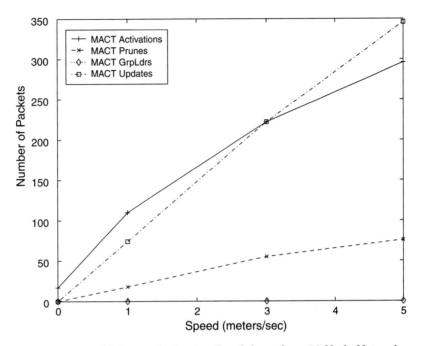

Figure 6.18. Multicast Activation Breakdown for a 50-Node Network

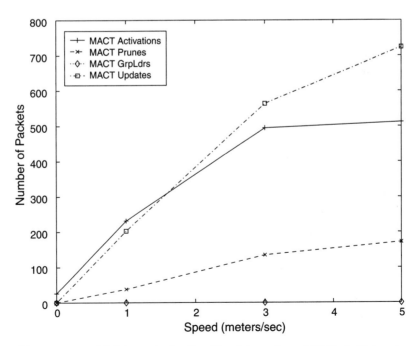

Figure 6.19. Multicast Activation Breakdown for a 100-Node Network

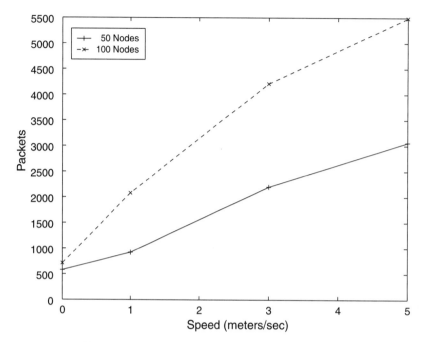

Figure 6.20. Number of Multicast Tree Repairs

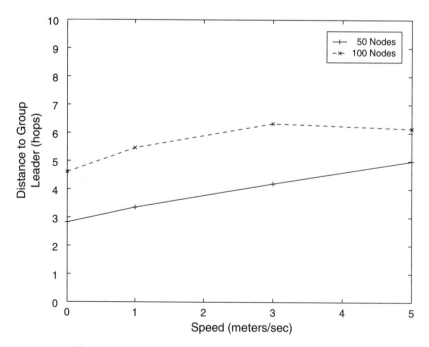

Figure 6.21. Average Distance to the Group Leader

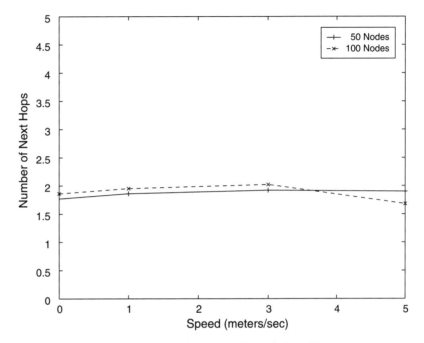

Figure 6.22. Average Number of Next Hops

tree branches in this network, tree link breaks are more likely to occur and hence more repairs are needed. The increased number of repairs results in a lower packet delivery ratio and a greater amount of control overhead, as was shown in Figures 6.14 and 6.15.

Finally, Figure 6.22 illustrates the average number of next hops for multicast group members. This graph gives an idea of the structure of multicast trees. The number of next hops in both networks is just under two, indicating that most group members are either leaf nodes or have just a couple of next hops.

6.6 OPTIMIZATIONS AND ENHANCEMENTS

Through simulation, AODV has shown excellent performance in various network scenarios (Section 6.5). However, there are still ways to improve it as well as to enhance it so that it can provide additional services and be more versatile. The following sections describe methods for optimizating and enhancing AODV.

6.6.1 Quality of Service

AODV defines extensions that can be used to request certain quality of service parameters—in particular, Maximum Delay and Minimum Bandwidth—which can be appended to a RREQ. To respond to a RREQ with such extensions, a node must be able to satisfy the indicated quality of service constraints in addition to the conditions described in Section 6.3.3.

If after the establishment of such a route, any node along the path detects that it can no longer maintain the requested quality of service parameters, it must send an ICMP QOS_LOST message back to the node that originally requested them.

For the Minimum Bandwidth extension, no additional processing is needed because intermediate nodes rebroadcast the RREQ message containing it. For the Maximum Delay extension, each intermediate node must subtract its own characteristic value for adding delay to the handling of future data packets. This characteristic value depends on measured processing time as well as time-varying queue lengths. It is expected that queue lengths for incoming data packets will be fairly volatile, so a conservative reported value is preferred. Moreover, a forwarding node wishing to offer such delay assurances may be required to reduce queue delays for incoming packets from the requesting node. Further work may be needed to allow the forwarding nodes to distinguish among flows of various types from the same IP source node. With the current design, no such distinction is made.

6.6.2 Subnet Routing

In many situations, a collection of nodes within the ad hoc network share a fixed relationship with one another with respect to both their IP addresses and their mutual reachability. If the nodes are all mutually reachable by a single hop and their IP addresses fall within a range that can be encompassed with a single convenient subnet prefix, and if all nodes with that subnet prefix are reachable in a single hop from all other nodes with the same subnet prefix, then the collection can be treated as a subnet. In this case, a route to any one of the nodes in the collection is nearly as good as a route to any other node, plus or minus one hop. Thus, route information to all of the nodes can be summarized by a single route table entry, and route aggregation is possible. Of course, this is the whole idea of subnets and CIDR in today's wide-area Internet [Rekhter+ 1993].

To work with AODV, routes to the subnet have to be assigned a destination sequence number just as multicast groups are assigned a sequence number. For subnets, all that is needed is that one of the nodes on the subnet take responsibility for creating and managing the sequence number. If there is a router on the subnet already, that node is the logical choice. If not, some other node has to be assigned this function as well as the function of forwarding traffic for other nodes on the subnet. The node managing the sequence number is called the *subnet leader,* and it must be considered the default router for all subnet nodes.

Nodes on the subnet that receive RREQs have to forward them to the subnet leader. The subnet leader creates a reverse route to its subnet nodes in the same way as to any other node in the network. RREP messages through any node on the subnet must be sent back to the source through the subnet leader. Other operations, including multicast tree maintenance, are handled similarly.

Notice that there is no notion of periodic route advertisement defined for AODV. Even with subnets, all route establishment is on demand only.

6.6.3 AODV and Mobile IP

The design motivation for AODV arises from the need to manage network connectivity for nodes that do not necessarily have access to any *network infrastructure*, which is typically taken to mean the backbone of the Internet. However, if some nodes within the ad hoc network actually do have access to the Internet, they can perform the role defined for *mobility agents* in Mobile IP [Perkins 1996]. There is more than one approach to offering Mobile IP to an ad hoc network. The approach described here was treated more fully in a previous publication [Lei+ 1997].

Suppose that an ad hoc node connected to the Internet agrees to serve as a *foreign agent* [Perkins 1996]. It is then expected to issue periodic advertisements to the wireless nodes within its range, indicating to them the availability of Mobile IP service and any relevant service conditions. For all nodes within the ad hoc network to have the service, the nodes neighboring the foreign agent must agree to rebroadcast the advertisements throughout. For the purposes of this rebroadcast, those neighboring nodes may assign the IP `ident` field of the advertisement, concatenated with the advertisement sequence number, as the 32-bit sequence number for the advertisement.

With this approach, each mobile ad hoc node can determine whether Mobile IP is available. For the hop count metric to be handled correctly, the foreign agent should allow registrations from mobile nodes that are farther than one hop from its wireless interface. This relaxation of the Mobile IP rules must not be enabled for registrations that arrive from any of the foreign agent's wired interfaces. Given the lack of security specified for any of the current ad hoc protocols, this is the only way to protect against remotely mounted denial of service attacks on the foreign agent.

With these modifications, Mobile IP can work. However, route table management turns out to be quite tricky if the ad hoc algorithms and the Mobile IP daemon do not have coordinated access to the route table. For this reason, in our previous work we implemented a route table manager, `rtmgr`, that had sole access to the route table. The `rtmgr` had to apply certain rules to keep a logical separation between routes to a foreign agent and those to its default router, and so on [Lei+ 1997].

6.7 FUTURE WORK

In this section, we mention a few important areas for future and planned development.

6.7.1 Security

As with any routing protocol, security for AODV will become important as soon as there are deployments and applications that require routing stability in the face of enemies with access to the basic communications medium. We have not taken any steps to provide this security up until now, hoping that any necessary support would be provided at the layers below IP. Unfortunately, such methods may not always be available. We believe that authentication and privacy methods adopted for other routing protocols will be sufficient for AODV and that our protocol has not introduced any special vulnerabilities to new protocol attacks.

6.7.2 Asymmetric Routing

There are many cases in which the assumption of link symmetry between neighboring nodes is not valid. Sometimes, unfortunately, a source might not be able to find any route to a destination where all links are symmetric. Thus, whenever AODV is deployed in a network where there are likely to be asymmetric links, care must be taken to prevent RREPs from being sent back to a last hop that will never hear them. For this purpose, we have defined an extension to the Hello message that includes the node's list of known neighbors. If a node receives several such Hello messages that do not contain its own IP address, it infers that it must not forward any data packets to the Hello messages' source.

Recent work in asymmetric routing has shown that some routes cannot be discovered with unicast messages sent in response to a broadcast route request. This is intuitively clear in cases in which the network is partitioned into two domains that are joined by two oppositely oriented asymmetric links. All other links can be symmetric and still no routes can be discovered between the domains, even though asymmetric routes enable perfect network connectivity in this example. It turns out that other asymmetric routing domains can be generically understood by similar arguments. The result is that for asymmetric routing domains, twice as many broadcasts are needed [Prakash 1999].

Asymmetric routing almost breaks IP whenever there is a need to resolve an IP address into a MAC (layer-2) address. Because ARP assumes bidirectional connectivity, it is useless in such cases, and address resolution has to proceed by unusual, special-case algorithms. Several such algorithms have been suggested, but none seem to be wholly satisfactory in our opinion.

Nevertheless, given the importance of establishing asymmetric routes, it is clear that AODV should be retooled to offer this feature. As detecting a broken asymmetric link is almost oxymoronic, any sort of route aging becomes problematic. To favor symmetric links by disabling asymmetric links, an acknowledgment strategy is required. Each recipient of a RREP then sends a RREP-ACK back to the sender (i.e., the next hop along the way to the desired destination listed in the RREP). If the recipient receives the RREP, it already knows that the link is bidirectional because the RREP is a response to the recipient's previous RREQ. The RREP-ACK thus guarantees bidirectionality to the next hop.

We would like to see simulations that establish the frequency of occurrence for asymmetric routes in general wireless topologies. Making a distance-vector protocol complicated for handling asymmetric routes must be justified by a large expected increase in applicability and/or throughput. If the work is justified, the challenge will be to allow complicated protocol actions in the asymmetric case while still allowing minimalist and nonintrusive protocol actions in the easier symmetric case.

6.8 CONCLUSION

We have presented AODV, our on-demand, distance-vector routing protocol for highly mobile wireless nodes. We claim that it offers excellent performance for both unicast and multicast routing and have exhibited some simulations to provide evidence for our assertion. We have presented the protocol details and interactions for AODV messages; message formats and bit assignments can be found in the appendix as well in the current Internet draft specification [Perkins+ 2000]. We will continue to explore the performance of AODV under new conditions of node mobility, density, traffic models, and radio propagation characteristics. We claim that AODV has the best chance to scale to large node populations; we know of only a couple of publications with results for node populations any greater than 100 or 200 [Pearlman+ 1999, Perkins+ 1999]. We have reported results for AODV with node populations as great as 10,000 nodes, including good delay and packet delivery measurements. We hope that our results will encourage further research and development for distance-vector routing protocols in general and AODV specifically.

References

[Bajaj+ 1997] L. Bajaj, M. Takai, R. Ahuja, K. Tang, R. Bagrodia, and M. Gerla. *GlomoSim: A Scalable Network Simulation Environment.* CSD technical report 990027, University of California at Los Angeles, 1997.

[IEEE 1994] IEEE Computer Society LAN MAN Standards Committee. *Wireless LAN Medium Access Control (MAC) and Physical Layer (PHY) Specification, IEEE Standard 802.11–1997.* International Society of Electrical and Electronics Engineers, New York, 1994.

[Lei+ 1997] H. Lei and C.E. Perkins. Ad Hoc Networking with Mobile IP. In *Proceedings of the Second European Personal Mobile Communications Conference,* October 1997, 197–202.

[Pearlman+ 1999] M.R. Pearlman and Z.J. Haas. Determining the Optimal Configuration for the Zone Routing Protocol. *IEEE Journal on Selected Areas of Communications* 17(8):1395–1414, August 1999.

[Perkins 1996] C. Perkins. IP Mobility Support. RFC 2002 (proposed standard), Internet Engineering Task Force, October 1996.

[Perkins+ 1994] C.E. Perkins and P. Bhagwat. Highly Dynamic Destination-Sequenced Distance-Vector Routing (DSDV) for Mobile Computers. *ACM SIG-COMM '94 Computer Communications Review* 24(4):234–244, October 1994.

[Perkins+ 1999] C.E. Perkins and E.M. Royer. Ad-hoc On-Demand Distance Vector Routing. In *Proceedings of the Second Annual IEEE Workshop on Mobile Computing Systems and Applications,* February 1999, 90–100.

[Perkins+ 2000] C.E. Perkins, E.M. Royer, and S.R. Das. *Ad Hoc On-Demand Distance-Vector (AODV) Routing.* IETF Internet draft (draft-ietf-manet-aodv-06.txt), July 2000 (work in progress).

[Prakash 1999] R. Prakash. Unidirectional Links Prove Costly in Wireless Ad Hoc Networks. In *Proceedings of the Third International Workshop on Discrete Algorithms and Methods for Mobile Computing and Communications (DIAL M),* August 1999, 15–22.

[Rappaport 1996] T.S. Rappaport. *Wireless Communications, Principles and Practices.* Prentice-Hall, Englewood Cliffs, N.J., 1996, 70–74.

[Rekhter+ 1993] Y. Rekhter and T. Li. An Architecture for IP Address Allocation with CIDR. RFC 1518 (proposed standard), Internet Engineering Task Force, September 1993.

[Royer+ 2000] E.M. Royer, P.M. Melliar-Smith, and L.E. Moser. An Analysis of the Optimum Node Density for Ad Hoc Mobile Networks (submitted for publication), 2000.

[Tobagi+ 1975] F.A. Tobagi and L. Kleinrock. Packet Switching in Radio Channels: Part II—The Hidden Terminal Problem in Carrier Sense Multiple-Access Models and the BusyTone Solution. *IEEE Transactions on Communications* COM-23(12):1417–1433, December 1975.

APPENDIX A: MESSAGE FORMATS

A.1 Route Request

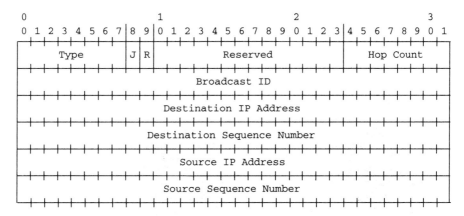

Figure 6.23. Route Request Message Format

The format of the Route Request (RREQ) message is illustrated in Figure 6.23 and contains the following fields:

Type—1

J—Join flag, set when a source node wants to join a multicast group.

R—Repair flag, set when a node wants to initiate a repair to connect two previously disconnected portions of the multicast tree.

Reserved—sent as 0, ignored on reception.

Hop Count—the number of hops from source IP address to the node handling the request.

Broadcast ID—a sequence number uniquely identifying the particular RREQ when taken in conjunction with the source node's IP address.

Destination IP Address—the IP address of the destination for which a route is desired.

Destination Sequence Number—the last sequence number received by the source for any route toward the destination.

Source IP Address—the IP address of the node that originated the route request.

Source Sequence Number—the current sequence number to be used for route entries pointing to (and generated by) the source of the route request.

When a node wishes to unicast the RREQ for a multicast group to the group leader, it includes the Multicast Group Leader extension (see Section B.2). When a node wishes to repair a multicast tree, it appends the Multicast Group Rebuild extension (see Section B.3).

A.2 Route Reply

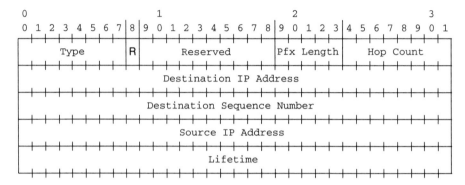

Figure 6.24. Route Reply Message Format

The format of the Route Reply (RREP) message is illustrated in Figure 6.24 and contains the following fields:

Type—2

R—Repair flag, set when a node is responding to a repair request to connect two previously disconnected portions of the multicast tree.

A—acknowledgment requests.

Reserved—sent as 0, ignored on reception.

Prefix Size—if nonzero, it specifies that the indicated next hop may be used for any nodes with the same routing prefix (as defined by Prefix Size) as that of the requested destination.

Hop Count—the number of hops from the source IP address to the destination IP address. For multicast route requests this indicates the number of hops to the multicast tree member sending the RREP.

Destination IP Address—the IP address of the destination for which a route is supplied.

Destination Sequence Number—the destination sequence number associated with the route.

Source IP Address—the IP address of the source node that issued the RREQ for which the route is supplied.

Lifetime—the time for which nodes receiving the RREP consider the route to be valid.

When the RREP is sent for a multicast destination, the Multicast Group Information extension is appended (see Section B.4).

Note that Prefix Size allows a subnet leader to supply a route for every host in the subnet defined by the routing prefix, which is determined by the IP address of the subnet leader and Prefix Size. To make use of this feature, the subnet leader has to guarantee reachability to all the hosts sharing the indicated subnet prefix. It is also responsible for maintaining the destination sequence number for the whole subnet.

A.3 Route Error

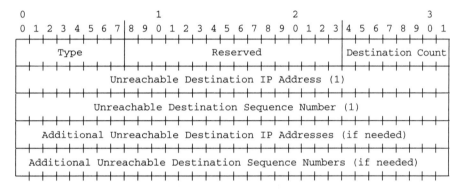

Figure 6.25. Route Error Message Format

The format of the Route Error (RERR) message is illustrated in Figure 6.25 and contains the following fields:

Type—3

Reserved—sent as 0, ignored on reception.

DestCount—the number of unreachable destinations included in the message; it must be at least 1.

Unreachable Destination IP Address—the IP address of the destination that has become unreachable because of a link break.

Unreachable Destination Sequence Number—the last known sequence number, incremented by 1, of the destination listed in the previous Unreachable Destination IP Address field.

The RERR message is sent whenever a link break causes one or more destinations to become unreachable. The unreachable destination addresses included are those of all lost destinations that are now unreachable because of the loss of that link.

A.4 Multicast Activation

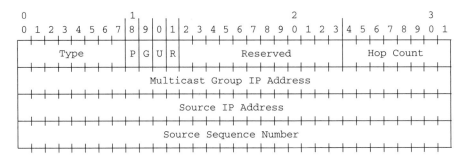

Figure 6.26. Multicast Activation Message Format

The format of the Multicast Activation (MACT) message is illustrated in Figure 6.26 and contains the following fields:

Type—4

J—Join flag, set when a node is joining the multicast group, as opposed to when finding a route to the group for the transmission of data messages.

P—Prune flag, set when a node wishes to prune itself from the tree and unset when the node is activating a tree link.

G—Group Leader flag, set by a multicast tree member that fails to repair a multicast tree link breakage. It indicates to the group member receiving the message that it should become the new multicast group leader.

U—Update flag, set when a multicast tree member has repaired a broken tree link and is now a new distance from the group leader.

R—Reboot flag, set when a node has just rebooted (see Section 6.3.5).

Reserved—sent as 0, ignored on reception.

Hop Count—the distance of the sending node from the multicast group leader. It is used only when the Update flag is set; otherwise, it is sent as 0.

Multicast Group IP Address—the IP address of the multicast group for which a route is supplied.

Source IP Address—the IP address of the sending node.

Source Sequence Number—the current sequence number for route information generated by the source of the route request.

To prune itself from the tree (i.e., to inactivate its last link to the multicast tree), a multicast tree member sends a MACT with the Prune flag set to 1 to its next hop on the multicast tree. A multicast tree member that has more than one next hop to the multicast tree should not prune itself from the tree.

A.5 Group Hello

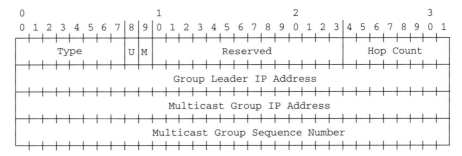

Figure 6.27. Group Hello Message Format

The format of the Group Hello message is illustrated in Figure 6.27 and contains the following fields:

Type—5

U—Update flag, set when there has been a change in group leader information.

M—**Off_Mtree** flag, set by a node receiving the GRPH which is not on the multicast tree.

Reserved—sent as 0, ignored on reception.

Hop Count—the number of hops the packet has traveled, used by multicast tree nodes to update their distance from the group leader when the **Off_Mtree** flag is not set.

Group Leader IP Address—the IP address of the group leader.

Multicast Group IP Address—the IP address of the multicast group for which the sequence number is supplied.

Multicast Group Sequence Number—the current sequence number of the multicast group.

APPENDIX B: EXTENSION FORMATS

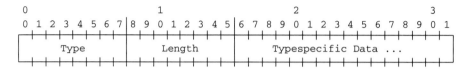

Figure 6.28. General Extension Format

RREQ and RREP messages have the extensions defined in Figure 6.28 and contain the following fields:

Type—the type of the extension.

Length—the length of the type-specific data, not including the Type and Length fields of the extension.

Extensions with types between 128 and 255 may *not* be skipped. The rules for extension, to be spelled out more fully, conform to those for handling IPv6 options.

B.1 Hello Interval

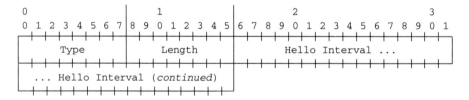

Figure 6.29. Hello Interval Extension Format

The format of the Hello Internal extension is shown in Figure 6.29 and contains the following fields:

Type—2

Length—4 .

Hello Interval—the number of milliseconds between successive transmissions of a Hello message.

The Hello Interval extension may be appended to a RREP message with TTL == 1. It is used by a neighboring receiver to determine how long to wait for subsequent RREP messages (i.e., Hello messages, as discussed in Section 6.2.5).

B.2 Multicast Group Leader

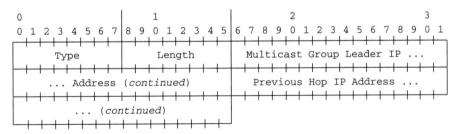

Figure 6.30. Multicast Group Leader Extension Format

The Multicast Group Leader extension is appended to a RREQ by a node wishing to repair a multicast tree. It is defined in Figure 6.30 and contains the following fields:

Type—3

Length—8

Multicast Group Leader IP Address—the IP address of the multicast group leader.

Previous Hop IP Address—the IP address of the node that previously received the RREQ; it is used when the RREQ is unicast to the group leader when a node wishes to join a multicast group.

    Each node receiving a RREQ updates the Previous Hop IP Address field to reflect its address.

B.3 Multicast Group Rebuild

Figure 6.31. Multicast Group Repair Extension Format

The Multicast Group Rebuild extension is appended to a RREQ by a node wishing to repair a multicast tree. It is defined in Figure 6.31 and contains the following fields:

Type—4

Length—2

Multicast Group Hop Count—the distance in hops between the node sending the RREQ and the multicast group leader.

This extension is used for rebuilding a multicast tree branch and to ensure that only nodes as least as close to the group leader as indicated by the Multicast Group Hop Count field respond to the request.

B.4 Multicast Group Information

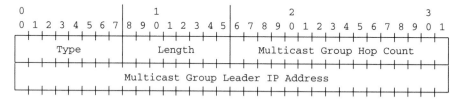

Figure 6.32. Multicast Group Information Extension Format

The Multicast Group Information extension is used to carry additional information for the RREP message (see Section A.2) when sent to establish a route to a multicast destination. It is defined in Figure 6.32 and contains the following fields:

Type—5

Length—6

Multicast Group Hop Count—the distance of the node from the multicast group leader.

Multicast Group Leader IP Address—the IP address of the current multicast group leader.

This extension is included when a node is responding to a RREQ to join a multicast group. The node places its distance from the group leader in the Multicast Group Hop Count field.

B.5 Maximum Delay

Figure 6.33. Maximum Delay Extension Format

The Maximum Delay extension is illustrated in Figure 6.33 and contains the following fields:

Type—6

Length—2

Max Delay—the number of seconds allowed for a transmission from the source to the destination.

This extension can be appended to a RREQ by a requesting node in order to place a maximum bound on the acceptable time delay experienced on any acceptable path from the source to the destination.

Before forwarding the RREQ, an intermediate node must compare its `node_traversal_time` to the (remaining) maximum delay indicated by the Maximum Delay extension. If the Max Delay is less, the node must discard the RREQ without processing it any further. Otherwise, the node subtracts its `node_traversal_time` from the Max Delay value in the extension and continues processing the RREQ, as specified in Section 6.2.1.

B.6 Minimum Bandwidth

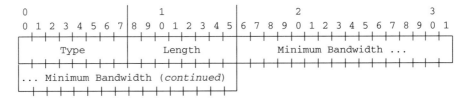

Figure 6.34. Minimum Bandwidth Extension Format

The Minimum Bandwidth extension is illustrated in Figure 6.34 and contains the following fields:

Type—7

Length—4

Minimum Bandwidth—the amount of bandwidth (in kilobits/sec) needed for acceptable transmission from the source to the destination.

The Minimum Bandwidth extension can be appended to a RREQ by a requesting node to specify the minimal amount of bandwidth that must be made available along an acceptable path from the source to the destination.

Before forwarding the RREQ, an intermediate node must compare its available link capacity to the minimum bandwidth indicated in the extension. If the requested amount of bandwidth is not available, the node must discard the RREQ without processing it any further. Otherwise, the node continues processing the RREQ, as specified in Section 6.2.1.

APPENDIX C: CONFIGURATION PARAMETERS

This section gives defaults for some important values associated with the AODV protocol operations (see Table 6.1). A particular mobile node may wish to change certain of the parameters—in particular, `net_diameter`, `my_route_timeout`, `allowed_hello_loss`, `rreq_retries`, and possibly `hello_interval`. In the last case, the node should advertise the `hello_interval` in its Hello messages by appending a Hello Interval extension to the RREP. The choice of parameters may affect the performance of the protocol.

`net_diameter` measures the maximum possible number of hops between two nodes in the network. `node_traversal_time` is a conservative estimate of the average one-hop traversal time for packets and should include queueing delays, interrupt processing times, and transfer times. `active_route_timeout` should be set to a longer value (at least 10,000 milliseconds) if link layer indications are used to detect link breakages such as in the IEEE 802.11 standard [IEEE 1994]. `ttl_start` should be set to at least 2 if Hello messages are used for local connectivity information. Performance of the AODV protocol is sensitive to the chosen values of these constants, which often depend on the characteristics of the underlying link layer protocol, radio technologies, and the like.

Table 6.1. AODV Parameters and Values

Parameter Name	Value
active_route_timeout	3,000 milliseconds
allowed_hello_loss	2
bcast_id_save	30,000 milliseconds
broadcast_record_time	rrep_wait_time
delete_period	See equation on page 219
group_hello_interval	5,000 milliseconds
hello_interval	1,000 milliseconds
mtree_build	2 × rev_route_life
my_route_timeout	2 × active_route_timeout
net_diameter	35
next_hop_wait	node_traversal_time + 10
node_traversal_time	40 milliseconds
prune_timeout	active_route_timeout
rev_route_life	rrep_wait_time
rrep_wait_time	3 × node_traversal_time × net_diameter / 2
rreq_retries	2
ttl_start	1
ttl_increment	2
ttl_threshold	7

delete_period should be an upper bound on the amount of time an upstream node A can have a neighbor B as an active next hop for destination D when B has invalidated the route to D. Until this time, B is required to maintain the latest information it has about D's destination sequence number. Beyond it, B can delete all information about its route to D. The determination of the upper bound depends somewhat on the characteristics of the underlying link layer. For example, if the link layer feedback is used to detect the loss of a link, delete_period must be at least active_route_timeout. If there is no feedback and Hello messages must be used, delete_period must be at least the maximum of active_route_timeout and allowed_hello_loss × hello_interval. If Hello messages are received from a neighbor but data packets to that neighbor are lost (e.g., because of temporary link asymmetry), we have to make more concrete assumptions about the underlying link layer. We assume that such asymmetry cannot persist beyond a certain time—say, a multiple k of allowed_hello_loss × hello_interval. In other words, it can never be the case that a node A receives k subsequent Hello messages from a neighbor if that same neighbor B fails to receive any data packet from node A in this period. This is a reasonable assumption because this AODV specification works only with symmetric links. Covering all possibilities,

$$
\begin{aligned}
\texttt{delete\_period} \;=\; &k \times \max(\texttt{active\_route\_timeout}, \\
&\texttt{allowed\_hello\_loss} \times \texttt{hello\_interval})
\end{aligned}
$$

($k = 5$ is recommended).

ZRP
A Hybrid Framework
for Routing in
Ad Hoc Networks

Zygmunt J. Haas
Marc R. Pearlman
Cornell University

Abstract

We introduce here a novel routing protocol for a special class of ad hoc networks, which we term reconfigurable wireless networks (RWNs). The main features of RWNs are increased mobility of network nodes, a larger number of nodes, and a large network span. We argue that current routing protocols do not provide a satisfactory solution for routing in this type of environment. We propose a scheme, called the Zone Routing Protocol (ZRP), which dynamically adjusts itself to operational conditions by sizing a single network parameter—the zone radius. More specifically, ZRP reduces the cost of frequent updates to the constantly changing network topology by limiting the scope of the updates to the immediate neighborhood of the change. We study the performance of the scheme, evaluating the average number of control messages required to discover a route within the network. Furthermore, we compare the scheme's performance with reactive flood search and proactive link-state classes of routing protocols.

7.1 RECONFIGURABLE WIRELESS NETWORKS

A reconfigurable wireless network (RWN) is an ad hoc network architecture that can be rapidly deployed without relying on a pre-existing fixed network infrastructure. The nodes in an RWN can dynamically join and leave the network frequently, often without warning and possibly without disruption of other nodes' communication. Finally, the nodes in the network can be highly mobile and thus can rapidly change the node constellation and the presence or absence of links. Examples of the use of the RWNs follow.

- *Tactical operation*—fast establishment of military communication during the deployment of forces in unknown and hostile terrain.
- *Rescue missions*—communication in areas without adequate wireless coverage.
- *National security*—communication in times of national crisis, when the existing communication infrastructure is nonoperational because of a natural disaster or a global war.
- *Law enforcement*—fast establishment of communication infrastructure during law enforcement operations.
- *Commerce*—communication for exhibitions, conferences, sales presentations, and so forth.
- *Education*—operation of wall-free (virtual) classrooms.
- *Sensor networks*—communication between intelligent sensors (e.g., micro-electromechanical systems, or MEMS) mounted on mobile platforms.

Nodes in the RWN exhibit nomadic behavior by freely migrating within some area, dynamically creating and tearing down associations with other nodes. Groups of nodes that have a common goal can create formations (clusters) and migrate together, similar to military units on missions or to guided tours on excursions. Nodes can communicate with each other at any time, without restrictions, except for connectivity limitations and subject to security provisions. Carriers of network nodes might be pedestrians, soldiers, or unmanned robots. Examples of mobile platforms on which the network nodes might reside are cars, trucks, buses, tanks, trains, planes, helicopters, or ships.

RWNs are intended to provide a data network that is immediately deployable in arbitrary communication environments and that is responsive to changes in network topology. Because ad hoc networks are intended to be deployable anywhere, existing infrastructure may not be present. The mobile nodes, thus, are likely to be the sole elements of the network. Differing mobility patterns and radio propagation conditions that vary with time and position can result in intermittent and sporadic connectivity between adjacent nodes, resulting in a time-varying network topology.

RWNs are distinguished from other ad hoc networks by rapidly changing network topologies, influenced by network size and node mobility. Typically, such networks have a large span and contain hundreds to thousands of nodes. The RWN nodes exist on top of diverse platforms that exhibit quite different mobility patterns. Within an RWN, there can be significant variations in nodal speed (from stationary nodes to high-speed aircraft), direction of movement, acceleration and/or deceleration, or restrictions on paths (e.g., a car must drive on a road, but a tank does not). A pedestrian is restricted by built objects, while airborne platforms have free movement within some range of altitudes. In spite of such volatility, the RWN is expected to deliver diverse traffic types ranging from pure voice to integrated voice and image and even possibly some limited video.

7.2 THE COMMUNICATION ENVIRONMENT AND THE RWN MODEL

The following list presents assumptions about the communication parameters, network architecture, and network traffic in an RWN.

- Nodes are equipped with portable communication devices, which may be powered by lightweight batteries. Limited battery life can restrict the transmission range, communication activity (both transmitting and receiving), and computational power of these devices.
- Connectivity between nodes is *not* a transitive relation; that is, node A can communicate directly with node B and B can communicate directly with node C, but A *may not* necessarily be able to communicate directly with C. This leads to the hidden terminal problem [Tobagi+ 1975].
- A hierarchy in network routing and mobility management procedures may improve network performance measures, such as the latency in locating a mobile node. However, a physical hierarchy may cause areas of congestion and is very vulnerable to topological reconfigurations.
- Nodes are identified by fixed IDs (perhaps based on IP addresses [Postel 1981]).
- All network nodes have equal capabilities. This means that they are all equipped with identical communication devices and are capable of performing functions from a common set of networking services. However, all nodes do not necessarily perform the same functions at the same time. They may be assigned specific functions in the network that can change over time.
- Although the network should allow communication between *any* two nodes, it is envisioned that a large portion of the traffic will be between those that are geographically close. This assumption is clearly justified in a hierarchical organization. For example, it is much more likely that communication will take place between two soldiers in the same unit than between two soldiers in different brigades.

A RWN is a peer-to-peer network that allows direct communication between any two nodes if adequate radio propagation conditions exist between them and subject to their transmission power limitations. If there is no direct link between the source and the destination nodes, multihop routing is used. In multihop routing, a packet is forwarded from one node to another until it reaches the destination. Of course, appropriate routing protocols are necessary to discover routes between the source and the destination or even to determine the presence or absence of a path to the destination node. Because of the lack of central elements, distributed protocols must be used.

The main challenges in the design and operation of RWNs, compared to more traditional wireless networks, stem from the lack of a centralized entity, the potential for rapid node movement, and the fact that all communication is carried over the wireless medium. In standard cellular wireless networks, there are a number of centralized entities (e.g., base stations, mobile switching centers (MSCs), the Home Location Registry (HLR), and the Visitor Location Registry (VLR)). In ad hoc networks, there is no pre-existing infrastructure and these centralized entities do not exist. In cellular networks, the centralized entities perform coordination. Their absence in RWNs requires distributed algorithms to do this. In particular, the traditional algorithms for mobility management, which rely on a centralized HLR/VLR, and the medium access control (MAC) schemes, which rely on the base-station/MSC support, become inappropriate.

All communications between all network entities in our ad hoc networks are carried over the wireless medium. Because of the radio communications' vulnerability to propagation impairments, connectivity between network nodes is not guaranteed. In fact, intermittent and sporadic connectivity may be quite common. Additionally, the wireless bandwidth is limited, so its use should be minimized. Finally, as some mobile devices are expected to be handheld with limited power sources, the required transmission power should be minimized as well. For these reasons, the transmission radius of each mobile is limited and channels assigned to them are typically spatially reused. Consequently, given that the transmission radius is much smaller than the network span, communication between two nodes often needs to be relayed through intermediate nodes—that is, multihop routing.

Because of the possibly rapid movement of the nodes and variable propagation conditions, network information, such as a route table, becomes obsolete quickly. Frequent network reconfiguration may trigger frequent exchanges of control information to reflect the network's current state. However, the short lifetime of this information means that a large portion of it may never be used, and thus the bandwidth used for its distribution will be wasted. In spite of these attributes, the design of RWNs must still allow for a high degree of network reliability, survivability, availability, and manageability.

On the basis of the preceding discussion, we require the following features for RWNs:

- *Robust routing and mobility management algorithms* to increase the network's reliability and availability—for example, to reduce the chances that any network component will be isolated from the other components.
- *Adaptive algorithms and protocols* to adjust to frequently changing radio propagation, network, and traffic conditions.
- *Low-overhead algorithms and protocols* to preserve the radio communication resource.
- *Multiple (distinct) routes* between a source and a destination to reduce congestion in the vicinity of certain nodes and to increase reliability and survivability.
- *Nonhierarchical physical network architecture* to avoid susceptibility to network failures, congestion around high-level nodes, and the penalty incurred by inefficient routing.

7.3 THE ZONE ROUTING PROTOCOL

In this section, we concentrate on the design of a routing protocol for the RWN. We propose the *Zone Routing Protocol* (ZRP), which allows efficient and fast route discovery in the RWN communication environment (that is, large geographical network size, large number of nodes, fast nodal movement, and frequent topological changes). ZRP requires a small amount of routing information to be maintained at each node, and the cost in wireless resources for maintaining routing information of inactive routes is low. The protocol identifies multiple, loop-free routes to the destination, which increase reliability and performance. Routing is flat rather than hierarchical, reducing organizational overhead, allowing optimal routes to be discovered, and reducing the threat of network congestion. However, the most appealing feature of ZRP is that its behavior is adaptive, based on the mobility and calling patterns of the mobile users.

In what follows, we explain the elements of ZRP. First, however, we clarify the difference between *reactive* and *proactive* routing schemes.

7.3.1 Reactive versus Proactive Routing

The challenge in designing a routing protocol for RWNs stems from the fact that, on the one hand, at least the reachability information[1] for the source's neighbors needs to be known to the source node for it to determine

---

[1]The reachability information indicates whether a destination node can be reached from the node in question, what is the next neighbor on that path, and what is the "cost" of the path. The cost may be based on criteria such as delay, number of hops, and traffic congestion along the path.

a packet route. On the other hand, in an RWN this topology may change quite often. Furthermore, as the number of network nodes can be large, the potential number of destinations can be large also, requiring large and frequent exchanges of data (e.g., routes, route updates, or route tables) among the network nodes. Thus, the amount of update traffic is quite high, which is appropriate because all updates in the wireless communication environment travel over the air and use scarce bandwidth.

Routing protocols can be classified as either proactive or reactive. Proactive protocols attempt to continuously evaluate the routes within the network so that when a packet needs to be forwarded the route is already known and can be immediately used. Examples are OSPF [Moy 1997], WRP [Murthy+ 1996], and DSDV [Perkins+ 1994]. Reactive protocols, such as TORA [Park+ 1997], AODV [Perkins+ 1999], and DSR [Johnson+ 1996], invoke route determination only on demand.

The advantage of proactive schemes is that when a route is needed there is little delay before it is determined. In reactive protocols, because route information may not be available at the time a route request is received, the delay before a route is determined can be quite significant. Furthermore, the reactive global search procedure requires significant control traffic. Because of this long delay and the excessive control traffic, pure reactive protocols may not be applicable to realtime communication. However, pure proactive schemes are not appropriate for the RWN environment either as they continuously use a large portion of network capacity to keep the routing information current. Because nodes in an RWN move quite fast and because the changes may be more frequent than the route requests, most of this routing information is never used. Again, this results in an excessive waste of network capacity. What is needed is a protocol that initiates the route determination procedure on demand but at a limited search cost.

Our answer is ZRP, a hybrid reactive/proactive routing protocol [Haas+ 1998, Pearlman+ 1999]. ZRP limits the scope of the proactive procedure to the *node's local neighborhood,* but the search throughout the network, although global, is done by querying only a subset of the network nodes. Regarding updates in the network topology, for a routing protocol to be efficient, changes in the network topology should have local effect only. In other words, creation of a new link at one end of the network is an important local event but is usually not a significant piece of information at the other end. Proactive protocols tend to distribute information about topology changes widely in the network, incurring large costs. ZRP, on the other hand, limits their propagation to their own neighborhood, thereby limiting their cost. ZRP is based on the notion of a *routing zone,* which we introduce next.

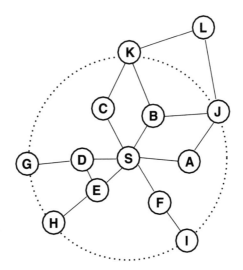

Figure 7.1. A Routing Zone of Radius 2

7.3.2 Routing Zones and Intrazone Routing

In ZRP, a node proactively maintains routes to destinations within a local neighborhood, which we refer to as a *routing zone*. More precisely, a node's routing zone is defined as a collection of nodes whose minimum distance (in hops) from the node in question is no greater than a parameter referred to as the *zone radius*. An example of a routing zone (for node S) of radius 2 hops is shown in Figure 7.1. Nodes A through K are members of node S's routing zone, whereas node L lies outside. *Peripheral nodes* are those nodes whose minimum distance to the node in question is equal to the zone radius. Nodes G through K are peripheral, whereas nodes A through F are interior. We note that each node maintains its own routing zone. As a result, routing zones of nearby nodes may overlap heavily.

Related to the definition of a zone is the coverage of a node's transmitter, which is the set of nodes in direct communication with the node in question. These are referred to as *neighbors*. The transmitter's coverage depends on propagation conditions, transmitter power, and receiver sensitivity. In our simulation, we define a radius, d_{xmit}, that is the maximal distance at which a node's transmission will be received without errors. Of course, it is important that each node be connected to at least one other node. However, more is not necessarily better. As the transmitter's coverage includes all the nodes with a distance of one hop from the node in question, the larger the d_{xmit} is, the larger its routing zone population is. A large routing zone requires a larger amount of update traffic. For the purpose of illustration, we will depict zones as circles around the node in question. However, one should keep in mind that the zone is not a description of physical distance but rather of node connectivity (hops).

Each node is assumed to maintain the routing information to all nodes within its routing zone and those only. Consequently, even though a network can be quite large, the updates are only locally propagated. The node learns the topology of its routing zone through a localized proactive scheme, which we refer to as the *Intrazone Routing Protocol* (IARP). In this chapter, we use a basic link-state algorithm, where link-state updates are localized within the routing zone radius. Other link-state and distance-vector variants may be modified to serve as an IARP by properly restricting the propagation of topology updates to the extent of a node's routing zone.

7.3.3 Interzone Routing and the Zone Routing Protocol

The *Interzone Routing Protocol* (IERP) is responsible for reactively discovering routes to destinations beyond a node's routing zone. IERP distinguishes itself from standard flood search route discovery protocols by exploiting the structure of the routing zone. Routing zones increase the probability that a node can respond positively to a route request. This is beneficial for traffic that is destined for geographically close nodes. More important, knowledge of local routing zone topology can be exploited to efficiently relay a query through the network. This is achieved through a packet delivery service, called *bordercasting,* which directs messages from one node out to its peripheral nodes.

The nature of bordercasting lends itself to a multicast implementation. One approach is for a node to compute its bordercast (multicast) tree and append the corresponding packet forwarding instructions to the bordercast packet. Alternatively, each node may reconstruct the bordercast tree of its interior routing zone members by proactively maintaining the topology of an *extended zone.* In particular, if IARP maintains an extended zone of radius $2\rho - 1$ (where the "basic" routing zone radius is ρ), bordercast messages can be relayed without the need for explicit directions from the bordercast source.

IERP route discovery operates as follows. The source node first checks whether the destination is within its zone. If so, the path to the destination is known and no further route discovery is required. If the destination is not within the source routing zone, the source bordercasts a *route request* to its peripheral nodes. In turn, the peripheral nodes execute the same algorithm—checking whether the destination is within their zone. If so, a *route reply* is sent back to the source, indicating the route to the destination (more about this in a moment). If not, the peripheral nodes forward the route request to *their* peripheral nodes, which execute the same procedure.

An example of this *route discovery* procedure is shown in Figure 7.2. Source node S sends a packet to destination D. To find a route within the

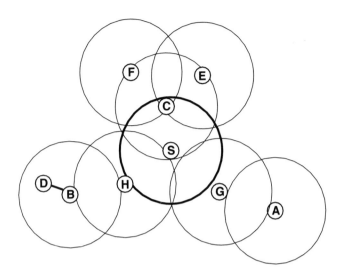

Figure 7.2. An Example of IERP Operation

network, S first checks whether D is within its routing zone. Because D does not lie within S's routing zone, S bordercasts a route request to all of its peripheral nodes—that is, to nodes C, G, and H. Nodes C, G, and H then determine that D is not in their routing zones and therefore bordercast the request to *their* peripheral nodes. One of H's peripheral nodes, B, recognizes D as being in its routing zone and responds to the route request, indicating the forwarding path S→H→B→D.

To complete the route discovery process, a reply is sent back to the route query's source, providing it with the desired route. It is the responsibility of the route accumulation procedure to acquire sufficient information during the route request phase so that the route response can be routed back to the source. In the basic route accumulation procedure, a node appends its address to a received route request packet. The sequence of addresses specifies a route from the query's source to the current node. By reversing this sequence, a route back to the source may also be obtained. In this way, a route reply may be sent back to the source through strict source routing. Given sufficient storage space, nodes may remove the routing information accumulated in the route request packet and store it in a temporary route query cache. This has the benefit of reducing the length of the request packet, thereby decreasing the query-response time. When all nodes adopt this caching policy, the route reply can be relayed back to the source through next-hop routing.

A nice feature of this distributed route discovery process is that a single route query can return multiple route replies. The quality of these returned routes can be determined on the basis of hop count or any other path metric accumulated during the propagation of the route request. The best route can be selected on the basis of relative quality (i.e., the route with the smallest hop count or the shortest accumulated delay).

The cost of route discovery can be significantly reduced by initiating a global route search only when there is a substantial change in the network topology. When such a change causes a broken link within an active path, a *local* path repair procedure is initiated. This procedure replaces a broken link with a minipath between the link ends. A path update is then generated and sent to the path's endpoints. Local path repair procedures tend to reduce path optimality (e.g., increasing the length for shortest-path routing). Thus, after some number of repairs the path endpoints initiate a new route discovery procedure to replace the path with a new, optimal one.

Querying can be performed more efficiently than flooding by directing route requests to target peripheral nodes. However, because neighboring routing zones heavily overlap, each node may forward a route request multiple times, resulting in more control traffic than flooding incurs. The challenge is to "steer" the query outward from the original routing zone (see Figure 7.3) rather than return it to areas that it has already covered. This desired query propagation behavior is achieved by properly extending the query forwarding and termination strategies from traditional flooding algorithms to the context of a routing zone architecture.

Redundant querying occurs when a route request packet arrives in a previously queried routing zone. To prevent this, nodes should be able to detect when a routing zone to which they belong has been queried already. Clearly, a node that bordercasts a route request is aware that its zone has

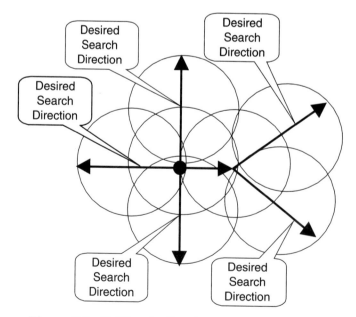

Figure 7.3. Guiding the Search in Desirable Directions

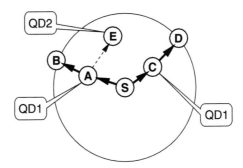

Figure 7.4. Advanced Query Detection(QD1/QD2)

been queried. If bordercasting is implemented below the routing protocol (i.e., by the network layer), the query will not be detected until it reappears at the target peripheral nodes. To notify the remaining routing zone nodes without introducing additional control traffic, bordercasting must be performed by ZRP itself. The first level of query detection—QD1—allows nodes to detect queries as they relay them to the edge of the routing zone. In networks that use a single broadcast channel, it may be possible for queries to be detected by any node within the range of a query-relaying node. This extended query detection capability—QD2—can be implemented through IP and MAC neighbor broadcast (or multicast) as a vehicle for relaying a route request to the downstream neighbors. Figure 7.4 illustrates both levels of advanced query detection. In this example, node S bordercasts to two peripheral nodes, B and D. The intermediate nodes A and C can detect passing route request packets and record that S's routing zone has been queried. In single-channel networks, node E may also be able to receive A's transmission and record the query information as well.

Standard flood search protocols terminate packets that are targeted for (or arrive at) previously queried nodes. We can extend this idea to ZRP by discarding route request packets before they arrive at bordercast recipients belonging to the routing zone's previously queried nodes. More precisely, a node will not relay a query packet to a target bordercast recipient either if that recipient lies inside the routing zone of a previously bordercast node or if this node has already relayed the query to this recipient. This scheme, which we refer to as *early termination* (ET), relies on query detection to identify which local nodes have already bordercast the query. To identify the nodes that lie within the routing zones of these bordercast nodes, the topology of an extended zone of radius $2\rho - 1$ hops (where ρ is the radius of the "basic" routing zone) must be maintained. Conveniently, IARP already maintains this extended information in support of multicast-based bordercasting. Figure 7.5 illustrates the operation of ET. Node B first detects

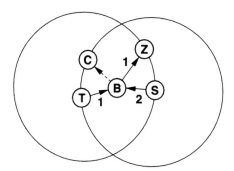

Figure 7.5. Early Termination

(and relays) a route request packet bordercast by node T. Later, B receives a route request packet to be relayed to the bordercast recipient node C. B recognizes that node C belongs to the previously queried routing zone of node T and therefore withholds transmission.

7.4 ZRP—FORMAL DESCRIPTION

The placement of ZRP in the OSI protocol stack is shown in Figure 7.6. The proactive maintenance of the routing zone topology is performed by IARP through exchange of route update packets. Route updates are triggered by the MAC-level Neighbor Discovery Protocol (NDP), which notifies IARP when a link to a neighbor is established or broken. IERP reactively acquires routes to nodes beyond the routing zone using a query-reply mechanism. It forwards queries to its peripheral nodes through the bordercast delivery service, keeping track of the peripheral nodes through up-to-date routing zone topology information provided by IARP. IERP also makes use of IARP routing zone information to determine whether a queried-for destination belongs to its routing zone.

We now turn to the formal definitions of NDP, IARP, and IERP.

7.4.1 Neighbor Discovery Protocol

Nodes advertise their presence to their neighbors by periodically transmitting Hello beacons. Upon receipt of a beacon, a node records the beacon's source ID in its *neighbor table,* which it scans at regular intervals to check the status of each of its neighbors. If no beacon was received from a neighbor during the previous MAX_LAST_RECORDED intervals, the neighbor is considered lost. If a beacon was received, and the neighbor was previously unrecorded, it is considered found. When a neighbor is either lost or found, IARP is notified of this new link status. The protocol is shown in Figures 7.7 and 7.8.

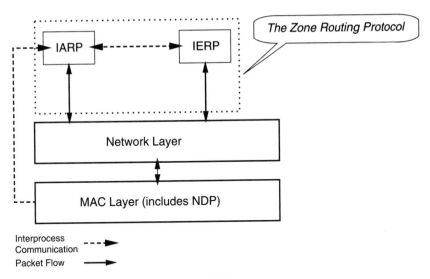

Figure 7.6. ZRP Architecture

Packet Format

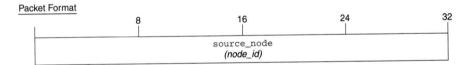

Structures

       `Neighbor_Table`

Neighbor *(node_id)*	Arrival *(boolean)*	Last recorded *(int)*

Initialization

```
beacon_xmit_timer = rand_uniform (2 • T_beacon);
table_update_timer = rand_uniform (2 • T_beacon);
```

Beacon Transmission

```
// Transmit periodic HELLO beacon
source_node = my_id;
load(packet);        /*load packet fields with corresponding local variables */
broadcast(packet);
beacon_xmit_timer += T_beacon;
```

Figure 7.7. The Neighbor Discovery Protocol (Part 1)

Beacon Reception
```
// Record detected neighbor (from received beacon) in Neighbor Table
extract(packet); /* extract packet fields into local variables of the same name */
if (source_node ∈ Neighbor_Table)
    Neighbor_Table[source_node].Last_recorded = -1;
Neighbor_Table[source_node].Arrival = TRUE;
```

Neighbor Table Update
```
// Identify lost neighbors and remove them from the Neighbor Table
for each neighbor in Neighbor_Table
{
    if (Neighbor_Table[neighbor].Arrival == FALSE)
    {
        if (Neighbor_Table[neighbor].Last_recorded ≥ MAX_LAST_RECORDED)
        {
            // If a neighbor's beacon hasn't been received in MAX_LAST_RECORDED update cycles
            // then remove neighbor from Neighbor Table
            remove (Neighbor_Table[neighbor]);
            load_intrpt_params(neighbor);
            set_intrpt(IARP, "Neighbor Lost", "Update Intrazone Routing Table");
        }
        else
        {
            // Increment number of cycles that neighbor's beacon has not been received
            Neighbor_Table[neighbor].Last_recorded++;
        }
    }
    else
    {
        // If a new neighbor was found, alert the IARP
        if (Neighbor_Table[neighbor].Last_recorded == -1)
        {
            load_intrpt_params(neighbor);
            set_intrpt(IARP, "Neighbor Found", "Update Intrazone Routing Table");
            Neighbor_Table[neighbor].last_recorded = 0;
        }
        Neighbor_Table[neighbor].arrival = FALSE;
    }
    table_update_timer + T_beacon;
}
```

Figure 7.8. The Neighbor Discovery Protocol (Part 2)

7.4.2 The Intrazone Routing Protocol

In this version of IARP (Figures 7.9 and 7.10), nodes compute intrazone routes based on the link state of each (extended) routing zone node. A node may receive link-state updates either from an IARP link-state packet or from an interrupt generated by the NDP. Link states are maintained in a link-state table. When all pending link-state updates have been received (full link-state updates may contain multiple links and span multiple packets), the route table is recomputed, using a minimum spanning tree algorithm. The link-state table is then updated to remove links that lie outside of the (extended) routing zone. Newly received link-state updates for link sources within the node's (extended) routing zone are forwarded to all of

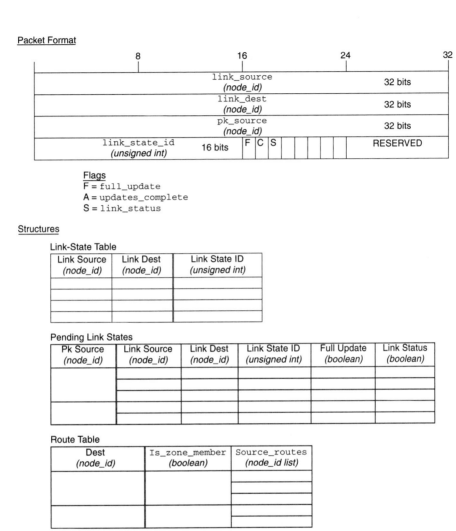

Figure 7.9. The Intrazone Routing Protocol

the node's neighbors. In addition, any new neighbor discovered by the node is sent the link states of all nodes that lie inside of the node's (extended) routing zone.

7.4.3 The Interzone Routing Protocol

The Interzone Routing Protocol (Figures 7.11 through 7.16) is responsible for discovering routes to hosts beyond a node's routing zone. A route request is triggered at the network layer when a data packet is to be sent to a

<u>Update Intrazone Route Table</u>
```
// IARP may be triggered by either a link state packet update or an interrupt from the NDP
if (packet arrived)
{
    extract(packet);              /* extract packet fields into local variables of the same name */
    my_link_changed = FALSE;
}
else
{
    extract_intrpt_params(&link_dest);
    link_source   = my_id;
    pk_source     = my_id;
    link_state_id = my_link_state_id;
    full_update   = FALSE;
    updates_complete = TRUE;
    if (type(intrpt) == "Neighbor Found")
    {
        link_status = UP;
        // Send all link state information that lies inside my (extended) routing zone to each new neighbor
        if(!is_neighbor(Link_State_Table, my_id, link_dest))
        {
            send_link_state_table(Link_State_Table, link_dest);
            my_link_state_id++;
        }
    }
    else
    {
        link_status = DOWN;
        if(is_neighbor(Link_State_Table, my_id, link_dest))
            my_link_state_id++;
    }
}

// Buffer link state updates until all updates from pk_source have arrived
add_to_Pending_Link_States(pk_source, link_source, link_dest, link_state_id,
        full_update, link_status);

// Once all link state updates have arrived from pk_source, transfer those link states to the Link_State_Table
if(updates_complete)
{
    link_states_list = remove_from_Pending_Link_States(pk_source);
    for each link_state ∈ link_states_list
        add_to_Link_State_Table(link_state);
}

// The link state table should not contain links that lie beyond my (extended) routing zone
// The routing table is recomputed until all outlying links have been removed from the routing table
rebuild = TRUE;
while(rebuild)
{
    Routing_Table = construct_spanning_tree(Link_State_Table);
    rebuild = prune(Link_State_Table);
}

// Broadcast all new link state information for link sources that lie inside my (extended) routing zone
broadcast_new_link_state_updates(Link_State_Table);
```

Figure 7.10. The Intrazone Routing Protocol

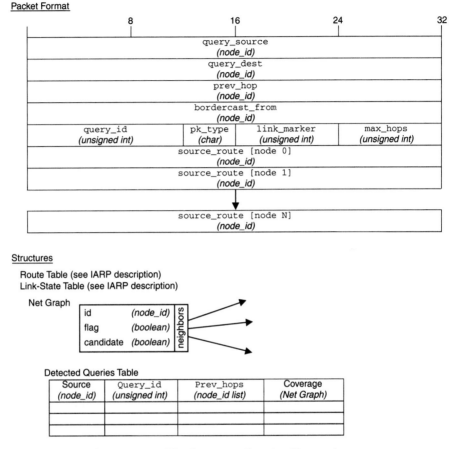

Figure 7.11. The Interzone Routing Protocol

destination that is not recorded in its route table. It is assigned a query ID that is unique to the source node. The combination of source node ID and query ID uniquely identifies any route query in the network. After recording the query source and query ID in the request packet, the packet is bordercast to all peripheral nodes.

When a node receives a route request packet, the query ID, query source, bordercasting node, and previous hop are all recorded in the detected queries table. The node then searches its route table to see if the requested destination lies within its routing zone. If so, the node responds with a route reply returned to the query source, along a path specified by the previous hop information cached in the detected queries table. If the destination does not belong to the node's routing zone, the node

<u>Initiate Route Discovery</u>

```
extract_intrpt_params(&query_dest);
        pk_type         = ROUTE_REQUEST;
        query_id        = my_query_id++;
        query_source    = my_id;
        bordercast_from = my_id;
        prev_hop        = NULL;
        source_route    = NULL;

        // the path repair is a route query with limited depth
        if(type(intrpt)== "Path Repair")
        {
           max_hops      = MAX_REPAIR_HOPS;
           link_marker   = 0;
        }
        else
        {
           max_hops      = MAX_REQUEST_HOPS;
           link_marker   = NULL;
        }
        // bordercast route request to all peripheral nodes
        load(packet);                /* load packet fields with corresponding local variables */
        load_intrpt_params(packet);
        set_intrpt(IERP, "Receive IERP Packet", " ");
```

Figure 7.12. The Interzone Routing Protocol (Part 1)

forwards the route request down its bordercast tree to the target peripheral nodes.

Without sufficient query control mechanisms, the bordercasting mechanism can result in far more traffic than that caused by flooding. A combination of advanced query detection (QD) and early query termination (ET) techniques are employed to realize the potential of zone-based querying. On the basis of the information cached in the detected queries table, a node will *not* relay a route request packet on an outgoing link if none of the intended bordercast recipients need to receive it. Specifically, a node can refrain from forwarding a route request to a bordercast recipient if the recipient lies within a previously queried routing zone *or* if the current node has already relayed a query packet to that recipient.

In addition to discovering new routes, IERP also repairs broken routes. When a broken link is detected, IERP is immediately notified and attempts a repair (by means of a route discovery). Because it is very likely that the lost host is just beyond the routing zone, the depth of a link repair route discovery can be restricted. Upon receipt of link repair route reply, all routes containing the broken links can be updated. If no route reply is received within a reasonable amount of time, all routes containing the broken link are removed.

Invalid links detected by the network layer in the routes of incoming data packets are rerouted on the basis of the local route repairs. While the

Receive IERP Packet (Part I)

```
extract(packet);        /* extract packet fields into local variables of the same name */
route_length = length(source_route);
switch(pk_type)
{
    case: ROUTE_REQUEST
    // If a route to the query destination is known, forward route replay back to query source
    if(dest ∈ Routing_Table)
    {
        source_route = get_route(Routing_Table, query_dest);
        pk_type = ROUTE_REPLY;
        load(packet);    /* load packet fields with local variables of the same name */
        send(packet, prev_hop);
    }
    else
    {
        // If this is the first received copy of this query, add it to the Detected Queries Table,
        // along with a copy of my extended routing zone graph (for recording the detected
        // coverage of this query)
        if(!∃ Detected_Queries_Table[query_source, query_id])
        {
            add_to_Detected_Queries_Table(query_source, query_id);
            t = Detected_Queries_Table[query_source, query_id];
            t.coverage = create_graph_from_Link_State_Table(Link_State_Table);
        }
        t = Detected_Queries_Table[query_source, query_id];

        // Add query packet's previous hop to the Detected_Queries_Table
        add_to_NodeID_List(&t.Prev_hops, source_route[prev_hop]);

        // Mark all nodes within bordercast_from's routing zone as having been covered.
        // This is achieved simply by a breadth-first search of the t.coverage graph, starting at
        // bordercast_from, and limited to a depth of zone_radius −1
        mark_interior_nodes as_covered(t.coverage, bordercast_from);

        // If I am a peripheral node of bordercast_from, then I will re-bordercast the query
        if(is_peripheral_node(bordercast_from, my_id))
        {
            bordercast_from = my_id;
            mark_as_covered(t.coverage, bordercast_from, zone_radius-1);
        }

        // Determine the neighbors to whom I should relay the query
        downstream_neighbors = get_downstream_neighbors(t.coverage, bordercast_from);

        prev_hop = my_id;
        load(packet);
        for each neighbor ∈ downstream_neighbors
            send(packet, neighbor);
    }
    break;
```

Figure 7.13. The Interzone Routing Protocol (Part 2)

route repair process can be transparent to the packet source, hiding this information may result in a costly route selection by the packet source. To address this problem, IERP sends the packet source a link repair report. The packet source then updates its route tables accordingly.

Receive IERP Packet (Part II)

```
case: ROUTE_REPLY
case: PATH_REPAIR_REPORT
   if(pk_type == PATH_REPAIR_REPORT)
   {
       // replace broken link in routing table with path repair
       bad_link = source_route[link_marker] + query_dest;
       path_repair = source_route[link_marker : length(source_route)-1];
       replace(Routing_Table, bad_link, path_repair);
   }
   else
   {
       // record route in routing table
       add(Routing_Table[query_dest], route);
   }

   if query_source ≠ my_id)
   {
       // look up the next hop back to the query source (from the Detected Queries cache)
       // and forward reply back to query source
       prev_hop = Detected_Queries_Table[query_source, query_id].prev_hops[0];
       source_route = prev_hop + source_route;
       load(packet);   /* load packet fields with corresponding local variables */
       send(packet, prev_hop);
   }
break;
} /*end switch*/
```

Figure 7.14. The Interzone Routing Protocol (Part 3)

7.5 EVALUATION OF ZRP

We use the OPNET Network Simulator from OPNET Technologies^{TM}, an event-driven simulation package, to evaluate the performance of ZRP over a range of routing zone radii (ρ), from reactive flood-search routing ($\rho = 1$) to proactive link-state routing ($\rho \rightarrow \infty$). Performance is gauged by measuring the control traffic generated by ZRP and its effects on the average session delay. Our results can be used to determine the optimal ZRP routing zone radius for a given nodal velocity and for a given route query rate.

Control traffic includes intrazone route update packets and interzone route request/reply/failure packets. The neighbor discovery beacons can be considered control overhead, but this additional traffic is independent of both mobile velocity and routing zone radius. Furthermore, the neighbor discovery process is not an exclusive component of ZRP, but is the foundation of various MAC protocols as well. Given that, the beacons do not contribute to the relative performance of ZRP and are not accounted for in our analysis. We measure the average arrival rate of both interzone and intrazone control packets separately and then add the two to produce the total average arrival rate.

A meaningful measure of ZRP delay is the average route query-response time ($\overline{T}_{rqr}$), defined as the average duration from the time a route is

```
node_id list  get_downstream_neighbors (Net_Graph graph, node_id bordercast_from)
{
    root_node = find_node(graph, bordercast_from);
    bordercast_downstream(root_node, 0, my_downstream_neighbors);
    clear_visited_flags(root_node);
    return(my_downstream_neighbors);
    }

boolean    bordercast_downstream (Net_Graph node,
           int depth, node_id list downstream_neighbors)
{
    insert = FALSE;

    if(!node.visited)
    {
    // mark nodes to prevent looping in this depth-first search
    node.visited = TRUE;

    if(depth == zone_radius)
    {
        // If this peripheral node is a candidate bordercast recipient, then the query should be relayed to it.
        if(!node.covered)
        {
            node.candidate = FALSE;
            insert = TRUE;
        }
    }
    else
    {
        // Nodes inside of the routing zones of previously bordercast nodes are not candidate bordercast recipients
        node.candidate = FALSE;
        // Determine which neighbors of node.id have downstream bordercast recipients.
        // If at least one neighbor has a downstream bordercast recipient, then this node is part
            // of the root's bordercast tree.
        for each neighbor ∈ node.neighbors
        {
        if(bordercast_downstream(neighbor, depth+1, my_downstream_neighbors))
        {
            insert = TRUE;
            // If this node is my node, then record the neighbors which belong the root's bordercast tree
            if(node_id == my_id)
            add_to_node_id_list(my_downstream_neighbors, neighbor.id);
            }
            }
        }
    }
    return(insert);
}
```

Figure 7.15. The Interzone Routing Protocol (Part 4)

initially[2] requested by the network layer until it is discovered. If the destination appears in the route tables (which will occur with probability $P_{route-disc}$), the query is immediately answered and the query-response time is assumed to be zero.[3] Otherwise, a route discovery is required, which will

---

[2]This delay metric does not reflect the delays associated with subsequent route repairs. We assume here that routes can be adequately repaired through the local route repair procedure described earlier. These limited-depth queries produce much less control traffic and much lower delays compared to the initial full-depth query.

[3]For simplicity, we assume that the local processing time (e.g., table lookup) is negligible compared to transmission delays.

```
extract_intrpt_params(&route);
// locate "my_id's" broken link in source route [my_id, next_hop]
last_hop = 0;
while (route[last_hop] ≠ my_id)
     last_hop++;
next_hop = route[lat_hop+1];

// replace broken link with new segment from Routing Table
repaired_path = Routing_Table[next_hop].route(0);

// relay route repair report back to source, through all nodes along the reverse route
source_route = route[0:last_hop] + repaired_path;
pk_type = PATH_REPAIR_REPORT;
link_marker = last_hop;
load(packet);      /*load packet fields with local variables of the same name */
send(packet route[last_hop-1]);
```

Figure 7.16. The Interzone Routing Protocol—Report Path Repair

occur with probability $(1 - \mathrm{P}_{route-disc})$, and the query-response time is measured as the time elapsed between the generation of the route request and the reception of the first route reply, $T_{route-reply}$.

$$\overline{T}_{rqr} = (1 - \mathrm{P}_{route-disc}) \times 0 + \mathrm{P}_{route-disc}$$
$$\times \overline{T}_{route-reply}$$
$$= \mathrm{P}_{route-disc} \times \overline{T}_{route-reply}$$

For a fixed network size and a fixed nodal density, the probability of a route discovery for an initial query is dependent only on the routing zone radius. The behavior of the route reply time is far more complicated—dependent not only on the arrival rate of control packets but also on such factors as the network traffic load and the average length of IERP control packets. Our study provides some insight into the effect of these factors on ZRP delay.

Our simulated RWN consists of 200 mobile nodes, whose initial positions are chosen from a uniform random distribution over an area of 1,000 [m] by 1,000 [m]. Each node j moves at a constant speed, v, and is assigned a new direction, θ_j,[4] uniformly distributed between 0 and 2π. When a node reaches the edge of the simulation region, it is reflected back into the coverage area by setting its direction to $-\theta$(horizontal edges) or $\pi - \theta$(vertical edges). The magnitude of the velocity is not altered.

The duration of each simulation is 125 seconds. No data is collected for the first 5 seconds to avoid measurements during the transient period and to ensure that the initial intrazone route discovery process stabilizes.

---

[4]Direction is measured as an angle of the velocity vector relative to the positive v_x-axis.

To measure the delay resulting only from the ZRP overhead, the network load is assumed to be low. Route failures are detected and acted on. The route queries are generated according to a Poisson arrival process, with the arrival rate a simulation parameter. They represent both the initial query performed at the beginning of a session and subsequent queries due to reported route failures. Each route query is for a destination selected from a uniform random distribution of all other nodes in the network. Because the average time between a node's query for the same destination is longer than the expected interzone route lifetime, discovered interzone routes are effectively used only once and then discarded.

In the absence of a packet collision, we assume that background channel interference and receiver noise limit the transmission range of packets and busy tones to a physical radius of $d_{xmit} = 500$ [m]. Within a range of d_{xmit}, the average power of the desired signal, and the resulting average signal-to-interference ratio (SIR), rapidly increases to support reliable packet transmission. As significant improvements can be realized through the addition of error control coding, we approximate the rapid increase of packet reliability by a simple threshold packet delivery model. *Once access to the channel has been established,* a packet can be delivered (error free) to any receiver within d_{xmit} of the transmitting node. Receivers farther than d_{xmit} will not receive the packet.

In single-channel networks, nodes contend for a channel on the basis of the Dual Busy Tone Multiple Access (DBTMA) protocol [Deng+ 1998]. Prior to transmitting a data packet, a node secures access to the channel through an RTS/CTS handshake (performed on a separate control channel). After the handshake, the transmitter sends the data packet while simultaneously activating a *transmit busy tone.* The intended receiver then activates a separate *receive busy tone* as soon as this data transmission is detected. The dual busy tones are used to block attempts by neighboring nodes to access a channel already in use. In particular, the transmit busy tone prevents the transmitter's neighbors from accepting incoming RTS requests, and the receive busy tone prevents the receiver's neighbors from initiating the RTS/CTS handshake. This effectively prevents the "hidden terminal problem" associated with wireless channel access. In addition, DBTMA inherently avoids the "exposed terminal problem" by permitting neighboring nodes to transmit data simultaneously to different (and available) receivers.

We assume that channel access in our multichannel networks, in contrast to single-channel networks, is contention free. The underlying medium access control is responsible for assigning to each incoming/outgoing link a locally unique channel (to avoid channel contention). Although there are no packet collisions, retransmissions are still possible, as a receiving node may be busy receiving or transmitting another packet.

Table 7.1. Fixed Simulation Parameters

Parameter	Symbol	Value
Number of Nodes	N	200
Network Coverage Area	A	1,000 meters × 1,000 meters
Transmission Radius	d_{xmit}	105 meters
Beacon Period	T_{beacon}	0.2 second
Transmission Rate	R_{xmit}	1.0 Mbps

In our model, neighbor discovery is based on the reception of Hello beacons that are broadcast at the MAC layer. These short beacons (containing only the source address) are transmitted at random intervals of mean $T_{beacon} = 0.2$ seconds. Neighbor connectivity is determined by the reception of the Hello beacons. If a new beacon fails to arrive within $2T_{beacon}$ of the most recent beacon's arrival, a link failure is reported. Because the links are bidirectional, the need for a more complex Hello→I-Hear-You packet exchange is eliminated. Furthermore, we assume that neighbor discoveries are given highest transmission priority and are not destroyed by collisions. This prevents inaccurate reporting of link failures for the allowed $2T_{beacon}$ window. Table 7.1 lists the relevant fixed simulation parameters.

7.6 PERFORMANCE RESULTS

The results of our simulation are presented in the following figures. Figure 7.17 illustrates the dependence of proactive IARP control traffic on the routing zone radius, ρ. All else being equal, the rate at which the network reconfigures increases linearly with the speed of the nodes. Therefore, we express the amount of IARP traffic produced by each node for each meter/second of node mobility. Because each node needs to construct the border-cast trees for its interior nodes, a routing zone radius of ρ hops actually corresponds to an exchange of link-state information over a range of $2\rho - 1$ hops. For unbounded networks with a uniform distribution of nodes, we expect the amount of intrazone control traffic to be $O(\rho^2)$ However, because our network is of finite size, the resulting boundary effect makes this dependence less than ρ^2. It should be noted that there is no intrazone control overhead for $\rho = 1$. For $\rho = 1$, the routing zone and extended routing zone both have a one-hop radius and consist solely of neighbor nodes. Therefore, the NDP provides all of the information needed to maintain connectivity within the routing zone. As we might expect, significantly more packet transmissions are required for multiple-channel networks, as the MAC level broadcast used to advertise link-state information to neighbors must be replaced with individual unicasts to each neighbor.

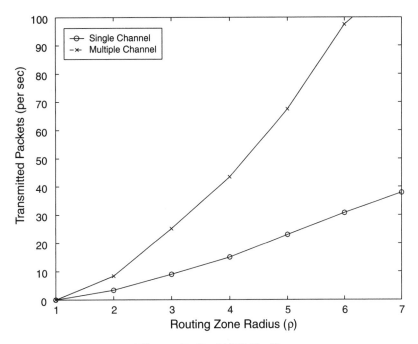

Figure 7.17. IARP Traffic

Reactive IERP performance is demonstrated by the average traffic produced by each route query as shown in Figure 7.18. In the case of $\rho = 1$, the peripheral nodes are neighbors. Consequently, the IERP route query operates as a basic flood search. As we increase the routing zone radius, the reactive route discovery operates with increased efficiency. This improvement is due to the query detection (QD) and early termination (ET) query control mechanisms, which combine to guide the route requests outward from previously queried regions. For multiple-channel networks, IERP can control which nodes relay route requests and on which outgoing links the requests are forwarded. A routing zone radius of just two hops can produce 50% less route query traffic than a simple flood search. The improvement is less dramatic for single-channel networks, since each node has only a single (broadcast) outgoing link. In these networks, a zone radius of two hops reduces the amount of route discovery traffic but only by 15%.

The total ZRP control traffic (i.e., the sum of the control packets from the intrazone and interzone protocols), depicted in Figures 7.19 and 7.20, indicates the performance of our hybrid routing scheme. The amount of control traffic depends on both node mobility and route query rate. However, we can characterize the relative traffic on the basis of the call-to-mobility

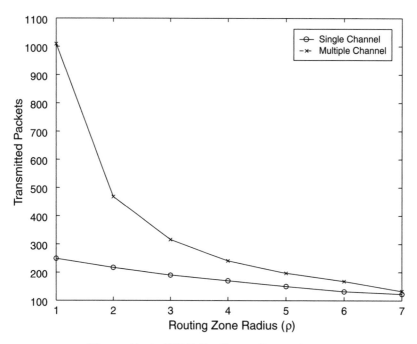

Figure 7.18. IERP Traffic per Route Query

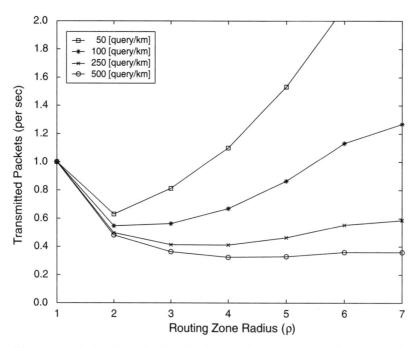

Figure 7.19. ZRP Traffic Relative to Flood Search (Multiple Channels)

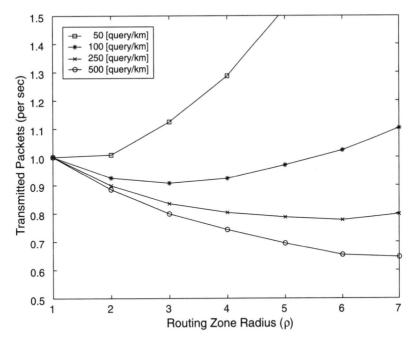

Figure 7.20. ZRP Traffic Relative to Flood Search (Single Channel)

ratio (CMR) (measured as the ratio of route query rate to node speed). As the CMR increases, the ZRP configuration favors larger routing zone radii. For large CMR scenarios, node mobility is relatively low and the cost of maintaining larger routing zones is justified by the resulting reduction in route discovery traffic. In contrast, a lower CMR corresponds to relatively higher mobility scenarios, where routing zone maintenance becomes more costly. In these simulated networks, a ZRP configuration of $\rho = 1$ (equivalent to flood searching) is appropriate for a CMR below 15 [query/km] (multiple channels) or 100 [query/km]. For a larger CMR, routing zones provide an improvement in the overall amount of routing traffic. For example, an optimally configured ZRP for a CMR of 500 [query/km], produces 70% less routing traffic than flood searching for multiple-channel networks and 20% less traffic than flood searching for single-channel networks. As another example, we note that for multiple-channel networks with a CMR of 100 [query/km], a routing zone radius of two hops produces 40% less routing traffic than flood searching ($\rho = 1$) and more than 50% less traffic than a purely proactive link-state routing protocol ($\rho \rightarrow \infty$).

Results of our simulation are presented in Figures 7.21 and 7.22, which show the performance of ZRP as measured by the average route

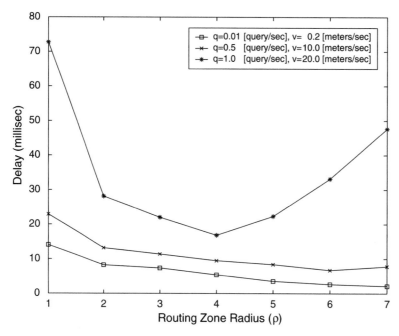

Figure 7.21. ZRP Route Query-Response Time CMR = 50[query/km]
(Multiple Channels)

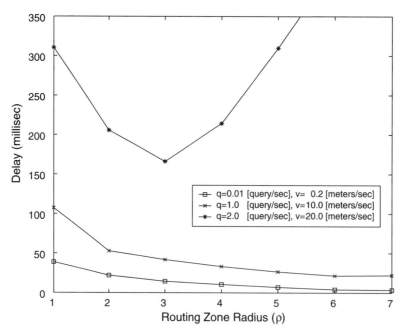

Figure 7.22. ZRP Route Query-Response Time CMR = 100[query/km]
(Single Channel)

query-response time. For low network load, the delay characteristics appear to be heavily influenced by the traffic generated by the present route query. As the network topology becomes more volatile and as the demand for new routes increases, overall ZRP control traffic grows and begins to have a noticeable impact on the instantaneous network load, which is generally more reactive than the average network load (because of the strong contribution of the current route query). The route query-response time is therefore minimized by using routing the zone radius that minimizes overall ZRP control traffic. Neglecting the effects of additional data traffic, we find that ZRP can provide routes, on demand, in about half the time achieved by flood search routing protocols. Optimizing ZRP for control traffic sacrifices some delay performance, but the ZRP response time is still noticeably less than the flood search response time.

Increased route demand and node mobility contribute to additional protocol overhead traffic. In spite of the fact that zone-based querying outperforms traditional proactive and reactive routing protocols, there are limits to what can be achieved by routing protocols in the RWN environment. Given the network's bandwidth limitations, it may not be possible to support routing in extremely dynamic networks. However, the improvements provided by ZRP help to push this threshold higher.

7.7 CONCLUSION

ZRP provides a flexible solution to the challenge of discovering and maintaining routes in the RWN communication environment. It combines two radically different methods of routing in one protocol. Interzone route discovery is based on a reactive route request/route reply scheme. By contrast, intrazone routing uses a proactive protocol to maintain up-to-date routing information to all nodes within its routing zone.

The amount of intrazone control traffic required to maintain a routing zone increases with the routing zone's size. However, through a mechanism that we refer to as bordercasting, we are able to exploit the knowledge of the routing zone topography to significantly reduce the amount of interzone control traffic. For networks characterized by highly mobile nodes and very unstable routes, the hybrid proactive-reactive routing scheme ($\rho > 1$) produces less average ZRP control traffic than do purely reactive flood search routing protocols ($\rho = 1$). Purely reactive schemes appear to be more suitable for networks with greater route stability. For highly active networks (frequent route requests), more proactive networks produce less overhead (i.e., larger routing zones are preferred).

We note that for networks with low activity, the instantaneous network load is generally dominated by the control traffic from a single route discovery. Consequently, ZRP exhibits minimum delay for relatively large routing zone radii, even for cases in which reactive routing minimizes average ZRP control traffic. By minimizing the amount of routing control traffic, ZRP can provide routes that are about 1.5 to 2.0 times faster than flood search routing protocols.

References

[Deng+ 1998] J. Deng and Z.J. Haas. Dual Busy Tone Multiple Access (DBTMA): A New Medium Access Control for Packet Radio Networks. In *Proceedings of ICUPC '98,* October 1998.

[Haas+ 1998] Z.J. Haas and M.R. Pearlman. The Performance of Query Control Schemes for the Zone Routing Protocol. In *Proceedings of SIGCOMM '98,* September 1998, 167–177.

[Johnson+ 1996] D.B. Johnson and D.A. Maltz. Dynamic Source Routing in Ad Hoc Wireless Networks. In *Mobile Computing,* T. Imielinski and H. Korth, eds. *The Kluwer International Series in Engineering and Computer Science* (vol. 35), Kluwer Academic Publishers, Norwood, Mass., 1996, 153–181.

[Murthy+ 1996] S. Murthy and J.J. Garcia-Luna-Aceves. An Efficient Routing Protocol for Wireless Networks. *ACM/Baltzer Mobile Networks and Applications Journal* 1(2):183–197, October 1996.

[Moy 1997] J. Moy. OSPF Version 2. RFC 2178 (draft standard), Internet Engineering Task Force, July 1997.

[Park+ 1997] V.D. Park and M.S. Corson. A Highly Adaptive Distributed Routing Algorithm for Mobile Wireless Networks. In *Proceedings of IEEE Conference on Computer Communications (INFOCOM '97),* April 1997.

[Pearlman+ 1999] M.R. Pearlman and Z.J. Haas. Determining the Optimal Configuration of the Zone Routing Protocol. *IEEE Journal on Selected Areas of Communications (Special Issue, Ad-Hoc Networks)* 17(8), August 1999.

[Perkins+ 1994] C. Perkins and P. Bhagwat. Highly Dynamic Destination-Sequenced Distance-Vector Routing (DSDV) for Mobile Computers. *ACM SIGCOMM '94 Computer Communications Review* 24(4):234–244, October 1994.

[Perkins+ 1999] C.E. Perkins and E.M. Royer. Ad-Hoc On-Demand Distance Vector Routing. In *Proceedings of the Second Annual IEEE Workshop on Wireless and Mobile Computing Systems and Applications (WMCSA),* February 1999.

[Postel 1981] J. Postel. Internet Protocol. RFC 791 (standard), Internet Engineering Task Force, September 1981.

[Tobagi+ 1975] F.A. Tobagi and L. Kleinrock. Packet Switching in Radio Channels: Part II—The Hidden Terminal Problem in Carrier Sense Multiple Access and the Busy Tone Solution. *IEEE Transactions on Communications* COM23(12):1417–1433, December 1975.

APPENDIX: CORRECTNESS PROOF OF ZRP

The following proofs demonstrate the correctness of ZRP. For analysis of the route query mechanism, we assume that the network topology remains static during the propagation of the query and that IARP has already converged to prior topology changes.

These proofs indirectly apply to ZRP enhancements such as route caching and local route repair. It is true that cached routes are not guaranteed to be valid and that limited-depth route repair may not be successful. However, failure of these mechanisms will result in a new full-depth route query, which discovers a route to any reachable network node. An important feature of this proof is that it does not rely on any assumptions about the size of any node's routing zone. Consequently, it applies to networks in which every node's routing zone radius is the same and to networks in which each node independently adjusts its own routing zone.

Let $X(t)$ be the set of reachable nodes that belong to the routing zones of all bordercast recipients, at time t. We refer to these as *covered* nodes. Likewise, the complementary set of nodes, $X^c(t)$, represents the remaining set of *uncovered* nodes. Let $P(t)$ be a subset of $X(t)$ such that each node in $P(t)$ has at least one neighbor in $X^c(t)$. These *frontier* nodes, are the covered nodes that form a boundary between covered and uncovered regions in the network.

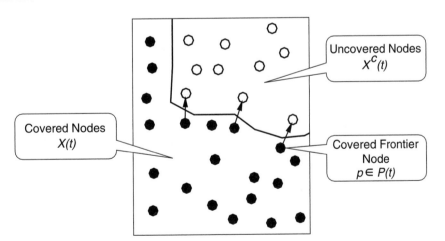

Figure 7.23. Covered, Uncovered, and Frontier Nodes

Theorem 1: $X(t_1) \subset X(t_2)$ and $X^c(t_2) \subset X^c(t_1)$, for $t_1 \leq t_2$.

Proof: Once a node has been covered by a query, it cannot be uncovered. Therefore, $X(t_1) \subset X(t_2)$. From basic set theory, it also follows that $X^c(t_2) \subset X^c(t_1)$. □

Theorem 2: If $|X^c(t)| > 0, |P(t)| > 0.$

Proof: Because all $x \in X^c(t)$ are reachable from any other node, there exists a node $x \in X^c(t)$ that has a neighbor $p \in P(t)$. □

Theorem 3: Every $p \in P(t)$ is a peripheral node of a bordercast recipient.

Proof: Because $p \in P(t)$, $p \in X(t)$ (p belongs to the set of covered nodes). Because p was covered by a query, it belongs to the routing zone of a bordercast recipient. Thus, p must be either a peripheral node or an interior node of the bordercast recipient's routing zone. If p is an interior node, then all of p's neighbors belong to a queried routing zone and are considered covered as well. However, by definition at least one of p's neighbors is uncovered ($x \in X^c(t)$). Therefore, p must be a peripheral node of a bordercast recipient. □

Theorem 4: If there exists a node $p \in P(t_1)$ such that $p \notin P(t_2)$, then $|X^c(t_2)| < |X^c(t_1)|$.

Proof: Let N_p be the set of nodes that are neighbors of node p. Because $p \in P(t_1), X^c(t_1) \cap N_p \neq \emptyset$. Because $p \notin P(t_2), X^c(t_2) \cap N_p = \emptyset$. It follows that $X^c(t_1) \neq X^c(t_2)$. We have already shown that $X^c(t_2) \subset X^c(t_1)$, so $|X^c(t_2)| < |X^c(t_1)|$. □

Theorem 5: If a node p is a bordercast recipient and receives the route query message at t_2, then $p \notin P(t_2)$.

Proof: When node p receives the bordercast route query at t_2, it checks its routing zone for the queried destination, thereby covering all members of its routing zone. Consequently, all of node p's neighbors will be covered and $p \notin P(t_2)$. □

Our protocol is said to provide full coverage if a route query for a nonreachable destination results in every reachable node belonging to at least one queried routing zone (i.e., $X^c(t_k) = 0$, for some $(t_k < \infty)$).

If our protocol provides full coverage, it follows that a route query for any reachable destination will discover at least one route to that destination.

Theorem 6: ZRP permits at least one node in $P(t_{k-1})$ to receive a route query bordercast by time $t_{k-1} < t_k < \infty$.

Proof: For each covered frontier node, $p \in P(t_{k-1})$, there exists at least one bordercast recipient, n, that will launch a bordercast to p. If the query is relayed along the designated path between nodes n and p, then node p will receive the route query packet.

An intermediate relaying node, m, may terminate the query for one of two reasons. In the first case, m may determine (on the basis of its detected query information) that p is no longer a covered frontier node. However, p was a covered frontier node at time t_{k-1}. The only way for p to have been removed from the frontier is if another covered frontier node, $p' \in P(t_{k-1})$, already received a route query bordercast at some time $t_{k-1} < t_k < \infty$.

In the second case, m recognizes that it has already relayed a query packet to node p. If nodes m and p are a distance of d hops apart, the query packet has already progressed to $d - 1$ hops from p. For the case of $d = 1$, the query packet is relayed directly to p. It follows, by induction, that as long as p remains on the frontier, it will successfully receive a route query bordercast by time $t_{k-1} < t_k < \infty$. □

Theorem 7: ZRP provides full coverage.

Proof: From Theorem 6, we know that at least one node in $P(t_{k-1})$ will receive a route query by time $t_k < \infty$.

Each time, t_k, that a query arrives at a node $p \in P(t_{k-1})$, the number of uncovered nodes decreases ($|X^c(t_k)| < |X^c(t_{k-1})|$). Consequently, there exists an increasing sequence of times $\{t_k\}$ for which the corresponding number of uncovered nodes $\{|X^c(t_k)|\}$ decreases, ultimately reaching 0.   □

8

Link Reversal Routing

M. Scott Corson
Institute for Systems Research
University of Maryland
at College Park

Vincent Park
Naval Research Laboratory

Link Reversal Routing (LRR) is a highly adaptive form of routing originally intended for use in networks with rapidly changing topologies. A key concept behind LRR is the decoupling of far-reaching control message propagation from the dynamics of the network's topology. Conceptually, it can be thought of as appropriate for use in networks where the rate of topological changes is not so fast as to make flooding the only possible routing method, but not so slow as to make algorithms capable of supporting a shortest-path computation applicable. By "flooding," we mean a distributed process of broadcasting a packet to all nodes in the network. Practically, results obtained thus far for one LRR algorithm indicate that the technique's range of applicability—relative to other methods—is not so simply stated; rather, it is a function of network size, network topology, rate of topological changes, and available bandwidth.

There have been three contributions to the development of LRR technology, which this chapter will discuss in turn. First we describe the general approach common to all.

8.1 GENERAL APPROACH

The objective of the LRR approach to highly adaptive routing is to *minimize*—to the greatest extent possible—the amount of routing overhead that must be exchanged between nodes when reacting to changes in a network's topology (e.g., link activations and failures). This is achieved by

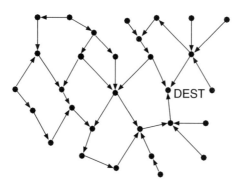

Figure 8.1. A "Routing DAG" Relative to the Destination

localizing the algorithm's reaction to topological changes. Instead of maintaining distributed network state sufficient to support a shortest-path routing computation for a destination of interest, LRR algorithms forgo this possibility and instead maintain only state sufficient to constitute a directed acyclic graph (DAG) rooted at the destination (see Figure 8.1). A directed graph is acyclic if it contains no cycle or loop. By "rooted at the destination," we mean that the destination is the only node that may have *only* incoming links—all other nodes that have incoming links must also have outgoing links.

Maintenance of a distributed DAG is desirable, as it guarantees loop-free routing and can provide participating nodes with multiple, redundant routes to the destination. However, a node's position in the DAG relative to the destination is *unknown* to the node. In other words, there is no multihop propagation and maintenance of an additive distance metric as in distance-vector algorithms; nor is there any multihop propagation of topology composition information, as in link-state and path finding approaches. Thus, the node does not know its distance to the destination or which nodes—other than its one-hop neighbors—are in its proximity or along paths between it and the destination. This differentiates LRR from approaches such as link state, path finding, and distance vector. It is not possible for a node to continuously estimate its distance to the destination or to perform a shortest-path computation, which probably turns out to be a mixed blessing. On the one hand, it can result in less optimal routing; on the other hand, it permits definition of algorithms that are potentially very efficient, in terms of routing overhead communication complexity, and hence very adaptive and scalable. Later on it will be seen that lower delivery latencies can also be achieved relative to some other approaches.

A clarification of the term *loop freedom* as used in this chapter is needed. It is meant here in an "academic" sense. That is, during the execution of a protocol (assuming correct, instantaneous, in-order, reliable delivery of control messages), the set of routes for a given destination never forms a cycle.

This is clearly an idealized set of assumptions regarding delivery of control packets. During the finite interval required for control packet transmission between neighbors (which may be lengthened arbitrarily because of losses of control packets), loops may exist in the route tables. Consequently, during periods of routing protocol convergence, data packets may retrace their paths in the network (i.e., loop). This chapter concentrates on the logic of LRR algorithms and omits discussion of mechanisms required to ensure reliable packet delivery between neighbors and their subsequent effect on protocol behavior.

Assuming that a routing DAG has been constructed for a particular destination, a common thread present in all LRR protocols thus devised is the definition of the event that *triggers* route maintenance (shown in Figure 8.2). A node i is shown initially with three upstream (UP) and two downstream (DN) neighbors in Figure 8.2(a). Note that when a link is directed from a node i to a node j, i is said to be "upstream" of j and is referred to as an "upstream neighbor" of j, while j is said to be "downstream" of i and is referred to as a "downstream neighbor" of i. In Figure 8.2(b), the node loses the link to its downstream neighbor j. In LRR, this results in no algorithmic reaction, as it suffices for a node to have only one downstream neighbor. However, in Figure 8.2(c), when node i loses the link to its *last* downstream neighbor k, an LRR protocol must react to inform node i's upstream neighbors *not* to route information through node i and to reestablish a route for node i if required.

Thus, reaction to the failure of a node's last downstream link triggers route maintenance. Of course, the same event triggers route maintenance in many other approaches, as does a link activation event. What differentiates LRR from approaches, such as link state, path finding and distance vector, is the *frequency* with which algorithmic reaction becomes necessary and the *scope* of each reaction. Typically in link-state approaches, each topological change (and hence each link failure) generates a network-wide, link-state

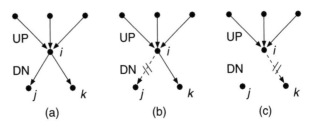

Figure 8.2. Route Maintenance "Trigger"—Failure of i's *Last* Downstream or Outgoing Link to Node k in (c)

update involving all nodes. With path finding, each link change must be communicated to all nodes for which that link forms a part of their shortest-path spanning trees. Similarly in distance-vector approaches, the effects of a link change must be communicated to all nodes whose shortest-path estimates are modified by the change. For LRR approaches, the reaction to a link failure is limited to the set of nodes for which all prior directed paths to the destination included the failed link. Thus, the redundancy in the routing DAG minimizes the frequency and scope of algorithmic reactions due to link failures. Each LRR protocol maintains its DAG in a different fashion, and there are advantages and disadvantages to each approach.

Source-initiated route construction, *on-demand* route construction, and *reactive* route construction all refer to a routing philosophy in which routes are built only when necessary in response to data traffic demands at a source node. Early work in this field came from military-sponsored research [Weber+ 1983, Li+ 1986, Corson+ 1989] and more recent work [Corson+ 1995, Johnson+ 1996, Toh 1996, Park+ 1997, Gracia-Luna-Aceves 1993, Perkins+ 1999]. It can also be referred to as *traffic-driven* route construction. The presumption is that in a dynamic topology it may not be desirable to maintain routes between all source–destination pairs at all times. The overhead expended to establish a route between a given source and destination will be wasted if the source does not require the route prior to its invalidation due to topological changes. This approach is in contrast to the traditional *table-driven* routing methods (e.g., [Merlin+ 1979, Jaffe+ 1982, Moy 1998, Garcia-Luna-Aceves 1993]), which *proactively* seek to compute and maintain routes between all possible source–destination pairs at all times.

Recent work on LRR technology [Corson+ 1995, Park+ 1997] has adopted an on-demand approach to route construction perhaps leading to the impression that LRR is fundamentally a reactive form of routing. Such is *not* the case. LRR is neither proactive nor reactive but refers to the method used to maintain routing in response to topological changes. LRR may be used either proactively or reactively, just as many other traditionally proactive algorithms can be implemented reactively if desired. Herein, when statements are made comparing LRR with other techniques, it is assumed that those techniques are running proactively unless otherwise stated.

8.2 THE GAFNI-BERTSEKAS ALGORITHM

Gafni and Bertsekas produced perhaps the first work on highly adaptive, loop-free multipath routing [Gafni+ 1981]. They considered the problem of routing in packet radio networks (PRNets) and introduced a class of algorithms intended to solve the following problem, P:

Given a connected, destination-disoriented DAG, transform it into a destination-oriented DAG by reversing the directions of some of its links.

Using their terminology, we say that a DAG is *destination oriented* if for every node there exists a directed path originating at the node and terminating at the destination. Otherwise, we say that the DAG is *destination disoriented*. It is easy to see that a connected DAG is destination disoriented, if and only if there exists a node other than the destination that has no outgoing link. The importance of *efficiently* solving problem P, and its relevance to the problem of routing in mobile ad hoc networks, is apparent.

There are two algorithms that solve this problem, the Full Reversal method and the Partial Reversal method [Gafni+ 1981]. We focus on the latter, as it tends to be the more efficient of the two and forms a portion of the conceptual basis necessary to understand a subsequent algorithm [Park+ 1997]. We note that the Gafni-Bertsekas (GB) algorithms—as originally presented—are proactive and actively maintain routing from all nodes to a given destination.

The following, which loosely describes the second algorithm, is from Gafni's [1981] article.

Partial Reversal Method (list-based): Every node i, other than the destination, keeps a list of its neighboring nodes j that have reversed the direction of the corresponding links (i, j). At each iteration, each node i that has no outgoing links reverses the directions of links (i, j) for all j that do not appear on its list and empties the list. If no such j exists (i.e., the list is full), node i reverses the directions of all incoming links and empties the list.

Full Reversal differs from this in that when a node has no outgoing links, it always reverses the directions of *all* of its links. Thus, no list is required in the Full Reversal algorithm.

Figure 8.3 [Gafni+ 1981] provides an example of the link-reversal process of successive iterations of the partial reversal algorithm (starting with empty lists). A node reverses its incoming links by broadcasting an update (U) packet to its neighbors. Readers can convince themselves through other examples that in most networks (particularly those with relatively high connectivity) the reversal process will be initiated infrequently and will typically not require a long chain of iterations. In Section 8.5, we will return to the issue of low versus high network connectivity and its effect on the relative performance of LRR protocols.

Transformation of the Partial Reversal algorithm from a list-based form to a numeric, or "height-based," form permits ready addition of new directed links that may result from mobility. The following algorithm, which is taken directly from [Gafni+ 1981], is defined now.

Partial Reversal Method (height-based): At each stage of the algorithm, we associate with every node i a triple (α_i, β_i, i), where α_i and β_i are integers.

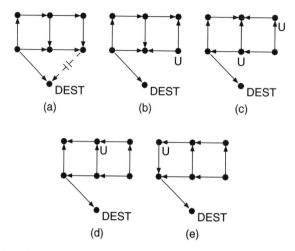

Figure 8.3. Reaction to a Link Failure in the Partial Reversal Method

The set of triples $\{(\alpha_i, \beta_i, i)\}$ is ordered lexicographically. Let N denote the set of nodes in the network. The initial set of triples $\{(\alpha_i^0, \beta_i^0, i) \mid i \in N\}$ satisfies $\alpha_i^0 = 0$ for all i, and for any link (i, j) we have $(\alpha_i^0, \beta_i^0, i) > (\alpha_j^0, \beta_j^0, j)$ if and only if link (i, j) in the initial DAG is directed from i to j. Assuming that each node ID i is unique, the set of triples forms a total order and the directed graph is seen to be loop free, regardless of the values for α_i and β_i. Conceptually, the triple associated with each node can be viewed as a "height," and links are directed on the basis of the relative heights of neighboring nodes—that is, from higher to lower. Information flows downstream from higher to lower nodes according to these heights. The parameter α_i can be viewed as a "reference level," while β_i and i differentiate the relative node heights with a common reference level.

A new iteration of the distributed algorithm is triggered whenever one or more of the nodes each find themselves with no downstream links. Let N_i denote the set of one-hop neighbors of node i. The kth iteration is implemented as follows:

- A node i, other than the destination, for which $(\alpha_i^0, \beta_i^0, i) < (\alpha_j^0, \beta_j^0, j)$, $\forall j \in N_i$, *increases* α_i^k to

$$\alpha_i^{k+1} = \min\{\alpha_j^k \mid j \in N_i\} + 1$$

and sets β_i^{k+1} as follows:

$$\beta_i^{k+1} = \min\{\beta_j^k \mid j \in N_i, \alpha_i^{k+1} = \alpha_j^k\} - 1$$

if there exists a neighbor j with $\alpha_i^{k+1} = \alpha_j^k$; otherwise, $\beta_i^{k+1} = \beta_i^k$.
- All other nodes j maintain the same integers α_j and β_j; that is, $\alpha_j^{k+1} = \alpha_j^k$ and $\beta_j^{k+1} = \beta_j^k$.

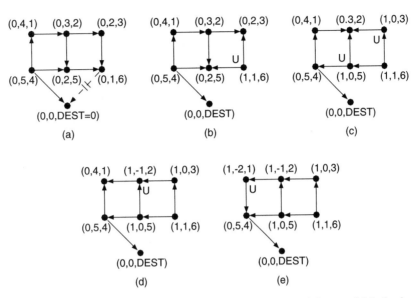

Figure 8.4. Reaction to a Link Failure in the Partial Reversal Method
Showing Height Modification

The preceding algorithm may appear abstract at first glance, but Figure 8.4 portrays the example of Figure 8.3 as a modification of the triples. Figure 8.4(a) shows the state of the algorithm just after the link failure but prior to height modification and subsequent link reversals. As mentioned, the triples can be viewed as heights, and Figure 8.5 depicts Figure 8.4(a) with relative elevations shown. The initial set of heights in Figure 8.4(a) is only one possible set—other sets can be chosen as long as they obey the constraint that links are directed from higher to lower heights. The destination is always the lowest node, shown here with height $(0,0,\text{DEST}=0)$. When a node loses its last downstream link, the rules of the algorithm operate so as to make this node—which has become a local minimum (i.e., it is "lower" than all of its one-hop neighbors)—higher than *at least one* of its one-hop neighbors, thus reversing the directions of its links with one or more neighbors. This is apparent from the aforementioned description of the kth iteration of the algorithm wherein a node chooses its new α value to be greater than the minimum of its neighbors' α values.

In the example, this occurs first at node 6, which changes its height from $(0,1,6)$ to $(1,1,6)$ and broadcasts its new height in an update packet. This causes nodes 3 and 5 to become local minima and thus choose new heights as well. The process of new height selection continues until finally node 1 selects a new height, at which time the DAG is transformed from destination disoriented to destination oriented (using terminology from the beginning

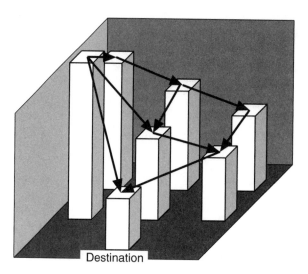

Figure 8.5. Conceptual Illustration of the Directed Acyclic Graph Formed by the Relative "Heights" of the Nodes

of this section). No node that has a valid route to the destination ever participates in the reversal process. Note that a "valid" route is defined here as a sequence of directed links leading from a given node to the destination.

The GB algorithm is deadlock free and loop free at all times [Gafni+ 1981]. The protocol runs independently for each destination, and the lexicographic ordering property of the triples requires that the DEST be the *lowest*-numbered node. The algorithm maintains a DAG and hence maintains one or more routes from each node to the destination provided that such routes exist. Maintenance of multiple routes provides redundancy—a potentially advantageous characteristic for mobile ad hoc networks.

As long as the network remains connected, the GB algorithm converges after a finite number of iterations. However, in network portions disconnected from the destination, the algorithm is unstable and *never* converges. This nonconvergence is the protocol's critical shortcoming and is a principal reason that subsequent LRR algorithms have been developed.

8.3 THE LIGHTWEIGHT MOBILE ROUTING ALGORITHM

Corson and Ephremides [Corson+ 1989, Corson+ 1995] also considered the routing problem in mobile packet radio networks where topological connectivity is subject to frequent, unpredictable change. They noted that there are differing approaches to distributed routing depending on the rate of topological change. If the rate is very high, little can be done in terms of routing—since structured algorithms cannot react fast enough—and the only viable alternative is *flooding*. If the rate is relatively low (i.e., the network is "quasi-static"), there are many suitable shortest-path algorithms such as Distributed Bellman-Ford [Bertsekas+ 1992] and Floyd-Warshall [Bertsekas+ 1992]. If the rate of change is somewhat higher, more adaptive shortest-path algorithms [Merlin+ 1979] and subsequent improvements [Jaffe+ 1982, Garcia-Luna-Aceves 1987, Garcia-Luna-Aceves 1988, Garcia-Luna-Aceves 1989, Garcia-Luna-Aceves 1992, Garcia-Luna-Aceves 1993, Rajagopolan+ 1989] or approximate Bellman-Ford implementations [Awerbuch+ 1991] or many of the link-state-based protocols [Moy 1998, Garcia-Luna-Aceves+ 1995, Ogier 1999] become appropriate.

The work of Carson and Ephremides [Corson+ 1989, Corson+ 1995] considered routing in networks when the rate of change is not fast enough to make flooding the only option but not slow enough to make one of the shortest-path algorithms applicable. In this realm, changes occur too frequently to allow the shortest-path algorithms to converge. On the other hand, enough consistency remains to suggest that more efficient routing than flooding is possible. The GB protocol is well suited to such highly dynamic networks. However, as mentioned, if the network becomes partitioned, this protocol exhibits instability in network portions that are separated from the desired destination. One expects network partitioning to be a common event given the frequency and arbitrary nature of the topological changes envisioned in mobile ad hoc networks.

It was conjectured [Corson+ 1989] that in a highly dynamic mobile ad hoc network, the objectives should be:

- To build routes only *when necessary.*
- To build them *quickly* so that they may be used *before* the topology changes.
- To react *quickly,* establishing new routes when a topological change destroys existing routes—again, only *when necessary.*

This has come to be known as "on-demand" routing. Here, *routing optimality is of secondary importance;* what matters is simply finding a route. Because of the changing topology, it is not worthwhile to construct and maintain routes to *all* nodes. If a node does not currently desire or need a path, the routing information gained in its construction may be outdated before the node needs to use this path, and the expended control overhead is wasted.

To these ends, Corson and Ephremides developed an adaptive algorithm [Corson+ 1989, Corson+ 1995]—termed Lightweight Mobile Routing (LMR)—based, in part, on a concept first presented in [Weber+ 1983]. To quickly build a set of routes, the nodes exchange short control packets using a query-reply process. As the topology changes and existing routes are destroyed, the nodes use a second type of exchange—in combination with the basic query-reply process—to erase invalid routes and construct a new set. As we will see, the protocol enables nodes to maintain multipath routing only to desired destinations with minimal overhead in networks with arbitrarily changing connectivity.

Garcia-Luna-Aceves [1993] introduced a family of shortest-path algorithms based on "diffusing computations" [Dijkstra+ 1980]. Diffusing computations also employ query-reply processes. For example, as Garcia-Luna-Aceves [1993] states, "A diffusing computation started by a node grows by sending queries and shrinks by receiving replies along a directed acyclic graph rooted at the source of the computation." The LMR protocol is similar in that the source floods a query (expanding the computation) and receives replies (shrinking the computation). However, it differs in that the process builds a directed acyclic graph rooted at a desired destination that is *not* the source of the computation.

The LMR algorithm is distributed and deadlock free, and maintains routes that are loop free at all times to each desired destination. Furthermore, the protocol proceeds independently of the number and location of topological changes (even those that partition the network) and, provided that the changes eventually cease, builds the desired routes in finite time. The protocol is localized in the sense that nodes do not have global connectivity information but are only aware of connections to adjacent nodes ("neighbors"). Thus, nodes do not have global routing knowledge and must assume that a route passing through one of their neighbors ultimately leads to the intended destination. Similar to a traditional distance-vector algorithm, the protocol runs independently for each destination in the network.

The algorithm is "source initiated" and demand driven. For a given DEST, instead of maintaining routes from *all* sources to the DEST, the protocol guarantees route maintenance only for those sources that actually desire routes. This property reduces unnecessary control overhead, particularly in conditions with light traffic and high rates of topological change. Furthermore, there are no routing "updates" to support a shortest-path computation, further reducing communication complexity. Control overhead is expended in route computation only when desired by a source or when necessary in response to topological changes. The basic LMR protocol does not support a shortest-path computation, although one may (optionally) be *approximated* within the basic protocol by including a distance metric in the reply propagation.

In essence, the LMR protocol attempts to adapt to topological changes with a *minimal* amount of overhead while maintaining multipath routing only between desired source–destination pairs. This efficiency permits it to be very reactive in chaotic network topologies. It also permits it to function effectively in *very large* mobile networks with more slowly changing topologies. The LMR protocol sacrifices routing quality under light traffic conditions to reduce complexity; this strikes a balance between shortest-path routing and no routing at all (flooding).

The protocol has similarities to previous work on highly adaptive routing [Gafni+ 1981], most notably in its definition of the event that triggers reaction to link failures. At the time of its publication, it was unique in its ability to maintain source-initiated, loop-free multipath routing only to desired destinations with minimal overhead in a randomly varying topology. A subsequently developed protocol [Park+ 1997] also has these characteristics. The Ad Hoc On-Demand Distance Vector (AODV) [Perkins+ 1999, see also Chapter 6] protocol now shares many of these characteritics as well, except that it supports only single-path routing.

8.3.1 Protocol Description

The LMR protocol's execution consists of two logical processes: route "construction" and route "destruction." Of course, in a dynamic topology these two processes occur simultaneously. The protocol will be described in two phases: "initialization" and "maintenance," and it is most easily described as though the initialization phase occurs in a static topology, during which only route construction occurs. Afterwards, the maintenance phase ensures loop-free routing in the face of arbitrary topological changes, erasing routes and rebuilding new ones when necessary.

Because the topology is assumed to be changing rapidly, the protocol does not provide an explicit mechanism for *initiating* destruction of existing routes. Rather, the routes remain intact until severed by a topological change (i.e., a link failure), at which time the protocol erases any invalid routes. This erasure process is an integral part of the maintenance phase and is described as such. An alternative to this would be a data-driven, soft-state-based timeout mechanism to age away unused routes, as in AODV, but this was not specified for LRR. Before focusing on the two phases, we first describe our model.

Network Model and Terminology

We consider a graph $G = (N, L)$ consisting of a finite set of nodes N and a set of initially undirected (or, *unassigned*) links L, which may, however, become directed (*assigned*) in one of two possible directions. The assumption is that every pair of *neighboring* nodes can communicate with each other in either direction.

For each node $i \in N$, we assume a unique node identifier. We define a set of nodes, $N_i \subset N$, as all those adjacent to node i that are known as the *neighbors* of node i. For each neighbor $j \in N_i$, there exists a link $l_{i,j}$

between node i and its neighbor j, which may be either directed or undirected.

An underlying, link-level protocol is assumed that provides the following assurances:

- Each node i is aware of its neighbors in N_i or can discover this set as necessary.
- A packet transmitted by a node is received correctly by all its neighbors regardless of the "assignment" status of its links.

The protocol utilizes three types of control packets: query (QRY), reply (RPY), and failure-query (FQ). A QRY consists of a source node identifier (SID); a destination node identifier (DID); a sequence counter (SEQ), which is assumed to never roll over; and a transmitting node identifier (XID). This no-rollover assumption does not make the protocol impractical, as it was shown [Awerbuch+ 1994] that any protocol using unbounded registers can be transformed to work with bounded registers in a self-stabilizing fashion. The SID identifies the node originating the QRY. The DID identifies the algorithm's destination, which for this description is always DEST. Each source keeps a separate SEQ for each destination. The triple (SID,DID,SEQ) forms a unique identifier that distinguishes a QRY from all others. A XID identifies the node that most recently broadcast the packet and is updated as the QRY propagates. Both RPYs and FQs consist only of a DID and a XID.

The protocol contains, at each node, a QRY/FQ timer Q that once initialized with an implementation-dependent QRY/FQ timeout period T, controls the time between successive QRY broadcasts. The protocol maintains a "query-seen" array entry QS_j for each source j, which holds the QRY SEQ number most recently received from that source.

The protocol utilizes a transmission queue TQ that holds only a single packet. If a new control packet must be queued for transmission and the queue is already full, the old packet is discarded.

The node maintains a link status table entry LS_j for each potential neighbor j. The status of an active link is one of the following: unassigned (UN), upstream (UP), downstream (DN), downstream-blocked (DN-B), unassigned-waiting (UN-W), and awaiting-broadcast (A-BR). Links marked UN, UN-W, or A-BR are undirected; otherwise, they are directed either to or from the node. The precise meaning of the link status will become more apparent later.

Initialization Phase
In the beginning, the network is "unassigned," meaning that all nodes except those neighboring DEST have no routes to DEST; consequently, all

their links are unassigned (undirected) (see the example beginning with Figure 8.6(a)). A node is said to have a route if it has *at least one* downstream link (i.e., a link marked DN). This is in contrast to having an entire path of directed links leading to the DEST (also referred to as "source routing"). In this protocol, "having a route" implies *acting as if* such a path does exist through the downstream neighbor. We assume that eventually some node i not neighboring the DEST will desire a route and subsequently transmit a QRY, thereby starting the initialization phase (Figure 8.6(b)).

A QRY is a control packet broadcast by a node desiring a route to the DEST, which is flooded (see Figure 8.6(b)–(d)) throughout the network in search of nodes that have such a route. By flooding, we mean a node-to-node broadcast such that no node broadcasts any individual packet more than once. Conceptually, QRYs travel over paths of unassigned links. Nodes without routes that receive a QRY rebroadcast or *forward* the QRY (e.g., node j in Figure 8.6(c)), whereas nodes with routes broadcast an RPY in response to a QRY reception (e.g., node k in Figure 8.6(d)). Upon initiating a QRY flood, a source node waits for reception of an RPY; reception of an RPY implies obtaining a route, as the node marks the "unassigned" link over which the RPY was received as "downstream." If no RPY arrives after

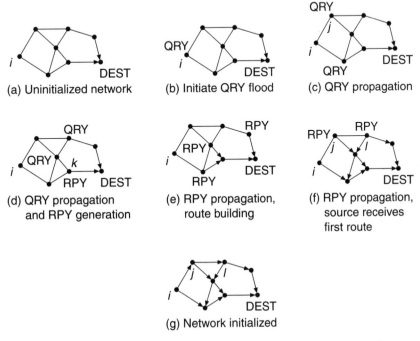

Figure 8.6. Route Construction Phase (QRY-RPY Mechanism)

some time period (possibly because of a network partition), the node is free to broadcast a new QRY, thereby starting a new QRY flood. The source node may continue this process of periodic QRY transmission until the node either hears an RPY or no longer desires a route. Any intermediate nodes that forwarded the QRY do not themselves generate new QRYs unless they also desire routes. Although not in the original algorithm, a QRY suppression timer should be added to the protocol to limit the frequency with which nodes generate new QRYs if they recently forwarded a QRY for the DEST.

An RPY is a control packet broadcast by a node, which has a route, in response to receiving either a QRY or an FQ; it is propagated back toward the QRY's source (Figure 8.6(d)–(g)). RPY propagation can be thought of as a "directed flood." RPYs travel through network portions consisting of unassigned links, transforming these portions into a DAG rooted at the RPY's origin. As an RPY propagates back toward the QRY's source, one or more routes are created at each node within the DAG participating in the RPY flood, each (possibly) weighted with a distance estimate to the DEST over that route. Route creation is somewhat arbitrary, depending on the order of RPY transmission, but the final result is always loop free. For example, the routing obtained in Figure 8.6(g) assumes that node l transmitted its RPY *before* node j in Figure 8.6(f). Otherwise, the link between nodes j and l would be directed toward node j.

If the QRY's source, node i, resides in the network portion containing the DEST, some node neighboring the DEST will eventually receive a QRY and subsequently generate an RPY. The subsequent RPY flood results in node i obtaining one or more loop-free routes. Also, some nodes that do not desire routes but that participated in the RPY flood may obtain them as well. Conceptually, RPY flood termination signals completion of the protocol's initialization phase, and the network portion that participated is considered "initialized" or "assigned."

Maintenance Phase

The maintenance phase begins when some node loses its *last* route because of an adjacent link failure.

• If the node has no other nodes routing through it (i.e., no upstream neighbors), it broadcasts a QRY *only* if it desires a route to the DEST. As in the initialization phase, the node now uses the QRY-RPY mechanism to discover and build new routes, because the motivation is to replace a needed route that was lost. An example is illustrated in Figure 8.7. Here, the failure destroys node i's last downstream link and triggers a QRY broadcast.

• If, however, the node has upstream neighbors (which it assumes may be routing through itself), it will broadcast an FQ *regardless* of whether or

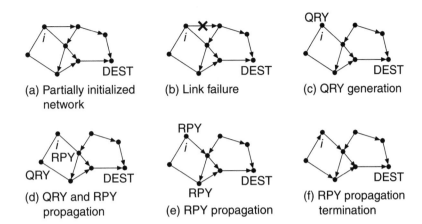

Figure 8.7. Route Reconstruction after Failure of Last Downstream Link
(QRY-RPY Mechanism)

not it currently desires a route. The FQ erases invalid routes. A route is termed "invalid" if it is not rooted at the DEST.

An FQ is transmitted to tell any upstream neighbors not to route through the node and, at the same time, to ask them if they have any alternate routes. This action differentiates an FQ from a QRY in that the latter asks neighbors for alternate routes but does not simultaneously erase routes. Upon reception of an FQ by an upstream neighbor, the neighbor determines whether it still has a route. FQ reception over a link erases the route present on that link (i.e., a directed link becomes undirected). If it does have an alternate route remaining, the neighbor will broadcast an RPY. However, if the FQ reception caused the neighbor to lose its last route, that node will rebroadcast or forward the FQ if it has upstream neighbors. An example of FQ-RPY propagation is shown in Figure 8.8.

In this way, once an FQ is transmitted, the upstream FQ propagation will continue, erasing invalid routes, until a node is found that has an alternate route and subsequently generates an RPY (both nodes i and j in Figure 8.8), or until the FQ propagation halts, having erased all invalid routes without finding a node with an alternate path because the network has become partitioned (see Figure 8.9). In the first case, the subsequent RPY flood creates a new set of loop-free routes for the nodes affected by the link failures. In the second case, the disconnected network portion affected by the failures becomes unassigned. Any disconnected node that desires a path must periodically broadcast QRYs, as in the initialization phase, until network reconnection occurs.

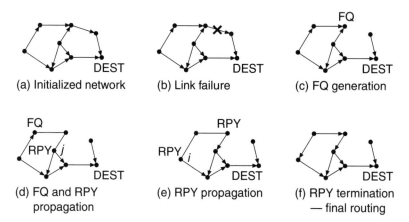

Figure 8.8. Invalid Route Erasure, Route Reconstruction Phase
(FQ-RPY Mechanism)

Loop Freedom

It has been proven [Corson+ 1995] that the protocol builds and maintains
loop-free routes. To summarize here, in a static topology, loop freedom is a
direct result of RPY propagation, which builds a DAG rooted at the DEST.
However, in a dynamic topology the following "downstream-blocking rule"
must be added to ensure loop freedom.

> When a node receives an RPY over an unassigned link, it checks to see if
> it has any upstream links. If not, the node marks the link over which the
> RPY was received as downstream; otherwise, the node marks the link as
> "downstream-blocked (DN-B)."

The blocking marker "-B" forces the node to ignore the existence of
the downstream link for the purpose of routing. It can thus be seen that
loops are prevented because, for a loop to form, a node i, which received
an RPY, must choose as a downstream neighbor node j that has a route
that runs through i. This choice is not possible, as node i cannot add a new
downstream neighbor if it already has upstream neighbors.

The blocking markers will not remain indefinitely if the node does not
have any downstream links available for routing. If topological changes do
not destroy the existing upstream links, the protocol will ensure that these
links are eventually erased and become unassigned. At that point, all blocking markers are removed and the resulting downstream links are available
for routing.

An example is a node that has several upstream and unassigned links
but no downstream links. If the node receives an RPY over an unassigned

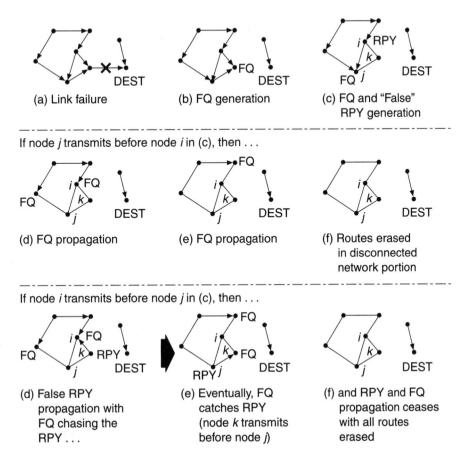

Figure 8.9. Invalid Route Erasure with False RPY Propagation, Route Reconstruction Phase (FQ-RPY Mechanism)

link, it must mark it as blocked to guard against loop formation. It may not yet consider this as a valid downstream link. According to the protocol's rules, such a node already has an FQ queued for transmission prior to the RPY reception. Reception of the RPY will not alter the transmission queue. Once the FQ has been transmitted—an action that erases all upstream links—the blocking marker is removed and the downstream link is available for routing.

The example in Figure 8.9 highlights a typically transient, although potentially unbounded, instability within the basic protocol. It begins with a link failure that partitions the network and generates an FQ broadcast. Upon receiving the FQ, node i queues an RPY for transmission (because it "believes" it still has a valid route through node j) and node j queues an

FQ for transmission (because j's FQ reception erased its last route). There are now two possibilities:

- If node j transmits *before* node i, the protocol quickly converges. Upon receiving the FQ, node i *replaces* its queued RPY with an FQ (because it just lost its last route); subsequently, only FQs remain in the transmission queues of disconnected nodes (see Figure 8.9(d)). This latter condition guarantees convergence and ensures erasure of all invalid routes in the disconnected nodes.

- If node i transmits *before* node j, reception of the RPY at node k *extends* the invalid route one more hop. RPYs that build or extend invalid routes are termed "false RPYs" (FRPY). Any RPY in a disconnected network segment is inherently false. The FQ about to be broadcast at node j will have to "chase" the false RPY, first erasing the route on link $l_{j,i}$ and then being rebroadcast by node i to erase the route on link $l_{i,k}$. False RPY propagation will continue until it is overtaken by FQ propagation. The pursuit will not last long in a network segment with a tree-like topology. In particular, in a partitioned portion with a pure tree topology (i.e., n nodes and $n-1$ links) it is not possible to generate an FRPY. In non-tree segments, quenching FRPY propagation may take some time because FQs may be chasing RPYs around in circles. This behavior is related to the "counting-to-infinity" behavior of the Bellman-Ford algorithm [Bertsekas+ 1992].

Such behavior can be eliminated by using node labels [Garcia-Luna-Aceves 1992] for loop detection, but doing so is also undesirable because it results in increased RPY packet length. It is shown [Corson+ 1995] by a probabilistic argument that FQ propagation will eventually erase all invalid routes (thus overtaking RPYs)—whether or not the network graph remains connected—provided that the scheduling of packet transmissions is *random*.

The potential for transient periods of instability, combined with the lack of any protocol mechanism that discourages their longevity, is the protocol's principle shortcoming and the major reason for subsequent work [Park+ 1997] (see Section 8.4).

Deadlock Freedom
The deadlock issue arises because of the "FQ wait rule," which states,

> A node that transmits an FQ and has upstream neighbors will wait and not transmit another control packet until it has received a transmission from each of those neighbors.

This waiting action creates a possible deadlock situation. The purpose of the FQ wait rule is to ensure that when both valid and invalid routes are present, the invalid routes are eventually erased and only the valid routes remain.

Like the downstream blocking rule, this rule is implemented through link markers. When a downstream node transmits an FQ, it temporarily marks each of its upstream links as "unassigned-waiting" (UN-W). Similarly, whenever an upstream node receives an FQ over a downstream link, the link is temporarily marked "awaiting-broadcast" (A-BR). The presence of a UN-W marker places a node in a "wait state" and prevents it from transmitting until it has received either an RPY or an FQ transmission over each of the UN-W links. Similarly, the presence of an A-BR marker forces a node to eventually broadcast either an RPY or an FQ. It is shown [Corson+ 1995] that a waiting node will eventually receive a transmission and not wait indefinitely because it is impossible for a loop of waiting nodes to form.

As the topology changes, the QRY-RPY and FQ-RPY mechanisms operate indefinitely. It is shown [Corson+ 1995] that once the topology stabilizes the protocol terminates in a finite time. During the maintenance phase, a node desiring a route, having broadcast an FQ but not having received an RPY within a certain time period, may revert to the periodic QRY transmission process, as in the initialization phase. This process guarantees that all nodes that desire a route, but that did not obtain one as the result of an FQ-RPY exchange, will eventually obtain a route via a QRY-RPY exchange.

8.3.2 Properties of the Protocol

We now discuss some of the protocol's properties and characteristics.

Flooding

The protocol utilizes two forms of flooding during its QRY-RPY exchange process. Here, flooding has the obvious advantage of not requiring a priori topological knowledge. This is essential given that the network has no assumed topology and that any knowledge gleaned through protocol operation has only short-term applicability.

It is argued [Gafni+ 1981] that flooding is unsuitable for rapidly changing networks on the premise that it "triggers nearly simultaneous bursts of broadcast messages throughout the network," resulting in collisions and retransmissions that can lead to network overload and collapse. However, the presence or absence of collisions depends on the channel access mechanism and so has little to do with the relative merit of routing algorithms decoupled from the channel access function. Also, the failure reaction mechanisms of this protocol and the GB protocol both create localized, nearly simultaneous bursts of broadcast transmissions. As with many on-demand protocols, the true extent of flooding overhead depends on many factors, such as data traffic patterns and the particular mechanisms used (if any) to cut back flooding on the basis of knowledge gained earlier.

Source-Initiated, or Reactive, Operation

The source-initiated QRY-RPY method of "building routes only as needed" operates naturally within the highly mobile networks envisioned here. Instead of routes being maintained between all source–destination pairs, they are built only when necessary, minimizing communication overhead. Of course, the cost of this savings is having to construct a route *on demand* and incurring the corresponding time delay. Thus, the savings in bandwidth carries with it an increase in delay.

Reactive operation reduces reliance on proactive computation. This technique is especially useful in the case of temporary link additions. When two nodes come within range of one another, both may record the other's presence through link availability notifications from link-level protocols without transmitting a network-level control packet. Should the nodes subsequently separate, this is similarly noted and no network layer control packets are transmitted unless, during the connection, routes were constructed through the link and the disconnection destroys the last existing routes. In this way, the protocol adapts to large amounts of topological change without necessitating any network-wide transmissions, as might occur in proactive approaches such as link-state routing. When a newly arriving node desires a route, it simply queries its neighbors that may know of a route and that promptly broadcast an RPY.

The QRY-RPY sequence guarantees that all nodes participating in the RPY flood obtain one or more routes. When only one route is required, the extras provide increased reliability through redundancy and, if an optional distance metric is used, make possible an improved routing decision during periods of light traffic. When a distance metric is used, the distance information is piggybacked on the RPYs without increasing message complexity. Because there is no attempt to maintain shortest-path routing, there is no need for an "update" message when estimates change [Garcia-Luna-Aceves 1993], so message complexity is low. Also, although shortest-path routing is not performed, the nature of RPY propagation makes it unlikely that the minimum-hop path will not be included in a node's initial set of paths.

Failure Reaction

The protocol's failure reaction mechanism differs from that in [Gafni+ 1981]; however, its trigger is the same and occurs whenever a node loses its last route because of an adjacent link failure. The triggering frequency depends on the rate of topological changes. Here, as in [Gafni+ 1981], only those nodes possessing routes materially affected by the topological changes must undergo route erasure; however, other nodes may participate in the failure reaction by broadcasting an RPY in response to either an FQ or a QRY.

The failure reaction process converges in all network portions whether or not the network has become partitioned [Corson+ 1995]. In portions disconnected from the DEST, all routes are erased and those portions return to the initial, unassigned state. The algorithm implicitly performs "distributed partition detection," meaning that all nodes in these portions lose their routes and cease message transmissions.

The original GB protocol does not possess this characteristic. In portions separated from the DEST, the algorithm is unstable and partitioned nodes exchange control packets in an unending sequence of transmissions, which congest the control channel. Furthermore, since that algorithm relies on directed link reversals (as opposed to first erasing and then building new routes), these nodes continue to possess downstream links during the route discovery process. These links constitute invalid routes, so these nodes continue misdirected message transmissions, wastefully congesting the message channel. In fairness to the GB protocol, it is clear that it was not intended for use in disconnected networks. Its instability could be addressed by using counters, although this would not stop the nodes from sending messages when no valid route exists.

Performance

LMR was compared by simulation with both pure flooding and the GB Partial Reversal method [Corson+ 1995]. The performance results indicated that LMR is preferable for heavy traffic conditions. For light traffic conditions, LMR is preferable for low rates of change, whereas GB is preferable for high rates. Both LMR and GB significantly outperform flooding for all rates of change until the rate becomes so high that only flooding is possible.

8.4 THE TEMPORALLY ORDERED ROUTING ALGORITHM

Following essentially the same design philosophy of Corson and Ephremides [Corson+ 1995], Park and Corson developed the Temporally Ordered Routing Algorithm (TORA) [Park+ 1997] principally to address the shortcomings discovered in [Corson+ 1995, Gafni+ 1981]. In so doing, they developed a protocol that can be viewed conceptually as a merger of the query-reply mechanism of LMR and the partial link-reversal mechanism of GB. However, in the process each mechanism was also modified. The periodic nature of LMR's query process was replaced with a propagation mechanism that removes the need for periodic retransmissions. Also, the partial reversal mechanism of GB was enhanced with a temporal marker permitting distributed partition detection, hence providing stability and convergence in the face of network partitions. The protocol is adaptive, reasonably efficient, and scalable, making it potentially well suited for use in large, dynamic, bandwidth-constrained networks.

The protocol's key feature is its reaction to link failures. In short, its reaction is structured as a temporally ordered sequence of diffusing computations, with each computation consisting of a sequence of directed link reversals. Each link reversal sequence effectively conducts a *search* for alternative routes to the destination. This search mechanism often involves only a *single pass* of the distributed algorithm because it simultaneously modifies the routing tables *during the outward phase of the search procedure* itself.

This is in contrast to other approaches such as LMR, which uses a *two-pass* procedure (FQ/RPY), or DSR and AODV, which utilize *three-pass* procedures (i.e., route error/route-request/route-reply) to discover new routes when a node loses its last route. DSR and AODV (1) erase routes with route error packets, (2) search for new routes in an expanding outward search phase (route request), and (3) rebuild new routes in a contracting, inward phase (route reply). Alternatively, LMR combines phases 1 and 2 (route erasure and search) into a single expanding phase (with the FQ packet) and then builds new routes in a contracting phase (with the RPY packet). TORA attempts to combine all three phases—erasure, search, and rebuilding—into a single phase (UPD processing) in response to link failures.

TORA's aggressive single-pass route search and rebuilding capability is unique among protocols that are stable in the face of network partitions. It can result in high localization and low communication complexity operation in highly connected networks. This behavior is achieved through the use of a "physical or logical clock" to establish a temporal order of topological change events, which is used to structure the protocol's reaction to changes. Of course, during initial on-demand route construction, TORA utilizes a two-pass search and build procedure (with QRY and UPD packets) in a fashion equivalent to that in LMR, AODV, and DSR.

8.4.1 Protocol Description

Except as noted, the network model assumed and the notation used are the same as for the LMR protocol. The following is taken directly from Park and Corson [Park+ 1997] with only minor modifications.

A logically separate version of TORA is run for each destination to which routing is required. The following presentation focuses on a single version running for a given destination. The protocol can be separated into three basic functions—creating, maintaining, and erasing routes. During route creation and maintenance, nodes use a metric to establish a DAG rooted at the destination. Conceptually, as with the GB protocols, this metric can be viewed as the "height" of the node. Links are assigned a direction (upstream or downstream) based on the relative heights of neighboring nodes—that is, from higher to lower. Links to neighboring nodes with an unknown or "null" height are considered undirected and cannot be used for routing. The route creation process essentially corresponds to the selection of node heights to establish a directed sequence of links leading to the destination in a previously undirected network or portion of the network. Following a topological change (e.g., the loss of some node's last downstream link), some directed paths may no longer lead to the destination. The route maintenance process acts as a sequence of directed link reversals (caused by the reselection of node heights), which re-orients the DAG such that all directed paths again lead to the destination. Route erasure is initiated when a node perceives that it has detected a network partition. During this process, nodes set their heights to null and their adjacent links become undirected. TORA accomplishes these three functions through the use of three distinct control packets: query (QRY), update (UPD), and clear (CLR).

At any given time and for each destination, an ordered quintuple, $H_i = (\tau_i, oid_i, r_i, \delta_i, i)$, is associated with each node $i \in N$. The quintuple associated with each node represents the node height as defined by two parameters: a "reference level" and a "delta," or offset, with respect to the reference level. The reference level is represented by the first three values in the quintuple, while the delta is represented by the last two. A *new* reference level is defined each time a node loses its last downstream link because of a link failure. The first value representing the reference level, τ_i, is a time tag set to the "time" of the link failure. Initially we assume that all nodes have synchronized clocks, as it simplifies the description. As will be discussed in Section 8.4.2, this time tag need not actually indicate or be the "time," nor will any lack of clock synchronization invalidate the protocol. The second value, oid_i, is the originator ID (i.e., the unique ID of the node that *defined* the new reference level). This ensures that the reference levels can be totally ordered lexicographically, even if multiple nodes define reference levels due to failures that occur simultaneously (i.e., with *equal* time tags). The third value, r_i, is a single bit used to divide each of the unique reference levels into two unique "sub-levels," which distinguish the "original" reference level from its corresponding, higher "reflected" reference level. When a distinction is not required, both original and reflected reference levels are simply referred to as "reference levels." The first value representing the delta, δ_i, is an integer used to order nodes with respect to a common reference level. This value is instrumental in a levels' propagation. How δ_i is selected will be clarified in a subsequent section. Finally, the second value representing the delta, i, is the unique ID of the node itself. This ensures that nodes with common reference levels and equal values of δ_i (and, in fact, all nodes) can be totally ordered lexicographically at all times.

Each node i (other than the DEST) maintains its height H_i with respect to the DEST. Initially, the height of each node i in the network (other than the destination) is set to null, meaning that $H_i = (-, -, -, -, i)$. Subsequently, the height of each node i can be modified in accordance with the rules of the protocol. The height of the destination is always zero, meaning that $H_{\text{DEST}} = (0, 0, 0, 0, \text{DEST})$, where DEST is the destination ID (i.e., the unique ID of the destination for which the algorithm is running). In addition to its own height, each node i maintains a height array with an entry $HN_{i,j}$ for each neighbor $j \in N_i$. Initially the height of each neighbor is set to null, $HN_{i,j} = (-, -, -, -, j)$. If the destination is a neighbor of i (i.e., $\text{DEST} \in N_i$), node i sets the height entry of the destination to zero, $HN_{i,\text{DEST}} = (0, 0, 0, 0, \text{DEST})$.

Each node i (other than the destination) also maintains a link status array with an entry $LS_{i,j}$ for each link $(i, j) \in L$, where $j \in N_i$. The status of the links is determined by the heights H_i and $HN_{i,j}$ and is directed from the higher to the lower node. If a neighbor j is higher than node i, the link is marked upstream (UP). If j is lower than i, the link is marked downstream (DN). If the neighbor's height entry, $HN_{i,j}$, is null, the link is marked undirected (UN). Finally, if the height of node i is null, then any neighbor's height that is not null is considered lower and the corresponding link is marked downstream. When a new link $(i, j) \in L$ is established (i.e., node i has a new neighbor $j \in N_i$), node i adds entries for the new neighbor to the height and link status arrays. If the new neighbor is the destination, the height entry is set to zero, $HN_{i,\text{DEST}} = (0, 0, 0, 0, \text{DEST})$; otherwise, it is set to null, $HN_{i,j} = (-, -, -, -, j)$. The corresponding link status, $LS_{i,j}$, is set as outlined above. Nodes need not communicate any height information at link activation, but they may transmit QRY packets, as will be seen subsequently.

Creating Routes

As with LMR, creating routes requires the use of two packets, QRY and UPD. A QRY packet consists of a DEST field, which identifies the destination for which the algorithm is running. An UPD packet consists of a DEST field and the height of the node i that is broadcasting the packet, H_i.

Each node i (other than the destination) maintains a route-required flag, RR_i, which is initially assigned the value zero. Each node i (other than the destination) also maintains the time at which the last UPD packet was broadcast and the time at which each link $l_{i,j} \in L$, where $j \in N_i$, became active.

When a node i with no directed links and $RR_i = 0$ requires a route to the destination, it broadcasts a QRY packet and sets $RR_i = 1$.

When a node i receives a QRY packet, it reacts as follows:

- If $RR_i = 1$, it discards the QRY packet, as this means that it has already broadcast a QRY for the DEST.
- If $RR_i = 0$ and H_i is non-null with $r_i = 0$, it first compares the time the last UPD packet was broadcast by this node to the time the link (over which the QRY packet was received) became active. If a UPD packet has been broadcast since the link became active, it discards the QRY packet; otherwise, it broadcasts a UPD packet that contains its current height H_i. This ensures that UPD packets are not repeatedly (and unnecessarily) broadcast in response to nearly simultaneous QRY receptions.
- If $RR_i = 0$ and H_i is *either* null or non-null with $r_i = 1$, but has a neighbor node j whose height is non-null with $r_j = 0$, the node

1. Sets its height to $H_i = (\tau_j, oid_j, r_j, \delta_j + 1, i)$, where $HN_{i,j} = (\tau_j, oid_j, r_j, \delta_j, j)$ is the minimum height of its non-null neighbors with $r_j = 0$.

2. Updates all the entries in its link status array LS.

3. Broadcasts a UPD packet that contains its new height H_i.

In this case the node updates its (null or invalid $r_i = 1$) height with that from a neighbor j with a non-null $r_j = 0$ height, and broadcasts its height in the UPD packet. This is necessary, as the protocol does not build routes from nodes with null or $r = 1$ heights.

- If none of the above conditions hold true, the receiving node rebroadcasts the QRY packet and sets $RR_i = 1$.

Also, if a node has $RR_i = 1$ when a new link is established, it broadcasts a QRY packet. This ensures that the search for a route to the destination continues to propagate as the network topology changes, when the destination may have initially been unreachable from the source that initiated the query.

When a node i receives a UPD packet from a neighbor $j \in N_i$, it first updates the entry $HN_{i,j}$ in its height array, with H_j contained in the received UPD packet, and then reacts as follows:

- If $RR_i = 1$ and $HN_{i,j}$ is non-null with $r = 0$, the node

1. Sets $H_i = (\tau_j, oid_j, r_j, \delta_j + 1, i)$, where $HN_{i,j} = (\tau_j, oid_j, r_j, \delta_j, j) = H_j$.

2. Updates all the entries in its link status array LS.

3. Sets $RR_i = 0$.

4. Broadcasts a UPD packet that contains its new height H_i.

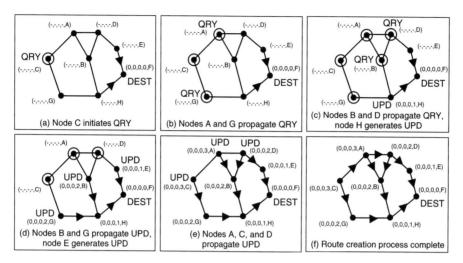

Figure 8.10. Creating Routes

• If the preceding condition does not hold true (i.e., either a route is not required or a neighbor does not offer a valid path), the receiving node simply updates the entry $LS_{i,j}$ in its link status array.

The Maintaining Routes subsection, which follows, discusses the additional reaction that occurs if the second condition results in loss of the *last* downstream link.

An example of the route creation process is depicted in Figure 8.10. The respective heights are shown adjacent to each node, and the destination for which the algorithm is running is marked "DEST." A circle around a node indicates that its route-required flag is set. Recall that the last value in each height is the unique ID of the node and that lexicographical ordering (where $0 < 1 < 2 \ldots$ and $A < B < C \ldots$) is used to direct links. Note that the height selected for node D in Figure 8.10(e) reflects an arbitrary assumption that node D received the UPD packet from node E before the packet from node B. Had node D instead selected a height in response to the packet from node B, the direction of link (A, D) in Figure 8.10(f) would have been reversed.

Maintaining Routes

Route maintenance is performed only for nodes that have a height other than null. Furthermore, any neighbor's null height is not used in any computations. A node with no downstream links must modify its height to re-orient the DAG. A node i is said to have no downstream links if $H_i < HN_{i,j}$ for all non-null neighbors $j \in N_i$. Thus, route maintenance proceeds following the loss of a node's last downstream link and can result from two possible events that trigger modification of the link status array LS: a link failure or a packet reception. First, in the event that a node i experiences the failure of an adjacent link $(i, j) \in L$, it removes the entries $HN_{i,j}$ and $LS_{i,j}$ in its height and link status arrays. Second, when a node i receives a UPD packet from a neighbor $j \in N_i$, it updates the entries $HN_{i,j}$ and $LS_{i,j}$ in its height and link status arrays. If either of these events results in the loss of node i's last downstream link, i must subsequently modify its height in accordance with the cases outlined next. It is also possible for a node to lose its last downstream link because of the reception of a CLR packet, that discussion is presented in the Erasing Routes subsection, which follows (see p. 284).

Each node i (other than the destination) that has no downstream links modifies its height, $H_i = (\tau_i, oid_i, r_i, \delta_i, i)$, as follows.

Case 1 (Generate): If, because of a link failure, node i has no downstream links, it modifies its height as

$$
\begin{aligned}
(\tau_i, oid_i, r_i) &= (t, i, 0), \\
(\delta_i, i) &= (0, i)
\end{aligned}
$$

where t is the time of the failure.

In essence, node i *defines* a new reference level. The preceding assumes that node i has at least one upstream neighbor. If node i has no upstream neighbors, it simply sets its height to null.

Case 2 (Propagate): If, because of a link reversal following reception of an UPD packet from a node j, node i has no downstream links (note that a UPD reception triggers modification of link state entry LS_{ij}, which may cause loss of the last downstream link at node i), and the ordered sets (τ_j, oid_j, r_j) are *not equal* for all $j \in N_i$, then node i modifies its height as

$$
\begin{aligned}
(\tau_i, oid_i, r_i) &= \max\left\{(\tau_j, oid_j, r_j) \mid j \in N_i\right\}, \\
(\delta_i, i) &= \left(\min\left\{\delta_j \;\middle|\; \begin{array}{l} j \in N_i \text{ with } (\tau_j, oid_j, r_j) \\ = \max\{(\tau_j, oid_j, r_j)\} \end{array}\right\} - 1, \; i\right)
\end{aligned}
$$

In essence, node i *propagates* the reference level of its highest neighbor and selects a height that is lower than that of all neighbors with that reference level.

Case 3 (Reflect): If, because of a link reversal following reception of a UPD packet, node i has no downstream links, and the ordered sets

(τ_j, oid_j, r_j) are *equal* with $r_j = 0$ for all $j \in N_i$, then i modifies its height as

$$(\tau_i, oid_i, r_i) = (\tau_j, oid_j, 1),$$
$$(\delta_i, i) = (0, i)$$

In essence, the same level (which has *not* been "reflected") has propagated to node i from all of its neighbors. Node i *reflects* back a higher sublevel by setting the bit $r = 1$.

Case 4 (Detect): If, because of a link reversal following reception of a UPD packet, node i has no downstream links, and the ordered sets (τ_j, oid_j, r_j) are *equal* with $r_j = 1$ for all $j \in N_i$, and $oid_j = i$ (i.e., node i defined the level), then i modifies its height as

$$(\tau_i, oid_i, r_i) = (-, -, -),$$
$$(\delta_i, i) = (-, i)$$

In essence, the last reference level defined by node i has been reflected and propagated back as a higher sublevel from all of its neighbors. This corresponds to *detection* of a partition. Node i must initiate the process of erasing invalid routes—routes that are not rooted at the destination— as discussed in the next section.

Case 5 (Generate): If, because of a link reversal following reception of a UPD packet, node i has no downstream links, the ordered sets (τ_j, oid_j, r_j) are *equal* with $r_j = 1$ for all $j \in N_i$, and $oid_j \neq i$ (i.e., node i did not define the level), then i modifies its height as

$$(\tau_i, oid_i, r_i) = (t, i, 0),$$
$$(\delta_i, i) = (0, i)$$

In essence, node i experienced a link failure (which did *not* require reaction) between the time it propagated (i.e., relayed) a reference level and the time the reflected higher sublevel returned from all neighbors (this is not necessarily an indication of a partition). Node i *defines* a new reference level. The action is the same as in case 1; hence, it has the same case name, "generate."

Following determination of its new height in cases 1, 2, 3, and 5, node i updates all entries in its link status array LS, and broadcasts to all neighbors $j \in N_i$ a UPD packet that contains its new height H_i. This may cause one or more neighbors to lose their last downstream links, in which case

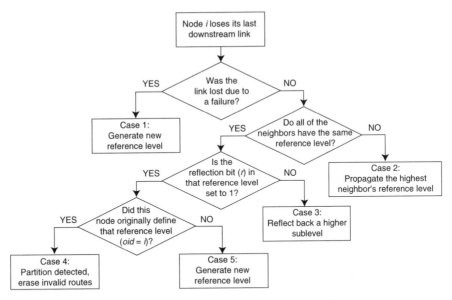

Figure 8.11. Decision Tree for Maintaining Routes

any such neighbors will modify their heights as outlined in the preceding cases. Figure 8.11 summarizes these five cases in the form of a decision tree, starting from the time a node loses its last downstream link.

Referring to Figure 8.11, the final test of whether node i itself defined the reference level is important. Definition of a new reference level equates to initiation of a new diffusing computation. Multiple diffusing computations may be active simultaneously. For each computation, only one node (the originator) is permitted to declare whether or not the computation has terminated in the detection of a partition. Relaxation of this constraint may result in many nodes in a dynamic topology declaring partition when the network is still connected. In fact, the originator may (falsely) detect a partition when the destination is still reachable (and always was so), but the probability of false detection is greatly lowered by restricting that role to the originator.

A disquieting aspect of distributed algorithm design is the (unfortunate) realization that many algorithm decisions must be made with only partial information. The more one tries to localize algorithmic reaction, the less information is made available for algorithmic processing.

The following examples illustrate how the algorithm works. Figure 8.12 provides an example where no reaction is required. The network is first depicted as at the end of Figure 8.10 except that link (D, E) is marked as failing. Because all nodes still have downstream links following the failure,

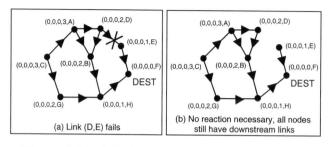

Figure 8.12. A Link Failure Requiring No Reaction

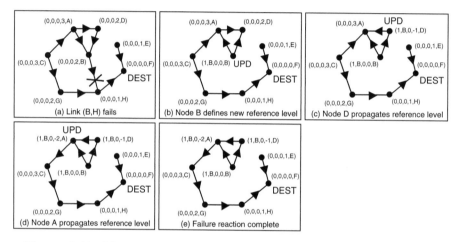

Figure 8.13. Maintaining Routes after a Link Failure Requiring a Reaction

no transmissions are required. The significance of this is greater for networks that are highly connected, as nodes with a greater number of downstream links can tolerate more failures before reacting. Figure 8.13 provides an example where a reaction is required. The network is first depicted as at the end of Figure 8.12 except that link (B, H) is marked as failing. The time of the failure, as depicted in the example, was arbitrarily selected to be 1.

Erasing Routes

Following detection of a partition (case 4), node i sets its height and the height entry for each neighbor $j \in N_i$ to null, updates all the entries in its link status array LS, and broadcasts a CLR packet. The CLR packet consists of a DEST and the reflected reference level of node i $(\tau_i, oid_i, 1)$. When a node i receives a CLR packet from a neighbor $j \in N_i$, it reacts as follows:

- If the reference level in the CLR packet matches the reference level of node i, it sets its height and the height entry for each neighbor $j \in N_i$ to null (unless the destination is a neighbor, in which case the corresponding height entry is set to zero), updates all entries in its link status array LS, and broadcasts a CLR packet.

- If the reference level in the CLR packet does not match the reference level of node i, it sets the height for each neighbor $j \in N_i$ (with the same reference level as that of the CLR packet) to null and updates the corresponding link status array entries.

Thus, the height of each node in the partitioned portion of the network is set to null and all invalid routes are erased. If the second condition causes node i to lose its last downstream link, i reacts as in case 1 of route maintenance. Figure 8.14 provides an example demonstrating partition detection and invalid route erasure. The network is first depicted as at the end of Figure 8.13 except that link (A, C) is marked as failing. The time of the failure, as depicted in the example, was arbitrarily selected to be 2.

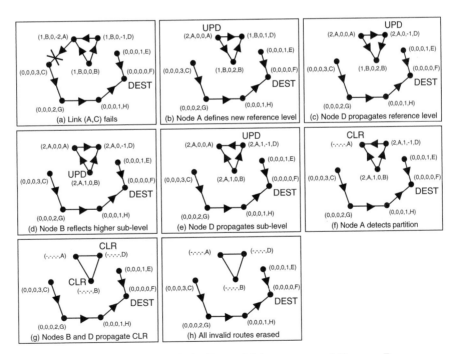

Figure 8.14. Examples of the Route Maintenance and Erasure Processes
Following a Network Partitions

The results illustrated by the examples can be summarized as follows. When a failure causes a node to lose its last downstream link, the node re-establishes a route to the destination in one pass of the set of nodes affected by the failure (provided that a path to the destination exists). If a path to the destination no longer exists, the node detects the partition in two passes of the set of affected nodes; all invalid routes are erased in three passes of that set.

8.4.2 Properties of the Protocol

Issues such as loop freedom and convergence must be examined to understand the operation and limitations of a protocol. Loop freedom and convergence within a finite time are desirable properties for routing protocols—protocols possessing them tend to perform well. We stress that these are generally desirable but not necessary conditions for good protocol performance. Whereas the key concept of TORA is the route maintenance function—which is simply a new algorithm in the general class of GB algorithms (and thus inherits the properties of that class)—the entire protocol includes other mechanisms that place it *outside* this class. For example, TORA adds the notion of a null height (which can be thought of as an *infinite* height), a method for assigning non-null heights to previously null nodes (creating routes), the ability to detect network partitions, and a method for assigning null heights to previously non-null nodes (erasing routes). The modification from null to non-null effectively *reduces* a node's height, which is not permitted in GB algorithms. Also excluded is the notion of an infinite height.

For these reasons, it is necessary to address the properties of loop freedom and convergence for TORA. In addition to the stated assumptions regarding packet transmission and reception, it is also assumed that events (e.g., topological changes or packet receptions) are processed by each node in the order in which they occur and that each individual event is processed within a finite time.

Loop Freedom

Consider any time when the control packets that were created by nodes that modified their heights have been correctly received by all of the neighboring nodes, and any such neighboring nodes have updated their corresponding height and link-state entries. At any such time, no two neighboring nodes can disagree on the direction (i.e., UP versus DN) assigned to a given link (although one neighbor may consider the link assigned while the other may consider it unassigned). This does not imply that all reactions have ceased. There may be any number of nodes that must subsequently modify their heights in accordance with the rules of the protocol (because of a link failure or a received control packet) and must broadcast additional control packets.

Claim: Loop freedom. The routes defined by the link-state arrays are loop free at every such instant in time.

Proof: This property is almost a direct result of the total ordering of the heights associated with the nodes and of the fact that these heights determine the direction of the links between nodes. The proof is by contradiction. Assume that a loop is formed (node 1 is considered downstream by node 2; node 2 is considered downstream by node 3; ... node $(k-1)$ is considered downstream by node k; and node k is considered downstream by node 1). A node i considers a neighbor j to be downstream on the basis of comparison of its stored values for the respective heights, H_i and $HN_{i,j}$. This is not possible if any of the corresponding entries in the height arrays $(HN_{i,j} \mid (i,j)$ is part of the loop) are null, as a neighbor with a height of null is never considered downstream. A non-null height array entry for a neighbor j implies prior reception of a UPD packet from that neighbor, which by the initial assumptions implies that $HN_{i,j} = H_j$, $\forall i = 1 \ldots k$, and that $j \in N_i \mid (i,j)$ is part of the loop. Furthermore, the height of all nodes that are part of the loop must be non-null. Therefore, the internal node comparisons that define the downstream links—$HN_{2,1} < H_2, HN_{3,2} < H_3, \ldots HN_{k,k-1} < H_k$, $HN_{1,k} < H_1$—can be rewritten $H_1 < H_2 < H_3 \ldots < H_{k-1} < H_k < H_1$. This is a clear contradiction because the heights are quintuples where the last value is the unique ID of the node (ensuring that heights can be totally ordered lexicographically).

Convergence and Stability

It would be comforting to show analytically that there is a finite bound on TORA's worst-case convergence time. However, this is not always true for the on-demand mode of the protocol; that is, in some circumstances the protocol can enter a cycle that, theoretically, can repeat indefinitely.

An example of this potential oscillatory behavior is depicted in Figure 8.15, where it can be seen that the protocol's state in Figure 8.15(f) and (r) is essentially equivalent. The protocol is kept in this cycle not by continuously occurring topological changes (after Figure 8.15(a) the topology is static) but by continuously occurring QRY packets being generated and transmitted by nodes at inopportune times—essentially building "invalid" routes rooted at nodes other than the destination. In this sense, the behavior is related to the transient instability exhibited in the LMR protocol.

It has been shown [Park 1997] that in the absence of route building TORA (as described) will converge within a finite time. Furthermore, the route creation process can be modified such that a finite bound on the worst-case convergence time can be established even in the presence of route building [Park 1997], but it is not clear that doing so is desirable.

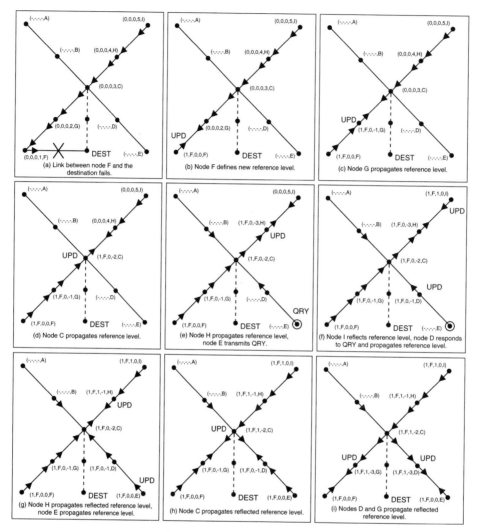

Figure 8.15. Example of Potential Oscillatory Behavior

Every mechanism we have devised to accomplish this task adversely impacts the protocol's communication complexity. In most cases, the protocol performs worse rather than better. Also, the oscillatory behavior illustrated in the previous example is highly dependent on the physical topology of the network, the state of the nodes at the time of the last topological change, and the timing of the packet transmissions. Examination of the phenomena shows that it is unlikely that any oscillations will persist very long. In essence, *TORA is biased toward convergence.* For the protocol to remain in the cycle requires an infinite sequence of perfectly timed QRY generations

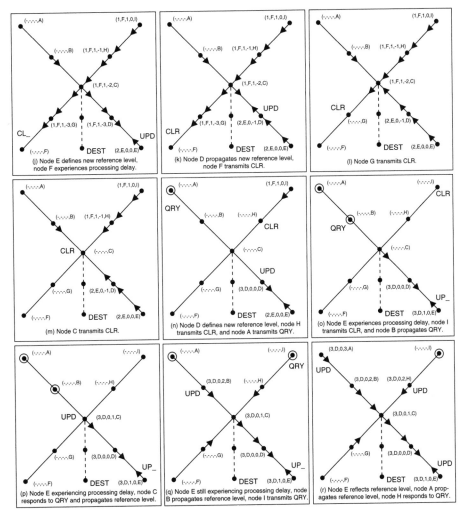

Figure 8.15. *(Continued)*

(something highly unlikely in any real network). Any deviation from such a sequence results in protocol convergence.

The simulations presented in [Park 1997, Park+ 1998] show that despite its unbounded worst-case convergence time, the protocol performs well under a wide variety of networking environments and never displays the traditional explosion of control or data message traffic that characterizes protocol instability. Throughout approximately 150 hours of simulated runtime under rather extreme and stressing scenarios, TORA's average performance remains consistently good (i.e., comparable to or better than an Ideal Link State (ILS) algorithm [Bertsekas+ 1992]). The amount of control overhead generated by TORA is less than that of ILS for every simulation scenario investigated.

One possible explanation for TORA's good performance, despite its unbounded worst-case convergence time, relates to internodal coordination— a technique used in distance-vector routing algorithms to prevent the counting-to-infinity problem [Jaffe+ 1982, Gracia-Luna-Aceves 1993]. In a distance-vector routing algorithm, nodes maintain (and exchange) estimates of their distance to the given destination. In a sense, this distance metric serves as a protocol's "anchor" to the destination and ensures global "stability." The counting-to-infinity problem can occur when nodes update their distance metrics on the basis of a node with outdated information (which is similar to building "invalid" routes as described herein and in prior work by Corson and Ephremides [Corson+ 1995]). With this conceptual view, it is apparent that the counting-to-infinity problem exhibited by some distance-vector algorithms is related to the unstable behaviors exhibited by TORA and LMR. By coordinating topological change reactions with surrounding nodes under certain circumstances, this problem can be prevented.

Although in a vastly different form, TORA also uses internodal coordination. Upon failure of the last downstream link, a node generates a new reference level, which the set of affected nodes propagate, essentially coordinating a structured reaction to the failure. In a sense, this set of nodes becomes "anchored" to the node that generated the reference level. Within an "unstable" section of the network (i.e., one where there are ongoing failure reactions anchored to different nodes), the coordinated group of nodes anchored to the node that generated the highest reference level will typically *dominate* (i.e., expand to include more nodes) until either all groups merge with it (and it joins a "stable" section of the network) or it detects a partition. If a partition is detected, all nodes with that reference level will be set to null. Thus, this coordination of nodes with a common reference level has a "stabilizing effect" within the protocol, significantly reducing the likelihood of an excessively long convergence time.

As mentioned earlier, the potential for oscillatory behavior stems from the fact that routes are built *on demand* and that the height metric used in TORA is not firmly anchored to the destination. Thus, oscillations may occur when multiple sets of coordinating nodes are simultaneously detecting partitions, erasing routes, and building new routes based on each other. However, permitting this potential—something forbidden in a traditional approach to protocol design—and then biasing the protocol away from oscillation is exactly what allows localization of TORA's communication in the midst of on-demand route construction. This makes it adaptive and well suited to the certain networking environments.

Recent Extensions

Thus far we have described the on-demand mode of TORA. However, proactive periodic route optimization is also possible. This mode of operation can be activated on a per-destination basis, under the control of the destination itself. Such functionality might be used when many (or all) nodes frequently require routes to a given destination, perhaps to a gateway router or a Mobile IP foreign agent [Perkins 1996]. We now describe the essential characteristics of this mode.

Proactively Optimized TORA   Optimized TORA requires the definition of a new packet type, the optimization (OPT) packet. OPT packets for a given destination are generated only by the destination itself. Each node maintains an indication of the mode of operation for routing to the destination. The Optimization Mode flag OM_i may be either OFF, PARTIAL, or FULL—determining the behavior of periodic optimizations (if any) for the destination. Each node also maintains an optimization sequence number OS_i, which indicates the most recently seen OPT packet received from the destination. For the optimization mechanism, the destination also maintains an optimization period, which determines the frequency with which periodic optimizations will occur.

The DEST controls the settings of the aforementioned parameters, which are disseminated to the nodes in OPT packets. The OPT packet contains several fields: the DEST identifier, the optimization mode set by the destination OM_{DEST}, the optimization sequence number set by the destination OS_{DEST}, and a delta value δ set by the node that broadcast the packet.

If optimization is turned ON (i.e., OM_{DEST} = PARTIAL or FULL) for a DEST, the DEST node periodically generates OPT packets with successively higher sequence numbers. The extent of their dissemination is determined by the OM_{DEST} setting and the heights in the network. When a node i receives an OPT packet from some neighbor j, it checks to see if the sequence number in the packet OS_{DEST} is higher than one it has previously seen, OS_i. If not, it discards the packet; if so, it updates its OS_i and OM_i values stored for the DEST and then proceeds as follows.

If OM_i = FULL, or if OM_i = PARTIAL, and the node's height is non-null, the node:

1. Sets its height to zero.
2. Sets its δ_i to $\delta_j + 1$, where δ_j is the delta value in the received OPT packet.
3. Updates its LS arrays for all nodes.
4. Sets its $RR_i = 0$.
5. Updates the time it last broadcast its height.
6. Broadcasts the OPT packet with its current value of δ_i.

This processing ensures that full optimizations travel throughout the network and that partial optimizations only reset the heights of non-null nodes. The affected portions of the network have their heights reset to a zero reference level and receive an updated estimate of their distance to the DEST.

While there is no explicit distance estimate maintained in TORA, when the DAG is initially formed upon route creation (i.e., before any subsequent link reversals) the fourth element of each node's height δ_i essentially contains the distance (in hops) from the destination to the node over the path traveled by the UPD packet (see Figure 8.10(f)). As links are reversed in reaction to a failure, this distance information is lost in these "reversed" portions (as δ no longer denotes distance to the destination when the reference level is not zero). The optimization mechanism described here restores the distance significance of δ_i in the height metric maintained by each node.

Synchronization   Up to now we have described the methods for modifying TORA heights assuming that the nodes participating in the computation have synchronized clocks. As described, if the nodes do not have synchronized clocks, the distributed computation can be shown to enter an erroneous condition in certain cases—resulting in the formation of invalid routes to the destination.

This erroneous condition can be described briefly as follows. In some cases, a node i with no downstream links selects a new height by defining a new reference level based on its locally perceived time. The use of synchronized clocks ensures that the newly selected height is higher than all previously defined heights in the network. Thus, selection of the new height for node i reverses the direction of all links incident on that node. However, in the absence of synchronized clocks the new height of node i may be lower than the heights of all the neighboring nodes—resulting in *none* of the links incident on node i being redirected. In this case node i becomes an additional sink (sometimes referred to as a "black hole") for traffic intended for the destination. That is, node i does not have a downstream link for forwarding traffic to the destination, and the set of directed paths in the network leads either to the destination or to node i.

For proper operation in the absence of synchronized clocks it is necessary to ensure that, when a node i with no downstream links selects a new height based on its locally perceived time, the direction of *at least one* of the links incident on that node will be reversed. The protocol can be modified as follows. Whenever a node i modifies τ_i to its locally perceived time and subsequently updates the directions of the link markings stored in LS, the protocol checks if there is at least one downstream link incident on the node. If there are no incident downstream links, τ_i is again modified in a manner that ensures the reversal of at least one downstream link. All that is required is that the new height metric be higher than the *lowest* neighbor height, thus ensuring that the direction of at least one link incident on the node will be reversed—for example, $\tau_i = \tau_j + 1$, where node j is the lowest non-null neighbor. Many alternative computations for the new height can be used, such as setting $\tau_i = \tau_j + 1$, where node j is the *highest* non-null neighbor as opposed to the lowest. This computation results in reversing *all* of the links incident on the node.

The behavior and performance of the protocol will be affected by the computation used. The approach chosen for implementation in actual systems makes use of a clock "bias." A local clock bias B is maintained (it is initially set to zero) and applied to the locally perceived time t such that when a node i with no downstream links selects a new height based on its adjusted local time, the reversal of at least one link is guaranteed. At each time t that a node i learns of a new neighbor j's height, it computes its local clock bias as $B = \max(B, \tau_j - t)$, where τ_j is the time tag associated with the new neighbor j's height. Then, when a node i must select a new height based on the current local time t, it simply sets $\tau_i = t + B$.

Performance

TORA was originally developed for possible use in military networks—principally large-scale, dynamic heterogeneous networks employing a mixture of physical layer and multiple access technologies. The military is also studying the use of link-state routing technology in this context because of its uniform convergence properties and its suitability for supporting QoS-based routing. Thus, TORA's initial performance comparison [Park+ 1998] was made relative to ILS. Because no particular multiple access layer could be assumed, the MAC layer was abstracted away—this was reasonable given that both TORA and ILS require the same underlying network support.

The Park and Corson study provided insight into the effects of varying network size, average rate of topological changes, and average network connectivity. While the average network connectivity was found not to be a significant factor, the relative performance of TORA and ILS was found to be critically dependent on the network size and the average rate of topological changes [Park+ 1998]. The results indicated that for a given available bandwidth—as either the size of the network increases or the rate of network topological change increases—the performance of TORA eventually exceeds that of ILS. Specifically, as the network size and/or rate of topological change increases, the amount of control overhead for ILS increases much more rapidly than for TORA—effectively congesting the communication channel and causing additional queuing delay for message traffic. Therefore, above some combination threshold of network size and rate of topological change, TORA provides lower end-to-end message packet delay on average for a given available bandwidth.

The point to be emphasized is that under some networking conditions, TORA—which is not a shortest-path routing algorithm—can outperform a shortest-path routing algorithm. ILS is but one approach for performing shortest-path routing. Nevertheless, for a given network size and rate of topological change, any shortest-path algorithm requires a minimum amount of control overhead to permit continuous shortest-path computation. Our conjecture is that, as the network size and/or rate of topological change increase, this minimum amount of control overhead to permit computation of the shortest path will increase more rapidly than the amount of control overhead for TORA. If so, there must be some threshold for network size and/or rate of topological change at which *any* shortest-path routing protocol will perform poorly relative to TORA. This is an admittedly strong conjecture, difficult to prove in general, but it can perhaps be shown to be valid for other existing shortest-path protocols.

If so, it will likely be so only relative to shortest-path protocols that require the *same* form of interactions with and support from lower layers as TORA does. TORA requires broadcast reliability of its routing information to its one-hop neighbor set—an expensive requirement in ad hoc networks although not an uncommon one [Murthy+ 1996, Ramanathan+ 1998]. It was shown [Broch+ 1998] that TORA performs poorly relative to DSR and AODV when implemented over 802.11-based link layers, principally because of this requirement. DSR and AODV require only unicast reliability to function effectively, which is efficiently provided by the 802.11 RTS-CTS-DATA-ACK exchange. It should be noted that neither DSR nor AODV support shortest-path routing, nor do they require the same underlying support from lower layers. Thus, they are not covered by the earlier conjecture.

In fairness, TORA was not designed for use over 802.11 MAC layers or for any particular MAC layer technology. Rather, it was intended for application in large-scale, dynamic heterogeneous networks that likely have more than one advanced form of multiple access, possibly TDMA based. The relative performance of MANET algorithms is highly dependent on the MAC layer. In networks composed of multiple MAC layers, comparison becomes more difficult. Nevertheless, more simulation study of TORA is required.

In some sense, LMR, TORA, DSR, AODV, and many other on-demand approaches are specific realizations of a general class of algorithms that forgo traditional support of shortest-path computations. Instead, they avoid reacting to many topology changes (often changes that potentially improve routing) to conserve network bandwidth. As mentioned earlier, this approach is akin to a *lazy computation,* albeit one implemented at the network protocol level. The idea is to *defer* reaction as long as possible.

8.5 COMPARISON OF LRR ALGORITHMS

A trend apparent in the progression of LRR routing technology is the movement away from "instability" (nonconvergence) toward "stability." The GB protocols are known to be convergent in portions of the network that are connected to the destination and nonconvergent in portions that are partitioned from it. Similarly, the LMR protocol is convergent in connected portions but may remain nonconvergent in partitioned portions for an arbitrary time period. The TORA approach is convergent in both connected and partitioned portions in the absence of route building, but it may remain nonconvergent in the presence of route building. However, TORA uses a form of internodal coordination to bias the computation toward convergence and to reduce the likelihood that any oscillations or nonconvergent behavior will persist.

It should be noted that TORA is stable by the traditional definition of stability in a distributed algorithm: "Once input to the algorithm ceases, the algorithm converges in a finite time." However, TORA's input consists of link activations and failures (topology driven) *and* QRY generation (demand driven). This last item is not commonly thought of as an input to a routing algorithm, as the development of on-demand routing technology is relatively recent.

The instability of the GB protocols in portions of the network that are partitioned from the destination limits their practical applicability. The relative suitability of LMR and TORA for any particular application will likely be dependent on the characteristics of the intended networking environment. The LMR reaction to link failures is more *pessimistic,* utilizing an erase and build mechanism. This has the advantage of erasing routes in a single pass in partitioned tree portions, but it requires two passes to re-establish routing when an alternative path exists. In contrast, the TORA reaction to link failures is more *optimistic,* reversing links to re-orient the DAG as a means of searching for an alternate path. When alternate paths exist, reactions typically require only a single pass of the distributed algorithm. However, partition detection and erasure of invalid routes requires three passes. The implication is that LMR may be better suited for sparse topologies while TORA may be better suited for dense topologies—although this is simply conjecture at this point. Further performance comparison is needed to better assess the relative suitablity of the two protocols.

8.6 CONCLUSION

This chapter described and compared several algorithms based on LRR technology. The protocols are adaptive, loop free, and distributed, and they possess different convergence properties when handling network partitions. All of the protocols can be implemented reactively (on demand) or proactively (traditionally).

These protocols are designed to decouple (to the greatest extent possible) far-reaching control message propagation from the dynamics of the network topology. Thus, none of them are "anchored" to a source or destination, as is common in other approaches through either additive cost metric propagation or multihop path topology information propagation. This allows the design of highly adaptive and potentially scalable algorithms, but requires care to ensure sufficiently quick convergence.

None support a shortest-path computation, but all may embed a secondary process of route optimization, as described for LMR [Corson+ 1989] (and in this chapter for TORA), wherein a periodic optimization wave is generated and sent out from the destination, which "re-orients" a DAG's link markings to point more uniformly toward the destination. This process can occur at a very low rate—one that is decoupled from the rate of topological changes—and can also serve as a method of soft-state route verification.

While both LMR and TORA are potentially suitable for practical applications, their relative performance has yet to be formally compared. Because of the differences in the mechanisms for failure reaction, it is anticipated that the characteristics of the underlying network topology may have a significant impact on the relative performance of the protocols. Thus, their regions of applicability may be nonoverlapping, with each best suited to different networking environments.

Acknowledgment

Some of the information in this chapter has been excerpted from Gafni, E., and D. Bertsekas, Distributed Algorithms for Generating Loop-free Routes in Networks with Frequently Changing Topology, *IEEE Transactions on Communications* 29(1):11–15, January 1981. Copyright © IEEE. Used with permission.

References

[Awerbuch+ 1991] B. Awerbuch, A. Bar-Noy, and M. Gopal. Approximate Distributed Bellmann-Ford Algorithms. In *Proceedings of IEEE INFOCOM '91*, April 1991.

[Awerbuch+ 1994] B. Awerbuch, B. Patt-Shamir, and G. Varghese. Bounding the Unbounded. In *Proceedings of IEEE INFOCOM '94*, June 1994.

[Bertsekas+ 1992] D. Bertsekas and R. Gallager. *Data Networks*, 2nd ed. Prentice-Hall, Englewood Cliffs, N.J., 1992.

[Broch+ 1998] J. Broch, D.A. Maltz, and D.B. Johnson. A Performance Comparison of Multihop Wireless Ad Hoc Network Routing Protocols. In *Proceedings of* the Fourth Annual ACM/IEEE International Conference on Mobile Computing and Networking (MOBICOM '98), October 1998.

[Corson+ 1989] M.S. Corson and A. Ephremides. A Distributed Routing Algorithm for Mobile Radio Networks. In Proceedings of the IEEE Military Communications Conference (MILCOM '89), October 1989.

[Corson+ 1995] M.S. Corson and A. Ephremides. A Distributed Routing Algorithm for Mobile Wireless Networks. ACM/Baltzer Wireless Networks Journal 1(1):61–82, February 1995.

[Dijkstra+ 1980] E. Dijkstra and C. Scholten. Termination Detection for Diffusing Computations. Information Processing Letters 11(1), August 1980.

[Dube+ 1997] R. Dube, C.D. Rais, K.-Y. Wang, and S.K. Tripathi. Signal Stability-Based Adaptive Routing (SSA) for Ad-Hoc Mobile Networks. IEEE Personal Communications 4(1):36–45, February 1997.

[Gafni+ 1981] E. Gafni and D. Bertsekas. Distributed Algorithms for Generating Loop-free Routes in Networks with Frequently Changing Topology. IEEE Transactions on Communications 29(1):11–15, January 1981.

[Garcia-Luna-Aceves 1987] J.J. Garcia-Luna-Aceves. A New Minimum-Hop Routing Algorithm. In Proceedings of IEEE INFOCOM '87, April 1987.

[Garcia-Luna-Aceves 1988] J.J. Garcia-Luna-Aceves. Distributed Routing Using Internodal Coordination. In Proceedings of IEEE INFOCOM '88, March 1988.

[Garcia-Luna-Aceves 1989] J.J. Garcia-Luna-Aceves. A Minimum-Hop Routing Algorithm Based on Distributed Information. Computer Networks and ISDN Systems 16(5), May 1989.

[Garcia-Luna-Aceves 1992] J.J. Garcia-Luna-Aceves. Distributed Routing with Labeled Distances. In Proceedings of IEEE INFOCOM '92, April 1992.

[Garcia-Luna-Aceves 1993] J.J. Garcia-Luna-Aceves. Loop-Free Routing Using Diffusing Computations. IEEE/ACM Transactions on Networking 1(1):130–141, 1993.

[Garcia-Luna-Aceves+ 1995] J. J. Garcia-Luna-Aceves and J. Behrens. Distributed, Scalable Routing Based on Vectors of Link States. IEEE Journal on Selected Areas of Communication SAC-13(8):1383–1395, 1995.

[Haas+ 1998] Z. Haas and M. Pearlman. The Zone Routing Protocol for Highly Reconfigurable Ad-Hoc Networks. In Proceedings of ACM SIGCOMM '98, August 1998.

[Jaffe+ 1982] J. Jaffe and F. Moss. A Responsive Distributed Routing Algorithm for Computer Networks. IEEE Transactions on Communications COM-30:1758–1762, July 1982.

[Johnson+ 1996] D. Johnson and D. Maltz. Dynamic Source Routing in Ad Hoc Wireless Networks. In Mobile Computing, T. Imielinski and H. Korth, eds. Kluwer Academic Publishers, Norwood, Mass., 1996.

[Li+ 1986] V.O.K. Li and R. Chang. Proposed Routing Algorithms for the US Army Mobile Subscriber Equipment (MSE) Network. In Proceedings of the IEEE Military Communications Conference (MILCOM '86), October 1986.

[Merlin+ 1979] P. Merlin and A. Segall. A Failsafe Distributed Routing Protocol. *IEEE Transactions on Communications* COM-27:1280–1287, 1979.

[Moy 1998] J. Moy. OSPF Version 2. RFC 2328, April 1998.

[Murthy+ 1996] S. Murthy and J.J. Garcia-Luna-Aceves. An Efficient Routing Protocol for Wireless Networks. *ACM/Baltzer Mobile Networks and Applications Journal* 1(2):183–197, October 1996.

[Ogier 1999] R.G. Ogier. An Optimized Link State Routing Algorithm. In *Proceedings of IEEE INFOCOM '99*, 1999.

[Park 1997] V. Park. A Highly Adaptive Distributed Routing Algorithm for Mobile Wireless Networks. Master's thesis, University of Maryland at College Park, 1997.

[Park+ 1997] V. Park and M.S. Corson. A Highly Adaptive Distributed Routing Algorithm for Mobile Wireless Networks. In *Proceedings of IEEE INFOCOM '97*, April 1997.

[Park+ 1998] V. Park and M.S. Corson. A Performance Comparison of TORA and Ideal Link State Routing. In *Proceedings of ISCC '98*, July 1998.

[Perkins 1996] C. Perkins. IP Mobility Support. RFC 2002, October 1996.

[Perkins+ 1999] C. Perkins and E. Royer. Multicast Using Ad Hoc On-Demand Distance-Vector (AODV) Routing. In *Proceedings of the Second Annual IEEE Workshop on Mobile Computing Systems and Applications*, February 1999.

[Rajagopolan+ 1989] B. Rajagopolan and M. Faiman. A New Responsive Distributed Shortest-Path Routing Algorithm. *ACM SIGCOMM Computer Communications Review* 19(4), September 1989.

[Ramanathan+ 1998] S. Ramanathan and M. Steenstrup. Hierarchically-Organized, Multihop Mobile Networks for Multimedia Support. *ACM/Baltzer Mobile Networks and Applications Journal* 3(1):101–119, January 1998.

[Toh 1996] C-K. Toh. *Wireless ATM and Ad-Hoc Networks: Protocols and Architectures*. Kluwer Academic Publishers, Norwood, Mass., 1996.

[Weber+ 1983] M. Weber (Bates) and A. Ephremides. A Simulated Performance Study of Some Distributed Routing Algorithms for Mobile Radio Networks. In *Proceedings of the Conference on Information Sciences and Systems (CISS '83)*, March 1983.

The Effects of Beaconing on the Battery Life of Ad Hoc Mobile Computers

C-K. Toh
Vasos Vassiliou
School of Electrical and Computer Engineering
Georgia Institute of Technology

Abstract

Mobile computing is evolving rapidly with advances in wireless communications and wireless networking protocols. However, despite the fact that devices are getting smaller and more efficient, advances in battery technology have not yet reached the stage where a mobile computer can operate for days without recharging. Many existing routing protocols use periodic transmission of route updates to maintain the accuracy of route tables. In wireless networks, beaconing can also be used to signify the presence of neighboring nodes and to indicate their *spatial, temporal, connection,* and *signal stability.*

In this chapter, we present the outcome of our research, in which a series of experiments was conducted to evaluate the effect of periodic beaconing on the battery life of an ad hoc mobile computer. We have found that it is imperative to select an appropriate beaconing interval that does not upset the overall power degradation characteristic of the system and, at the same time, causes no noticeable side effects for existing applications. We have also found that the actions taken by the system in preparation for power shutdown actually draw more power than usual. The impact of neighboring nodes' beacons on power life is also examined.

9.1 MOTIVATION

There is an increasing need for energy efficient systems in the wireless world because being wireless requires as much standalone operation as possible, including a self-sustaining power supply. Advances in battery technologies, however, have not reached the stage where batteries that power mobile computers can last for days or months without recharging. Although solar energy is abundant, solar cells are not cheap enough to be widely used. In addition, many solar cells are required to achieve the ampere-per-hour requirements for today's mobile computers, making their use impractical [SCET 1998]. Until the day when batteries are long-lasting and systems are self-sustaining, we will have to face the issue of power efficiency and conservation.

There have been two major aspects of research in power conservation for computers and computer networks—namely, *device* [Intel+ 1996, Intel+ 1999, Chan+ 1995, Katz+ 1996] and *communications* [Agrawal 1998, Scott+ 1996, Zorzi+ 1997, Woo+ 1998, Singh+ 1998]. The former is concerned with the hardware associated with the standalone mobile computer, such as LCD display, CPU, keyboard, memories, floppy disks, and hard drives. The latter is concerned with power conservation by the various layers of the protocol stack. With regard to the communication aspects, especially at the network layer, several existing link-state or distance-vector protocols [McQuillan+ 1980] employ periodic transmission of *Hello* messages to propagate route updates throughout the network. Beaconing has also been used to announce the presence of a node to surrounding nodes. Given that beaconing is used in wireless networks, it is important to examine its effects on battery life and to find suitable values so that it does not compromise power and communication performance. This forms the core motivation of our research work.

This chapter is organized as follows. Section 9.2 gives a brief introduction to wireless ad hoc networks and some background on power management (PM) techniques and battery characteristics. Section 9.4 describes the experimental environment for evaluating the effects of beaconing on battery life. Section 9.5 presents and discusses our experimental results. Lastly, Section 9.6 presents the conclusions drawn from this work.

9.2 AD HOC WIRELESS NETWORKS

In ad hoc wireless networks, no base stations exist and each mobile host (MH) acts as a router and a packet forwarder. Networks can be formed and fragmented on the fly without the intervention of a system administrator or the presence of fixed network devices.

Mobility and the constraints on power and bandwidth in ad hoc wireless networks have been the motivation for deriving a suitable routing protocol for such networks. Most protocols proposed can be classified as *table driven* [Perkins+ 1994] or *on demand* [Toh 1997b, Perkins+ 1999, Johnson+ 1996]. Some can be classified as *proactive* or *reactive*. The former constantly propagate route updates to maintain consistent and up-to-date route table information in all ad hoc mobile nodes. The latter discover routes on the basis of demand by the source node so that constant route udpates are avoided. In this chapter, we will discuss some details of the on-demand routing protocol that was used in our experimental testbed.

9.2.1 Power Issues

Mobile computers today are powered by battery while they are on the move. Thus, to ensure good continuity of system operation over time, several approaches are taken to enhance battery life. One such approach is known as *power management,* another relies on the *discharge and storage characteristics* of the battery used. We will discuss these in the following sections.

Power Management

Device manufacturers have always striven for lower power consumption in their products so that these devices are efficient to operate. Many such power-limiting efforts have concentrated on the individual device. A mobile computer, however, comprises different devices, such as hard and floppy disk drives, LCD displays, and CD/DVD ROMs, each of which has its own power requirements, operation characteristics, and usage patterns. This makes power management (PM) in the overall system complicated. Recent suggestions for more comprehensive power management include *Advanced Power Management* (APM) [Intel+ 1996], *Operating System Power Management* (OSPM), and *Advanced Configuration Power Interface* (ACPI) [Intel+ 1999].

Most of these techniques are incorporated into existing mobile computers and hence are worthy of mention here. In APM, one or more layers of software support power management in computers with power-manageable hardware. APM's objective is to control the power usage of a system on the basis of the system's activity. Power is reduced gradually as system resources become unused until the system suspends.

ACPI, on the other hand, defines new methods for power control. It enables an operating system to implement system-directed power management. The ACPI hardware interface is a standardized way to integrate power management throughout a portable system's hardware and OS and applications software. It gives the operating system direct control over the power management and plug-and-play functions of a computer.

9.2.2 Smart Batteries and Battery Characteristics

To facilitate power management in mobile computers, changes have to be made in batteries as well. One of the most important factors required in systems today is the ability to "read" the battery's remaining power. With

it, APM or ACPI can put the system in certain power-saving states when
the power level drops below a threshold.

Smart batteries can offer this feature. Through a series of specifications [SBSI 1999], the industry has come up with general guidelines for a
comprehensive approach to reading, selecting, and charging smart batteries. Several parameters are used to measure battery performance, such as
self-discharge rate, cycle life, operating temperature range, energy density,
and cell balancing.

A high-performance battery is expected to have a low self-discharge
rate, a long cycle life, a wide operating temperature range, and high energy
density. There are currently three major portable battery technologies to
choose from for mobile computers: nickel cadmium (NiCad), nickel metal
hydride (NiMH), and lithium-ion (Li-ion).

Li-ion batteries, which are the most commonly used, have the key advantage of higher energy density at a higher voltage than NiCad and NiMH
achieve. Their energy density is more than two times that of NiCad. To get
a higher voltage, Li-ion cells can be stacked from one (3.6 V nominal) to
eight (28 V nominal) cells in series.

Typical discharge and storage (self-discharge) characteristics of one
battery cell are shown in Figures 9.1(a) and 9.1(b), respectively. Both characteristics are highly dependent on surrounding temperature.

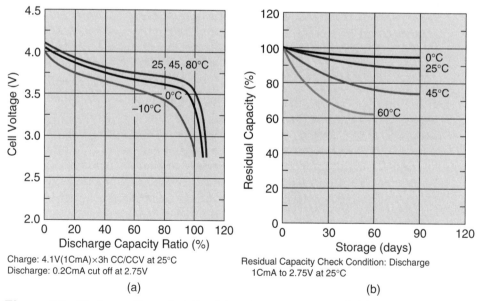

Charge: 4.1V(1CmA)×3h CC/CCV at 25°C
Discharge: 0.2CmA cut off at 2.75V

Residual Capacity Check Condition: Discharge
1CmA to 2.75V at 25°C

(a)   (b)

Figure 9.1. Discharge Characteristics (at various temperatures) (a), and Storage
Characteristics (100% charged state) (b), of Lithium-Ion Batteries

9.3 ASSOCIATIVITY BASED ROUTING

Associativity is related to the spatial, temporal, and connection stability of a mobile host. Specifically, it is measured by a node's connectivity relationship with its neighbors. A node's association with its neighbors changes as it moves, and its transition period can be measured by the associativity ticks, or counts. The migration may be such that after this unstable period there is a period of stability (i.e., a node is constantly associated with certain neighbors over time without losing connectivity with them). The mobile host will spend some dormant time[1] within a wireless cell before it starts to break its connectivity relationship with its surrounding neighbors and move outside the boundary of the existing wireless cell.

In *Associativity Based Routing* (ABR), each mobile host periodically transmits beacons to identify itself (like Hello messages) and constantly updates its associativity ticks in accordance with the mobile hosts sighted (i.e., hearing others' beacons) in the neighborhood. As an example, consider an ad hoc wireless network where each wireless cell is 10 m in diameter and where each mobile host is beaconing once every second. In this case, a mobile node migrating at pedestrian speed (2 m/sec) across a wireless cell with one or more mobile hosts will record an associativity tick of no more than five. This is $A_{threshold}$,[2] and any associativity ticks greater than this threshold imply periods of association stability.[3]

A mobile node is said to exhibit a high state of mobility when it has low associativity with its neighboring nodes. However, if high (i.e., greater than $A_{threshold}$) associativity is observed, the mobile host is said to be in a stable state.[4] This is the ideal point at which to select it to perform ad hoc routing.

The "longevity" of a route is of great importance in ad hoc mobile networks, as the merits of a shorter-hop but short-lived route will be reduced because of frequent data flow interruptions and the frequent need for route reconstructions. Because of the greater value of long-lived routes, the classical shortest-path metric is not necessarily applicable and useful in ad hoc wireless networks. From another perspective, even/fair route relaying load is also important, as no one particular mobile node should be unfairly burdened by supporting many routes and performing many packet relay functions.

---

[1]This may be true even while the mobile host is moving.
[2]The value where associativity transitions take place.
[3]"Stability" here refers to maintaining a connectivity relationship with surrounding mobile hosts over time.
[4]This does not imply that the mobile host is not moving.

9.3.1 ABR Protocol Description

ABR is a source-initiated on-demand routing protocol. It consists of a route discovery phase, a route reconstruction phase, and a route deletion phase. Initially, when a source node desires a route, the route discovery phase is invoked. Then, if any of the three kinds of nodes—SRC, source node; DEST, destination node; IN, intermediate node—move, or if subnet-bridging of a mobile host's migration occurs, reconstruction has to start. Finally, when the SRC no longer desires the route, it initiates the route deletion phase. These three phases will be discussed briefly in the sections that follow. A full description of the design of Associativity Based Routing is presented by Toh [Toh 1997a].

9.3.2 ABR Route Discovery Phase

The route discovery phase consists of a broadcast query (BQ) and an await reply (BQ-REPLY) cycle. Initially, only the DEST's neighbors have routes to the DEST. A node desiring a route to the DEST broadcasts a BQ message, which is propagated throughout the ad hoc mobile network in search of MHs that have such a route. Here, a sequence number uniquely identifies each BQ packet, and no BQ packet is broadcast more than once.

Once the BQ is broadcast by the SRC, all INs that receive the query check that they have processed this packet. If so, the query packet will be discarded; otherwise, the node will check if it is the DEST. If it is not the DEST, the IN appends its MH address/identifier to the IN Identifiers (IDs) field of the query packet and broadcasts the packet to its other neighbors (if any). The associativity ticks with its neighbors will also be appended along with its route relaying load, link propagation delay, and hop count.

The next succeeding IN will then erase its upstream neighbor's associativity ticks and retain only those concerned with itself and its upstream neighbor. In this manner, the query packet reaching the DEST will only contain the intermediate MH addresses (hence recording the path taken), their associativity ticks (hence recording the stability state of INs supporting the route), and their relaying loads, together with information on the route forwarding delay and hop count.

At an appropriate time after receiving the first BQ packet, the DEST will know all the possible routes and their qualities. It can then select the best route (on the basis of the selection criteria mentioned earlier) and send a REPLY packet back to the SRC via the route selected. This causes INs in the route to mark one route to the DEST as valid, which means that all other possible routes will be inactive and will not relay packets destined for the DEST, even if they hear the transmission. Therefore, duplicate packets do not arrive at the DEST.

9.3.3 Handling Mobility in ABR

Although the route selected using ABR tends to be long-lived, there are cases where the association stability relationship is violated. When this happens, route reconstruction (RRC) procedures are invoked to cope with mobility. The ABR route maintenance phase consists of partial route discovery, invalid route erasure, valid route update, and new route discovery (worst case). ABR handles unexpected moves by attempting to locate an alternative valid route quickly without resorting to a broadcast query unless necessary. The following description refers to Figures 9.2(a), (b), and (c), respectively.

Because the routing protocol is source initiated, any moves by the SRC will invoke an RRC process equivalent to that of a route initialization, that is, via a BQ_REPLY process. It will be clear later that this avoids multiple-RRC conflicts as a result of concurrent node movements.

When the DEST moves, its immediate upstream neighbor (the pivoting node) will erase its route. It then performs a localized query LQ[H] process to ascertain if the DEST is still reachable. 'H' here refers to the hop count

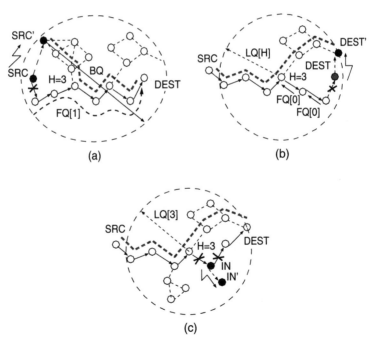

Figure 9.2. Route Maintenance When SRC (a), DEST (b),
and IN (c) Move

from the upstream node to the DEST. If the DEST receives the LQs, it will select the best partial route and send a REPLY; otherwise, the LQ_TIMEOUT period will be reached and the next upstream node will become the pivoting node. During the backtrack, the new pivoting node will erase the route through that link and perform an LQ[H] process until the new pivoting node is greater than half $hop_{src-dest}$ away from the DEST or until a new partial route is found. If no partial route is found, the pivoting node will send an RN[1] (route notification) packet back to the SRC to initiate a BQ process.

If any one of the INs in the route moves and breaks the association stability characteristics, an RRC process is necessary. The immediate upstream node will invoke an LQ process to quickly locate an alternate partial route. However, the immediate downstream node will immediately send a Route Erase message toward the DEST. In this manner, invalidated route entries are deleted. Again, multiple partial routes can exist, and the destination node will select the best possible route. If no partial routes to the DEST exist, the next upstream node invokes another LQ process. This backtracking proceeds until a partial route is found or until the number of backtrack steps exceeds half the route length. If all possible localized queries are unsuccessful, the source will timeout and may invoke a BQ instead.

Race conditions exist because of multiple invocations of RRC processes as a result of concurrent movements by the SRC, the DEST, and the INs. However, the ABR protocol is able to resolve the conflicts of multiple RRCs by ensuring that only one ultimately succeeds. Each LQ process is tagged with a sequence number so that earlier LQ processes will terminate when a new one is invoked. In the same vein, if nodes processing LQs hear a new BQ for the same connection, the localized query process is aborted.

9.3.4 ABR Route Deletion Phase

When a discovered route is no longer desired, a route delete (RD) broadcast will be initiated by the SRC so that all INs will update their route table entries. A full broadcast is used instead of a directed broadcast because nodes supporting an active route will have changed during route reconstruction. Similar to BQ, the RD control packet has a Live field of infinity to achieve a full wave-like broadcast. In addition to the *hard*-state approach, a *soft*-state approach is possible where the route entries are invalidated upon timeout when there is no traffic activity related to the route over a period of time.

9.4 EFFECTS OF BEACONING ON BATTERY LIFE

To investigate the effects of beaconing on the battery life of ad hoc mobile hosts, we conducted a series of experiments. Before we discuss those experiments, we describe the experimental hardware and software environment.

9.4.1 Experimental Hardware

The ad hoc wireless networking testbed setup at our laboratory comprises seven laptop computers (IBM and Compaq notebooks) equipped with Lucent Technologies' WaveLAN wireless PCMCIA adapters. Each of the laptops runs the Linux operating system version 2.0.30, which has a copy of the TCP/IP/Ethernet protocol suite enhanced with the ABR ad hoc networking software.

The Mobile Computer

The measurements of remaining power are taken on the IBM laptops, while the Compaqs are used as neighbors in multihop configurations. The IBM Thinkpad 600 laptop computer used in our experiments has an Intel Mobile Pentium II processor with built-in 64 MB memory, 2.5-inch 5.1 GB of hard disk drive, and an active 13.3-inch TFT color display with 1024-by-768 resolution. It is a lightweight laptop weighing only 5.01 pounds with an external floppy drive. It also comes equipped with standard I/O interfaces (such as serial, parallel, USB, diskette, keyboard/mouse, docking interface, audio I/O, external monitor connector) and an internal 56K modem. Finally, it has three power-saving modes controlled by the BIOS: *standby, suspend,* and *hibernation.*

The Battery Used

The IBM Thinkpad 600 uses a Li-ion battery with a nominal voltage of 10.8 Vdc and a capacity of 3.2 AH. The nominal voltage is the result of connecting three Li-ion cells in series.

The Wireless Adapter

The adapter used in the experiments to provide wireless ad hoc connectivity is the 2.4 GHz WaveLAN PCMCIA card by Lucent Technologies, which provides a fast and reliable solution for wireless client access applications.

As seen from Table 9.1, WaveLAN has the capability of operating in three modes, each having a different power consumption level. While in sleep mode, the card consumes only about 10% of the transmit or receive

Table 9.1. Power Specification of WaveLAN PCMCIA Cards

Power Consumption	2.4 GHz
Sleep Mode	0.175 W
Receive Mode	1.575 W
Transmit Mode	1.825 W

Table 9.2. Data Communications Specifications
of WaveLAN PCMCIA

Data Communications	Performance
Data Rate	2 Mbps
Media Access	Ethernet CSMA/CA
Bit Error Rate	Better than 10^{-8}

power. However, power management is not supported by WaveLAN in
ad hoc configurations because it requires dedicated support from Wave-
Point[5] access points; thus, it is not utilized during our experiments. The
communication specifications for WaveLAN are presented in Table 9.2.

Propagation Characteristics

All experiments were performed in a semi-open office environment in our
laboratory. In the experiments requiring multiple nodes beaconing at the
same time, the nodes are within 10 m of each other with no obstacles.
No nearby equipment was used at the same frequency as the WaveLANs
(2.4 GHz) and no WavePoint or similar network component, mobile phone,
or microwave oven was in operation. The experiments were performed in a
climate-controlled environment with an average temperature of 25°C.

9.4.2 Experimental Software

In this section, we give a general description of our platform software, including operating system, protocol stack, and ABR beaconing subsystem.

Linux Operating System

We chose Linux as the operating system platform for our ad hoc mobile
hosts because it allows us to easily incorporate our ABR code into the
system to support ad hoc wireless networking. Other useful features include
its complete multitasking, multiuser operation, which allows many users to
have access to the same machine and multiple processes to be supported.

The use of the X Window system is a plus for displaying networked applications. With the support of TCP/IP, a Linux machine is readily capable
of supporting networked applications.

---

[5]WavePoint is the name of the base station normally used in Lucent's Wireless LANs.

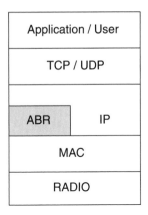

Figure 9.3. The ABR Protocol Implementation within TCP/IP
over Wireless Ethernet

Ad Hoc Routing Protocol

We implemented ABR within the IP/Ethernet protocol layers (Figure 9.3).
Basically, beaconing functions are implemented in the ABR layer, and mobile hosts periodically transmit a beacon identifying themselves. Those beacons, when received by the other nodes in the network, help those nodes
define the degree of link association with their neighboring nodes. Although
beacons allow one to derive long-lived routes, doubts arise as to what is an
appropriate beaconing interval and the impact this level will have on the
battery life of ad hoc mobile hosts. Therefore, before we delve into the details of these issues, it is necessary to reveal how beaconing was implemented
in our experiments.

Periodic Beaconing in Ad Hoc Mobile Hosts

The beacon structure is shown in Figure 9.4, which depicts the ABR base
header, with the Type field defined as BEACON, encapsulated by the data
link header (in our case, Ethernet). The ABR beacon is a network control
message generated at the ABR layer and broadcast[6] to the network. It
contains the identity of the beacon generator and its intended recipients.
The broadcast beacons are received at the destination nodes and are used
to derive connection stability information. This information is then used by
ABR to derive long-lived routes.

---

[6]This does not imply flooding of the network. The beacon is sent via radio and all nodes
within the radio cell range can therefore receive it.

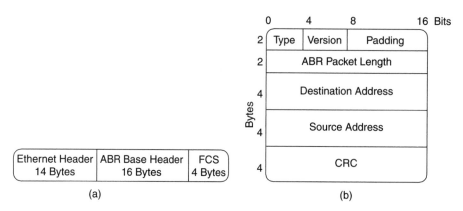

Figure 9.4. The ABR Beacon (a) and the ABR Base Header (b)

9.5 EXPERIMENTAL RESULTS AND OBSERVATIONS

With the hardware and software experimental platform described in the previous section, we performed the following experiments in order to understand the impact of periodic beaconing on the degradation of battery life:

- Standalone beaconing at high frequencies
- Standalone beaconing at low frequencies
- Beaconing in the presence of neighboring nodes at low and high frequencies

The parameter of interest to us is the percentage of battery life remaining over time for each beaconing period. In the following sections, we will explain the results and observations for each experiment conducted.

9.5.1 Standalone Beaconing at High Frequencies

In this experiment, a single mobile computer was set up to beacon at millisecond intervals. At the beginning of the experiment, the mobile computer's battery was fully charged. The computer was booted with the Linux-ABR kernel, and the Ethernet interface was configured. The beaconing process was activated soon after. As there were no other mobile computers in the neighborhood, the power usage was independent of receive power. The computer had X Window, `xload`, and `netstat` applications running. The Advanced Power Management daemon in the OS was disabled and the BIOS APM was prevented from operating.

Figure 9.5 shows the `netstat` program displaying the interface statistics of the system. WaveLAN cards were configured on interface `eth0`. The

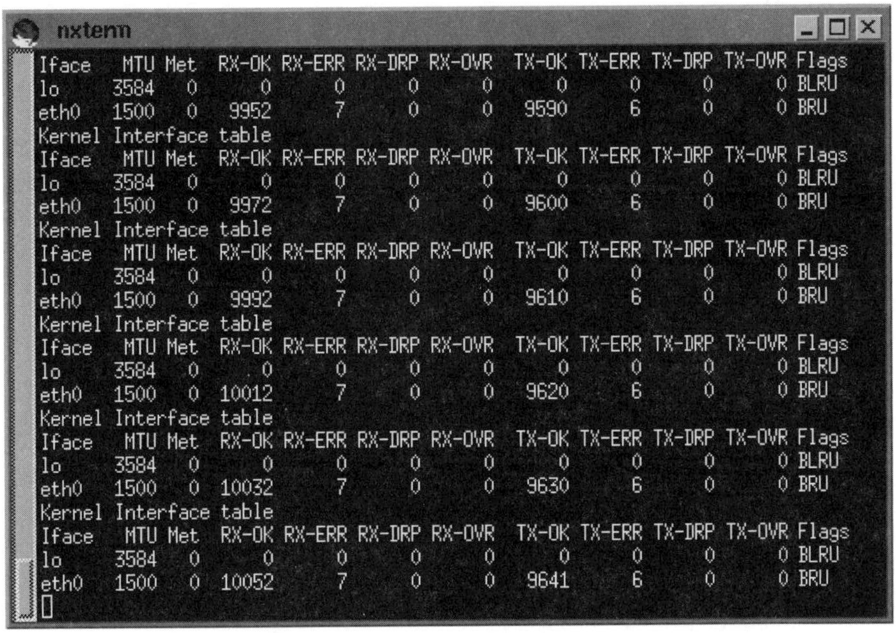

```
nxterm                                                              _ □ ✕

Iface  MTU Met  RX-OK RX-ERR RX-DRP RX-OVR  TX-OK TX-ERR TX-DRP TX-OVR Flags
lo     3584   0      0      0      0      0      0      0      0      0 BLRU
eth0   1500   0   9952      7      0      0   9590      6      0      0 BRU
Kernel Interface table
Iface  MTU Met  RX-OK RX-ERR RX-DRP RX-OVR  TX-OK TX-ERR TX-DRP TX-OVR Flags
lo     3584   0      0      0      0      0      0      0      0      0 BLRU
eth0   1500   0   9972      7      0      0   9600      6      0      0 BRU
Kernel Interface table
Iface  MTU Met  RX-OK RX-ERR RX-DRP RX-OVR  TX-OK TX-ERR TX-DRP TX-OVR Flags
lo     3584   0      0      0      0      0      0      0      0      0 BLRU
eth0   1500   0   9992      7      0      0   9610      6      0      0 BRU
Kernel Interface table
Iface  MTU Met  RX-OK RX-ERR RX-DRP RX-OVR  TX-OK TX-ERR TX-DRP TX-OVR Flags
lo     3584   0      0      0      0      0      0      0      0      0 BLRU
eth0   1500   0  10012      7      0      0   9620      6      0      0 BRU
Kernel Interface table
Iface  MTU Met  RX-OK RX-ERR RX-DRP RX-OVR  TX-OK TX-ERR TX-DRP TX-OVR Flags
lo     3584   0      0      0      0      0      0      0      0      0 BLRU
eth0   1500   0  10032      7      0      0   9630      6      0      0 BRU
Kernel Interface table
Iface  MTU Met  RX-OK RX-ERR RX-DRP RX-OVR  TX-OK TX-ERR TX-DRP TX-OVR Flags
lo     3584   0      0      0      0      0      0      0      0      0 BLRU
eth0   1500   0  10052      7      0      0   9641      6      0      0 BRU
```

Figure 9.5. Window Capture Showing Periodic ABR Beaconing
at 100 m/sec Intervals

`netstat` program updates its readings every second, so the increase by 10 in the transmitted packets (`TX-OK`) denotes transmission of beacons every 100 m/sec. The value `RX-OK` denotes the number of correctly received beacons in the same 1-second interval. In this case, no other laptops were operating in the same area, so the value was always zero.

Over regular time intervals (i.e., 20 minutes), we noted the percentage of battery life remaining for beaconing intervals of 10, 50, 100, and 500 ms. The results are shown in Figure 9.6a. At the 10-ms beaconing interval, battery life degrades at the fastest rate, while the 50-ms, 100-ms, and 500-ms intervals have relatively similar power degradation characteristics. In addition, it is noticeable that at the 10-ms beaconing interval the computer has a shorter lifetime (by about 40 minutes) compared to the other beaconing intervals. We also observe that at 10 ms the CPU load is high (as indicated by `xload`) and the computer seems to be slow in forking new applications and responding to commands.

An important observation was made at the last 20 minutes of the computers' operation. As shown in Figure 9.6a, there is a sudden and substantial decrease in remaining battery capacity before the computer eventually shuts down. This phenomenon can be attributed to the discharge characteristics of the battery, as shown in Figure 9.6b. The battery capacity changes significantly after a certain point in time for different current levels drawn from the battery. Note the last reading obtained is at shutdown.

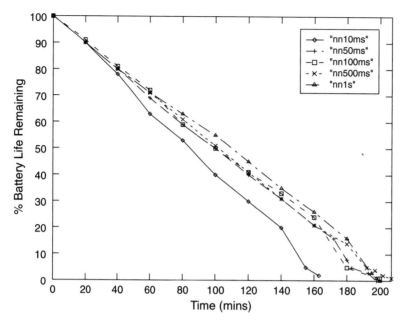

Figure 9.6a. Effects of Standalone High-Frequency Beaconing on Battery Life

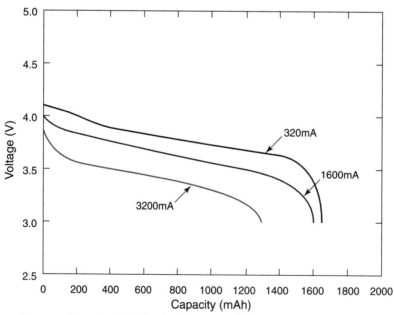

Charge conditions: Constant voltage/constant current, 4.2V, 1120mA (max.), 2 hrs, 20°C
Discharge conditions: Constant current up to 3.0V at 20°C

Figure 9.6b. Effects of High-Frequency Beaconing on Manufacturer's Battery Discharge Curves

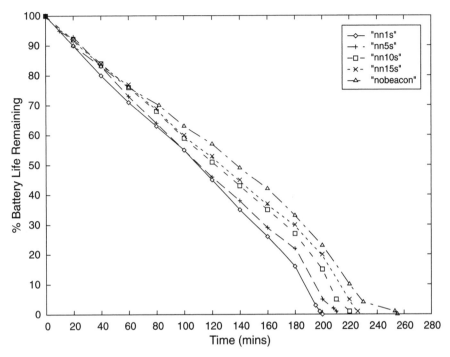

Figure 9.7. Effects of Standalone Low-Frequency Beaconing on Battery Life

9.5.2 Standalone Beaconing at Low Frequencies

In another experiment, the beaconing interval was increased in order to investigate the effects of slow beaconing on power consumption. We chose to observe remaining power life at beaconing intervals of 1, 5, 10, and 15 seconds. The system setup was essentially the same as in the earlier case and readings were taken at regular time intervals.

The results obtained are shown in Figure 9.7. For up to the first 40 minutes, the difference in power degradation for different beaconing intervals is not significant. Beyond this time, however, the curves begin to spread. At 180 minutes, the difference in remaining battery life between 1-sec and 15-sec beaconing intervals is about 15%. Although there is a noticeable difference in remaining battery life for a computer using different beaconing intervals, this may not affect ongoing applications and the user may not see any difference.

Figure 9.7 reveals an important observation. For 1-sec and 5-sec beaconing intervals, the remaining power life suddenly drops significantly at 180 minutes. This is similar to the phenomenon observed for high beaconing intervals and is a result of the actions taken by the OS and BIOS in preparation for power down. However, for 10-sec and 15-sec beaconing intervals, this phenomenon happens 20 minutes later—at 200 minutes. This shows that with a longer beaconing interval, the system will operate longer before it must prepare for power down. As a limiting case, it can also be observed from Figure 9.7 that for no beacons this phenomenon occurs at 230 minutes.

Comparison of Results

With reference to Figures 9.6 and 9.7, low-frequency beaconing results in a longer operating time. Comparing the results for 10-ms and 15-sec beaconing intervals, the difference in lifetime is about 60 minutes. This significant difference advocates careful selection of an appropriate beaconing interval for overall *usefulness, efficiency,* and *availability* of the mobile computer.

For both cases, we observed the interesting scenario in which a greater amount of power is drawn in the last 20 minutes of operation, during which the computer system invokes procedures and actions in preparation for power down. Such procedures actually draw more power than does pure beaconing alone. This is a result of additional I/O operations performed during the shutdown process.

9.5.3 Beaconing with Neighboring Nodes at High Frequencies

The experiments discussed so far involved a single mobile computer beaconing at periodic intervals. However, in ad hoc mobile network nodes rely on the presence of neighbors to forward packets to the destination. For this reason, we investigated the degree to which the presence of neighboring ad hoc nodes impacts the power life of mobile computers. Figure 9.8 reveals the difference between the earlier and the current setup.

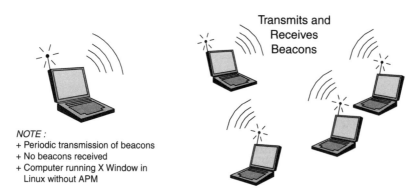

Figure 9.8. Standalone Beaconing (*left*) and Beaconing in the Presence of Neighbors (*right*)

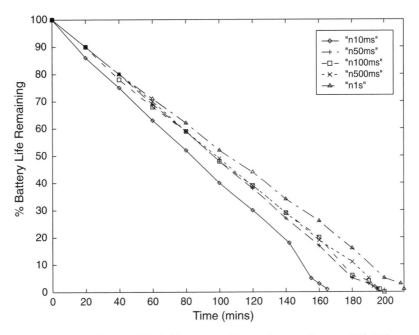

Figure 9.9. Effects of High-Frequency Beaconing on Battery Life When
One Neighbor Is Present

At high-beaconing frequency, the same intervals were used as in stand-alone beaconing: 10 ms, 50 ms, 100 ms, and 500 ms. The results obtained are shown in Figure 9.9. At a 10-ms beaconing interval, battery life degrades at the fastest rate while the 50-ms, 100-ms, and 500-ms intervals have relatively similar power degradation characteristics. In addition, the lifetime for a mobile computer beaconing at 10 ms is about 40 minutes shorter than those beaconing at 50 ms, 100 ms, and 500 ms. At 20 minutes after the initiation of the experiment, deviation of remaining power life for the 10 ms beaconing interval begins, while the rest have indistinguishable remaining battery life.

A sudden increase in power consumption in preparation for power down in the last 20 minutes of operation is also observed in this experiment.

Comparison of High-Frequency Beaconing with and without Neighbors

With the presence of neighbors, the computer's overall power degradation is a function of both *transmit* and *receiver* power, as neighboring beacons are being received. Compared to the results obtained for standalone beaconing, the remaining power life decreases at a faster rate at all beaconing intervals under test.

As shown in Figure 9.10(a), there are noticeable increases in power consumption for the 10-ms beaconing interval during the first 40 minutes of

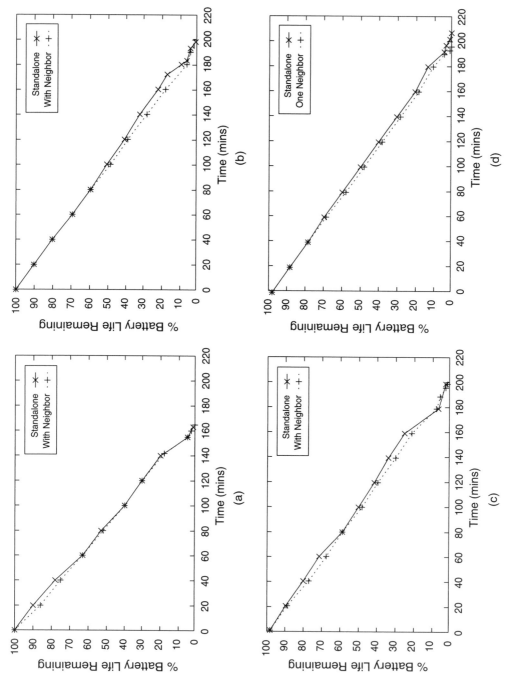

Figure 9.10. Comparing Power Degradation with and without Neighbors at HF Beaconing—(a) 10 ms, (b) 50 ms, (c) 100 ms, (d) 500 ms

316

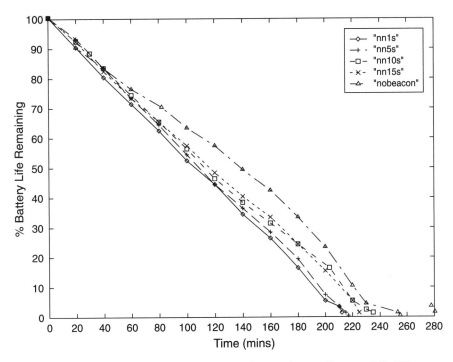

Figure 9.11. Effects of Low-Frequency Beaconing on Battery Life When One Neighbor Is Present

the experiment. Thereafter, the differences between the results are minute. Figure 9.10(b) shows the case for the 50-ms beaconing interval; here, the impact of an additional neighbor can be observed between 80 and 180 minutes of experimental time. For the 100-ms and 500-ms beaconing intervals, the difference in remaining power life for those with and without neighbors is noticeable over a wide range of experimental time (from 20 to 180 minutes). The worst-case percentage difference is observed to be about 7% at the 50-ms beaconing interval.

9.5.4 Beaconing with Neighboring Nodes at Low Frequencies

With the presence of a neighboring host beaconing at the same low frequency intervals used in earlier experiments, we recorded the results shown in Figure 9.11. Again, the results show that there are small differences in the remaining battery life at 1, 5, 10, and 15 seconds during the first minutes of the experiment. Compared to the high-frequency case with the presence of a neighbor, the computer system has a longer lifespan—about 50 minutes more if we compare the 10-ms and the 1-sec beaconing intervals. As in previous experiments, the same power down phenomenon is observed at the last measurement interval of operation.

Comparison of Low-Frequency Beaconing with and without Neighbors

In a final experiment, we compared the remaining battery life for the same beaconing interval with and without a neighbor. The differences are illustrated in Figure 9.12.

The first observation is that the differences in remaining battery life are insignificant except for the 10-sec and 15-sec beaconing intervals. At high beaconing intervals, transmit power contribution tends to overwhelm receiver power consumption. Because transmit power is greater than receiver power for WaveLAN radios, the difference in remaining power life is noticeable only at very high beaconing frequencies.

The second observation is that the computer system enters shutdown at about 180 minutes, which is similar to the case of no neighbors present. This shows that receiving additional beacons from a neighbor does not significantly change the power down time of the mobile host.

9.5.5 Deductions

On the basis of our experiments, we arrived at the following deductions:

- Beaconing at extremely high frequency (i.e., at 10-ms intervals) can significantly shorten the battery life of a mobile computer and can also affect application execution speed. This is not recommended in practical wireless ad hoc mobile systems.
- Only small differences are observed if a standalone ad hoc mobile host beacons at 50-ms, 100-ms, 500-ms, and 1-sec intervals.
- Beaconing at 1-sec, 5-sec, 10-sec, and 15-sec intervals does not significantly lengthen the lifetime of an ad hoc mobile host (only 20 minutes is gained, as seen from our experimental results).
- The power degradation of a standalone ad hoc mobile computer does not differ greatly from one that has a periodic beaconing interval of 5, 10, or 15 seconds.
- For both low-frequency and high-frequency beaconing, more power is drawn when the OS and BIOS take actions in preparation for system power down.
- With the presence of a neighbor, the receive power consumption as a result of receiving neighboring beacons does not contribute much to the overall power degradation when the beaconing interval is small. This is attributed to the fact that transmitting beacons consume

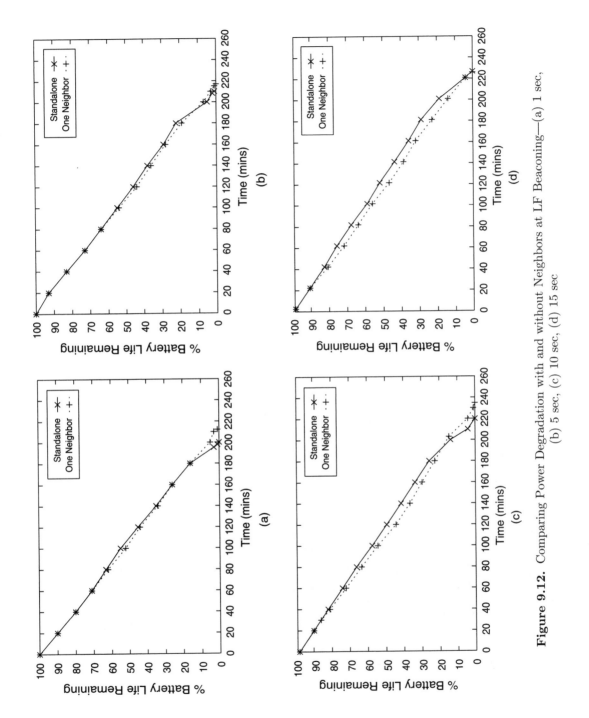

Figure 9.12. Comparing Power Degradation with and without Neighbors at LF Beaconing—(a) 1 sec, (b) 5 sec, (c) 10 sec, (d) 15 sec

319

much more power than do receiving beacons. In addition, because of the presence of collisions in the channel, not all transmitted beacons will be received.

9.6 CONCLUSION

Beaconing is a technique used by many routing protocols for ad hoc networks to update routing information or to simply denote the presence of a node in the network. It is important that the implementation of the network and its use should not be a limiting factor. One particularly challenging task in mobile computing is to design for low power consumption. Although much has been done in terms of limiting the power consumption of system hardware devices, the same has not been done for communication protocols, especially in relation to beacons.

In this chapter, we presented the findings of our experimental research in which we evaluated the effect of periodic beaconing on the battery life of an ad hoc mobile computer. We concluded that selecting an appropriate beaconing interval is imperative so as not to upset the overall power degradation characteristic of the system or to cause noticeable side effects for existing applications. We also concluded that the actions taken by the system in preparation for shutdown actually draw more power than usual. Future work is necessary to investigate the impact of more neighbors and the presence of APM on remaining battery life and to reveal the impact of beaconing on communication performance.

References

[Agrawal 1998] Prathima Agrawal. Energy Efficient Protocols for Wireless Systems. In *Proceedings of IEEE PIMRC '98*, September 1998.

[Chan+ 1995] E. Chan, K. Govil, and H. Wasserman. Comparing Algorithms for Dynamic Speed-Setting of a Low-Power CPU. In *Proceedings of the Fourth Annual ACM/IEEE International Conference on Mobile Computers and Networking (MOBICOM '95)*, 1995.

[Intel+ 1996] Intel and Microsoft Corporations. *Advanced Power Management (APM), BIOS Interface Specification Rev.1.2.* February 1996.

[Intel+ 1999] Intel, Microsoft, and Toshiba Corporations. *Advanced Configuration and Power Interface (ACPI) Specification.* February 1999.

[Johnson+ 1996] D.B. Johnson and D.A. Maltz. Dynamic Source Routing in Ad-Hoc Wireless Networks. *Mobile Computing,* T. Imielinski and H. Korth, eds. Kluwer Academic Publishers, Norwood, Mass., 1996.

[Katz+ 1996] R. Katz and M. Stemm. Reducing Power Consumption of Network Interfaces in Hand-Held Devices. In *Proceedings of the Third Annual International Workshop on Mobile Multimedia Communications (MoMuC-3)*, December 1996.

[McQuillan+ 1980] J. McQuillan, M. Richer, and E.C. Rosen. The New Routing Algorithm for the ARPANET. *IEEE Transactions on Communications* COM-28(5):711–719, May 1980.

[Perkins+ 1994] C. Perkins and P. Bhagwat. Highly Dynamic Destination-Sequenced Distance Vector Routing (DSDV) for Mobile Computers. *ACM SIG-COMM '94 Computer Communications Review* 24(4):234–244, October 1994.

[Perkins+ 1999] C. Perkins and E. Royer. Ad-Hoc On Demand Distance Vector Routing. In *Proceedings of the Second Annual IEEE Workshop on Mobile Computing Systems and Applications*, February 1999.

[SBSI 1999] Smart Battery Systems Implementers Forum Web Page—*http:// www.sbs-forum.org*, June 1999.

[SCET 1998] *Solar Cell Efficiency Tables (Version 12)—Progress in Photovoltaics: Research and Applications*. John Wiley and Sons, New York, 1998.

[Scott+ 1996] K. Scott and N. Bambos. Routing and Channel Assignment for Low Power Transmission in PCS. In *Proceedings of ICUPC '96*, October 1996.

[Singh+ 1998] S. Singh and C.S. Raghavendra. PAMAS: Power Aware Multi-Access Protocol with Signalling for Ad Hoc Networks. *ACM SIGCOMM '98 Computer Communications Review*, July 1998.

[Toh 1997a] C-K. Toh. *Wireless ATM and Ad Hoc Networks: Protocols and Architectures*. Kluwer Academic Publishers, Norwood, Mass., 1997.

[Toh 1997b] C-K Toh. Associativity-Based Routing for Ad-Hoc Mobile Networks. *Journal on Wireless Personal Communications* 4(2), March 1997.

[Woo+ 1998] M. Woo, S. Singh, and C.S. Raghavendra. Power-Aware Routing in Mobile Ad Hoc Networks. In *Proceedings of the Fourth Annual ACM/IEEE International Conference on Mobile Computing and Networking (MOBICOM '98)*, October 1998.

[Zorzi+ 1997] M. Zorzi and R. Rao. Error Control and Energy Consumption in Communications for Nomadic Computing. *IEEE Transactions on Computers (Special Issue, Mobile Computing)*, March 1997.

10

Bandwidth-Efficient Link-State Routing in Wireless Networks

J.J. Garcia-Luna-Aceves
University of California

Marcelo Spohn
Nokia Corporation

Abstract

This chapter presents the Source Tree Adaptive Routing (STAR) protocol as an example of bandwidth-efficient routing in ad hoc networks using link-state information. Routers in STAR communicate their source routing trees to their neighbors either incrementally or in atomic updates. Source routing trees are specified by stating the link parameters of each link belonging to any of the preferred paths used to reach every known destination. Hence, a router disseminates link-state updates to its neighbors only for those links along paths used to reach destinations. To reduce bandwidth utilization, updates to source routing trees are communicated only when routers determine that long-term loops can be created, when new destinations are found, or when destinations become unreachable. The performance of STAR is compared by simulation against table-driven and on-demand routing protocols. The simulation results show that STAR is an order of magnitude more efficient than traditional topology-broadcast protocols and that it can be as efficient as on-demand routing protocols.

Multihop packet radio, or ad hoc networks, consist of mobile hosts interconnected by routers that can also move. The deployment of such routers is ad hoc and the topology of the network is very dynamic because of host and router mobility, signal loss and interference, and power outages. Furthermore, the bandwidth available for the exchange of routing information in ad hoc networks is much less than that available in a wired internet.

Routing algorithms for ad hoc networks can be categorized according to the way routers obtain routing information and according to the type of information they use to compute preferred paths. In terms of the way routers obtain information, routing protocols can be classified as table driven and on demand. In terms of the type of information they use, they can be classified as link state and distance vector. Routers running a link-state protocol use topology information to make routing decisions; routers running a distance-vector protocol use distances and, in some cases, path information to destinations.

In an on-demand routing protocol, routers maintain path information for only those destinations that they need to contact as a source or as a relay of information. The basic approach consists of allowing a router that does not know how to reach a destination to send a flood search message to obtain the path information. The first routing protocol of this type was proposed to establish virtual circuits in the Mobile Subscriber (MSE) network [Li+ 1986], and there are several more recent examples of this approach (e.g., Ad Hoc On-Demand Distance-Vector (AODV) [Perkins+ 1999, see also Chapter 6], Associativity Based Routing (ABR) [Toh 1996, see also Chapter 9], Dynamic Source Routing (DSR) [Johnson+ 1996, see also Chapter 5], Temporally Ordered Routing Algorithm (TORA) [Park+ 1997, see also Chapter 8], and Signal Stability-Based Adaptive Routing (SSA) [Dube+ 1997]). Source tree bridges also use flood search packets to obtain source routes from source to destination. All of the on-demand routing protocols reported to date are based on distances to destinations, and no on-demand link-state protocols have yet been proposed. On-demand routing protocols differ in the specific mechanisms used to disseminate flood search packets and their responses, to cache the information heard from other nodes' searches, to determine the cost of a link, and to determine the existence of a neighbor.

In a table-driven algorithm, each router maintains path information for each known destination in the network and updates its route table entries as needed. Examples of table-driven algorithms based on distance vectors are the routing protocol of the DARPA packet radio network [Jubin+ 1987], the Destination-Sequenced Distance-Vector (DSDV) protocol [Perkins+ 1994, see also Chapter 3], the Wireless Routing Protocol (WRP) [Murthy+ 1996], the Wireless Internet Routing Protocol (WIRP) [Garcia-Luna-Aceves+ 1997], and least-resistance routing protocols [Pursley+ 1993]. Earlier table-driven approaches were based on topology broadcast. However, disseminating complete link-state information to all routers incurs excessive communication overhead in an ad hoc network because of the dynamics of the network and the small bandwidth available. Accordingly, all link-state routing approaches for packet radio networks have been based on hierarchical routing schemes [Ramamoorthy+ 1983, Ramanathan+ 1998, Steenstrup 1995, see also Chapter 4], The Zone Routing Protocol (ZRP) [Haas+ 1998, see also Chapter 7] is a hybrid of on-demand and table-driven techniques.

Up to now, the debate about whether a table-driven or an on-demand approach is best for wireless networks has assumed that table-driven routing must provide optimum (e.g., shortest-path) routing, when in fact it cannot do so. The Distance Routing Effect Algorithm for Mobility (DREAM) [Basagni+ 1998] was proposed to address the perceived limitations of earlier on-demand and table-driven routing protocols. DREAM uses node coordinates rather than identifiers for routing, disseminating coordinate information to all nodes and using directed flooding to forward data packets to destinations. At each router, a data packet for a given destination is forwarded to all neighbor routers in the destination's direction. Another approach based on location information is Location-Aided Routing (LAR) [Ko+ 1998]. LAR is an on-demand protocol that uses location information to reduce the scope of the flood search needed to obtain a route to a destination.

This chapter presents the Source Tree Adaptive Routing protocol as an approach to efficient routing in packet radio networks using link-state information. In STAR, a router sends updates to its neighbors regarding the links in its preferred destination paths. The links along these paths constitute a *source tree* that implicitly specifies the complete paths from the source to each destination. Each router computes its source tree on the basis of information about adjacent links and the source trees reported by its neighbors; it reports changes to its source tree to all its neighbors incrementally or atomically. The aggregation of adjacent links and source trees reported by neighbors constitutes the partial topology known by a router. Unlike any of the current hierarchical link-state routing schemes for packet radio networks [Steenstrup 1995], STAR does not require backbones, the dissemination of complete cluster topology within a cluster, or the dissemination of complete intercluster connectivity. Furthermore, it can be used with distributed hierarchical routing schemes proposed for both distance-vector or link-state routing [Kleinrock+ 1977, Steenstrup 1995, Murthy+ 1997, Behrens+ 1998].

Earlier proposals for link-state routing using partial link-state data without clusters [Garcia-Luna-Aceves+ 1995, Garcia-Luna-Aceves+ 1998] required routers to explicitly inform their neighbors of which links they use and which links they stop using. In contrast, because STAR sends only changes to the structure of source trees, and because each destination has a single predecessor in a source tree, a router needs to send only updates for those links that are part of the tree and a single update for the root of any subtree of the source tree that becomes unreachable because of failures. Routers receiving a STAR update can correctly infer all the links that the sender of an update message has stopped using without the need for explicit delete updates.

Section 10.1 describes two approaches that can be used to update routing information in wireless networks: the Optimum Routing Approach (ORA) and the Least-Overhead Routing Approach (LORA); it also explains why STAR is the first table-driven routing protocol that can adopt LORA. Section 10.2 describes STAR and how it supports ORA and LORA. Section 10.3 compares STAR's performance against the performance of other table-driven and on-demand routing protocols. The simulation results show that STAR is four times more bandwidth-efficient than the best-performing link-state routing protocol, an order of magnitude more bandwidth-efficient than topology broadcasting, and more bandwidth-efficient than DSR, which has been shown to incur the smallest amount of routing packets transmitted per data packet delivered to a destination [Das+ 2000]. To our knowledge, this is the first time that any table-driven routing protocol has been shown to be more efficient than on-demand routing protocols in wireless networks. Our simulation experiments use the same methodology first described by Broch et al. to compare on-demand routing protocols [Broch+ 1998a].

10.1 UPDATING ROUTES IN WIRELESS NETWORKS

We can distinguish two main approaches to updating routing information in the routing protocols that have been designed for wireless networks: the *optimum routing approach* and the *least-overhead routing approach*. With ORA, the protocol attempts to update route tables as quickly as possible to provide paths that are optimal with respect to a defined metric. With LORA, the routing protocol attempts to provide viable paths, which need not be optimal, causing the least amount of control traffic.

This chapter addresses shortest-path routing as the only type of service supported for ORA. Furthermore, given that optimality of the paths is not important in LORA, we assume that all links have the same cost—that is, ORA uses minimum-hop routing.

On-demand routing protocols, such as DSR, follow LORA in that they attempt to minimize control overhead by maintaining path information for only those destinations with which the router needs to communicate and by using the paths found after a flood search as long as those paths are valid, even if they are not optimal. ORA is not an attractive or even feasible approach in on-demand routing protocols because flooding the network frequently as a way to optimize existing paths consumes the available bandwidth and make the paths worse.

The flood search messages used in on-demand protocols can be viewed as a form of polling of destinations by sources. In table-driven protocols, it is the destinations that poll the sources, meaning that the sources obtain their paths to destinations as a result of update messages that originate at the destinations. It is apparent that flooding occurs in both approaches, so it should be possible to obtain a table-driven protocol that polls as infrequently as on-demand routing protocols do to limit its overhead.

Interestingly, table-driven routing protocols reported to date for ad hoc networks adhere to ORA and, admittedly, have been adaptations of protocols developed for wired networks. A consequence of adopting ORA in table-driven routing within a wireless network is that, if the topology of the network changes frequently, the number of update messages increases dramatically, consuming bandwidth needed for user data. The two methods used to reduce the update rate in table-driven protocols are clustering and periodic updates. Clustering is attractive to reduce overhead due to network size; however, if the affiliations of nodes with clusters change too often, clustering itself introduces unwanted overhead. Sending periodic updates after long timeouts reduces overhead; it is a technique that has been used since the DARPA packet radio network was designed [Jubin+ 1987]. However, control traffic still has to flow periodically in order to update route tables.

A nice feature of protocols, such as DSR [Johnson+ 1996] and WIRP [Garcia-Luna-Aceves+ 1997], is that they remain quiet when no new update information has to be exchanged, having no need for periodic updates. Both take advantage of promiscuous listening of any packets sent by a router's neighbors to determine the neighborhood of the router. A key difference is that DSR follows LORA whereas WIRP follows ORA, which means that WIRP may incur substantial overhead when the network topology is unstable and routers are forced to update their optimal paths.

Given that both on-demand and table-driven routing incurs flooding in one way or another, a table-driven protocol could be designed that incurs similar or less overhead than that incurred by on-demand routing protocols by limiting the polling done by the destinations to the same or less than that done by the sources in on-demand routing protocols.

However, there has been no description of a table-driven protocol that can truly adhere to LORA—that is, one that has no need for periodic updates, uses no clustering, and remains quiet as long as the paths available at the routers are valid, if not optimal. The reason is that, with the exception of WIRP and WRP, earlier protocols used either distances to destinations, topology maps, or subsets of the topology to obtain paths to destinations, and none of these types of information permits a router to discern whether the paths it uses are in conflict with those its neighbors use. Accordingly, routers must send updates after they change their route tables in order to avoid loops, and the best that can be done is to reduce the control traffic by sending such updates periodically. Furthermore, the validation of update messages in some approaches (e.g., topology broadcast) requires periodic updates in order to correctly age out old information.

STAR is the first table-driven protocol that can implement LORA because it uses routing trees that can signal a router when its paths have become prone to loops and because it does not require periodic updates to validate paths.

10.2 STAR DESCRIPTION

In STAR, the topology of a network is modeled as a directed graph $G = (V, E)$, where V is the set of nodes and E is the set of edges connecting the nodes. Each node has a unique identifier and represents a router with input and output queues of unlimited capacity, updated according to a FIFO policy. In a wireless network, a node can have connectivity with multiple nodes over the same physical radio link. In route table updating, a node A and another node B are adjacent (we call such nodes "neighbors") if there is link-level connectivity between them and A receives update messages from B reliably. Accordingly, we map a physical broadcast link connecting multiple nodes into multiple point-to-point bidirectional links defined for these nodes. A functional bidirectional link between two nodes is represented by a pair of edges, one in each direction and with a cost associated that can vary in time but is always positive.

Routers maintain a partial topology map of their network. In this chapter we assume that there is no aggregation of topology information into areas or clusters.

All messages, changes in the cost of a link, link failures, and new-neighbor notifications are processed one at a time within a finite time and in the order in which they are detected. Routers are assumed to operate correctly, and information is assumed to be stored without errors.

Each router reports the characteristics of every link it uses to reach each known destination to its neighbors. The set of links used by a router in its preferred path to a destination is called its *source tree*. A router knows its adjacent links and the source trees reported by its neighbors; the aggregation of a router's adjacent links and the source trees reported by its neighbors constitute a partial *topology graph*. Therefore, the links in the source tree and in the topology graph are those adjacent to the router and those reported by at least one of the router's neighbors. The router uses the topology graph to generate its own source tree. Each router derives a route table specifying the successor to each destination by running a local *route selection algorithm* on its source tree.

Because each router communicates its source tree to its neighbors, the deletion of a link that is no longer used to reach a given destination is implicit with the addition of the new link that is used to reach the same destination. The only case in which a router needs to explicitly inform its neighbors about link deletions is when a deletion causes the router to have no paths to one or more destinations. In this case the router tells its neighbors about the failed link as well as about any new links needed to reach the neighbor or other destinations.

The basic update unit used to communicate changes to source trees is the link-state update (LSU). An LSU reports the characteristics of a link; an update message contains one or more LSUs. For a link between router u and router or destination v, router u is called the *head node* of the link in the u-to-v direction. The head node of a link is the only router that can report changes in the parameters of that link.

By means of sequence numbers, routers can determine that an LSU contains more recent link-state information for a given link than that stored locally for the link. Each router erases a link from its topology graph if the link is not adjacent to the router and is not present in the source trees reported by any of its neighbors. The head of a link does not periodically send LSUs for the link because link-state information never ages out.

LSUs are exchanged among routers in update messages. How update messages are sent among routers depends on the services provided by the link layer and whether ORA or LORA is implemented. We describe the exchange of update messages in the following sections.

10.2.1 Information Stored and Exchanged

We describe STAR assuming that Dijkstra's Shortest Path First (SPF) algorithm [Dijkstra 1959] is used locally at each router to compute preferred routes.

An LSU for a link (u, v) in an update message is a tuple (u, v, l, sn) reporting the characteristics of the link, where l represents the cost of the link and sn is the sequence number assigned to the LSU.

A router i maintains a topology graph TG_i, a source tree ST_i, a route table, the set of neighbors N_i, the source trees ST_x^i reported by each neighbor $x \in N_i$, and the topology graphs TG_x^i reported by each neighbor $x \in N_i$. The record entry for a link (u, v) in the topology graph of router i is denoted $TG_i(u, v)$ and is defined by the tuple of attributes (u, v, l, sn, del). A specific attribute p in such a tuple is denoted by $TG_i(u, v).p$. The same notation applies to a link (u, v) in ST_i, ST_x^i, and TG_x^i. $TG_i(u, v).del$ is set to TRUE if the link is not in the source tree of any neighbor.

A vertex v in TG_i is denoted $TG_i(v)$. It contains a tuple $(d, pred, suc, suc')$ whose values are used in the computation of the source tree. $TG_i(v).d$ reports the distance of the path $i \leadsto v$; $TG_i(v).pred$ is v's predecessor in $i \leadsto v$, $TG_i(v).suc$ is the next hop along the path toward v, and suc' holds the address of the previous next hop toward v. The same notation applies to a vertex v in ST_i, ST_x^i, and TG_x^i.

The source tree ST_i is a subset of TG_i. The route table contains an entry for each destination in ST_i, each of which consists of the destination address, the cost of the path to the destination, and the address of the next hop toward the destination.

The topology graph TG_x^i and the source tree ST_x^i reported by neighbor x of router i differ when router i receives an update message from x. TG_x^i contains all the links in ST_x^i, plus the links reported by neighbor x in the message being processed by router i. $TG_x^i \equiv ST_x^i$ immediately after router i completes its processing of the update message from neighbor x.

A router i running LORA also maintains the last reported source tree ST_i'.

The cost of a failed link is considered to be infinity. The cost of a link can simply be the number of hops or the addition of the latency over the link plus some constant bias. The way costs are assigned to links does not change the way STAR operates.

In the rest of our description of STAR, we refer to a link-state update that has a cost infinity as a RESET, $TG_i^i \equiv TG_i$, and $ST_i^i \equiv ST_i$. MSG_i is the ith message.

10.2.2 Validating Updates

Because of delays in the routers and links of an internetwork, update messages sent by a router may propagate at different speeds along different paths. Therefore, a given router may receive an LSU from a neighbor with stale link-state information, and a distributed termination detection mechanism is necessary for a router to ascertain when a given LSU is valid and to avoid the possibility of LSUs circulating forever. STAR uses sequence numbers to validate LSUs. A sequence number associated with a link consists of a counter that can be incremented only by the head node of the link. For convenience, a router i needs to keep only a single counter SN_i for all the links for which it is the head node, which simply means that the sequence number a router gives to a link for which it is the head node can be incremented by more than 1 each time the link parameters change value.

A router receiving an LSU accepts it as valid if it has a larger sequence number than that of the LSU stored from the same source or if there is no entry for the link in the topology graph and the LSU is not reporting an infinite cost. Link-state information for failed links consists only of the LSUs erased from the topology graph because of aging (which is on the order of an hour after having processed the LSU). LSUs for operational links are erased from the topology graph when the links are erased from the source tree of all the neighbors.

Because LSUs for operational links never age out, there is no need for the head node of a link to send periodic LSUs to update the link's sequence number. This is very important because it means that STAR does not need periodic update messages to validate link-state information, unlike OSPF [Moy 1994] and routing protocols based on sequence numbers or time stamps.

10.2.3 Exchanging Update Messages

How update messages are exchanged depends on the routing approach used (ORA or LORA) and the services provided by the link layer. The rest of this section describes how LORA and ORA are supported in STAR, assuming that

- An underlying neighbor protocol ensures that a router detects within a finite time the existence of a new neighbor and the loss of connectivity with a neighbor.
- An update message is broadcast to all neighbors of a router without experiencing hidden terminal interference.

The following discussion addresses the impact of not having a neighbor protocol and having to rely on an unreliable link layer that does not eliminate hidden terminal interference in broadcast transmissions.

For ORA to be supported in STAR, the only requirement for update messages is that a router send an update message every time its source tree changes.

In an on-demand routing protocol, a router can continue using a path found as long as the path leads to the destination, even if it does not have optimal cost. A similar approach can be used in STAR because each router has a complete path to every destination as part of its source tree. To support LORA, router i running STAR reports updates to its source trees in the event of unreachable destinations, new destinations, the possibility of permanent routing loops, and the cost of paths exceeding a given threshold. Router i accomplishes this by comparing its source tree against the source trees it has received from its neighbors after any input event and by sending the updates to its source tree according to the following three rules.

1. Router i sends a source tree update when it finds a new destination or when any of its neighbors reports a new destination.
2. Router i sends a source tree update when the change in the cost of the path to at least one destination exceeds a threshold Δ for router i or any of its neighbors.
3. Router i sends a source tree update after processing an input event if
   - A path implied in the source tree of router i leads to a loop.
   - The new successor chosen to a given destination has an address greater than the address of router i.
   - The reported distance from the new chosen successor n to a destination j is longer than the reported distance from the previous successor to the same destination. However, if the cost of the link (i, j) increases and $n \neq i$ is a neighbor of j, no update message is needed regarding j or any destination whose path from i involves j.

The first rule is needed to disseminate the existence of a new destination. The second rule is needed to disseminate the fact that one or more destinations may be unreachable. The third rule is needed to eliminate permanent looping.

Whenever a router hears from a new neighbor that is also a new destination, it sends an update message that includes the new LSUs in its source tree. Obviously, when a router is first initialized, or after a reboot, the router itself is a new destination and should send an update message to its neighbors.

When a router processes an input event (e.g., a link fails or an update message is received) that causes *all* of its paths through all of its neighbors to one or more destinations to be severed, it sends an update message that includes an LSU specifying an infinite cost for the link connecting to the head of each subtree of the source tree that becomes unreachable. The update message does not have to include an LSU for each node in an unreachable subtree because a neighbor receiving the update message has the sending node's source tree and can therefore infer that all nodes below the root of the subtree are also unreachable, unless LSUs are sent for new links used to reach some of the nodes in the subtree. When at least one destination becomes unreachable by any of the router's neighbors and the router has a path to that destination, the router sends an update message reporting the changes to its source tree.

The loop prevention mechanisms of rule 3 in the preceding list assume that the local route selection algorithm prevents a router from adding a link (u, v) to its new source tree, choosing neighbor k as the successor to v if (u, v) is not in the source tree reported by k. This is easily done by labeling each link in the topology graph with the neighbors that reported the link and by allowing a link (u, v) to be added to the new source tree only if the neighbor k used in the path from the root of the source tree to (u, v) is one of the link's reporting neighbors.

To explain the need for the first part of rule 3, we observe that, in any routing loop among routers with unique addresses, one of the routers must have the smallest address in the loop. Therefore, if a router is forced to send an update message when it chooses a successor whose address is greater than its own, it is not possible for all routers in a routing loop to remain quiet after choosing one another because at least one of them is forced to send an update message, which causes the loop to break when routers update their source trees.

The last part of rule 3 is needed when link costs can assume different values in different directions, in which case the first part of the rule may not suffice to break loops because the node with the smallest address in the loop may not have to change successors when the loop is formed.

To ensure that the rules in the preceding list work with incremental updates that specify only changes to a source tree, a router must remember the source tree that was last advertised to its neighbors. If any of the rules are satisfied, the router must do one of two things:

- If the new source tree includes new neighbors other than those present in the source tree that was last updated, the router must send its entire source tree in its update so that those new neighbors learn about all of the destinations the router knows.
- If the two source trees contain the same neighbors, the router sends only the updates needed to obtain the new tree from the old one.

The preceding rules are sufficient to ensure that every router obtains loopless paths to all known destinations without having to send updates periodically [Garcia-Luna-Aceves+ 2001]. In addition to a router's ability to prevent loops in STAR, the two key features that enable STAR to adopt LORA are the ability to validate LSUs without the need of periodic updates and the ability to either listen to neighbors' packets or use a neighboring protocol at the link layer to determine the neighbors of a router.

Figures 10.1 and 10.2 specify the main procedures of STAR (for both LORA and ORA) used to update the route table and the link-state database at a router i. The descriptions assume that the link layer provides reliable broadcast of network-level packets and that update messages consequently specify only incremental changes to the router's source tree instead of to the complete source tree. Procedure `NodeUp` is executed when a router i starts up. The neighbor set of the router is initially empty, and the sequence number counter is reset to zero.

If the neighbor protocol reports a new link to a neighbor k (procedure `NeighborUp`), the router then runs procedure `Update` with the appropriate message as input; the LSU in the message is given a new sequence number. The same approach is used for link failures (procedure `NeighborDown`) and changes in link costs (procedure `LinkCostChange`). When a router establishes connectivity to a new neighbor, it sends its complete source tree to that neighbor. The LSUs that must be broadcast to all neighbors are inserted into MSG_i.

Procedure `Update` is executed when router i receives an update message from neighbor k or when the parameters of an outgoing link change. The topology graphs TG_i and TG_k^i are updated first, and then the source trees ST_k^i and ST_i are updated, which may cause the router to update its route table and send its own update message. The information of an LSU reporting the failure of a link is discarded if the link is not in the topology graph of the router. A shortest-path algorithm based on Dijkstra's SPF (procedure `BuildShortestPathTree`) is run on the updated topology graph TG_k^i to

```
NodeUp()
description
// Node i initializes itself
{
    TG_i ← ∅;
    ST_i ← ∅;
    ST'_i ← ∅;
    N_i ← ∅;
    M_i ← FALSE;
    NS_i ← FALSE;
}

NeighborUp(k)
description
// Neighbor protocol reports connectivity
// to neighbor k
{
    N_i ← N_i ∪ {k};
    TG^i_k ← ∅;
    ST^i_k ← ∅;
    sendST ← TRUE;

    if ( LORA and k ∈ TG_i and TG_i(k).pred ≠ null )
    {
        NS_i ← TRUE;
        sendST ← FALSE;
    }

    Update(i, (i, k, l^i_k, T_i));

    if ( sendST )
    {
        MSG_i ← ∅;

        for each ( link (u, v) ∈ ST_i )
            MSG_i ← MSG_i ∪ {( u, v, TG_i(u, v).l,
                              TG_i(u, v).t)};
    }

    Send();
}

NeighborDown(k)
description
// Neighbor protocol reports link
// failure to neighbor k
{
    N_i ← N_i - {k};
    TG^i_k ← ∅;
    ST^i_k ← ∅;

    Update(i, (i, k, ∞, T_i));

    Send();
}

LinkCostChange(k)
description
// Neighbor protocol reports link
// cost change to neighbor k
{
    Update(i, (i, k, l^i_k, T_i));

    Send();
}

Update(k, msg)
description
// Process update message msg
// sent by router k
{
    UpdateTopologyGraph(k, msg);

    if ( k ≠ i )
        BuildShortestPathTree(k, null);

    BuildShortestPathTree(i, k);
    UpdateRoutingTable();

    if ( k ≠ i )
        Send();
}
```

```
UpdateTopologyGraph(k, msg)
description
// Update TG_i and TG^i_k from LSUs in msg
{
    for each ( LSU (u, v, l, t) ∈ msg )
    {
        if ( l ≠ ∞ )
            ProcessAddUpdate(k, (u, v, l, t));
        else
            ProcessVoidUpdate(k, (u, v, l, t));
    }
}

ProcessAddUpdate(k, (u, v, l, t))
description
// Update topology graphs TG_i and TG^i_k from LSU
{
    if ( (u, v) ∉ TG_i or t > TG_i(u, v).t )
    {
        if ( (u, v) ∉ TG_i )
        {
            TG_i ← TG_i ∪ {(u, v, l, t)};
            if ( LORA and k ≠ i and u = i )
                TG_i(u, v).l ← ∞;
        }
        else
        {
            TG_i(u, v).l ← l;    TG_i(u, v).t ← t;
        }
    }
    if ( k ≠ i )
    {
        if ( ∃ (r, s) ∈ TG^i_k | r ≠ u and s = v )
            TG^i_k ← TG^i_k - {(r, s)};
        if ( (u, v) ∉ TG^i_k )
            TG^i_k ← TG^i_k ∪ {(u, v, l, t)};
        else
        {
            TG^i_k(u, v).l ← l;    TG^i_k(u, v).t ← t;
        }
    }
    TG_i(u, v).del ← FALSE;
    if ( TG_i(u, v).l = ∞ ) Start aging (u, v);
}

ProcessVoidUpdate(k, (u, v, l, t))
description
// Update topology graphs TG_i and TG^i_k from LSU
{
    if ( (u, v) ∈ TG_i )
    {
        if ( t > TG_i(u, v).t )
        {
            TG_i(u, v).l ← l;    TG_i(u, v).t ← t;
            Start aging (u, v);
        }
        if ( k ≠ i and (u, v) ∈ TG^i_k )
        {
            TG^i_k(u, v).l ← l;    TG^i_k(u, v).t ← t;
        }
        TG_i(u, v).del ← FALSE;
    }
}

Send()
{
    if ( MSG_i ≠ ∅ ) Broadcast message MSG_i;
    MSG_i ← ∅;
}

InitializeSingleSource(k)
{
    for each ( vertex v ∈ TG^i_k )
    {
        TG^i_k(v).d ← ∞; TG^i_k(v).pred ← null;
        TG^i_k(v).suc' ← TG^i_k(v).suc;
        TG^i_k(v).suc ← null; TG^i_k(v).nbr ← null;
    }
    TG^i_k(k).d ← 0;
}
```

Figure 10.1. STAR Specification

```
BuildShortestPathTree(k, k')
{
  InitializeSingleSource(k);
  Q ← set of vertices in TG_k^i;
  u ← ExtractMin(Q); newST ← ∅;
  while ( u ≠ null and TG_k^i(u).d < ∞ )
  {
    if ( TG_k^i(u).pred ≠ null and TG_k^i(u).pred ∉ newST )
    {
      (r, s) ← TG_k^i(u).pred; newST ← newST ∪ (r, s);
      if ( LORA and k = i )
      {
        if ( k' ≠ i and TG_{k'}^i(u).suc = i and TG_i(u).suc' = k' )
          M_i ← TRUE;        // LORA-3 rule
        if ( TG_i(u).suc ≠ TG_i(u).suc' and TG_i(u).suc > i )
          M_i ← TRUE;        // LORA-3 rule
        if ( ∄ (x, y) ∈ ST_i' | y = u )
          M_i ← TRUE;        // LORA-1 rule
        if ( | TG_i(u).d − TG_i(u).d'' | > Δ )
        {
          M_i ← TRUE;        // LORA-2 rule
          TG_i(u).d'' ← TG_i(u).d;
        }
        if ( k' ≠ i and TG_{k'}^i(u).pred = null )
          M_i ← TRUE;        // LORA-2 rule
        w ← TG_i(u).suc;
        if ( w ≠ i )
          path_w_u_cost ← TG_i(u).d − TG_i(i, w).l;
        else path_w_u_cost ← 0;
        if ( path_w_u_cost > TG_i(u).d' )
        {
          if ( r = w or TG_i(r).nbr = i )
            TG_i(s).nbr ← i;
          if ( TG_i(s).nbr ≠ i )
            M_i ← TRUE;        // LORA-3 rule
        }
        TG_i(u).d' ← path_w_u_cost;
        TG_i(u).suc' ← TG_i(u).suc;
      }
    }
    for each ( vertex v ∈ adjacency list of TG_k^i(u)
             | TG_k^i(u, v).l ≠ ∞ and NOT TG_i(u, v).del )
    {
      if ( k = i )
      {
        if ( u = i ) suc ← i;
        else if ( TG_i(u).suc = i )
          suc ← {x | x ∈ N_i and x = u};
        else suc ← TG_i(u).suc;
      }
      else
      {
        if ( u = k )
        {
          if ( v = i )   suc ← i;
          else          suc ← k;
        }
        else suc ← TG_i(u).suc;
        if ( k ≠ i or u = i or (u, v) ∈ ST_{suc}^i )
          RelaxEdge(k, u, v, Q, suc);
      }
      if ( Q ≠ ∅ )   u ← ExtractMin(Q);
      else          u ← null;
    }
  }
  UpdateNeighborTree(k, newST);
  if ( k = i )
  {
    if ( LORA and M_i )
    {
      ReportChanges(ST_i', newST);
      ST_i' ← newST;   NS_i ← FALSE;
    }
    else if ( ORA )
      ReportChanges(ST_i, newST);
    for each ( link (u, v) ∈ TG_i | TG_i(u, v).del = TRUE )
      if ( ORA or ( LORA and ( M_i or (u, v) ∉ ST_i' ) ) )
        TG_i ← TG_i − {(u, v)};
    M_i ← FALSE;
  }
  ST_k^i ← newST;   newST ← ∅;
}
```

```
RelaxEdge(k, u, v, Q, suc)
{
  if ( TG_k^i(v).d > TG_k^i(u).d + TG_k^i(u, v).l or
     ( k = i and TG_k^i(v).d = TG_k^i(u).d + TG_k^i(u, v).l and
       (u, v) ∈ ST_i ) )
  {
    TG_k^i(v).d ← TG_k^i(u).d + TG_k^i(u, v).l;
    TG_k^i(v).pred ← TG_k^i(u, v);
    TG_k^i(v).suc ← suc;
    if ( LORA and k = i and TG_i(v).suc' = null )
    {
      // v was an unknown destination
      TG_i(v).suc' ← suc;
      TG_i(v).d'' ← TG_i(v).d;
      if ( suc ≠ i )
        TG_i(v).d' ← TG_i(v).d − TG_i(i, suc).l;
      else
        TG_i(v).d' ← 0;
    }
    Insert(Q, v);
  }
}
```

```
ReportChanges(oldST, newST)
description
// Generate LSUs for new links in the router's source tree
{
  for each ( link (u, v) ∈ newST )
    if ( (u, v) ∉ oldST or newST(u, v).t ≠ oldST(u, v).t
       or NS_i )
      MSG_i ← MSG_i ∪ {( u, v, TG_i(u, v).l, TG_i(u, v).t)};
}
```

```
UpdateNeighborTree(k, newST)
description
// Delete links from TG_k^i and report failed links
{
  for each ( link (u, v) ∈ ST_k^i )
  {
    if ( (u, v) ∉ newST )
    {
      // k Has removed (u, v) from its source tree
      if ( LORA and TG_k^i(v).pred = null )
      {
        // LORA-2 rule: k has no path to destination v
        M_i ← TRUE;
        if ( k = i )
          for each ( link (r, s) ∈ TG_i | s = v )
            if ( TG_i(r, s).l = ∞ )
              MSG_i ← MSG_i ∪ {( r, s, TG_i(r, s).l, TG_i(r, s).t)};
      }
      if ( ORA and k = i and ( u = i or TG_i(v).pred = null ) )
      {
        // i has no path to destination v or i is the head node
        if ( TG_i(v).pred = null )
          for each ( link (r, s) ∈ TG_i | s = v )
            if ( TG_i(r, s).l = ∞ )
              MSG_i ← MSG_i ∪ {( r, s, TG_i(r, s).l, TG_i(r, s).t)};
        else if ( TG_i(u, v).l = ∞ )
          // i Needs to report failed link
          MSG_i ← MSG_i ∪ {( u, v, TG_i(u, v).l, TG_i(u, v).t)};
      }
      if ( LORA and k = i and TG_i(v).pred = null )
      {
        TG_i(v).d' ← ∞;
        TG_i(v).d'' ← ∞;
        TG_i(v).suc' ← null;
      }
      if ( NOT ( k = i and u = i ) )
      {
        if ( (u, v) ∈ TG_k^i )
          TG_k^i ← TG_k^i − {(u, v)};

        if ( TG_i(u, v).l ≠ ∞ and ∄ x ∈ N_i | (u, v) ∈ TG_x^i )
          TG_i(u, v).del ← TRUE;
      }
    }
  }
}
```

Figure 10.2. STAR Specification   *(Continued)*

construct a new source tree ST_k^i; it is then run on the topology graph TG_i to construct a new source tree ST_i.

If a destination v becomes unreachable, LSUs are broadcast to the neighbors for each link in the topology graph TG_i that has v as the tail node of the link and a link cost equal to infinity.

The new router's source tree is compared to the last reported source tree (ST_i' for LORA and ST_i for ORA) (procedure `ReportChanges`), and an update message is constructed from the differences of the two trees. For the case of a router running LORA, the source trees are compared only if at least one of the three rules given earlier applies.

10.2.4 Example

The following example illustrates the working of STAR based on LORA. Consider the seven-node wireless network shown in Figure 10.3. All links and nodes are assumed to have the same propagation delays, and all the links have unit cost. The figure shows only the LSUs with new information transmitted in update messages to the neighbors; these LSUs appear in parentheses located next to the node that generates them. The third element in an LSU corresponds to the cost of the link (a RESET has cost infinity).

Figures 10.3(b)–(d) show the source trees according to STAR at the routers indicated with filled circles for the network topology depicted in Figure 10.3(a). Arrowheads on solid lines indicate the direction of the links stored in the router's source tree. When the link (f, g) fails (Figure 10.3(e)), the neighbor protocol at node f triggers the execution of procedure `NeighborDown`, the link (d, g) is inserted into f's source tree, and no update message is generated because f's new successor toward g has an address smaller than f. Figure 10.3(f) shows the new source tree of node d after the failure of link (d, g); because d has an address smaller than the new successor toward g, it is forced to send an update message reporting the new link added to the source tree and the failure of link (d, g). Nodes c, e, and f do not generate any update message after processing d's message because a path exists to all destinations in the network and no routing loop was formed.

This example illustrates that link failures do not cause the generation of update messages by nodes that have the failed link in their source trees as long as the nodes have a path to all destinations.

10.2.5 Impact of the Link Layer

If the link layer provides efficient, reliable broadcast of network-level packets, STAR can send an update message only once to all neighbors specifying

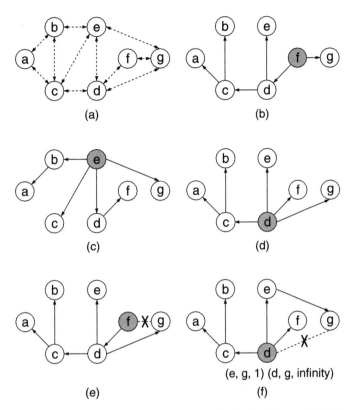

Figure 10.3. An Example Topology with Links Having Unit Cost

only incremental changes to the router's source tree. The link layer will retransmit the packet as needed to reach all neighbors, so that it can guarantee that a neighbor receives the packet unless the link is broken.

A reliable broadcast service at the link layer can be implemented very efficiently if the medium access control (MAC) protocol guarantees collision-free transmissions of broadcast packets. TDMA is a typical example of MAC protocols that can make this guarantee, and there are several recent proposals that need not rely on static assignment of resources (e.g., FPRP [Zhu+ 1998] and CATS [Tang+ 2000]).

Unfortunately, reliable broadcasting from a node to all of its neighbors is not supported in the collision-avoidance MAC protocols that have been proposed and implemented for ad hoc networks [Bharghavan 1994, Fullmer+ 1997, IEEE 1996, Karn 1990]. IEEE 802.11 [IEEE 1996] appears to be the only commercial alternative at the MAC layer in ISM bands today. Indeed, any link-level or network-level strategy for reliable exchange of broadcast update messages over a contention-based MAC protocol requires substantial retransmissions under high-load conditions and rapid changes to the connectivity of nodes.

For these reasons, if the underlying MAC protocol does not provide collision-free transmission over which efficient, reliable broadcasting can be built, STAR, and any table-driven routing protocol for that matter, is better off relying on the approach adopted in the past in the DARPA packet radio network. For STAR this means that a router broadcasts its update messages to its neighbors unreliably, and each update message contains the entire source tree. To operate correctly with this approach under LORA, STAR routers must avoid situations in which permanent loops are created because an update message is not received by a neighbor. A simple example is a two-node loop between two neighbor routers, A and B. The neighbor with the smaller address, A, sends an update to its neighbor B specifying that A is using B to get to at least one destination D, but the message does not reach B, which then starts using A to reach D.

Additional simple rules for sending an update message can be used to eliminate permanent looping due to lost packets using unreliable broadcasting [Garcia-Luna-Aceves+ 1999]. One such rule is that a packet must specify the path it has traversed; another is that a router must send its update reliably to the neighbor that caused the router to change its source routing tree.

10.3 PERFORMANCE EVALUATION

We ran a number of simulation experiments to compare STAR's average performance against that of table-driven and on-demand routing protocols. The protocol stack implementation in our simulator runs the same code used in a real embedded wireless router; IP (Internet Protocol) is used as the network protocol.

The link layer implements a MAC protocol similar to the IEEE 802.11 standard, and the physical layer is based on a direct-sequence spread-spectrum radio with a link bandwidth of 1 Mbit/sec. The neighbor protocol is configured to report loss of connectivity to a neighbor if the candidate of the link fails in a period of about 10 seconds.

The simulation experiments use 20 nodes forming an ad hoc network, moving over a flat space (5,000 m × 7,000 m) and initially randomly distributed at a density of one node per square kilometer. Nodes move in the simulation according to the *random waypoint* model [Broch+ 1998a]. Each node begins the simulation by remaining stationary for *pause time* seconds.

It then selects a random destination and moves toward it at a speed of 20 m/sec for a period of time uniformly distributed between 5 and 11 seconds. Upon reaching the destination, the node pauses again for pause time seconds, selects another destination, and proceeds there as previously described, repeating this behavior for the duration of the simulation.

The simulation study was conducted in the C++ Protocol Toolkit (CPT) simulator environment. Two sets of simulations were run. First, STAR based on ORA is compared against two other table-driven routing protocols. Second, STAR based on LORA is compared with DSR, which has been shown to be one of the best-performing on-demand routing protocols.

10.3.1 Comparison with Table-Driven Protocols

We chose to compare STAR against ALP (Account, Login, Password) and the traditional link-state approach [Garcia-Luna-Aceves+ 1998]. The traditional link-state approach (denoted TOB for "topology broadcast") corresponds to the flooding of link states in a network or within clusters coupled with flooding of intercluster connectivity among them. ALP is a routing protocol based on partial link-state information that we have shown elsewhere to outperform table-driven distance-vector and link-state protocols. For these simulations STAR uses ORA, as both ALP and TOB attempt to provide paths that are optimal with respect to a defined metric. The three protocols rely on the reliable delivery of broadcast packets by the link layer.

We ran our simulations with movement patterns generated for five pause times: 0, 30, 45, 60, and 90 seconds. A pause time of 0 seconds corresponds to continuous motion. The simulation time in all the simulation scenarios is 900 seconds.

As the pause time increases, we expect the number of update packets sent to decrease because the number of link connectivity changes decreases. Because STAR and ALP generate LSUs only for those links along paths used to reach destinations, we expect STAR and ALP to outperform any topology broadcast protocol.

A router running ALP does not report to its neighbors the deletion of a link from its preferred paths if the cost of the link has not increased (the state of the link transitions from 1 to 2). Consequently, all routers that have a link in state 2 in their topology graphs must forward to their neighbors an LSU that announces the failure of the link. Unlike ALP, routers running STAR have link-state information in their topology graphs only for those links that are in the preferred paths of their neighbors. That is, the failure of a link will make a router send an update message reporting the failure only if the link is in the router's preferred paths. Because the dynamics of

Table 10.1. Average Performance of STAR, ALP, and
TOB for Different Pause Times

Pause Time	Connectivity Changes	Packets Generated		
		STAR	ALP	TOB
30	154	411	1,765	5,577
45	102	262	1,304	3,908
60	90	239	1,144	2,502
90	50	138	623	1,811

link connectivity change in a wireless mobile network, we expect STAR to
outperform ALP.

Figures 10.5 and 10.4 depict the performance of STAR, ALP, and TOB
in terms of the number of update packets generated as a function of simulation time for four pause times. The ordinates represent the simulation time.
Table 10.1 summarizes the behavior of the three protocols according to the
pause time of the nodes. It shows the number of link connectivity changes
and the total number of update packets generated by the routing protocols.
ALP generates on average more than four times the update packets that
STAR generates; TOB generates more than 10 times that of STAR.

10.3.2 Comparison with On-Demand Routing Protocols

We compare STAR using LORA with DSR because DSR has been shown to
be one of the best-performing on-demand routing protocols [Broch+ 1998a,
Das+ 2000].

As we stated, our simulation experiments used the same methodology that was used recently to evaluate DSR and other on-demand routing
protocols [Broch+ 1998a]. To run DSR in our simulation environment, we
ported the *ns-2* code available from [Monarch 1998] into the CPT simulator. Our DSR implementation is different from that used in Broch et al.
[Broch+ 1998a] in two respects: (1) in the embedded wireless routers and
simulated protocol stack we used there is no access to the MAC layer and
the simulated stack cannot reschedule packets already scheduled for transmission over a link (however, this is the case for all the protocols we simulate); (2) routers cannot operate their network interfaces in *promiscuous
mode* because the MAC protocol operates over multiple channels—a router
does not know on which channels its neighbors are transmitting unless the
packets are meant for it. Both STAR and DSR can buffer 20 packets that
are awaiting discovery of a route through the network.

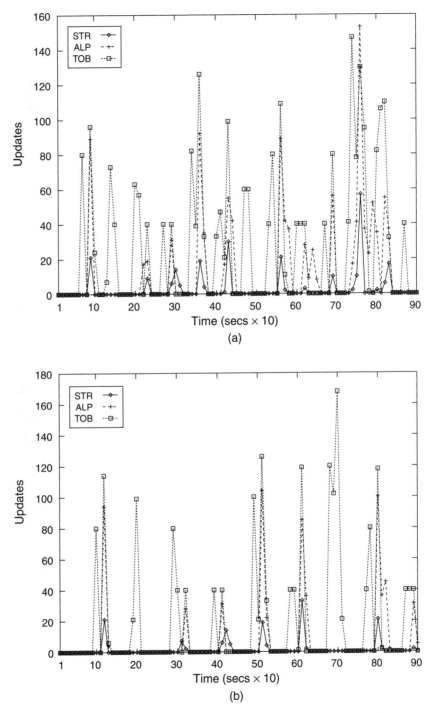

Figure 10.4. Comparison of STAR, ALP, and TOB Update Packet Generation for Pause Time 60 (a) and Pause Time 90 (b)

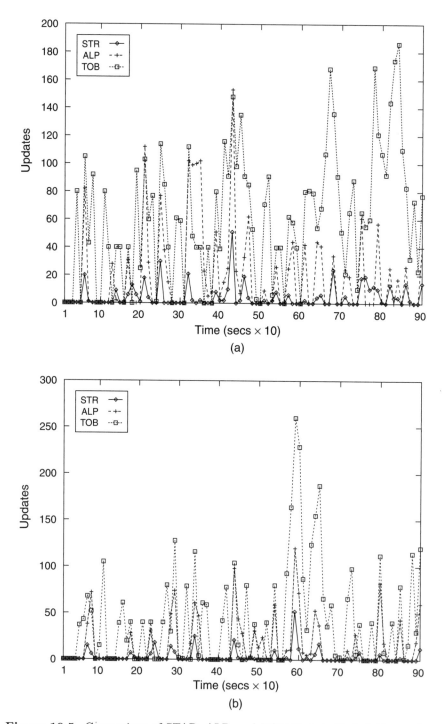

Figure 10.5. Comparison of STAR, ALP, and TOB Update Packet Generation for Pause Time 30 (a) and Pause Time 45 (b)

The overall goal of the simulation experiments was to measure the ability of the routing protocols to react to changes in the network topology while delivering data packets to their destinations. To measure this ability we applied to the simulated network two different communication patterns corresponding to 8 and 20 data flows. The total workload in both scenarios was the same and consisted of 32 data packets/sec. In the scenario with 8 flows, each continuous bit rate (CBR) source generated 4 packets/sec; in the scenario with 20 sources, each CBR source generated 1.6 packets/sec. In both scenarios the number of unique destinations was 8 and the packet size was 64 bytes. The data flows were started at times uniformly distributed between 20 and 120 seconds. (We chose to start the flows after 20 seconds of simulated time to give the link layer some time to determine the set of nodes that were neighbors of the routers.)

The protocol evaluations are based on the simulation of 20 wireless nodes in continuous motion (pause time 0) for 900 and 1,800 seconds of simulated time.

Tables 10.2 and 10.3 summarize the behavior of STAR and DSR according to the simulated time. They show the total number of update packets transmitted by the nodes and the total number of data packets delivered to the applications for the two simulated workloads. The total number of update packets transmitted by routers running STAR varies with the number of changes in link connectivity, whereas DSR generates control packets on the basis of both the variation in connectivity changes and the type of workload inserted in the network. Routers running STAR are able to deliver more

Table 10.2. Average Performance of STAR and DSR
Total Changes in Link Connectivity: 1,464

Number of Flows	Update Packets Sent*		Data Packets Delivered		Data Packets Generated
	STAR	DSR	STAR	DSR	
8	1,054	791	15,797	14,740	24,100
20	1,050	3,122	9,631	6,830	23,718

*Nodes moving during 900 seconds of simulated time

Table 10.3. Average Performance of STAR and DSR
Total Changes in Link Connectivity: 2,788

Number of Flows	Update Packets Sent*		Data Packets Delivered		Data Packets Generated
	STAR	DSR	STAR	DSR	
8	1,705	1,963	34,805	32,650	52,900
20	1,707	6,605	27,050	10,175	52,518

*Nodes moving during 1,800 seconds of simulated time

than 1,000 data packets, more than DSR when 8 data flows are present in the network for 900 seconds; however, routers running DSR transmit about 300 fewer update packets. When the 8 destinations receive that same data rate during a period of 1,800 seconds, STAR transmits 250 fewer control packets than DSR transmits and can deliver more than 2,000 data packets to the applications. When we increase the number of data sources from 8 to 20 nodes, while inserting the same number of data packets in the network (32 packets/sec), we observe that DSR transmits about three times more control packets than STAR and that routers running STAR can deliver from 40% to 160% more data packets.

The MAC layer discards all packets scheduled for transmission to a neighbor when the link to the neighbor fails. This contributes to the high loss of data packets seen by nodes. In DSR, each packet header carries the complete ordered list of routers through which the packet must pass and may be updated by nodes along the path toward the destination. The low throughput achieved by DSR for the case of 20 sources of data is due to the routers' poor choice of source routes, leading to a significant increase in the number of route error packets generated. Discarding of data packets is also due to the lack of routes to the destinations because the network may become temporarily partitioned or because the route tables do not converge in the highly dynamic topology we simulate.

Figures 10.6(a) and (b) show the cumulative distribution of packet delay experienced by data packets during 900 seconds of simulated time, for a workload of 8 and 20 flows, respectively. Figures 10.7(a) and (b) show the cumulative distribution of packet delay during 1,800 seconds of simulated time. The higher delay introduced by DSR when relaying data packets is not directly related to the number of hops traversed by the packets (as shown in Tables 10.4 and 10.5) but rather to the poor choice of source routes when the number of flows increases from 8 to 20.

In all of the simulation scenarios, the number of destinations was set to just 40% of the number of nodes in the network so as to be fair to DSR. For cases in which all of the network nodes receive data, STAR would introduce no extra overhead but DSR could be severely penalized. It is important to note the low ratio of update messages generated by STAR compared to the number of changes in link connectivity (see Tables 10.2 and 10.3).

We have not shown scenarios in which routers fail or in which the network becomes partitioned for extended periods. In such cases, the bandwidth consumed by STAR is much the same as in those in which no router fails, because all that must happen is that updates about the failed links to unreachable destinations propagate across the network. In contrast, DSR continues to send flood search messages in an attempt to reach the failed destination.

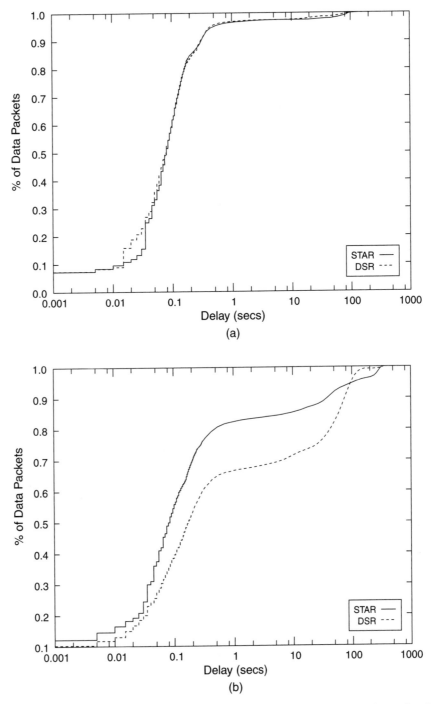

Figure 10.6. Cumulative Distribution of Packet Delay during 900 Seconds of Simulated Time for a Workload of (a) 8 Flows and (b) 20 Flows

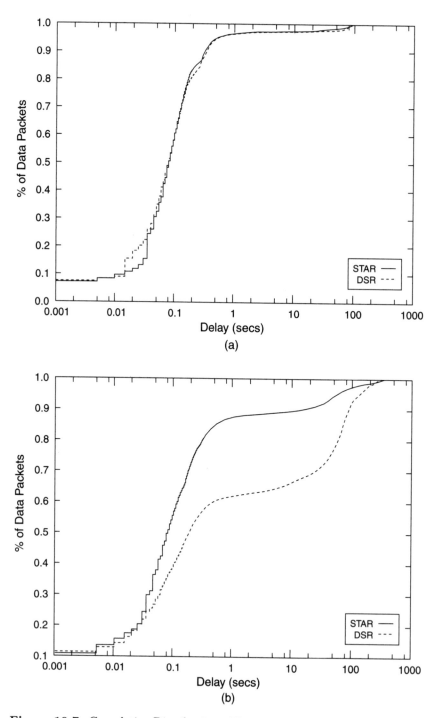

Figure 10.7. Cumulative Distribution of Packet Delay during 1,800 Seconds of Simulated Time for a Workload of (a) 8 Flows and (b) 20 Flows

Table 10.4. Distribution of Data Packets Delivered According to the Number of Hops Traversed from the Source to the Destination

Number of Flows	Protocol	Number of Hops*					
		1	2	3	4	5	6
8	STAR	91.1	8.0	0.8	0.1		
	DSR	64.9	31.2	2.6	1.3		
20	STAR	89.8	8.5	1.7			
	DSR	61.9	32.4	5.1	0.3		0.3

*Nodes moving during 900 seconds of simulated time

Table 10.5. Distribution of Data Packets Delivered According to the Number of Hops Traversed from the Source to the Destination

Number of Flows	Protocol	Number of Hops*					
		1	2	3	4	5	6
8	STAR	91.0	7.2	1.6	0.2		
	DSR	64.3	29.2	5.9	0.6		
20	STAR	91.0	7.0	1.7	0.3		
	DSR	67.5	28.7	3.5	0.2		0.1

*Nodes moving during 1,800 seconds of simulated time

10.4 CONCLUSION

STAR is a link-state protocol that incurs the smallest communication overhead of *any* table-driven routing protocol and that incurs an amount of overhead similar to that of on-demand routing protocols. It achieves this by allowing routes to deviate from the optimum. STAR accomplishes its bandwidth efficiency by disseminating only the link-state data needed for routers to reach destinations; by exploiting that information to ascertain when update messages must be transmitted to detect new destinations, unreachable destinations, and loops; and by allowing paths to deviate from the optimum without creating permanent loops.

Our simulation experiments show that, in terms of the number of update packets sent, STAR is an order of magnitude more efficient than the traditional link-state approach and more than four times more efficient than ALP (which has been shown to outperform earlier table-driven routing protocols). The results of our experiments also show that STAR is as bandwidth-efficient as DSR. Because STAR can be used with any clustering mechanism so far proposed, these results clearly indicate that it is a very attractive approach for routing in packet radio networks.

The main contribution of this chapter is not so much the description of a specific protocol but more the illustration that both on-demand and table-driven routing approaches can be attractive. Many interesting research avenues should be explored with respect to least-overhead routing over ad hoc networks. Examples include multiple types of services together with the requirement to conserve bandwidth, investigating ways in which on-demand routing protocols can be made even more bandwidth-efficient, and combining on-demand and table-driven routing approaches.

References

[Basagni+ 1998] S. Basagni et al. A Distance Routing Effect Algorithm for Mobility (DREAM). In *Proceedings of the Fourth Annual ACM/IEEE International Conference on Mobile Computing and Networking (MOBICOM '98)*, October 1998.

[Behrens+ 1998] J. Behrens and J.J. Garcia-Luna-Aceves. Hierarchical Routing Using Link Vectors. In *Proceedings of IEEE INFOCOM '98*, March/April 1998.

[Bharghavan+ 1994] V. Bharghavan, A. Demers, S. Shenker, and L.Z. Ang. MACAW: A Media Access Protocol for Wireless LANs. In *Proceedings ACM SIGCOMM '94*, August 1994.

[Broch+ 1998a] J. Broch et al. A Performance Comparison of Multi-Hop Wireless Ad Hoc Network Routing Protocols. In *Proceedings of the Fourth Annual ACM/IEEE International Conference on Mobile Computing and Networking (MOBICOM '98)*, October 1998.

[Broch+ 1998b] J. Broch, et al. *The Dynamic Source Routing Protocol for Mobile Ad Hoc Networks* (draft-ietf-manet-dsr-01.txt), December 1998.

[Das+ 2000] S. Das, C. Perkins, and E.M. Royer. Performance Comparison of Two On-Demand Routing Protocols for Ad Hoc Networks. In *Proceedings of IEEE INFOCOM 2000*, March 2000.

[Dijkstra 1959] E.W. Dijkstra. A Note on Two Problems in Connection with Graphs. *Numerische Math.* 1:269–271, 1959.

[Dube+ 1997] R. Dube, C. Rais, K.-Y. Wang, and S.K. Tripathi. Signal Stability-Based Adaptive Routing (SSA) for Ad Hoc Mobile Networks. *IEEE Personal Communications* 4(1):36–45, February 1997.

[Fullmer+ 1997] C.L. Fullmer and J.J. Garcia-Luna-Aceves. Solutions to Hidden Terminal Problems in Wireless Networks. In *Proceedings of ACM SIGCOMM '97*, September 1997.

[Garcia-Luna-Aceves+ 1995] J.J. Garcia-Luna-Aceves and J. Behrens. Distributed, Scalable Routing Based on Vectors of Link States. *IEEE Journal on Selected Areas of Communications* SAC 13(8):1383–1395, 1995.

[Garcia-Luna-Aceves+ 1997] J.J. Garcia-Luna-Aceves et al. Wireless Internet Gateways (WINGS). In *Proceedings of the IEEE Military Communications Conference (MILCOM '97)*, November 1997.

[Garcia-Luna-Aceves+ 1998] J.J. Garcia-Luna-Aceves and M. Spohn. Scalable Link-State Internet Routing. In *Proceedings of the IEEE International Conference on Network Protocols (ICNP '98)*, October 1998.

[Garcia-Luna-Aceves+ 1999] J.J. Garcia-Luna-Aceves and M. Spohn. Source Tree Routing in Wireless Networks. In *Proceedings of the IEEE International Conference on Network Protocols (ICNP '99)*, October/November 1999.

[Garcia-Luna-Aceves+ 2001] J.J. Garcia-Luna-Aceves and M. Spohn. Transmission-Efficient Routing in Wireless Networks Using Link-State Information. *ACM Mobile Networks and Applications (Special Issue, Energy Conserving Protocols in Wireless Networks)*, 2001.

[Haas+ 1998] Z. Haas and M. Pearlman. The Zone Routing Protocol for Highly Reconfigurable Ad Hoc Networks. In *Proceedings of ACM SIGCOMM '98*, August 1998.

[IEEE 1996] IEEE Computer Society LAN MAN Standards Committee. *P802.11—Unapproved Draft: Wireless LAN Medium Access Control (MAC) and Physical Specifications*. Institute of Electrical and Electronics Engineers, New York, 1996.

[Johnson+ 1996] D. Johnson and D. Maltz. Protocols for Adaptive Wireless and Mobile Networking. *IEEE Personal Communications* 3(1):34–42, February 1996.

[Jubin+ 1987] J. Jubin and J. Tornow. The DARPA Packet Radio Network Protocols. *Proceedings of the IEEE* 75(1):21–32, January 1987.

[Karn 1990] P. Karn. MACA—A New Channel Access Method for Packet Radio. In *Proceedings of the ARRL/CRRL Amateur Radio Ninth Computer Networking Conference*, September 1990.

[Kleinrock+ 1977] L. Kleinrock and F. Kamoun. Hierarchical Routing for Large Networks: Performance Evaluation and Optimization. *Computer Networks* 1(1):155–174, 1977.

[Ko+ 1998] Y-B. Ko and N. Vaidya. Location-Aided Routing (LAR) in Mobile Ad Hoc Networks. In *Proceedings of the Fourth ACM/IEEE International Conference on Mobile Computing and Networking (MOBICOM '98)*, October 1998.

[Li+ 1986] V.O.K. Li and R. Chang. Proposed Routing Algorithms for the US Army Mobile Subscriber Equipment (MSE) Network. In *Proceedings of the IEEE Military Communications Conference (MILCOM '86)*, October 1986.

[Monarch 1998] Carnegie-Mellon University Monarch Project. Wireless and Mobility Extensions to ns-2—Snapshot 1.0.0-beta (*http://www.monarch.cs.cmu.edu/cmu-ns.html*), August 1998.

[Moy 1994] J. Moy. OSPF Version 2. RFC 1583. Network Working Group, March 1994.

[Murthy+ 1996] S. Murthy and J.J. Garcia-Luna-Aceves. An Efficient Routing Protocol for Wireless Networks. *ACM Mobile Networks and Applications Journal (Special Issue, Routing in Mobile Communication Networks)* 1(2):183–197, October 1996.

[Murthy+ 1997] S. Murthy and J.J. Garcia-Luna-Aceves. Loop-Free Internet Routing Using Hierarchical Routing Trees. In *Proceedings of IEEE INFOCOM '97*, April 1997.

[Park+ 1997] V. Park and M. Corson. A Highly Adaptive Distributed Routing Algorithm for Mobile Wireless Networks. In *Proceedings of IEEE INFOCOM '97*, April 1997.

[Perkins+ 1994] C. Perkins and P. Bhagwat. Highly Dynamic Destination-Sequenced Distance-Vector Routing (DSDV) for Mobile Computers. *ACM SIG-COMM '94 Computer Communications Review* 24(4):234–244, October 1994.

[Perkins+ 1999] C. Perkins and E. Royer. Ad-hoc On-Demand Distance Vector Routing. In *Proceedings of the Second Annual IEEE Workshop on Mobile Computing Systems and Applications*, February 1999.

[Pursley+ 1993] M. Pursley and H.B. Russell. Routing in Frequency-Hop Packet Radio Networks with Partial-Band Jamming. *IEEE Transactions on Communications* COM-41(7):1117–1124, 1993.

[Ramamoorthy+ 1983] C.V. Ramamoorthy and W. Tsai. An Adaptive Hierarchical Routing Algorithm. In *Proceedings of IEEE COMPSAC '83*, November 1983, 93–104.

[Ramanathan+ 1998] R. Ramanathan and M. Steenstrup. Hierarchically-Organized, Multihop Mobile Wireless Networks for Quality-of-Service Support. *ACM/Baltzer Mobile Networks and Applications* 3(1):101–119, January 1998.

[Steenstrup 1995] M. Steenstrup (ed.). *Routing in Communication Networks*. Prentice-Hall, Englewood Cliffs, N.J., 1995.

[Tang+ 2000] Z. Tang and J.J. Garcia-Luna-Aceves. Collision-Avoidance Transmission Scheduling for Ad-Hoc Wireless Networks. In *Proceedings of IEEE ICC 2000*, June 2000.

[Toh 1996] C-K. Toh. *Wireless ATM and Ad-Hoc Networks: Protocols and Architectures*. Kluwer Academic Publishers, Norwood, Mass., 1996.

[Zhu+ 1998] C. Zhu and S. Corson. A Five Phase Reservation Protocol (FPRP) for Mobile Ad Hoc Networks. In *Proceedings of IEEE INFOCOM '98*, March 1998.

11

Summary and Future Work

Charles E. Perkins
Nokia Research Center

In this last chapter, I try to wrap up a subject that is still wide open and thus defies any attempt at a real conclusion. I describe some of the open questions that still face designers of ad hoc networks and give a thumbnail description of a few approaches that are not represented in this book. Finally, I attempt to give some idea of where the deployment of ad hoc networks may lead.

11.1 FUTURE WORK

Many questions about ad hoc networks remain unanswered, even after so many answers are suggested by the work represented in this book. The areas inviting further investigation include:

- *Scalability*—how large can an ad hoc network grow?
- *Quality of service*—can bandwidth- or delay-constrained applications operate well?
- *Client–server model shift*—what happens when a client cannot count on traditional methods to locate a suitable server?
- *Security*—is there a good way to protect against attacks from malicious ad hoc nodes?
- *Interoperation with the Internet*—how can an ad hoc network take advantage of evanescent or dynamically changing points of connection to the Internet?
- *Power control*—how can battery life be maximized?

Some of these questions will be briefly considered here. In my conclusion, I present some more extravagant ideas about the future benefits of ad hoc networking.

11.1.1 Scalability

Because of many interacting factors, no one knows just how large an ad hoc network can grow. It is safe to say that such a network cannot grow to the size of the Internet, which has tens of millions of IP addressable devices. So far, most simulations have been done with only 50 or 100 nodes, and even these small populations have exhibited fairly poor performance using the routing techniques available today. We have run simulations of ad hoc networks with up to 10,000 nodes, but the simulation environment definitely interferes with such experiments. One simulation can easily take over a gigabyte of memory and equal amounts of disk storage depending on which parameters are being measured.

With on-demand protocols, one can deploy larger populations of mobile nodes in the ad hoc network by accepting worse performance for route acquisition latency. Looking at it the other way around, demanding very short latencies for route acquisition can place heavy (or impossible) constraints on network size. Starting from a network without structure or valid route cache entries, the minimum route acquisition latency that allows full connectivity is the product of the maximum diameter of the network multiplied by the minimum node traversal time for route requests. At any point, the average route acquisition latency can be much better or much worse than this depending on average dissemination of valid route information and network congestion.

Lastly, I should mention that ad hoc networking ideas that exhibit sufficient scalability while still allowing subnet aggregation may find natural application in the Internet at large. This would help the problem of route thrashing in the Internet, which is partially caused by routes that change too fast to be faithfully managed by the routing protocols in use [Deering+ 2000]. Conversely, we might find that continued scalability to larger node populations may require some advanced routing techniques from wide-area routing protocols. However, I believe that such techniques are rendered unnecessary by the on-demand nature of several leading ad hoc network protocols. It seems less likely that the Internet will ever borrow this idea of on-demand route acquisition.

11.1.2 Quality of Service

Many of the candidate protocols in this book operate to establish end-to-end connectivity between network applications by finding a communications path between the endpoints without regard to the quality of the physical links between intermediate points. Thus, for these approaches it would be difficult to know whether any particular application bandwidth or delay requirements can be supported by the communications path.

For many traditional audio and video applications, specifically two-way voice communications (i.e., telephony), it is quite likely that the chosen communications path between the endpoints will have to meet additional constraints. The application will have to supply its constraint parameters (i.e., its QoS parameters) to the routing layer so that a suitable path can be found.

The path can be found in several ways. For instance, with a protocol that maintains full link-state information dynamically for every link in the ad hoc network, the well-known Dijkstra's algorithm can be applied, taking into account whether each link under consideration meets the application's requirements. Alternatively, almost any on-demand protocol can be equipped with extensions describing the requirements so that only appropriate paths are returned during route discovery. This is the approach taken by AODV (see Chapter 6). A more sophisticated link-state approach to the problem is discussed in Chapter 10.

All approaches are vulnerable to dynamic link quality variations between neighboring nodes. Thus, a route between two endpoints that initially meets the application's QoS constraints may soon fail to meet them. Methods for detecting and reporting these dynamic failure conditions need to be investigated and integrated into existing protocols. For instance, a new ICMP message (perhaps named ICMP QOS_LOST) might be defined to inform one or both endpoints that a new route discovery operation should be initiated.

11.1.3 Is the Client–Server Model Viable?

For many years, network applications have been designed to offer their users a *client–server* model. Typically, this means that a network client is configured to use a server (often, a remote server) as its partner (or sometimes as its adult supervisor) for network transactions. More advanced programs allow the network client to be automatically configured with the identity of an appropriate server (e.g., the DNS name or perhaps the IP address). Most recently, standards have been produced to enable clients to perform dynamic discovery algorithms that carry out the automatic configuration.

However, when the network is itself dynamic, and when its structure is no longer defined by techniques for collecting IP addresses into subnets, existing techniques for static and automatic configuration break down almost completely. Static configuration is out of the picture because an ad hoc network is characterized by its dynamic nature. Automatic configuration often depends on client transactions with a configuration server such as DHCP, and DHCP typically manages client parameters based on the subnet to which the client is connected. This makes today's deployed systems for automatic configuration inappropriate for ad hoc networks.

Where do services reside? That question is often not easy to answer, especially when the answer changes over time. Recent proposals have suggested integrating service discovery with the general route discovery mechanism. This can be done by specifying that only a particular kind of service (or perhaps only an application at a particular TCP or UDP port) be allowed to answer the broadcast request. Such an approach may have three deficiencies:

- Inserting application service discovery into a network layer protocol may be a violation of modular network protocol design.
- It may not be possible for the client to specify the exact service it desires in a way that can be naturally included in a network layer request.
- It may be difficult to make any determination about authorization at the network layer.

Other possibilities include the use of well-known multicast addresses for services and the Service Location Protocol [Guttman+ 1999]. The former approach may be more appropriate for very basic services such as DNS and DHCP. However, the question of administering and maintaining such servers in an ad hoc network is completely open, as far as I know. More esoteric services such as certificate authorities and SNMP management agents are completely off the map.

One further idea: Whenever some of these more basic questions are answered, a next step might be to maintain a *grid* of well-known services, with new candidate servers dynamically appearing in order to preserve a minimum number of hops to the closest service (e.g., of the above-mentioned types).

11.1.4 Connecting to the Internet

It is now possible to say a few things about how an ad hoc network can establish overall connectivity to the global Internet, but many (or perhaps most) of the answers are very poorly understood.

If any node in an ad hoc network also has connectivity to the global Internet, it is advantageous for that node to offer Internet connectivity to the other nodes. This can be done in several ways. We might think of having the Internet "gateway" advertise itself as a default router, which will have the desired effect if the other nodes in the ad hoc network can consider themselves connected to the default router by way of a multihop path through other ad hoc network nodes. However, this idea contrasts sharply with the traditional model of a default router.

One resolution to this problem might be to consider the entire ad hoc domain as a "single hop" from the point of view of Internet connectivity

[Royer+ 2001]. This view may be considered analogous to the way BGP characterizes an entire administrative system (AS) as a single hop in its route advertisements. However, given that multihop wireless connectivity incurs significant overhead, it is more important to minimize unnecessary hops in an ad hoc network than in a high-speed wired AS. I admit my bias toward counting each hop and generalizing the meaning of a default router. This has the effect of defining the previously noted problems out of existence. Moreover, it simplifies the choice between several possible points of attachment to the Internet (i.e., several default routers).

If we can agree that we can find a default router for an ad hoc node within an ad hoc network, then we may as well consider how to make the default router a *foreign agent* for Mobile IP. Then every node in the ad hoc cloud can appear to be as accessible as if it were still located on its home network. This has been investigated by multiple researchers [Lei+ 1997, Broch+ 1999]. In the Lei and Perkins project, we found that the route management for ad hoc networks had to be carefully distinguished from that for default routers (i.e., the foreign agents in Mobile IP). This same problem surfaces for any attempt to maintain routes to one of several interchangeable service points even if the service is something other than the offer of a default route.

11.1.5 Security

Clearly, security has so far not been satisfactorily investigated for ad hoc network protocols. Security for any routing protocol is always difficult, mainly because of the difficulties of key distribution and refresh. A quick scan through the chapters of this book will show that the topic of security for ad hoc protocols is impressive by its almost total absence. I cannot even suggest whether public key methods or symmetric key methods are more unwieldy in ad hoc networks because both seem so devilishly difficult. Use of public key infrastructure (PKI) algorithms have disadvantages stemming from using algorithms that are more CPU intensive than are symmetric key algorithms. Furthermore, it may be difficult to make good use of certificate revocation lists (CRLs) in an ad hoc network without an infrastructure. Symmetric key algorithms, however, rely on secure distribution of secret keys shared between partners, which amounts to a key distribution problem that scales as the square of the number of partners. Applied to the neighborhood ad hoc network scenario, this means quite a few phone calls between neighbors as the size of the community grows.

Multicast data distribution in ad hoc networks is another important consideration with security implications. There will always be many different trust relationships between neighbors in any large community and many different reasons for personal relationships. As groups of people collaborate and wish to establish private video distribution channels, multicast will become crucial. Given any reasonable solution to the QoS control problem, as outlined in Section 11.1.2, an adaptation of that solution to multicast will probably be realized without too much procrastination. However, thinking about keys for multicast groups is almost beyond the pale given the current state of the art. And solutions for byzantine agreements seem truly byzantine.

11.1.6 Power Control

There are two aspects to power control for wireless mobile nodes: Reducing power to the communications interfaces and entering *sleep mode* are both valuable ways to extend battery life for mobile units. These power-saving techniques are crucial to the viability of existing cellular telephones and other wireless PDAs. However, both of these techniques have the effect of making communication with the mobile device more difficult.

To enable sleep mode with wireless devices, the ad hoc routing algorithm will require some scheduling so that the wireless nodes can determine when to exit sleep mode and start listening for messages. Alternatively, a special signaling channel could wake up the wireless nodes.

The scheduling strategy requires synchronization between the wireless nodes, but achieving and maintaining synchronization is a problem that deserves significant study. For example, what happens when two ad hoc clouds collide? Changing the routing paths seems fairly straightforward, especially with an on-demand protocol. However, changing the synchronization is a whole different story.

The alternative strategy of reserving a special signaling channel is used in modern cellular telephone networks in conjunction with a paging subsystem. Besides requiring that sleeping nodes wake up, often unnecessarily, to process signals that are actually targeted to some other node, this method requires that some bandwidth be reserved just for paging, which reduces the amount of bandwidth available for data transfers. To further complicate matters, hybrid approaches that combine the advantages and disadvantages of both paging and synchronized sleep modes are possible.

In some wireless systems (notably CDMA), it is possible to vary the transmission power between stations so that the signal is just powerful enough to be correctly decoded at the receiver. Reducing the transmission power has at least these advantages:

- Power savings at the mobile nodes
- Noise reduction at all other neighboring stations
- Increased frequency re-use for the transmission channel

These are powerful incentives for introducing power control into the system design for wireless network nodes.

There is an interaction between transmission power control and routing—increasing the transmission power at a network node is likely to increase the number of other nodes that are directly reachable. Thus, it is possible that some routing paths will be available only at relatively high transmission power levels; sometimes high power is required before any routing path becomes available. One can imagine algorithms that attempt to stabilize the transmission power at a threshold level that just barely enables data transfer, but then these minimally powered links might be much more easily broken or vulnerable to errors and other disruptions.

Abstractly, power control seems to belong to layer 2, but from the preceding discussion we can see that it also has direct effects on the network layer protocol (i.e., IP). This is a puzzle that still needs to be sorted out. From this perspective, transmission power control is slightly more complex than handling sleep modes, but given the complication introduced by synchronization, it seems that both are quite challenging.

11.2 OTHER APPROACHES

In this section, I briefly describe other proposals for ad hoc network protocols that I find interesting. It would not be feasible given existing constraints to provide an exhaustive list, but I think that at least these few additional flavors should be added to the smorgasbord of protocol treats.

11.2.1 Location-Assisted Routing

Consider a routing path between a source S and a destination D that traverses a link from X to Y. Suppose that the link X → Y breaks. In the absence of local repair, we might profitably reduce route discovery traffic by directing it along the route that was previously known to work. This localization could be managed by keeping track of the position and velocity of the mobile node. The route request for a new route to destination D could then be accompanied by the last-known location information for D. Nodes not in that general direction might then be excluded from relaying the broadcast route request. This idea has been investigated with good results by researchers at Texas A&M University [Ko+ 1998].

11.2.2 Fisheye Routing

In trying to improve scalability for a routing protocol, it makes sense to put the most effort into gathering data on the topology information that is most likely to be needed soon. Assuming that nearby changes to the network topology are those most likely to matter, we might try to focus our view of the network so that nearby changes are seen with high resolution in time and more distant changes are seen at lower resolution and less often. We might compare this objective to "fisheye" vision—nearby things are clear and distant things are blurry. With this model in mind, researchers at UCLA have proposed *fisheye routing* [Iwata+ 1999], whereby a node has progressively less path information about nodes that are farther away. We might think of fisheye routing as blurring the sharp boundary defined in the network model used by ZRP.

11.2.3 CEDAR

Some scalability improvements involve creating a backbone for disseminating route requests, thereby avoiding the necessity for system-wide (i.e., *all-nodes*) broadcast [Sinha+ 1997]. The difficulty comes when core nodes move relative to each other so that they no longer form a convenient backbone. Managing the detection of such conditions and dynamically maintaining the backbone are challenges that can have a substantial payoff, measured by taking the number of nodes in the spanning tree containing all of the backbone nodes and comparing it to the total population of the ad hoc network. The payoff can also be measured by taking the number of packets broadcast when there is no backbone and comparing it to the number of packets unicast along the spanning tree. Both measures are of interest, and further research in these directions is warranted.

11.3 A POSSIBLE VISION OF THE FUTURE

Suppose that the low-level protocol details have all been worked out and that we can count on peer-to-peer connectivity wherever we go. Further suppose that ad hoc networks scale to tens or hundreds of thousands of nodes as desired. This could open the way to a new sense of community networking. Each home could support forwarding of voice and data to neighbors without the need for Internet service providers (ISPs). ISPs might be relegated to a sort of long-distance service, and private neighborhood matters could easily be handled locally. This would apply especially to neighborhood telephony, which might be viewed as a sort of expanded intercom service.

There is no reason that this sort of community-based ad hoc network cannot be extended to broadband communications, serving as the basis for a whole new understanding of what it means to be part of a community. Of course, there will be privacy concerns, but these will most likely be settled as the ad hoc neighborhood network rolls out. Any particular application with specific privacy requirements (e.g., remote webcam viewing) will probably require authentication before access is granted and encryption before data is delivered. Above either of these, however, is trust in the recipient as an obvious social requirement.

When the local community can manage its own needs for connectivity, using locally owned resources, control of local networking will again be located where it belongs. This may be the basis for yet another revolution in the way we understand telecommunications. Previous revolutions, including the telephone network and the Internet, caused local communities to rely on remote, centralized control facilities as the basis of their operations—we cannot call our friend down the street or even our closest neighbor if the telephone company has a problem downtown. Viewed in this way, Internet connectivity is even more reliant on the correct operation of distant network elements. However, I believe that it will be much more healthy to view networking as a bottom-up, community-based service. It should be possible to establish neighborhood connections without absolute reliance on external authorities. Occasional testing and system administration can be handled on a contract basis with no loss of local control.

In my vision of the future, local telephone calls via ad hoc Voice-over-IP will be made without tariff, and motivated neighbors will install higher-speed wireless LAN equipment for high-speed sharing. If a family goes on vacation and their equipment fails while they are away, ad hoc network reconfiguration will easily be able to adjust to the changed network topology. All of these functions will still be available locally even though the application endpoints establish communications based on global IP (or IPv6) addresses obtained from more traditional ISPs. The idea is to make the local network more robust against remote failures and to avoid payments to remote agencies for local communications. Local e-mail, local web pages, and local telephone calls will not be under the necessary and absolute jurisdiction of remote charging administrations.

What part does mobility play in the neighborhood network? The answer is simple and natural—almost the same role for computing devices as it does for people. This is natural because, generally speaking, it is the movement of people that makes mobile networking interesting in the first place. Furthermore, the computing and communications devices that people carry with them are the mobile devices that will need to establish dynamic interconnections to the local ad hoc network. In this vision of the future, the community controls a large population of ad hoc computers, most of which are static and friendly. But many of the most used devices are mobile, and almost all devices (even televisions) are potentially so. Certainly, video cameras and digital still cameras are mobile and should be able to establish network communications with local display devices whether in the owner's home or in someone else's. Viewed in this light, the close relationship between mobile networking and automatic configuration becomes obvious.

It is my hope that ad hoc networks will begin to place control of computer networks largely in the hands of the local community and that local communities will begin to see the benefits of using tax dollars to create online benefits and services for their ad hoc computing environments.

11.4 FOR MORE INFORMATION

The IETF has a working group, `manet`, which is concerned with ad hoc networking. Many of the protocols described in this book have been discussed at length on the `manet` mailing list, whose contributors come from academic, industrial, and military backgrounds. This diversity of opinion and expertise has made for many stimulating and enlightening discussions. Remarkably, there has been very little flaming and spam on the list, greatly improving its overall usefulness.

For more information, consult this URL: *http://www.ietf.org/html. charters/manet-charter.html,* which has the latest information about the working group, including access to the mailing list archives and instructions on subscription. To subscribe, send a message, with the word `subscribe` in the message body, to `manet-request@itd.nrl.navy.mil`.

For years, ad hoc networking has been a popular topic at the MobiCom conferences sponsored by ACM SIGMOBILE and the IEEE. Almost any one of the conference proceedings will provide interesting papers to read. Now there is the Mobiltoc workshop, also sponsored by these groups, that is devoted entirely to ad hoc networks. The first meeting was held in August 2000, and definitely far exceeded initial expectations. This is a further indication of the viability of ad hoc networking as a subject for continued research and development. I hope this book has inspired the reader to participate in that overall effort.

References

[Broch+ 1999] J. Broch, D.A. Maltz, and D.B. Johnson. Supporting Hierarchy and Heterogeneous Interfaces in Multi-Hop Wireless Ad Hoc Networks. In *Proceedings of the Fourth International IEEE Symposium on Parallel Architectures, Algorithms, and Networks (ISPAN '99), Workshop on Mobile Computing,* June 1999, 370–375.

[Deering+ 2000] S. Deering, S. Hares, C. Perkins, and R. Perlman. Overview of the 1998 IAB Routing Workshop. RFC 2902, Internet Engineering Task Force, August 2000.

[Guttman+ 1999] E. Guttman, C. Perkins, J. Veizades, and M. Dago. Service Location Protocol, Version 2. RFC 2608 (proposed standard), Internet Engineering Task Force, June 1999.

[Iwata+ 1999] A. Iwata, C.-C. Chiang, G. Pei, M. Gerla, and T.-W. Chen. Scalable Routing Strategies for Ad Hoc Wireless Networks. *IEEE Journal on Selected Areas of Communications* 17(8):1369–1379, August 1999.

[Ko+ 1998] Y. Ko and N.H. Vaidya. Location-Aided Routing (LAR) in Mobile Ad Hoc Networks. In *Proceedings of the Fifth Annual ACM/IEEE International Conference on Mobile Computing and Networking (MOBICOM '98)*, August 1998.

[Lei+ 1997] H. Lei and C.E. Perkins. Ad Hoc Networking with Mobile IP. In *Proceedings of the Second European Personal Mobile Communications Conference*, October 1997, 197–202.

[Maughan+ 1998] D. Maughan, M. Schertler, M. Schneider, and J. Turner. Internet Security Association and Key Management Protocol (ISAKMP). RFC 2408 (proposed standard), Internet Engineering Task Force, November 1998.

[Royer+ 2001] E. M. Royer and C. Perkins. Transmission Range Effects on AODV Multicast Communication. *ACM/Baltzer* (accepted for publication), 2001.

[Sinha+ 1997] P. Sinha, R. Sivakumar, and V. Bharghavan. CEDAR: Core Extraction Distributed Ad Hoc Routing. In *Proceedings of IEEE INFOCOM '97*, April 1997.

Index

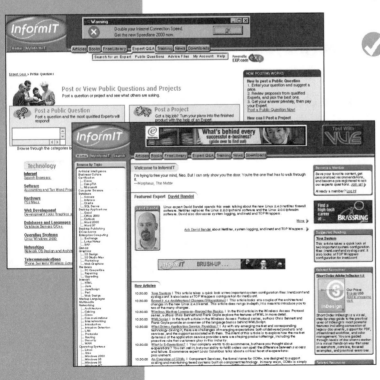
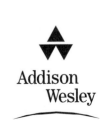

Malet Street, London WC1E 7HX
020-7631 6239
e-mail: library-renewals@bbk.ac.uk
Items should be returned or renewed by the latest date stamped below.
Please see Library Guide 1 or visit the Library website
http://www.bbk.ac.uk/lib/ for information about online renewals.

26/6/03

30 MAY 2004

0 2 MAR 2006

0 7 JUN 2007